The Royal Throne of Mercy and British Culture in the Victorian Age

The Royal Throne of Mercy and British Culture in the Victorian Age

James Gregory

BLOOMSBURY ACADEMIC
LONDON • NEW YORK • OXFORD • NEW DELHI • SYDNEY

BLOOMSBURY ACADEMIC
Bloomsbury Publishing Plc
50 Bedford Square, London, WC1B 3DP, UK
1385 Broadway, New York, NY 10018, USA

BLOOMSBURY, BLOOMSBURY ACADEMIC and the Diana logo
are trademarks of Bloomsbury Publishing Plc

First published in Great Britain 2020
Paperback edition published 2022

Copyright © James Gregory, 2020

James Gregory has asserted his right under the Copyright, Designs
and Patents Act, 1988, to be identified as Author of this work.

For legal purposes the Acknowledgements on p. xi constitute
an extension of this copyright page.

Cover image: Portrait of Queen Victoria by Thomas Benjamin Kennington, 1898. Oil on
canvas. Retford Town Hall. The Picture Art Collection/Alamy Stock Photo.

All rights reserved. No part of this publication may be reproduced or transmitted in
any form or by any means, electronic or mechanical, including photocopying, recording,
or any information storage or retrieval system, without prior permission
in writing from the publishers.

Bloomsbury Publishing Plc does not have any control over, or responsibility for,
any third-party websites referred to or in this book. All internet addresses given in
this book were correct at the time of going to press. The author and publisher
regret any inconvenience caused if addresses have changed or sites have
ceased to exist, but can accept no responsibility for any such changes.

A catalogue record for this book is available from the British Library.

A catalog record for this book is available from the Library of Congress.

ISBN:	HB:	978-1-3501-4243-5
	PB:	978-1-3502-1355-5
	ePDF:	978-1-3501-4244-2
	eBook:	978-1-3501-4245-9

Typeset by Integra Software Services Pvt. Ltd.

To find out more about our authors and books visit www.bloomsbury.com
and sign up for our newsletters.

To F and H.

Contents

List of Figures	viii
Acknowledgements	xi
Introduction	1
1 Royal Mercy's Constitutional Context	21
2 Victoria's Merciful Predecessors	41
3 Public Views of Victoria's Mercy	69
4 Victoria's Mercy in the Archives	93
5 Victoria's Mercy: Rebellion and Attempted Assassination	107
6 Victoria Beatrix: Victoria's Empire of Mercy	125
7 Victoria Humana: Representing Victoria as Merciful	137
Conclusion	151
Notes	156
Select Bibliography	224
Index	241

Figures

I.1 'Mr Henry Irving as Shylock, and Miss Ellen Terry as Portia, in 'The Merchant of Venice' by N. Stretch, *The Illustrated Sporting and Dramatic News*, 20 December 1879, p.348. Author's collection — 4

I.2 Gennaro Amato, 'Queen Victoria and the Poor: Her Majesty Visiting a Cottage Home', *Illustrated London News Record of the Glorious Reign of Queen Victoria* (London: Illustrated London News, 1901), p.19. Author's collection — 9

1.1 'Sir James Graham', *Illustrated London News*, 1 October 1842, p.333. Courtesy of the University of Plymouth, Rare Books Collection — 30

1.2 Robert Barnes, 'Sketches in the Royal Courts of Justice. A Common Jury', *The Graphic*, 11 January 1890, p.49. Author's collection — 33

1.3 Lord Mansfield, engraving by W. Holl after Joshua Reynolds, in H. Brougham, *Historical Sketches of Statesmen Who Flourished in the Time of George III* (London: Knight, 1839), 1st series, before p.101. Image courtesy of the University of Plymouth, Rare Books Collection — 38

2.1 'A View of the Manner of Beheading the Rebel Lords in Tower Hill London, in the Reign of George II'. An engraving by John Goldar after the drawing by Robert Dodd and originally appearing in Barnard's *New Complete & Authentic History of England* (1781–83). Author's collection — 45

2.2 'Advice to a Great K–g', *Oxford Magazine*, December 1771, opposite p. 216. Image courtesy of the University of Michigan — 50

2.3 Portrait of Robert Perreau. Engraving, *London Magazine; or, Gentleman's Monthly Intelligencer*, 1 July 1775. Author's collection — 52

2.4 Etching with aquatint of George III crowned by Mercy and Justice, with a sash of benevolence, published 6 August 1786, by W. Holland, Drury Lane, London. Royal Collection Trust/© Her Majesty Queen Elizabeth II 2020 — 55

2.5 'Princess Charlotte of Wales and Prince Leopold of Saxe Coburg'. An engraving by Henry Meyer, after a design by Burney, published by Edward Baines of Leeds, 1 November 1816. Author's collection — 64

Figures

3.1	A late-Victorian rendition of Queen Victoria's first parliament from *Illustrated London News Record of the Glorious Reign of Queen Victoria*, p.4. Author's collection	71
3.2	Detail of the coronation admission ticket for George IV, 19 July 1820. Image courtesy of Toovey's Fine Art Auctioneers and Valuers	73
3.3	'The first death warrant', G.A. Henty, *Queen Victoria. Scenes from Her Life and Reign* (London: Blackie, 1901), p.33. Author's collection	79
3.4	Illustration by Robert Barnes, in R. Wilson, *The Life and Times of Queen Victoria* (London: Cassell, 1893), p.249. Author's collection	80
3.5	'The Penge Mystery', *Illustrated Police News*, 1 December 1877, p.1. Newspaper image © The British Library Board. All rights reserved. With thanks to the British Newspaper Archive (www.britishnewspaperarchive.co.uk)	82
4.1	John Tenniel, 'The garotter's friend. "Let go, Bill, can't yer – it's our kind non-interfering friend, Sir George Grey !!!"', *Punch*, 29 November 1862, p.221. Author's collection	96
4.2	Sir William Vernon Harcourt MP. Steel engraving by W. Roffe after the photograph by Elliott and Fry, and published by William Mackenzie. Author's collection	98
4.3	Wood engraving of Henry Matthews Q.C., the new Home Secretary, *Illustrated London News*, 14 August 1886. Author's collection	100
4.4	'The Trial of Mrs Maybrick at Liverpool. Mrs Maybrick making her statement to the Court'. *The Graphic*, 17 August 1889. Author's collection	102
5.1	Engraving by J.W. Orr, in *Caroline Almanack and Freeman's Chronicle for 1840* (Rochester, NY: Mackenzie Gazette Office, 1840), p.3. Image courtesy of Lande Canadiana Collection, Rare Books and Special Collections, McGill University Library	110
5.2	John Tenniel, 'Justice', *Punch*, 12 September 1857, p.109. Author's collection	115
5.3	'O God of Battles! Steel My Soldiers' Hearts', *Punch*, 10 October 1857, p.151. Author's collection	116
5.4	Wood engraving showing John Francis aiming a pistol at the Queen's carriage, as it passes Constitution Hill, 30 May 1842, *Illustrated London News*, 4 June 1842, p.49. Author's collection	121
5.5	'Roderick Maclean, after his attempt to shoot the Queen at Windsor, taken to the police station', *Extra Supplement to the Illustrated London News*, 11 March 1882. Author's collection	123

7.1	'Marble group in the Prince's Chamber, House of Lords. Her Majesty Queen Victoria. Supported by Justice and Clemency. John Gibson, R.A., Sculptor', *Illustrated London News*, 7 March 1857, p.207. Wood engraving. Author's collection	139
7.2	'The Art-Union Prize Cartoon, by Mr Selous. – "Queen Philippa Interceding for the Burgesses of Calais"', wood engraving of prize-winning design by H.C. Selous in *Illustrated London News*, 7 February 1846, p.96. Author's collection	141
7.3	John Leech, 'Elizabeth and Victoria', *The Illuminated Magazine*, May 1843, p.3. Image courtesy the University of Plymouth, Rare Books Collection	142
7.4	'Mercy v Justice'. A commentary on the reprieve for Thomas Burke, in *Judy, or the London Serio-Comic Journal*, 5 June 1867, p.71. © The British Library Board. General Reference Collection P.P.5270.c	143
7.5	'The Statue of Queen Boadicea, to be placed on the Thames Embankment', *The Sketch*, 28 January 1898, p.9. Author's collection	146
7.6	'The Nightingale Jewel', *Illustrated London News*, 2 February 1856, p.109. Author's collection	147
7.7	Obverse of the second form of the Afghanistan medal in bronze, designed by William Wyon (1842). Metropolitan Museum of Art, accession X.14.23. Image assigned public domain status. https://www.metmuseum.org/art/collection/search/208753	148
C.1	'The Sword of Mercy. Coronation 1911'. Cigarette card in 'Coronation Series 1911. Published by Salmon and Gluckstein of London. Author's collection	154

Acknowledgements

This study of British culture through the perspective of mercy began with monarchs' acts of mercy over the 'long nineteenth century', a development of my interest in Victorian opposition to capital punishment. Tracing the background to Victoria's performance of mercy showed the discourse of royal mercy was related to political struggles at home and the wider British world. I am grateful to Bloomsbury's editorial board for their enthusiasm and to the anonymous readers for insightful comments and advice. I acknowledge the gracious permission of Her Majesty the Queen for quotation from material in the Royal Archives studied in 2011, later supplemented by access to the digitized material from Queen Victoria's journal and other royal papers. I am grateful for the archivists' kind assistance. Much primary material came from digitized collections in archive.org, Bibliothèque et Archives nationales du Québec, British Newspaper Archive, findmypast.co.uk, Google books, Hathi Trust, JISC Historical Texts, the National Library of Australia's Trove, Old Bailey Online, and South Asia Open Archives, whose contribution to my research I acknowledge. I thank the following for permission to reproduce images: the Royal Collection Trust, Lande Canadiana Collection, the Rare Books and Special Collections at McGill University Library, the British Library, Toovey's Auctioneers, and the University of Plymouth. It is a pleasure to thank my colleagues and former colleagues: Darren Aoki, Nick Barnett, Harry Bennett, James Daybell, Rebecca Emmett, Claire Fitzpatrick, Daniel Grey, Lucy Huggins, Richard Huzzey, Elaine Murphy, Angela Smith, Simon Topping, who read, listened to, challenged, and responded to my musings on mercy over the years.

James Gregory, Plymouth, 2020

Introduction

Mercy, like other virtues, has a history.[1] An important aspect of modern Britain's self-image and discourse, it has not been studied in depth before. This book is part of a project of writing a cultural history reflecting my interest in how Britons thought about mercy involving national acts, such as the abolition of slavery or global conflict, and small-scale acts, such as the reprieve for a criminal condemned to death or a soldier's behaviour on a battlefield. Here I focus on a central figure in the nineteenth-century imaginary, Queen Victoria, to explore the relationship between monarchy and that quality which encyclopaedias and dictionaries defined as a 'willingness to spare and save, to pardon and forgive, to kindness, clemency, compassion, sympathy, pity', and also (for one is at the mercy of another) of being 'in the power of that which is irresistible'.[2] Concentrating on this royal aspect, the study highlights mercy's central relationship to power. The religious poet's idea of mercy's reign or sway brought to people's minds the idea of a merciful ruler – whether divine or mundane.[3] This idea relied on its antitheses: involving choices between acts of mercy and mercilessness or (what is sometimes presented as antithetical) between 'strict justice' and mercy. So a history of royal mercy is a history of royal justice and cruelty too.[4] Decisions about lawbreakers might be made directly by earlier monarchs, but Victoria's ministers, operating through bureaucratic rules, extended or denied mercy in her name in dealing with criminals. But popular belief in the ongoing power of royal clemency in the British world obscured the decline in royal power.

Mercy, monarchy, and Victorian culture

The metaphors by which it was understood, its artistic representation as historic act or ideal, and the rituals by which it was acknowledged as a cultural value entangled mercy with monarchy and key aspects of Victorian culture. This is most obvious in considering the religious dimension, expressed in coronation ritual and in simile when discussing the Christian theology of atonement.

As a virtue, mercy was extolled and dissected in eighteenth- and nineteenth-century sermons and other forms of Christian commentary.[5] It was an inevitable keyword of religious instruction and worship. The historian of the eighteenth-century law Douglas Hay notes that English people were 'schooled in the lessons of Justice, Terror and

Mercy'.[6] Hay referred to mercy's role in the legal system and as an instrument of elite control, but its place in the operation of mundane and divine power was conveyed in pulpit, Sunday school, and by other modes of religious instruction. Its association with the sympathy and pity that motivated philanthropy – those 'acts of mercy' of traditional Christian discourse – means it should be recognized as one of the values (and emotions or dispositions) associated with that typical Victorian philanthropic impulse. Yet while Samuel Smiles, in passing, valued mercy in those key Victorian texts of *Self Help* and *Character*, it scarcely figures as a 'Victorian value' in the historical mind.[7] Popularly, the Victorians and their religion were associated in the next century with harsh or judgemental, rather than merciful, attitudes.[8]

The association between monarch and divine mercy was a trope of Christian argument continuing in the Victorian age.[9] So *On and Off Duty*, a Christian journal for policemen (1886), defended the doctrine of atonement thus: 'You, Policemen of London, think what would happen in this realm supposing Queen Victoria exercised her prerogative of mercy to-morrow morning, and turned out all the criminals from our jails, and let them enjoy their liberty.'[10] Using royal and earthly clemency to explain divine mercy was common, and metaphorical clichés led one essayist at the start of Victoria's reign to cry *Sauvez moi du metaphore!* in pointing out the contrast between the hyperbole of 'this godlike attribute of sovereigns' and practical reality of ministerial discretion.[11]

Despite this sensible critique, Victorians refused to abandon regal figures of speech when discussing theology. They inherited the ideas of a literal or figurative 'mercy seat' and heavenly throne of mercy.[12] Texts such as John Bunyan's posthumously published *The Throne of Grace; or, The Saints' Privilege and Profit* (1692) linked 'throne' and mercy. This worried one Victorian commentator, Robert Philip, who was clear that 'no earthly throne ever was, or ever can be, a throne of grace, or a mercy-seat'. Human thrones could only be of justice or equity 'for, whenever the British throne shews mercy to the condemned, the act is the exception, not the rule; and rather the private than the official act of the sovereign'.[13] Moreover, while mercy might appear 'mild-eyed' and 'amiable', the description was lurid when it related to Christ's crucifixion: in 1817 the Original Secession Church minister George Stevenson of Ayr, quoting Psalm 89, described the throne of mercy 'sprinkled with the blood of an atoning sacrifice'.[14]

Mercy entwined with royalty through the symbolism of the regalia, which, because of the monarchy's prominence in British culture, had metaphorical force in public discourse. The reader of this study may be overfamiliarized with the figure of speech of mercy as a jewel in the sovereign's crown – to be dimmed or made more lustrous by use or abuse.[15] Thus for the poet Sarah Ann Stowe of Hereford in 1895, 'Forbearance, compassion and tenderness are jewels which shine conspicuously in the diadem of mercy'.[16] Writers extolled the mercy functions and clement disposition of rulers in the present and past, in Europe and outside Christian culture through the metaphor of a coronal jewel.[17] There was the phrase 'crowning mercy' too – most famously associated with the regicide Oliver Cromwell's verdict on the battle of Worcester in 1651.[18] Nor are the metaphorical and symbolic associations of regalia and mercy exhausted with the crown, since the idea of justice tempered with mercy, a metallurgical metaphor, was linked to those swords of justice and mercy metaphorically wielded by princes and their representatives or present as symbols during British coronation rituals.

While the meaning of mercy may change over time, durable elements in a British context included the coronation ritual, where antiquity was deliberately sought through the oath and emblems of royal mercy (which also included rods, sceptres, and orbs). If one turns to the figure consecrated as a ruler in justice and mercy in June 1838, and whose behaviour after the loss of her husband was to eschew state robes and crown on grand public occasions for widow's weeds and bonnet (while still delighting in actual jewels), what was Victoria's understanding of the symbolism and meaning of mercy?[19]

Victoria's upbringing, including reading in history, religious, or moral instruction and attendance at divine service, educated her in the Christian language of mercy. While her education reflected her status as heir apparent, the religious instruction exposed Victoria to conventional ideas about mercy.[20] Her status as a Christian monarch was confirmed through the rituals of coronation, which included an oath where mercy was invoked and the rehearsal of the Ten Commandments and litany imploring mercy on miserable sinners.[21] The impact of these words and the material symbols of justice and mercy on Victoria during her lengthy ceremony in Westminster Abbey in June 1838 is unknown.[22] But we can register and gauge the frequency with which mercy in the religious sense appears in the queen's extensive personal and official writing. Throughout her life, the queen's diary recorded thanks for divine mercy and support. She wrote of the balm and consolation of belief in an 'all-merciful Redeemer'[23] and conventional acknowledgement of God's mercy appeared in *More Leaves from the Journal of a Life in the Highlands*.[24]

Another dimension to mercy's handling in Victorian culture is its cultural representation outside formal religious settings, in stage play, poetry, and prose. Scripture underlay thinking about mercy, but a religious perspective was also conveyed in frequent quotation of Portia's lines on the 'quality of mercy' in *The Merchant of Venice*, which, for trivial and profound reasons such as thespian set-piece and courtroom rhetoric, resonated through the period (see Figure I.1). The verse was picked out in flowers in genteel mid-Victorian charity bazaars; was phonographically recorded a year after Victoria's death, to compare the beauty of the female voice around the world; and was taught in the schools of the empire.[25]

Victoria knew the speech; in her diary entry dated 5 January 1877, she noted a private performance by the Biddulphs (the Keeper of the Privy Purse's family) where 'Betty had to give the celebrated speech on the qualities of "Mercy", which she did so well.'[26] If we accept *Pall Mall Gazette*'s anecdote, reprinted in provincial papers in May 1889 (and in colonial papers), Victoria prompted Ellen Terry quietly and then 'rather more loudly and encouragingly' when the celebrated actor performed at Sandringham.[27]

So far, I noted mercy's cultural presence as a familiar religious word of the age, its place in a monarchical state underscored through the coronation oath and its metaphorical location in the crown, and on the stage. Reference to dramatic verse shows mercy's performance beyond its real exercise in matters of life and death (or liberty and imprisonment). Through artistic representation, mercy appeared elsewhere, unsurprisingly in sites where executive and judicial powers were wielded.

Figure I.1 'Mr Henry Irving as Shylock, and Miss Ellen Terry as Portia, in 'The Merchant of Venice' by N. Stretch, *The Illustrated Sporting and Dramatic News*, 20 December 1879, p.348. Author's collection.

It figured alongside justice and other ideals as sculpture and painting in public sites of judgement and authority: in those (royal) courts of justice and civic halls constructed by Victorians. The template for its decorative presence, in an age tricking out its values in medieval or classical costume and validating the present through depictions of constitutional milestones and inspiring national episodes, was the rebuilt Palace of Westminster – a treasure house for the nation's moral and artistic elevation.

The penultimate chapter examines the prominent sculpture of Queen Victoria as arbiter of justice and mercy, in Pugin's and Barry's Westminster. Schemes to embellish the edifice with allegorical and historical subjects incorporated other depictions of royal mercy. It was argued that the brief's objective to represent 'the relations of the Sovereign to the state' was fulfilled by showing the prerogative of mercy as 'the brightest jewel in the crown … pleasingly exemplified by the Sovereign interposing between a rigorous law and a penitent offender.'[28] Designs on the themes of justice and religion included one on the act of mercy to illustrate the text 'Naked and Ye clothed me'.[29] Another, by Ford Madox Brown, a 'constitutional, and not a moral, representation of Justice', included mercy.[30] Designs for frescoes portraying historical clemency included a rendering of Edward III and the Black Prince's alms to the besieged poor of Calais of 1346, awarded £300 in the Westminster Hall exhibition in 1847, and engraved in the *Illustrated London News* with verse referencing the brightest gem in the crown.[31] Several representations of mercy were executed. The Irish artist Daniel Maclise showed angels of mercy and retribution in a fresco on justice alluding to abolition of slavery, in the Stranger's Gallery of the Lords in 1848.[32] The Scottish artist William Dyce included mercy among the chivalric virtues in a mural in the Robing Room. 'Mercy: Sir Gawaine Swearing to Be Merciful and Never to Be Against Ladies' (finished in 1854) portrayed the knight, after causing a lady's death, taking an oath after the queen passed sentence. 'The homage to women here illustrated', the artist and writer Thomas Gullick said, 'as well as the duty of showing mercy was perhaps the most remarkable characteristic of that French chivalry which gave the final colouring to the Mort d'Arthure'.[33]

Gullick's commentary, as well as suggesting a possible boost to mercy's cultural estimation in the Gothic revival, leads to another feature of the Victorian representation of mercy: its gendering. This appeared in sculpture, painting, and in drama where Shakespeare's texts on mercy, uttered by the female characters of Portia and Isabella (the latter, in *Measure for Measure*), created echoes and imitations. The *English Review*, appraising Robert Browning's anti-aristocratic play, 'Colombe's Birthday', in June 1849, selected its seventeenth-century hero Valence's words: 'There is a vision in the heart of each | Of justice, mercy, wisdom; tenderness | To wrong and pain, and knowledge of its cure – | And these, embodied in a woman's form | That best transmits them, pure as first received, | From God above her, to mankind below.' The *Review* added, 'Our royal mistress Queen Victoria would scarcely disapprove of this description.'[34]

The tendency in European treatment was to represent mercy in feminine form as a virtue and propensity in human nature most closely associated with women. Moreover it was seen as a characteristic of female rule and of the exercise of power by women more generally, so that mercy became a value to invoke when women started to be admitted to public political roles in the later nineteenth century. Queens regnant and queens consort were identified as merciful by nature: Marie Leckzinska's aphorism 'The mercy of Kings is to do justice; and the justice of Queens is to exercise mercy' appears in an English biography of Marie Antoinette.[35] Victoria was assumed to be responsive to appeals for mercy; a natural feminine sympathy is identified as 'one of the most prominent factors in Victoria's portrayal throughout her reign'.[36] Poetry presented the young Victoria as a monarch with a 'woman's heart' in promotion of native Indians' rights in a Quaker journal, for example.[37] State-inflicted violence in a woman's name was disturbing. Tellingly, in referring to 'hideous and bloody deeds' in Jamaica in official responses during the rebellion of 1865, it was noteworthy and problematic that this was done 'in the name of our own beloved and merciful Queen'.[38]

The word 'mercy' was often referenced in discussion of that female-driven humanitarianism which, from the earlier anti-slavery campaigns onwards, was prominent in the Victorian self-image. While this book also discusses other contexts for royal mercy, much of it was extended or withheld, and thus controverted, in relation to the death penalty. Reports of early anti-capital punishment activities before Victoria's reign connected these with the 'interest which the female heart naturally takes in any thing relating to the cause of humanity'.[39] Belief that female political power aided abolition was voiced throughout Victoria's reign. Female suffragists assumed that, in the words of one in 1866, 'the appalling sight of the gallows in a Christian land is owing to the exclusion of women from its political councils'.[40] Women as spectators before the gallows was hidden inside prisons, deviated from the template established by scriptural patterns of mercy such as Esther and the Virgin Mary.[41] A writer in 1839 condemned 'hardened profligate viragoes' clustering around the scaffold and observed that 'Mercy, the chief beauty of the female character, dwelt not with such companions'.[42]

The social critic John Ruskin famously extolled women's power as a throne 'founded on the rock of Justice, and descended from only by steps of mercy' in 'Of Queen's Gardens' (1864).[43] Later, 'when women [made] the weight of their opinion felt' in working as poor-law guardians, it was claimed they were a force for tempering justice with mercy.[44] The formal role of women in local government was defended on 'humanitarian' grounds by no less a figure than the Prime Minister Lord Salisbury, in 1899, citing their 'sympathetic' nature and high philanthropic motives.[45]

Mercy must also be related to Victorian ideas about race and the dealings in practice between the imperial power and the colonized. Mercy was the rhetorical partner in claims to rule in justice, and monarchy was entangled here – by apologists eulogizing the healing and binding power of royal clemency and by the colonized who made tactical appeals to the merciful British sovereign. Mercy was presented as an imperial concern by a range of reformers from slavery abolitionists in 1838 onwards, and petitions to the throne of mercy in domestic capital cases were echoed on behalf of lawbreakers facing punishment elsewhere in the British world.

In the early nineteenth century the 'jewel in the crown' was understood as mercy and not British rule in India. But the two ideas were neatly associated when the satirical *Punch* imagined a vocal Koh-i-noor, resplendent at the Great Exhibition in June 1851, fondly hoping it had 'taken the shine out of the prerogative of mercy itself, and was regularly installed as the brightest jewel of the British Crown'.⁴⁶ Miles Taylor's exploration of the Victorian monarchy in India shows how the queen was 'as much an Indian maharani as a British monarch'.⁴⁷ One element of her presence in the Indian imaginary was her role as source of mercy: extravagantly praised as unparalleled in 'mercy and forbearance' in Syad Latif's late-Victorian history of the Punjab for instance (Latif was discussing royal forgiveness for the deposed Sikh maharajah Duleep Singh's intriguing, in 1885).⁴⁸ As a boasted feature of British royalty and thus of the self-image of the imperial state (perhaps also recognized as an ideal shared with indigenous rulers), the mercy claims of imperial masters could be manipulated. In India, 'orientalist' ideas about the native imagination's awed response to gestures of executive clemency in the name of the queen-empress and successors were appealed to when campaigning for release of imprisoned anti-colonial leaders. My broader examination of mercy studies race more closely (considering, for example, how non-European races might be seen as inherently merciless, refashioned through missionary activity as merciful Christians, or recognized within their own cultures as expressing similar merciful values).

Among the nineteenth century's philanthropic innovations and reform movements was animal welfare. Opposition to animal cruelty included vegetarianism and, responding to the activities of a 'new priesthood' in science, antivivisection. These aspects to Victorian mercy efforts are not discussed here: but it is worth noting that once again, mercy was associated with the monarchy. Though the poet William Somervile eulogized George II and mercy as 'best prerogative of power' for sparing a stag, in *The Chace* (1735), royal association with animal welfare was a Victorian development.⁴⁹ Victoria's statement in the Albert Hall in July 1887, 'No civilization is complete which does not include the dumb and defenceless of God's creatures within the sphere of charity and mercy', was totemic for the Anglo-American animal welfare movement.⁵⁰

How did Victoria's subjects discuss mercy? It follows from its commonplace status in orthodox Christianity that mercy was often an unexceptionable value, though its position in the economy of divine punishment and forgiveness was subject to controversy and its relative weight changed as atonement theology was eroded by 'milder' doctrinal inflexions. Related to this was the treatment of clemency or lenity in judicial and penological contexts. There was no anxious and extensive philosophizing in the manner of modern philosophers and political theorists such as Nussbaum, Tuckness and Parrish, and Bull. John Stuart Mill was eloquent on liberty not mercy – although the philosopher's utilitarian forebear Jeremy Bentham wrote pungently on mercy, as Chapter 1 notes. The prolific Ruskin, writing little on mercy, defined it as 'in its fullest sense … delight in perceiving nobleness, or in doing kindness'.⁵¹ Other references can be discovered in the private and public utterances of eminent Victorians, and in *Mercy and British Culture, 1760–1960*, I look at philosophical, scientific, and literary treatments. Less eminent Victorians evoked the virtue in clichés in prose and poetry, often related to the operation and display of royal power, triggered by royal events such as accession or death. For the monarchy was an important part of culture, and claims for the queen's mercy were related to the mercifulness of British society.

A merciful queen for a merciful age

In 1854 the Irish poet William Allingham asked whether hope in progress was justified, before concluding it was a 'goal eternal', with 'Mercy's chart unrolling' through time.[52] This section introduces connections between this Victorian sense of the progressive or humanitarian present and the monarch. Victoria was described as humane. The novelist Charles Reade connected the statute book with a nation ruled by 'the most humane sovereign the world has ever witnessed on an earthly throne' in 1856.[53] Two decades later, banners designed to show her East End subjects' affection linked her supposed character, 'a humane Queen makes a loving people', with [mis]quotations from Shakespeare's Portia speech, when she visited London Hospital.[54] Jubilee fervour generated some scepticism, *The Referee* admitting the half-century of 'improvements', doubted an 'upward march of events is all the result of "beneficent sway" on the part of "good and gentle Queen Victoria"'.[55]

Despite such doubts, people expressed exalted notions of their monarch's virtues and sensibilities. 'Millions still half enslaved and bitterly oppressed are seeking now for succour and relief from her benignant clemency. Every sophism that can be used by sinners trained to cruelty and bloated with the fruit of their oppression will be employed to dry up all the fountains of her compassion', cautioned a sermonist in 1837.[56] An Austrian writer, John Lhotsky, appealed to her as *Victoria humana*.[57] For one Briton, long abroad on missionary work in Burma, writing in 1870, 'The workingmen of England owe more to Queen Victoria than to all the previous monarchs that have sat on the throne since the days of Alfred. Her name will go down to posterity on more acts for doing justice and loving mercy to the wronged, oppressed, and suffering, than can elsewhere be found in the statute books all put together.'[58]

Reformers dedicated schemes of mercy to her. The *Spectator* appealed to the queen during agitation against duelling in 1843. 'Few opportunities are given to Monarchs in these unchivalrous days', it suggested, 'to gain immortal renown. Such an enviable opportunity is however happily afforded to Queen Victoria and her amiable husband'. Royal support against duelling was 'as consistent with the character as becoming to the sex of our gracious Sovereign'.[59] By the time of her jubilee in 1897, her benevolence was a pretext for inaugurating local charities and philanthropic enterprise.[60]

Huddersfield Chronicle in 1880, writing on the queen's sympathy with victims of railway accidents, was convinced humane gestures were not the 'cool calculations of policy … from no desire to give mere lustre to the Crown and éclat to her reign'.[61] Anecdotes and engravings promoted Victoria's Christian benevolence (and 'condescending goodness') in visiting humble peasants and parishioners in Balmoral and Osborne (see Figure I.2).[62] She transmitted her 'tenderest sympathy' in the midst of 'her own overwhelming grief' after mining disasters. The *Belfast Newsletter* in 1897 reminded readers of her 'tender love and solicitude for children' and that from her infancy she delighted in spontaneous 'acts of charity and benevolence'.[63]

The extent of her humane feeling in relation to human or non-human suffering was debated. While the poet Lillian (Mrs F.G.V. Lawford) praised the Gentle Queen, who 'hath wept and mourned with those who weep', others thought she

Figure I.2 Gennaro Amato, 'Queen Victoria and the Poor: Her Majesty Visiting a Cottage Home', *Illustrated London News Record of the Glorious Reign of Queen Victoria* (London: Illustrated London News, 1901), p.19. Author's collection.

was hard.[64] The republican *Reynolds's Newspaper* in 1855 lambasted a failure to use her prerogative to safeguard the peasantry from aristocratic predation and for not pardoning Chartist rebels and Irish nationalists: 'judging by the experience of the present reign, mercy constitutes no part of the prerogative of Queen VICTORIA.'[65]

It poured cold water over claims for humanitarianism in relation to the royal buckhounds' welfare in what it bracingly called the 'fag end of the Queen's reign' in 1889 – arguing that this was for mercenary reasons (economizing in the Royal Household).[66]

Reynolds's harsh comments went against an international tide of 'flunkeyism' and extravagant praise for the queen's humane and merciful nature. Thus writers in Australia lauded her benevolence towards animals as the 'brightest jewel' in 1883.[67] In India, it was alleged, rural folk believed she was a benevolent power that even they could appeal to with success. The *Pall Mall Gazette* printed a tale by George Forrest (of the Government of India Records) concerning a peasant with a grievance in a north Indian village, whose letter to the 'Good Lady of England' reached the queen's hands in Balmoral. The anecdote illustrated the 'far-reaching influence of the Queen's private and personal virtues. She can have been little more than a name to millions of her native subjects, but that name always carried with it the associations of benignity and mercy'.[68] Jubilee-year eulogists attempted to popularize the title of 'Victoria the Good'.[69]

'Though mercy is certainly one of the greatest ornaments of human nature'. Charlotte Badger wrote in 1803, 'it unfortunately appears to be almost excluded from the catalogue of fashionable virtues'.[70] Is there evidence that the virtue of mercy waxed and waned in its cultural approval in the nineteenth century? A writer in *The Times* in 1842 pointed to a 'march of mercy' like intellect and education.[71] In 1864 verse appearing in several Irish newspapers on mercy's reign – using the idea of a diamond-crowned figure of mercy – asserted its sway in this 'latter age', on the basis of battlefield humanity (presumably the American civil war).[72] The Anglican clergyman Frederic Farrar stated it as 'a historic fact that this is a pre-eminently a merciful age'.[73] The nineteenth century saw calls to expand the claims or entitlement to human mercy and forbearance. Philanthropists linked the Christian value of mercy with their concerns – for example, in relation to fallen women and infanticides.[74] Mercy could be enacted by legislation, in Shaftesbury's phrase, describing one early measure of child protection.[75] 'Mercy' figured in the discourse and titles of philanthropic societies parodied by contemporaries: Ford Brown notes the 'Forlorn Females Fund of Mercy' as an example – a real early-nineteenth-century society offering 'temporary relief of females who shew evident marks of penitence' but had no relief in penitentiaries or other institutions, and destitute but virtuous servants.[76]

The nuances of Victorian reactions are reflected in offhand comment – swipes against 'sentimental mercy' taken to an absurd degree in judicial contexts for example.[77] A related point might be the perception of merciless and merciful pasts – the miscellany *The Percy Anecdotes*, in 1822, noted that the era of Anglo-Saxons, Danes, and even Normans demonstrated the 'great mercy of our ancestors'.[78] A more eminent source, the historian Thomas Macaulay, contrasting the England of 1685 and his present (1848), argued, 'the more we study the annals of the past the more shall we rejoice that we live in a merciful age'.[79] Late Victorians saw the amelioration of the capital code coinciding with the accession of Victoria as a 'great moral key-note of our new era'.[80] By the late-Victorian period progressive developments such as the Humanitarian League made usage of the word 'humanitarian' more familiar though contentious, as an alternative to mercy. Yet the word still appeared in campaigns for humans and animals, such as the Liberal MP and QC Charles Hopwood's Humanitarian League pamphlet *A Plea for Mercy to Offenders* (1894).[81] Hopwood argued for mercy's effectiveness even with violent offenders. Late-Victorian anti-humanitarians, concerned about the nation's softening, spoke of the need to temper mercy with justice.[82] G.K. Chesterton treated the claim that the world was getting more merciful, as espoused, he thought, by Leo Tolstoy and the 'Humanitarians', as one of the extremes of the age.[83]

One final point, linking this keyword with Victorian people. In *Tom Brown's Schooldays* (1857), Thomas Hughes presents a still thriving Puritan tradition in the Berkshire vales, of naming children after biblical names or the 'cardinal and other virtues', including Mercy.[84] How many children were named 'Mercy' in the late nineteenth century, compared with the previous century or Commonwealth era? At a rough glance of the census data for England, those with 'Mercy' among their names gradually declined. With some doubtful orthography slipping in 'Marys' no doubt, there were almost 2,863 in 1841 (the era when Charles Dickens had Mr Pecksniff christen his daughters Mercy and Charity); 3, 535 in 1851; 1,960 in 1891; 1,469 in 1901; and 1,137 in 1911.[85] There were children named 'Justice', about 34 in 1851, but only 4 in 1911, although the orthography of the census suggests a few were 'Justin'. In one case 'Justice' followed the birth of 'Mercy', to a 'cotton spinner by power' born in Dublin, at Werneth in Cheshire in 1851.[86]

The organization of the book

This book principally considers the royal prerogative of mercy related to criminal cases when life and death were at stake. Chapter 1 starts with a brief discussion of the legal and constitutional framework, with eighteenth-century texts situating royal mercy within ideas about the English constitution. It turns to the reform in 1837 removing Victoria's direct role in discussions of capital cases in London and Middlesex. The monarch's role in balancing mercy and justice was echoed by representatives such as viceroys, judges, and justices of the peace. The latter two are studied in this chapter through discourses associated with their reputations and utterances in the sites over which they presided.

Chapter 2 examines the popular reputations of the monarchs of the House of Hanover in exercising the royal prerogative. For a book on Victorian culture, it may seem an excessive presentation of controversies in the preceding century, but it establishes some features of the mediated culture of mercy through official or popular poetry, sermon and biography, and political texts. These sources shaped individual and dynastic reputations. The chapter also shows the backward look and self-congratulation of Victorian commentators, defining their monarchy and themselves against a less merciful recent past.

Chapter 3 studies the public or mediated view, revealing how Victoria was perceived to make a commitment to reign in mercy, was imagined as a creature of mercy and benevolence, and how anecdotes developed about royal mercy relating to capital convicts. Chapter 4 concerns a different reality to that offered by newspapers and other 'public' texts, through material in the Royal Archives documenting Victoria's private views and relationship to her Home Secretaries in responding to capital and other crimes. Her diary and correspondence provide the sources for this chapter. She thought Charles Dickens's account in *Oliver Twist* of Sikes's murder of Nancy 'too horrid', she confided to her diary in 7 June 1839; correspondence with ministers exposed her to the details of actual homicide and violence towards women.[87]

From this perspective, the focus shifts in Chapter 5 to royal mercy responding to rebellion, acts of terrorism, or attempted assassination. The actions of Victoria's Governor-General in Canada, Lord Durham, and intercession to her at the same time in response to Chartist risings at home show that the appeal to a throne bearing a female monarch offered a powerful trope in these situations. A key moment when pity for women and claims for British mercy linked to the monarch were expressed was the Indian rebellion in 1857, so discourse on royal mercy in the Indian context is also briefly examined. Appeals to her clemency touched Victoria closely as the repeated target of regicidal attempts: her record in that regard provided a way for contemporaries to assess the monarchy.

The empire is the location for further treatment of royal mercy in Chapter 6, whose title derives from a phrase current in 1858 after the Government of India Act and proclamation concerning Victoria's rule after the rebellion. The chapter begins with the ways in which appeals to the new queen, drawing on mercy's gendered associations, figured in attempts to complete abolition of slavery and deal with its legacy in the British world. From the West Indies in the late 1830s, the chapter turns to royal mercy's place in capital-punishment abolitionism and public debates about claims to independent statehood in colonial Australia. The chapter ends by raising the gaze beyond the confines of empire, to see how appeals were made to mercy by non-Britons and how mercy was understood in British discourse as an attribute of monarchy in general, even if this was the quite different rule of the Egyptian sultan, Ethiopian kings, or Chinese empress.

Chapter 7 studies artistic representation of queenly mercy in the Victorian era, focusing on the colossal sculptural group by John Gibson in the Palace of Westminster, placing this in the context of depictions of intercessory and mercy-wielding monarchs. It also considers the ambiguities of Victoria's role in mercy – represented in the material artefacts of official medal, public sculpture, and personal commission – in the context of British bellicosity.

How did royal mercy continue in the new century? The conclusion links the prerogative of mercy to the waning of royal power, by considering the treatment of this prerogative by Edward VII and his heir and situates this study within the wider history of British mercy that I attempt.

A historiography of royal mercy

The monarchy's sovereign virtues traditionally included mercy, the mark of a true prince. Scholars of the medieval and early modern eras have examined its part in royal culture. Helen Lacey studied mercy in fourteenth-century England.[88] While Edmund

Spenser depicted Elizabeth I as Gloriana, her face the very appearance of peace and mercy, Mary Villeponteaux argues mercy was a 'problematic concept' for moralists and political theorists in Elizabeth's reign because quite apart from its wielding by a female monarch, its virtuous exercise might become merely emotion-driven 'pity'. Yet, as she notes, the idea of mercy was inseparable from pity and encompassed in a broader idea of *equity*.[89] For Cynthia Herrup, the royal prerogative of mercy exposes some of the 'challenges of kingship with two genders', whereby the monarch was understood to have masculine and feminine qualities regardless of actual gender. Like Villeponteaux, Herrup discerns the fear of a 'womanish' mercy based on pity rather than reason but emphasizes the particular problem for the 'female prince' lacking the cloak of wifely intervention for acts of grace.[90] For Krista Kesselring, mercy was a significant aspect to state-formation in the sixteenth century, through a theatre of power which incorporated a participatory element; the Tudor monarchy's use of this prerogative went largely unquestioned. Notions of mercy derived from Christian and classical texts appeared in pageants and plays, sermons and public speeches. Mercy's status as a virtue exercised by the monarch in tempering justice was not yet seen as a corruption of justice, as post-Enlightenment thinkers argued, although there were critics of 'vain pity'.[91] Kesselring suggests that Protestant theology (responding to Catholic penance, contrition, and forgiveness) had no 'discernible impact on perceptions of pardon, but confessional animosities resulting from the reformation clearly did'.[92]

Seneca's *De Clementia* argued that mercy was 'temperance' or self-control by the mind when it had the power to take vengeance. Mercy accompanied mildness and moderation in theorizing power.[93] Recent work complicates the early modern idea of 'moderation' – defined as not being violent and unreasonable – for Ethan Shagan reveals the opposite when exploring this idea's role in social, religious, and political power.[94] He emphasizes its 'intrinsically aggressive character' and in particular finds that moderation in Tudor and Stuart England 'often bore powerful connotations of coercion and control that have been lost over subsequent centuries, leaving behind only cosy connotations of equanimity and reasonableness'.[95] This is an important insight for my study: since mercy is an exercise in and justification of power.

A number of scholars examine European royal mercy in subsequent centuries.[96] Princely mercy was discoursed upon in peaceful times and stimulated in tumultuous times when its withholding or display in treason trials was part of the 'theatre of justice', which 'became a forum not simply for the performance of just kingship but for a public dispute over where justice lay and who was its most trustworthy custodian'.[97] Herrup describes 'widespread clemency [as] a critical tool for restoring order'.[98] Restoration panegyrists focused on Charles II's clemency, as Kevin Sharpe notes, citing the Tory Thomas Flatman's description of the late king as 'Charles the Merciful' and John Dryden's writings.[99] In reflecting later on the brutal punishment after Monmouth's rising, Sharpe refers to his successor's 'vocabulary of self-representation' including moderation and mercy, and the attempt to present Judge Jeffreys as an aberration from kingly mercy.[100] Sharpe also notes the presentation of the Stuart monarch as part of a tradition of mercy and gentleness exemplified by Edward the Confessor.[101]

Douglas Hay, in a famous essay, studied the political theatre of mercy.[102] 'Men were merciful and merciless in the eighteenth century: the historian's task is to answer the questions when, and why', he wrote.¹⁰³ The 'powerful psychic configuration' of a paternal king tempering justice with mercy was a distinctive element of criminal law, before nineteenth-century reform, that 'encouraged loyalty to the king and the state'.¹⁰⁴ Acts of mercy helped create the mental structure of paternalism and legitimized the social order. Mercy was 'part of the currency of patronage' or 'game of interest' in which success was a mark of social weight.¹⁰⁵ Hay looked at 'pardon-dealing [going] on at the highest levels only', so that mercy could be treated as mysterious, sacred, and absolute rather than merely another expression of interests.¹⁰⁶ There was a close role for monarchy in the staging of mercy: George III shortly after his accession ordered news of royal mercy to be revealed to a robber only at his execution site.¹⁰⁷ Hay's 'majesty of the law' was in the context of a loss of ideological props for the monarchy after the Glorious Revolution and reduced prestige for the Church of England: 'English justice became a more important focus of beliefs about the nation and the social order.' 'Benevolence', he asserted, 'was not a simple positive act: it contained within it the ever-present threat of malice'.¹⁰⁸ While public approval for a pardon might be directed at the monarch, mercy was not just bestowed by the king but 'ran through the administration of the criminal law, from the lowest to the highest level'.¹⁰⁹ The glory of a pardon was shared with respectable, aristocratic, propertied, and genteel intercessors. The papers of 'any large landed proprietor are peppered with appeals for pardons, and earnest thanks for them'.¹¹⁰ When there was uncertainty about a conviction, mercy could be feigned rather than reveal impotence on the part of the propertied ruling class.¹¹¹

John Beattie has also explored the role of royal pardons in a study looking at crime and the law over the 'long eighteenth century'.¹¹² Others, subsequently, have examined the process to recover the factors behind successful appeals and disputed Hay's stress on respectability as a key factor. Andrews, from the perspective of *ancien régime* France, succinctly described the English case thus: 'the monarch ceased to be remote and abstract. Royal mythology suddenly became real, exerting an indelible effect on the beneficiary and all his dependents.'¹¹³ The broader trend in European monarchy was a humanization in which anecdotes about actual rather than generic mercy contributed to a sense of an authentic personality.¹¹⁴ In an episode of mercy withheld, Andrew and McGowen's examination of the Rudd/Perreau forgery case in George III's reign sees an 'unprecedented' campaign to sway public opinion and influence the Crown through petitions and newspapers in 1776.¹¹⁵ But several scandals involved widespread press coverage.¹¹⁶ Carolyn Strange's edited collection of essays studies the politics of discretionary exercise of mercy in Britain, Australia, and Canada, thereby addressing the neglect of mercy by historians of crime since Hay and Beattie. For Strange, after the eighteenth century and monarchy's decline, the concept 'acquired an increasingly old-fashioned ring' yet was linked to democratic rule as a popular 'right' to be exercised by the Crown. Strange emphasizes the act of mercy as a political and ontological subject rather than as an absence of punishment.¹¹⁷

A sermonist in 1743 asserted,

> did Princes and Potentates consider how much the Throne is upholden by Mercy, how much it ennobles their Character, how it endears them both to Heaven and

Earth, and stamps upon them a double Image of him whose Vicegerents they are; as they surpass others in the Means and Power of doing Good, so they would endeavour to excel them in the actual Exercise of Beneficence.[118]

Royalty's role in those 'acts of mercy' that we would understand as philanthropy and charity is explored by Frank Prochaska.[119] One philanthropic body endorsed by late-Victorian royalty was the League (and Order) of Mercy. In this instance a key figure was the Prince of Wales, and a biographer in a chapter entitled 'The King as a Philanthropist' noted the stream of letters sent in the belief that he was able to right their writers' wrongs.[120]

Controversy over Victoria's failure to be merciful in high-profile capital cases involving working-class convicts is related to the scholarship on loyalism and royalism, republicanism and anti-monarchism.[121] Richard Williams studied the 'reverence and sentimentality' towards the royal family in the context of a republicanism 'always in a distinct minority': relating that veneration to the domestic virtues Victoria was seen to express but also noting the eulogies to royal sympathy and kindness.[122] Antony Taylor, who identifies an early honeymoon phase of Victoria's reign as 'just monarch', drawing on a cult of King Alfred and expressed in illustrations depicting her 'injecting a note of female compassion into the affairs of state', mentions the case of Samuel Wright, condemned to death in 1864, in his account of anti-monarchism.[123] He suggests a 'conscious crypto-medievalism at court and in the depictions of the royal family inspired a misguided faith', in royal mercy, for the working-class man.[124]

Political radicals of various types heightened the politicization of mercy in the nineteenth century. Discussion of ministerial advice and royal insulation from decision-making in capital cases seemingly exposed the monarch's developing powerlessness. Mercy tempering justice and a benign rule in the context of popular liberty and freedom were tropes of coronation poetry suggesting mercy figured in a 'popular constitutionalism' that has interested historians.[125] Attempts on her life became occasions for extolling a benign monarchy and expressing loyalty towards Victoria, moments of 'triumphant renewal', in the words of Paul Murphy.[126]

John Plunkett's work on the relationship between a developing mass media and the monarchy shows how the press was part of a 'royal culture industry' across a range of media that ensured Victoria's 'overarching presence' in her subjects' lives.[127] Plunkett considers the 'insinuating nature of Victoria's imaginative and affective impact' in an age when the monarchy (at least in the 'Albertine' phase) was more visible through a deliberate policy of visits and tours.[128] Publishers fed a fascination with anecdotes of royal benevolence, and tearful mercy was part of the cloying reportage of Victoria's life and reign at the century's end.

More recently, scholars look at imperial contexts. Miles Taylor has noted, in a wide-ranging essay on the royal family and empire, that the convention of petitioning – for mercy among other things – 'has seldom been looked at in a colonial context'. His monograph studies the Victorian monarchy in India, where claims were made for the critical role of Victoria's merciful sympathies.[129] There is also work on Victoria as source of justice for indigenes confronting settler power and the invocation of her memory as merciful Great White Queen.[130]

The scholarship on British ideas about mercy encompasses cultural histories of dramatic text and performance, literature such as religious poetry or novels, and pictorial or sculptural rendering. Some of these productions concerned royal or imperial mercy. Meyler's study of the politics and drama of seventeenth-century England examines pardoning power on stage.[131] The eighteenth-century stage performed clemency through the actions or utterances of Artaxerxes, Caesar, Titus Vespasian, or Alexander the Great as revealed in McGeary's work on opera librettos, which 'not only validate Britain's system of pardons, but align the routine, daily actions of judges, secretaries, and ministers with the great and noble figures shown in the ancient world'.[132] Both comic opera and the serious operatic 'mirror for princes' extolled mercy.[133]

Sources for the study of royal mercy

This book concentrates some of its attention on the public, partial, or inaccurate impressions of royal mercy through the press, to show the misperceptions and myths as well as the reality of state mercy. The official correspondence of monarchs and ministers – some of this printed, for instance in edited volumes for the reigns of George III and his successor – allows a glimpse of royal responses to appeals for clemency.[134] I looked at the official record in the exercise of mercy by Victoria through the Royal Archives, largely in criminal cases (with correspondence to and from her Home Secretaries). There are other sources for the official use of mercy *not* studied in depth here, including petitions in the Home Office, a few letters addressed to Victoria for more merciful sentences, and petitions addressed to the monarch in the East India Company records, and described in the National Archives' online catalogues.[135]

The digitization of George III's essays makes more accessible private documents conveying his awareness of Enlightenment work on the penal law, the passions, emotions, and moral obligations.[136] There are Victoria's diaries for a private discourse by this monarch – but mercy figures little in her published letters or versions of her diaries which her daughter Beatrice constructed. The study of unpublished archival sources has otherwise been limited to manuscript archives available digitally, such as the Churchill Archive – Winston Churchill being Home Secretary in the reign of her successor in 1910. Material in relation to the eighteenth-century pardoning process in the papers of members of the landed elite seeking reprieve (or for mercy to be withheld) as part of their patronage or expression of paternalism might also include reflections on the royal willingness or appetite for mercy.

The British monarchy was mediated through institutions, activities, and cultural artefacts, including public celebrations of accession and jubilees, printed eulogy, and newspaper gossip. The press played a crucial role in creating versions of the Victorian monarch, as it had done for her Hanoverian forebears, but now with rapidly advancing technological sophistication and enhanced popular accessibility to print media. Tales of royal compassion were present at the start of the reign, embroidered by parties interested in associating royalty with their own reformist projects and used by her subjects in sermons, poetry, and biography. The monarch was expected to be merciful and imagined in acts of mercy; even if the exact circumstances were unclear, such episodes were believed to be true.

In researching representations of royal mercy from c.1760 onwards, a variety of literary and visual sources available in digital form are used. Newspapers had an acknowledged role as witnesses to the operation of criminal justice and punishment especially when execution took place in prison after 1868. Before Victoria, the names of those reprieved in the Recorder's Reports before the King-in-Council and news of royal mercy anticipated or withheld were printed. This might be inaccurate as in news of a pardon for chief clerk George Skeene of Queen Square Police Office in 1812 (when the Marquess of Huntley unsuccessfully 'used uncommon exertions to procure the mercy of the Prince Regent'[137]). The press provided news about petitioning campaigns for mercy.[138] Newspapers also agitated for and against particular criminal-law reforms. One London paper at the beginning of Victoria's reign commented, 'we find it has become the fashion of the newspapers (especially in the provinces) to advocate the total abolition of capital punishment even for murder.'[139]

In George III's reign, press accounts provide occasional evidence of prisoners in court knowledgeable about the pardon process. At the start of his reign, the twenty-five-year-old John Brett, son of an Irish Protestant minister, addressed the Old Bailey court after sentence of death for forgery. He begged prosecutors would 'be humanely pleased to request the Gentlemen my Jurors to recommend me to your Lordships for a favourable report to be made to his Majesty for his royal mercy. The great efficacy that such report made to his Majesty would have I shall not pretend to describe to your Lordships' (Brett reiterated this point four times in the letter he read out but was executed).[140] The first chapter studies the record of Old Bailey trials for the public language of mercy in this important legal context.

The complex documentation of the messiness of actual intercession and official response is in the state archives of justice and mercy. Examination of mercy from the angle of monarchy must also consider hagiographies and eulogies.[141] Tales of mercy exposed the humanity and awful responsibility of princes; rival claimants after the Hanoverian succession disputed narratives of royal mercy and justice. A similarly challenging environment for royal mercy operated in the late eighteenth century. One writer in the French Revolution's shadow fretted about the French king's evasion of duties if, because of 'those pangs which every humane mind cannot but feel in inflicting punishment upon criminals, he suffers those laws to lose their effect'. Then justice would be sacrificed in a too merciful application of power.[142]

George III and his long-reigned granddaughter stimulated a large body of eulogy. Victoria was a major cultural figure, and anecdotes about her character and life proliferated in poetry, pamphlet, and book. Already in 1838, one newspaper referred to the 'vast quantity of nonsense published in all quarters concerning her Majesty'.[143] An American complained in 1846 of the difficulty of approaching the real character through the 'mass of adulation and incense offered her by the English press and people', judging her, however, among the more lovable of British monarchs.[144] 'I was amused at the literature through which I had to wade for my facts', Clare Jerrold wrote in 1911: 'Taken in the mass, it became a paean of praise with every trace of real human lovableness erased.'[145] Many of these texts were obscure and deservedly so, but anecdotes about royal clemency enjoyed a sustained existence in Victoria's reign.

A brief note on methodology

By quoting, Ruth Finnegan argues, 'we simultaneously enact past and present', that 'paradoxical duality' of nearness and distance created by bringing others' words into our text. Walter Benjamin suggested that to 'write history therefore means to quote history'.[146] Some discussion about the way primary material is used here is in order, given the decision to employ contemporaries' words with a frequency that might seem to pile on quotations, in addition to extensive paraphrase.[147] One doyen of cultural history, in attempting to uncover values or attitudes, is criticized for accumulating 'a mass of evidential snippets' and ending up merely presenting contemporary views 'in all their splendid variety'.[148] My approach to cultural history uses a wide range of textual and visual sources. In an analysis that also acts as an evocation of the richness of the discourse, quotation from and paraphrase of what people wrote on or spoke about mercy in a variety of locations (including court room and pulpit, and in the realm of the imagination) is foregrounded. Not that everything merits quotation, yet clichés convey the trite and lazy ways of presenting mercy as well as the words designed to secure attention and approval from those in power.[149]

Whether there is enough textual analysis, explanation, and argument in the narrative, I leave to the reader to decide. But the method employed has not been that of unstructured collage in the naïve belief that contemporaries transparently 'speak for themselves'. Indeed what is important is where they do not just speak for themselves. Thus I indicate where a pattern or tradition existed, as in the 'Whiggish' and anti-Jacobin discourse on mercy in relation to the constitution in the first chapter. Another instance, the recovery and liberal quotation of verse using the metaphor of the blunt sword, demonstrates the practice of using the regalia to add symbolic weight to coronation-time poetry. This does not mean mercy's exercise (royal or otherwise) was uncontested: as capital cases show, frequently the use or withholding of mercy elicited criticism in the press from journalists and members of the public. I am generally unsatisfied merely to find a comment on mercy unless others can be identified taking a similar stance or opposing it, to avoid the monologic and totalizing gaze.[150] Alighting on an eloquent treatment is one thing, but the historian needs a sense of typicality in a particular context: what is indicative and representative as well as what is unusual and startling usage. Selective quotation can convey assumptions, outlooks, and responses of significance in the wider field. The discovery of mercy through digitized searches must be balanced against the risk of finding it everywhere, the 'fallacy of misplaced familiarity'.[151] If the pitfall of over-quotation has not been avoided, this may be excused by the effort to demonstrate mercy's status as a neglected keyword, as well as common word, in the British 'long nineteenth century'.[152]

As to the changing meaning (the defining feature of Raymond William's concept of the 'keyword') of mercy over a longer period, I leave this to the broader view of my second book. Its thematic chapters provide particular contexts for my citations on mercy (theologies of mercy, mercy in war, mercy as applied to non-Europeans and non-human animals, mercy as gendered attribute, mercy as counter in imperial and anti-imperial discourse, mercy defended and 'outlawed' in radical revolution). Mercy's discursive or rhetorical uses changed with the context (or specific 'problem', e.g., Irish nationalism and associated discourse communities), rather than there being a startling transformation or unsettling of meaning over the eighteenth and nineteenth centuries.[153] There were debates about who was admitted to the 'pale of mercy' (and consider, in the fluctuating penal responses to crime, the oscillation between severity and leniency), but no radical change in the varied understandings of mercy is discernible until it undoubtedly became an old-fashioned word in the late twentieth century.[154] Until then, it was a culturally esteemed value, so that the contest over its use and possession that Daniel Rodgers sees as axiomatic of keywords represented not conflict over meaning so much as who could claim to have the upper hand in mercy stakes, as well as who merited mercy's withholding.

One can quantify the appearance of the word: the 'hits' in searching for the usage and the frequency of mercy in databases such as *Old Bailey Online* and the census data for mercy as a female first name (cited above) are two examples. Whether quantifying or not, I look for the occurrence of the word and variants (mercifulness, mercilessness, mercies) while aware that the word and the ideas constituting mercy even where the word is absent belong to a set of associations (including justice, humanity, pity, cruelty) and extend beyond the politico-legal and theological contexts into everyday discourse.[155] Yet this study focuses on the variants of the word 'mercy' rather than interrogate associated words such as 'benevolence'.[156]

To conclude this account of methodology, there is no better way to convey what people 'do' with a keyword – Daniel Rodgers's test of importance – than the direct quotation and paraphrase I am liberal with.[157] Mark Fortier's work on 'equity' as a keyword in the English-speaking world defends the 'myriad citation … to indicate the particular dynamics of its predominantly extensive usage', notes the problem of book length in stopping to study closely each occurrence and accumulates exemplification to 'give weight to equity's extensiveness as a keyword' and provide material for others.[158] I adopt this approach for the same reasons.

The monarchy was key to the performance and embodiment of mercy in British culture. It is important to see how the monarchy as prominent symbol of human mercy relates to large-scale demands on mercy such as global war, imperial rebellion, and national acts of moral reform such as abolition of slavery. Taking the focus in this book as the association of monarch with mercy and clemency particularly in response to homicide, attempted regicide, and rebellion, the first chapter establishes the legislative and constitutional context for Victoria's acts of mercy. As chief magistrate of the realm, the monarch supposedly administered justice with mercy and was the pinnacle of a structure of justice and mercy descending from the judiciary down to her Justices of the Peace.

1

Royal Mercy's Constitutional Context

British justice is administered in the monarch's name. Hence, a criminal trial is officially styled *Rex (or Regina) vs. Smith*. The monarch is also the fountain of mercy, in whose name the prerogative of mercy is exercised. Discussion of the constitutional (including judicial) and legislative aspects to royal mercy provides the natural introduction to a closer study of the 'throne of mercy'. This chapter maps out the monarch's constitutional role in the administering of mercy primarily in the context of domestic criminal law. It begins by considering mercy's associations with monarchical power in constitutional commentary and allusion from the seventeenth century. It then studies how one development in 1837 changed the new monarch's direct relationship to capital punishment and reinforced the Home Secretary's role. After this, the discussion turns to royal mercy on special occasions in the life of a monarch, from accession to jubilee. The final section shows how mercy featured in the discourses of judge, jury, and justices of the peace.

Royal power and the prerogative of mercy

Study of the historic language of mercy shows that commonplace metaphors included the idea of a crown – symbol of power – where mercy was the brightest gem. A sacred power emanated from it, represented as an aura in prints of royal figures in the eighteenth and early nineteenth-centuries.[1] The aureate crown adorned portraits of Victoria's grandfather, George III, and his spouse, Charlotte, in the 1790s.[2] A crown from which light emanates embellishes an engraving of the king's daughter Princess Elizabeth by Edward Scriven in 1806. The earthly diadem of a divinely appointed magistrate prefigures the celestial crown in sentimental imagery of the deceased Princess Charlotte of Wales in 1818.[3] A print decorating a commemorative mug after George III's death in 1820 included scales and sword of justice, and the light-shedding crown.[4] When artists represented the spirit of the English constitution, elements such as the scales of justice, sword, and sceptre, combined with the crown and documents such as Magna Carta.[5]

Such was the visual imagery of early-nineteenth-century loyalists. Just as with the 'kingcraft of benevolence', mercy was a calculated act.[6] Thomas Mortimer asserted, 'it likewise inspires love and veneration for the sovereign when it is exercised with discretion and impartiality as we have experienced in our own time', in 1801 in a companion to Blackstone's *Commentaries on the Laws of England*.[7] Mercy was understood to require power, to be kept in bounds and effective.[8] Theologians such as the seventeenth-century Puritan Stephen Charnock, discoursing on God's attributes, made clear the 'perfection of Divine power' as a precondition for mercy and justice.[9]

'Clemency is the distinguishing quality of Monarchs', stated the French dramatist and writer Louis-Sébastien Mercier in 1784.[10] But as Tuckness and Parrish argue, during the eighteenth century, demands for equality under the law arose, and 'a consequent rejection of the monarchical discretion that, during its ascendancy, had helped mercy to be seen as a virtue'.[11] Critics saw mercy as part of tyranny's apparatus: Jeremy Bentham in 1822 wrote that '[t]o the vocabulary of tyranny belongs the word mercy', seeing it as antagonistic to justice.[12] 'The distinction between justice and mercy', argued the radical poet Percy Bysshe Shelley in a manuscript essay on Christianity, 'was first imagined in the courts of tyrants. Mankind receive every relaxation of their tyranny as a circumstance of grace or favour'.[13] Mercy's bestowal and denial were acts of power operating on the powerless. Individuals, communities, and nations were 'at the mercy' of the powerful; moreover, mercy could be interpreted as weakness or fear.

The most fraught exercise of this power related to capital punishment. '[M]ercy shews that sovereigns are above the law, and that they have not only a power to take away, but also to give life', wrote an essayist in 1766.[14] The eighteenth-century nonconformist minister Philip Doddridge argued that the magistracy's chief use was to inflict this punishment in his gloss on 'holding not the sword in vain' (Romans 13.1) in his *Family Expositor*.[15] An early Victorian capital-punishment abolitionist asked, 'is the chief use of our beloved Queen to hang … unhappy wretches?'[16] From the opposite side of the debate, the barrister William Mawdesly Best answered in the affirmative when he told the Juridical Society in 1857 that 'capital punishment is the ultima ratio [final argument] between sovereign and subject as war is the ultima ratio between state and state'.[17]

The relationship between subject and state placed mercy prominently in constitutional discourse – treatises, sermons, loyalist essays and songs, and radical writings. Mercy's status as one of the Crown's 'amiable powers' was discussed by legal and constitutional commentators through the seventeenth and eighteenth centuries.[18] As an aspect of government, it distinguished monarchy from democracy. The high Tory Nathaniel Johnston eulogized Charles II's clemency in a work extolling kingly government in 1686.[19] The non-juror and anti-Whig Charles Leslie, at the beginning of the next century, also contrasted popular governments with monarchy. They tended to withhold mercy: 'they exclaim against tyrants for their cruelty and at the same time find fault with them for their mercy and prefer a constitution, wherein there can be no mercy'.[20] A king might condemn and pardon – in a monarchy, there was room for mercy – but where the people condemned, mercy was totally excluded.[21]

The lawyer Roger Acherley's discussion of the monarch's role in *The Britannic Constitution* (1727) summarized the theory of royal mercy, the danger of partiality in its use, and the expediency of mercy in some instances. The monarch was supreme governor, and therefore 'many of the Vertues and Perfections attributed to the great creator … ought, in a Human and Subordinate Sense, and Similitude, to be Attributed to the Person placed in this Supreme Regal Office; such as Fortitude, Goodness, Justice, Mercy, Wisdom, and Activity'. For Acherley, justice was the prize jewel and mercy, defined as 'a generous Pardoning Offenders, and Mitigation of Punishments, in such Cases where the Publick Weal should not suffer', should be denied when it 'would Encourage others to Offend, and Prejudice the State or People in General; there Mercy to one Man, would become Cruelty to Multitudes'. Acherley saw political value when its employment could 'Gratify many; and sometimes create Friends, who, at seasonable Times[,] may Afford Important Services and Assistance'.[22]

Sir Michael Foster, Recorder of Bristol and former judge of the King's Bench, in mid-century discourses on homicide, admitted the constitutional role of mercy 'as well as justice', as a result of coronation oaths 'antiently taken'.[23] Book IV of Blackstone's *Commentaries on the Laws of England* (published 1769) is the most famous exposition of English law's relationship to mercy. Queen Victoria was meant to study Blackstone, but whether she studied this commentary is unknown.[24] For Blackstone, the law was 'bound to be administered in mercy: this is promised by the king in his coronation oath, it is that act of his government, which is the most personal, and most entirely his own'.[25] Blackstone observed that royal courts of justice condemned people, whereas the royal sceptre's 'great operation' was mercy.[26] Monarchy's advantage was that someone was empowered to 'extend mercy wherever he thinks it is deserved, holding a court of equity in his own breast to soften the rigour of the general law in such criminal cases as merit an exemption from punishment'.[27] This allowed the sovereign the popular reputation as 'the fountain of nothing but bounty and grace' and 'repeated acts of goodness' coming from the royal hand brought endearment and 'contributes more than anything to … that filial affection and personal loyalty which are the sure establishment of a prince'.[28]

Whigs such as the historian Catherine Macaulay could summarize the role of government so that it included a place for mercy as one of the general attributes of good government. A statue of Macaulay was inscribed: 'Government is a power delegated for the Happiness of Mankind, when conducted by Wisdom, Justice, and Mercy.'[29] Whig concerns about power are present in Advocate Hugh Arnot's reflexions on royalty as remedy for deficiencies in Scottish criminal law, in 1779:

> In a country where such anxiety has been shown to guard against oppression from the crown, it surely will not be said, that the liberty of petitioning for royal mercy is a sufficient remedy against iniquity. Alas! although we live at present under a mild and gracious Prince, it must not be forgotten, that, from the influence of the crown, the chief danger is to be dreaded. 'Can a man, (as is well said by a writer on this subject), expect justice from his party, or mercy from his enemy?' Nay, although the royal mercy be extended, the reparation is not adequate to the injury. A royal pardon may, indeed, heal the wound, but it cannot remove the scar. We approach the throne, the humble suppliants for favour; but, before a court of law, we are entitled boldly to demand justice.[30]

Mercy and pardon by a condescending king were part of the old order that American rebels opposed in the 1770s. Yet presidential power of pardoning ought to have modified British commentary on American or other republics.[31] During the revolutionary era, the 'reverend Simon Olive-Branch', addressing the 'Association for Preserving Liberty and Property against Republicans and Levellers' in *The Looker-On* in 1792, spoke of the republican polity with its insecurity and jealousy requiring severe laws: the 'curtain of hopeless sorrow is drawn round their tribunals'.[32] The Reverend Richard Valpy, reflecting on mercy in an assize sermon at Reading in 1793, condemned 'the principle of the French constitution, which tore the brightest jewel from the crown of the sovereign – the privilege of MERCY. The philosophical legislators of France widely departed from the idea of their great master Voltaire'.[33] A patriotic prologue to O'Keefe's comedy *The World in a Village*, performed at Covent Garden also in that time of the Terror in the revolutionary France of 1793, asserted: 'Here on a rock, secure amid the storm, | Dwells Liberty in fair Monarchic form.' Justice animated 'equal laws', but her sword was 'by mercy check'd, as urg'd by might, | Her Crown the sanction of a People's Right'.[34] The third edition of the *Encyclopædia Britannica* (dedicated to George III) took to task the 'zealous democrat' William Godwin in its essay on 'Pardon', disputing his characterization of clemency as 'pitiable egotism'.[35] An essayist in the loyalist *Tomahawk* in 1795, arguing that democracy was more dangerous than the prerogative's abuse, thought that those who were tender about seditionaries must understand that to pardon those who gloried in their crime was a misuse of clemency. The criminal needed to repent for mercy to be reconciled with justice. The prerogative's wrongful exercise was the easiest constitutional method for the king to ruin the nation, and with 'so much the more facility, that he would certainly not have to combat the present opposition upon such occasions'.[36]

The king's oath was highlighted for its merciful aspect by a correspondent in the radical *Political Review* in August 1812, discussing judges' constitutional role as 'keepers of the king's oath' (and arguing for a more merciful judicial response to libel cases). Mercy was needed since Englishmen did not love 'strict justice' and therefore 'it is not by the rigour of the Law that their King is bound to govern them, but by Justice softened and mitigated by Mercy, which is a divine and amiable attribute'.[37] Republicans, well into the Victorian era, argued for the greater compassion of their favoured polity.[38] In 1849, parliamentary supporters of Hungarian nationalists sought British intervention against Austria, claiming that 'since Republican France has abolished capital punishment for political offences, it will not be wise to allow a contrast to be drawn unfavourable to the clemency of monarchical governments'.[39] As these late-eighteenth- and mid-nineteenth-century allusions to royal mercy indicate, the prerogative was examined in the context of wider concerns about the reform or preservation of the British Constitution.[40]

That the royal prerogative was so obviously controlled by Victoria's ministers reflected the monarchy's declining political power.[41] A dying George IV was the last monarch to act independently by reprieving a gentleman and sometime magistrate, Peter Comyn, convicted of arson on his residence in County Clare, in April 1830. With opposition from the Home Secretary, Peel, and Wellington, the king backed down. At the same time, the prerogative was politicized by party politics. The Tory William

Huskisson, speaking on the opposition MP Robert Grant's motion on a regency in July 1830 after William IV's accession, asserted the need for no break in the monarchy: 'In England the people have been properly taught to look to the Throne as the directing and constantly active power which puts every part of the political machine in motion and keeps each part in its right place'.[42] From prorogation and dissolution of Parliament, in law-making, in 'public power of every description', the throne was the final location of authority including, 'the tempering of that administration with mercy'. It was 'most unwise to weaken those feelings by exhibiting the Crown as a phantom' brought to life by some *senatus consultum* or Parliament, Huskisson argued.

At the accession of Victoria, anti-Whigs hoped the queen would escape the 'Lichfield House bondage' of Whigs and radicals, to enjoy 'something of independence and freedom in the exercise of her royal prerogatives'.[43] Despite partisan discourse on abuse of the prerogative, it was by now 'firmly subject to ministerial advice and responsibility'.[44] Walter Bagehot hyperbolically asserted in *The English Constitution* (1867) that the monarch must sign her own death warrant if Parliament willed it. Capital punishment was used here as a striking symbol of eroded monarchical power. In truth, the pardoning power was already, in the eighteenth century, diluted by being shared with lesser magistrates as sacral sovereignty made way for parliamentary, judicial, and jury involvement. As Whitman has expressed it, England was a 'place in which the criminal law was less obviously devoted to dramatizing the power of the monarchy and the leading men of the realm than was the case in France'.[45] When renewed debate on capital punishment in the 1860s brought in the royal prerogative's role, this 'purely sentimental' relationship, a 'false bond of union … between the Sovereign and people', was contrasted to the 'scientific jurist's' position.[46]

Female monarch, Recorder, and Home Secretary

Modern delicacy has forborne to burden the crown with this ungrateful office and it falls into the daily round of common red tape duty.[47]

The avowed reason was 'to relieve Her Majesty of a painful duty', but, in fact, her tender woman's heart was not to be trusted in such an awful piece of business.[48]

One major development in the royal use of mercy, according to Victorians, such as the writers of those two statements, was the capital code's alteration to remove the task of signing the death warrant from the monarch.[49] In fact this was an error that those in the 'know' in the press liked to point out. Voltaire was mistaken when his commentary on Cesare Beccaria asserted that in England no criminal was executed 'whose death warrant is not signed by the King'.[50] But one change at the start of Victoria's reign *did* reduce her role in the exercise of mercy.

The close involvement of Victoria's immediate predecessors in the capital code was limited to London. Capital cases at the Old Bailey were considered by the king-in-council following the report by the chief judge in London, the Recorder of the City of London, after each session.[51] The theatre of mercy included the report's presentation and discussion in the Council, petitioning directed at the king and others, and the publication of respite or reprieve.[52] Press coverage ensured awareness of all these processes. In July 1779, for example, the *Derby Mercury* reported 'His Majesty's Letter to Mr Recorder' was read to twenty-seven convicts whose lives were spared, their execution from 'Time to Time' being respited on condition they undertook hard labour, which 'they joyfully accepted, and received sentence accordingly'.[53]

Newspapers continued to give details in the next reign, reporting, for instance, of the decision at the end of one of the Councils when the Recorder 'was introduced into the presence of the King in Council', of fourteen capitally convicted convicts with a burglar and a man convicted of shooting a woman ordered for execution.[54] Newspapers reported the reasons, however vague they were in the absence of hard evidence, for decisions. In 1825 the *Bristol Journal*, commenting on the sugar refiner and convicted forger Henry Savery, declared that a 'knowledge of the grounds of the respite in this case is due, we conceive, to the public'.[55]

Occasionally the monarch's intervention produced public controversy. In the context of radical politicians' wider conflict with the Crown, when George III directed the Recorder Sir James Eyre to execute two Spitalfield weavers near to Bethnal Green church rather than the usual place, in November 1769, it stimulated the Wilkesite Sheriffs of London and Middlesex to query the decision. There followed the opinion of judges to ensure the king's fiat – designed to terrorize weavers in violent dispute over competition between engine looms and narrow looms – was followed. Letters in the controversy were reprinted.[56] The radical John Horne Tooke, who penned an anonymous pamphlet and whose opinion encouraged the sheriffs in their stance, claimed any variance from the sentence represented murder.[57]

In 1785 the magistrate and clergyman Martin Madan complained of the metropolitan system. Between sentence and execution, the convicts' connexions and friends – 'a brother who is servant to some member of parliament, or a sister who is mistress to such a one, or perhaps to some greater man' – attempted to reach 'the higher powers', and abuse the 'royal ear'. As a result royal mercy was 'extended to the greatest villainies' to reduce those on the 'dead-warrant' by two-thirds.[58] Problems due to the personal failings of a particular monarch are suggested by 'A Levee Day' by George Cruikshank, which depicts Recorder John Silvester waiting to present his report to the gouty Prince Regent in April 1814, behind ministers, tailors, wig makers, and others.[59] The barrister Charles Purton Cooper criticized the anomaly of the report in a book on the defective administration of justice in 1828 – copies being 'principally bought' by members of parliament. There were complaints about the anomaly, the delay and added uncertainty it gave to punishment, in Edward Gibbon Wakefield's work on the punishment of death in London in 1831.[60]

The last report in the newspapers was 26 April 1837. All those condemned to death in Newgate who were burglars and robbers had sentences commuted.[61] The notorious James Greenacre, who murdered and dismembered Hannah Brown, was executed, a broadsheet declaring 'RECORDER'S REPORT Fate of GREENACRE DECIDED'.[62] At the time, a few commentators were struck by this peculiarity – 'why the King or the law should be apparently more tender of the lives of metropolitan culprits than of offenders in other counties', the *Morning Herald* commented in 1834, 'it is impossible for human ingenuity to imagine'. The *Herald* attributed it to the Corporation of London's antiquated privileges.[63]

On 24 June 1837, four days after Victoria's accession, the Cabinet 'considered in what way we might obviate the necessity of the Queen's receiving the Recorder's Report'. The Home Secretary, Lord John Russell, introduced a bill in the Commons. After this, he exercised the royal prerogative as her representative. By 1.Vict.c.77 the Recorder no longer issued a warrant to the sheriff in conformity with orders received by the king-in-council commanding execution: no report was now made in council of any capital convict at the Central Criminal Court.[64] The prime minister, Lord Melbourne, according to the political diarist John Cam Hobhouse, did not think Victoria would hesitate to sign a death warrant 'when the culprit deserved death'.[65] Victoria's diary refers to the matter briefly, reporting a conversation with Melbourne in March 1839, about a recent murder at Newcastle and murders and trials having been previously reported to the sovereign by the Recorder: 'That was done away with at your Majesty's accession; it's much better done away with; he said.'[66]

The Courts of Aldermen and Common Council decided not to intervene, though critics saw an infringement of Londoners' prerogative and the privileges. The Recorder, Charles Ewan Law QC (a Conservative MP for Cambridge University and brother of the Earl of Ellenborough), regretted the demise of this 'ancient usage', which had extended to parts of Surrey, Kent, and Essex after the Central Criminal Court was formed. Explaining at length the alterations to the grand jury sworn in at the Central Criminal Court in October 1837, he defended that 'last investigation' as an 'example of mercy to all those in whose hands the administration of the law was confided … a precedent was at least established, that wherever doubt existed the milder and more merciful course should be adopted, and on which all the ministers of justice must feel themselves bound to act'.[67]

Newspapers informed their readers in late July of the change.[68] The *Cheltenham Looker-On* reported that the secret reason was that at the last session of the Criminal Court a man was convicted of a 'felonious assault upon a married woman'. As the law stood 'every tittle of the evidence must be read to the young Queen in council' surrounded only by male ministers, officers, and clerks. Precedents were sought 'with unceasing perseverance, and legal ingenuity has been tortured to the utmost', until legislation was resorted to.[69] The Recorder's report, in *Bell's Weekly Messenger*'s words (a day after the Cabinet discussion), though it brought crimes 'disgusting and offensive in their details' before the Crown, was useful in acquainting monarch and ministers with criminal law and 'human misery, and thus calling forth the mercies and charities of life'. For *Bell's*, the Privy Council might dispense with personal attendance when the 'evidence and the particular facts may be unsuitable to feminine delicacy and to royal feelings … as no law or practice can be allowed to supersede morals, or commit an undue blow, an indecent shock, upon natural feelings and female modesty, we should wish to see the practice of reading the recorder's report modified to certain extent'. But the task of 'selecting fit and proper cases only for the royal ear, – omitting such as are of a disgusting and offensive character, – such as would necessarily shock feelings which it is the common good of us all to preserve inviolate, pure, and unassailed', was not entertained.[70]

So Victorians were told that the contents of the reports 'were such that it was impossible for the Home Secretary to propose that it should be received by her'. The *London Saturday Journal* asserted, 'The accession of her present Majesty rendered necessary a change in the practice of reporting in Council the cases of those against whom sentence of death was recorded there being of course many cases the details of which could not be with propriety gone into in presence of the Queen'.[71] The *Era*, reporting the plight of one murderer, William Lees, spoke of the uncertainty caused by the alteration, in terms of the 'exact time when he would be executed' for murdering his wife at Ratcliffe Highway, in December 1839.[72] On other occasions press references to this procedural change assumed the early Victorian public had not grasped the fact. After the sentences passed on the attempted regicide by John Francis and the murderer Thomas Cooper in June 1842, one writer suggested it was 'probably known' by readers that this 'painful task' of directly ordering execution was removed from the sovereign – showing the writer's own confusion about the situation before 1837.[73]

The barrister Charles Purton Cooper commented in 1850 that it was 'obviously' necessary that the report's presentation should cease. 'It is to no rule, therefore in criminal legislation', he observed, 'that the enactment must be ascribed. We owe it to a circumstance – very long may it be a cause of congratulation – that England has no Salic Law'.[74] Alpheus Todd's *On Parliamentary Government in England* (1867), a constitutional primer by the librarian of the Legislative Assembly in Ottawa, glossed over the change as a process 'fallen into desuetude'.[75] The sense that the accession of a *female* monarch made this 'necessary' also appears in capital-punishment abolitionist literature. Charles Phillips, in *Vacation Thoughts on Capital Punishment* (1856), refers to it in an aside thus.[76] The abolitionist Alfred Dymond's *The Law on Its Trial* (1865) reported the alteration in passing, as a matter of course when there was a female sovereign.[77] Garbled into constitutional principle, late in the reign, *The Spectator* commented that by law 'the English Home Secretary is, during the reign of a female Sovereign, – for on the next vacancy in the throne the old right of the Kings will revive – placed in the position of a Revising Judge'.[78] For one of Victoria's best early biographers, Sidney Lee, a 'girl was obviously unfitted to perform this repugnant task'. The paradoxical effect of the accession of a woman, in his view, was that whilst reserving the royal prerogative of mercy, this practically annulled all that had remained of it.[79]

In fact, according to V.A.C. Gatrell's seminal study *The Hanging Tree*, it is a 'charming myth' that ministers were embarrassed by the prospect of discussing capital matters with a girl of eighteen: this was actually due to the reduced number of capital convicts on the list which made a report redundant.[80] What was true was that the new monarch was deliberately shielded by the Home Secretary's role. Petitions to her in capital cases went to the minister as the formal link between the monarch and the public (in the 1880s, the Secretary of State for Scotland was reported to possess this role in Scotland).[81] The minister would attract the odium for unpopular decisions for execution or reprieve. In the *Glasgow New Liberator* in 1838, the Whig Home Secretary Russell's decision about the Glasgow cotton spinners condemned to seven years' transportation for the death of John Smith led to Russell being described as 'cruel as the Dey of Algiers – stands like a frozen icicle between poor [Peter] Hacket and the clemency of the Queen'.[82]

The satirical magazine *Punch* saw the absurdity in 1843 of the duties set out in the coronation oath, as 'judgment in mercy' was now only at the Home Secretary's suggestion.[83] No longer did mercy present the 'gracious aspect' of the poets and painters' evocations in this official guise, according to the abolitionist *Douglas Jerrold's Weekly Newspaper* in 1847.[84] *Punch* ridiculed the *Advertiser*'s 'muzzy notions of mercy' in September 1859 when the newspaper claimed that it 'knew that the QUEEN was always ready to give a gracious response to an appeal for mercy'. Did the newspaper think she signed death warrants, had special red ink for her royal pen, or the Home Secretary crawled on knees to her and delivered a neat and pathetic speech based on Portia's 'quality of mercy' speech? Victoria, according to *Punch*, had not the faintest responsibility for or even acquaintance with criminal proceedings, so that the image of a queen dashing the pen away with the statement that she wished she had never learnt to write was nonsense.[85]

To judge from the evidence of newspapers and periodicals, people still assumed the monarch had a personal role in capital cases and hoped that, alongside deputations to the minister, petitioning her might help. Thus did Liverpudlians organize a petition to Sir James Graham (see Figure 1.1) at the Home Office to be forwarded to the queen in 1843 after learning 'with pain, that two of their fellow creatures have been sentenced to death' (they were executed).[86] The petition addressed to the queen on behalf of Mary Reid, sentenced to death at Dumfries for murdering Ann Hannah, appeared in the press in 1862: 'they are all the more encouraged to make this appeal because the unhappy object is a woman and mother'.[87] (The year before, 1861, the queen had been widowed.)

As a medium for discussing constitutional history, the newspaper press reflected on the royal prerogative when decisions by the Home Secretary were queried. Consider the *Newcastle Daily Journal*'s summary in January 1864, responding to the treatment of George Townley, convicted of the murder of Elizabeth Goodwin, but respited by Sir George Grey without consulting the queen, it was reported, because of insanity: 'the growth and development of the constitution ... has gradually curtailed the power of the Crown, and distributed power among the people, and made ministers of the Executive departments of the Government responsible for acts formerly done in person by the Crown'.[88] The *Morning Post* considered the throne freed from 'personal supplication by friends or relatives of the condemned ... its obvious liability to abuse was probably the primary cause of its abandonment'. This was a necessity of constitutional government, following historic abuses such as that exercised by Robert Carr, favourite of James I. It was an 'imperative transfer' to people who were 'bound to answer to the country'.[89] These included not only the Home Secretary but also the Secretaries of State for the Colonies and War, exercising the prerogative of mercy when capital cases came within their departmental view.[90] These ministers were criticized whenever there were capital-punishment controversies.[91] A later chapter shows that the minister's relationship with the queen in the handling of mercy could be tense. Happily, there were other less controversial exercises of royal mercy outside the field of capital crime, briefly detailed next.

Figure 1.1 'Sir James Graham', *Illustrated London News*, 1 October 1842, p.333. Courtesy of the University of Plymouth, Rare Books Collection.

Royal mercy during special occasions

The previous section studied changes in the normal operation of royal mercy whether in the special case of London or beyond the metropolis. I have not exhausted the occasions for mercy to lawbreakers. Royalty pardoned the non-capital criminal and displayed mercy by releasing prisoners, whether individuals or groups, at special times. These included royal jubilees, on the basis of David's amnesty, when he declared, 'Shall there any man be put to death this day in Israel, for do I not know that I am this day King of Israel?' (2 Samuel 19.22). It was asserted that Edward III was the 'first of our Kings who, in the exertion of the prerogative of mercy, proclaimed a general pardon, which has since been practised by succeeding Monarchs'.[92] The first royal jubilee of modern times in Britain was in 1809.[93] An appeal was made to release debtors and a song commemorated the gesture: 'While mirth and joy pervade the mind, | And loyal souls in union beat, | Pity with mercy are combin'd, | T'explore the debtors sad retreat. | In tears of joy behold the debtor free | On this our glorious Jubilee!'[94] Jubilee sermons extolled the king as a prince of mild and merciful disposition.[95]

Reduction to sentences for all 'good conduct' prisoners in the British Empire was suggested during the jubilee of 1887.[96] In India this was on a large scale, with 25,000 prisoners released across the sub-continent in February. The act was justified by the precedent of January 1877 when 10 per cent of prisoners were freed after Victoria was proclaimed empress, in an act of clemency which 'produced no evil results' and was 'in accordance, too, with Oriental usages and expectations'.[97] Victoria's mercy was aligned here with the 'practice of the native princes of India' from 'time immemorial'.[98] Its display of power was clear to *The Globe*; Lord Dufferin the Viceroy aimed to bring home to the native 'lower order', 'both the power and the clemency of the Empress Queen, for if her deputy could open prison doors to debtors with a word, how could the Kaiser-i-Hind's prerogatives be measured?'[99] While poets might praise this gesture, the socialist critic William Morris queried why they were in prison in the first place if they could be safely released, and condemned it as further jubilee flunkeyism.[100] How it might be extended elsewhere interested Irish nationalists concerned about political prisoners.[101] They hoped for the release of Fenians due to the assumption of the imperial title and after the return of the Prince of Wales from India.[102] Two decades later, the queen's own philanthropic intervention in diamond jubilee planning, expressed for her by the Prince of Wales in January 1897, was to propose concentrating on works of mercy, which one colonial newspaper described as 'specially suggestive of her gracious character'.[103]

A monarch's birthday could be linked to calls for mercy. Thus in the trial for high treason of George Weightman in Derby in October 1817, it was claimed there was encouragement to hope that an application for mercy would 'not be unavailing, and that which was the anniversary of our gracious Sovereign, would form a new aera in restoring good harmony to the country'.[104] The tradition remained alive in other parts of the empire: the newspaper *Truth* of Sydney sought to make Victoria's birthday an opportunity for mercy in May 1894.[105]

Coronations raised expectations of release for small offenders and others. In 1821, royal mercy was anticipated to be 'generously extended' at the time of George IV's coronation.[106] It had the air of medieval practice, 'matters ... almost obsolete', in the view of a critic of the Whig Viceroy in Ireland, the Marquess of Normanby in 1839.[107] Almost a century later, at King George V's accession, there was a similar, widely reported, gesture of clemency ('on the advice of the Secretary of State'). Punishment in military prisons and detention barracks was remitted and the sentences of civil prisoners in England, Wales, and Scotland, whose terms of imprisonment would expire within a month or more, with satisfactory conduct and industry, were partially remitted.[108] Even clemency towards a murderer was shown, in Dublin, after an appeal to the Lord Lieutenant that gestured towards the sense of mourning felt in the city at King Edward VII's death.[109] But in 1911 the Home Secretary, Winston Churchill, opposed any postponement of execution because of George V's coronation, when deciding Arthur Garrod's fate (he had killed the girlfriend whose immoral earnings he lived on).[110]

Royal marriages heralded debtors' release, as in January 1795 when the Prince of Wales was married.[111] Another wedding, of the Princess Royal in January 1858, stimulated unsuccessful appeals for clemency or respite for the German Christian Sattler, convicted of the murder of detective Charles Thain.[112] The arrival of royal children generated hopes of mercy. The birth of Victoria's son and heir Albert Edward in 1841 brought a display of clemency that surfaced in popular royal biographies.[113] At least one prisoner's parent made a plea for mercy and remission of sentence of transportation to Van Diemen's Land, on that basis.[114] The queen asked that those on the prison hulks who had behaved should be freed since she was 'desirous of showing an act of Royal clemency on the happy occasion of the birth of an heir to the throne'.[115]

Important royal visits could trigger acts of mercy. When George IV became the first reigning monarch to visit Scotland since 1633, clemency was shown to prisoners who had broken the excise laws, when the most deserving cases were identified through the Excise Office.[116] In May 1913 his great-great-nephew Kaiser Wilhelm released three English spies, on the visit of George V and Queen Mary, as a gesture to improve Anglo-German relations.[117] Other moments for royal mercy included the peace concluding the Crimean war, which was reported in the press as the opportunity for releasing political prisoners, including the Chartist Thomas Frost.[118] This was fitting given that Chartists used the queen's nuptials in 1840 as a justification for releasing the 'Welsh patriots'.[119]

The Law and Mercy

> The Mercy, recommended here under the Law, exactly corresponds with the Universal Benevolence or Charity of the Gospel; by which we are taught to be gentle, meek, patient, and merciful in all our dealings.[120]

Mercy discourse was shaped by Scripture (as the Reverend Ralph Heathcote's words in a manual for justice of the peace claimed, in the quotation heading this section), by literary texts, and applied or appealed for in law courts. The final part of this chapter on constitutional aspects turns to mercy discourse in English criminal law, a central institution in securing state and social stability. This is a field in which much has now been written: Carolyn Strange, Mark Fortier, and others have studied the 'quality of mercy' and the culture of equity which, to cite Heathcote again, corrected the 'false and unequal measures, which would often flow from the Universality of law'.[121] Here, I examine how judges, unpaid and stipendiary magistrates, juries, and others writing about their roles used this language of mercy.

The 'whole feeling of the court … is tender and merciful towards the prisoner', Home Secretary Sir George Cornewall Lewis asserted when the Commons debated the second reading of a bill for appeal in criminal cases in 1860.[122] The constitutional and popular justification for the jury was in terms of liberty and freedom (expressed in toasts to 'trial by jury'), rather than to ensure a more merciful outcome. The trial, after all, was intended to seek justice.[123] It was true that jurors were told that they were as responsible – as the English lawyer and political radical Joseph Gerrald reminded his jury at the High Court of Justiciary in Edinburgh in March 1794 when charged with sedition – for justice to be 'administered in mercy'.[124] Jurors *did* under the 'bloody code' mitigate the law's severity by partial verdicts and 'pious' perjury especially outside London. For as King and Ward have found, 'in certain parts of the periphery mercy was almost universally the rule'. In the 1770s the Genevan Jacques De Lolme's constitutional treatise considered that the jury 'in doubtful cases always decides for mercy'.[125] The press reported on jury recommendations for mercy (with headlines about 'merciful verdicts') and the weight accorded to these by the judges and Home Office.[126]

Public discourse on nineteenth-century juries (see Figure 1.2) discussed this mitigatory role. One writer in 1848 claimed that mitigation of the code was largely

Figure 1.2 Robert Barnes, 'Sketches in the Royal Courts of Justice. A Common Jury', *The Graphic*, 11 January 1890, p.49. Author's collection.

down to jurors refusing 'though on their oaths, to convict of the crime, because they did not approve of the severity of the punishment'.[127] A newspaper correspondent in 1839, signing 'A Friend to Humanity', even enjoined jurymen, in tempering justice with mercy, to 'cultivate more civilized and religious constructions of savage and ancient exactions'.[128] But it was no recommendation to the institution of the jury if 'as is perhaps commonly supposed', a *Westminster Review* essayist said in 1872, the accused had 'a better chance of escape' with them than with a trial by judges.[129]

Occasionally juries spoke more publicly. An Old Bailey jury in January 1819 asked the Recorder when reporting to the King's Privy Council to 'urge this divine injunction – "I will have mercy and not sacrifice"'.[130] One might call this *humane* rather than merciful; a commentator referred to the 'strong feeling of sympathy and humanity' in the jury system and judges referred to the 'humane interposition' of juries.[131] There were those who condemned a 'lottery' of jury quality, the 'capricious leniency', and morbid 'sympathies' or 'feelings' of the jury and others as part of the argument to end capital punishment.[132]

Apart from the newspaper reports of references to mercy by defendants and others in court, the digitized Old Bailey archive allows us to see how defendants' appeals to mercy figured in one important legal site.[133] From 1800 to 1913 the use of any phrase involving justice or judgement *tempered* by mercy (or, a variant, 'humanity') in statements made by defendants there was limited to four. The phrase 'justice and mercy' when appealed to by defendants (to judge and or jury) is found on three occasions (with few in the period before 1800). There are no references to the danger of an *unmerciful* judgement, and only a few reports of people 'begging' or 'imploring' for mercy (more asked for mercy to be shown or *hoped* for mercy).[134] I find one reference to 'the court' appealing to the jury's merciful disposition: 'I know, Gentlemen, your inclination is both for justice and mercy', when a master stated he was happy to take a servant with good character back.[135]

Yet the Shakespearian phrases 'justice tempered by mercy' and 'quality of mercy' were clichés of legal discourse, newspaper commentary, and report of activities from police courts to assize courts. Exasperation from judges when yet another speech (by the defendant or others) ended with a plea on justice tempered is occasionally heard. A thin 'march-of-intellect-looking man' found talk of tempering justice unavailing with the Marlborough Street magistrate in 1836, when charged with drunken oratory.[136] In Leamington in 1870 a defendant's attempt to read the lines was curtailed as 'it was not the slightest use to talk to the bench in that way' – at least this defendant, in court for begging, was a poet.[137] In 1913 at the trial of a peccant postman the presiding judge said, 'the phrase "temper justice with mercy" was a phrase used by somebody on some occasion as an oratorical flourish without any meaning. If justice were not tempered with mercy, it ceased to be justice and became injustice.'[138] When appointing new magistrates and eulogizing retired or deceased magistrates, the same phrases appeared. 'It was often said at the introduction of a magistrate that he would no doubt temper justice with mercy', it was noted in 1942.[139]

Biographical writings on judges, one might think, gave space to their subjects' merciful propensities, and with the growth in legal literature stimulated by Campbell's *Lives of the Lord Chancellors*, anecdotes accumulated. Campbell's *Lives* refers to the

Whig politician and Lord Chancellor Henry Brougham's merciless enmity.[140] Edward Foss's mid-Victorian *Judges of England* scarcely mentions mercy in the volumes covering the period from George III to Victoria (and nothing on clemency), the most apposite being a comment on John Patteson as a criminal judge, 'inflexibly just, and, where he could be, most merciful'.[141] William Townsend provided anecdotes on the merciless eighteenth-century judge Sir Francis Buller.[142] Later collective biographical studies such as Birkenhead's *Fourteen Judges* say little about judicial mercy in our period. His sketch of Lord Chancellor Bethell in the 1860s merely indicates lack of mercy to rivals.[143] Elsewhere there are references to tearful judges, as Thomas Dixon's study shows.[144]

Of rather more interest, unsurprisingly, were the 'terrors of the law'.[145] In newspapers and magazines, interested as they were in character and anecdote, there might appear items on historic figures such as the notorious Judge Jeffreys or, from the eighteenth century, the 'hanging judge' Sir Francis Page. Alexander Pope's words on the latter appear in a critical account of the judges sent under Special Commissions to deal with the riots and machine breaking in the English countryside in 1831.[146] Nineteenth-century obituaries and paragraphs refer to their subjects' merciful or severe reputations. These include 'Hanging Norbury', notorious anti-Catholic in Ireland ('scarce ever permitted one grain of mercy to be dropped into the scales of justice while he held the balance'; 'Mercy droops not beside his tomb; nor will justice, eloquence, or learning, stretch themselves within it'.)[147] John Gurney was criticized in *The Satirist* for merciless punishment of minor offences with transportation, and the same paper mocked William Maule in 1844 for sentence of death on Mary Furley, who attempted to kill herself and her child (and mocked the queen and Home Secretary for the *mercy* of transportation).[148] There were the mid- and later Victorian judges George Deas and Henry Hawkins.[149] Hawkins, who understandably 'winces under the name of a "hanging Judge"', was unmoved by mere sentiment.[150] Defenders of London anarchists would attack him as a 'hyena', leading to a court appearance for David Nicoll and Charles Mowbray, editors of the anarchist *Commonweal*, in 1892.[151] By contrast, the Recorder of Bombay, Sir James Mackintosh, who wrote about Judge Jeffreys's 'traffic in mercy', thought the arrangement in London of the Recorder's report a 'humane usage', and at least in his career as a historian, 'liked a maiden assize, and came away with white gloves', according to Thomas Macaulay. And there was Robert Wright, praised for his campaign against severe sentencing and 'judicial cruelty'.[152]

Serious books on crime, novels, ghost stories, melodrama on stage, and celluloid ('He has turned this justice of his into a Juggernaut – and cares not whom he crushes underneath its wheels', declared the intertitle to a film of the play *The Hanging Judge* by Hepworth Pictures in 1918) depicted the trope of the 'hanging' judge.[153] The hanging judge was seen as part of the apparatus of British power in Ireland. A splendid image of Robert Emmet pointing at a malevolent Norbury appeared as *The Weekly Freeman*'s Christmas number in 1902; almost a century before, the judge was depicted by an American artist as struck down by death, with the devil close behind, with broken scales and sword of justice joining the stricken man on the ground.[154] Of course, the judge was only one aspect of the exercise of justice and mercy in court, alongside the jury, and the merciful propensities or otherwise of the Home Secretary might be considered. At least in rhetoric, the ancient role as keeper of the king's conscience (inherited by the Lord Chancellor) meant an especial role for judges in representing the monarch's administration of justice and mercy.[155] Schomberg's constitutional treatise stated the judge as 'minister of the crown, is bound to remember mercy in the administration of justice', in 1824.[156]

Individual biographies can be studied for what they have to say about the judges' character and their leaning towards mercy. Judges might reflect on mercy privately, including in verse.[157] Manuals and commentary in journals for justices of the peace discussed mercy's importance. The advice was to err on lenity's side rather than oppression, given that such magistrates were called on to judge their own neighbours.[158] In public as opposed to legal discourse, we find comments on judicial mercy, as defendants threw themselves on the Bench's mercy. The *Universal Magazine* commented in 1793 on a judge's requirement to 'guard against extreme sensibility, which is unjust weakness, as well as against inflexible severity, in cases which may admit the exercise of mercy', citing Matthew Hale's dictum, 'When I find myself swayed to mercy, let me remember, that there is a mercy likewise due to the country.'[159]

The radical weekly *Examiner* published a series of articles in the 1840s on judicial leniency.[160] Satirical magazines attacked 'mad mercy' in judicial judgements.[161] The radical *Reynolds's Newspaper*, critical of judicial inconsistency in the late-Victorian period (both 'easy' and 'stern' judges), saw in operation spleen, sympathy, irritation, prejudice.[162] For eulogists, a merciful disposition, if not spelled out, was indicated by reference to fairness, absence of harshness: Russell of Killowen is thus characterized: 'never harsh to the unfortunate, and ever lenient to the convicted'.[163]

In an era of penological reform, the competing claims of justice and mercy figured in debates by opponents and critics of amelioration. Those whose task it was to remind the judiciary and juries of their duties reflected on the respective roles: the Reverend Jonathan Boucher's anti-liberal sentiments in one assize sermon were approved by the *Anti-Jacobin Review* in 1799: 'Modern philanthropy he justly styles the "ape of mercy;" and represents it as injurious to pure morals, legal justice, genuine loyalty, and true religion'. In enlightened and liberal times, jurors needed to beware the 'insinuating pleas of compassion and mercy'.[164] Critics of legal and penal reform debated the balance between mercy and punishment; advocates of greater severity in punishment decried mercy.[165]

The prison reformer Elizabeth Fry told a son about to become a Justice of the Peace that 'much rests with him, as to leaning on the side of *mercy*, and not of severity; and I know from my own experience with so very many magistrates, how much they do in the prisons, &c, &c. to *instigate* or *increase* suffering'.[166] Comments on the unmerciful behaviour of a particular category of JP appeared throughout the century. Radicals condemned clerical magistrates in the Peterloo era, as lacking disinterestedness and practical benevolence (as well as for being members of an established church). They were still being condemned, by a speaker in a Trades Union Congress, in the late-Victorian era.[167] It seemed incongruous to be a minister of peace and justice of the peace, to mix temporal (including politically partisan) and spiritual power.[168] 'The clerical nature draws one way', stated the *Morning Advertiser* in 1855, 'and the nature of the legal functionary the other, and violence must in every case be done, either to mercy or justice'.[169] The *Advertiser* believed the problem related to the character of Christian ministry which was to make the 'weak and wandering' feel the force of kindness and mercy. 'Anti-judicial' character was explained by the fact that reverend magistrates also meted out punishment for 'incidental sins of which justice had properly no cognizance', such as poaching on Sundays.[170] The Congregational Minister Edwin Paxton Hood's essay 'Measure Without Measure' asserted this in 1868.[171] Rather than 'messengers of mercy', they acted as fearsome squires judging harshly in matters such as poaching.[172] We are told that '[c]lerical magistrates are the most severe and merciless' and that invariably these men were the harsh dealers of the law (research on the 'English vice' also suggests clergymen were merciless as teachers wielding the birch).[173] Anglican apologists registered the damage to the church's popularity and explained the 'proverbial' severity as fear of laxity or wariness of 'mistaken mercy'.[174] The topic constantly cropped up and brought into doubt the Bench's mercy and the church's moral authority to preach mercy and forbearance.

The magistrate's mercy was otherwise appealed to, criticized, or hailed in newspapers.[175] Interventions and commentary ranged from eulogies of deceased magistrates;[176] dialect verse (Sam Mee's Lancastrian 'Temper Justice Wi Mercy. Tawk with the Magistrates' in 1913); to editorials with variants on 'Justice with Mercy' as the title, claiming to express a community's anxiety at a decision by county or borough magistrates.[177] Coverage of local crime and punishment appeared in terms of mercy and justice, shorthand for magisterial leniency or harshness, an unsurprising but important feature of the press into the post–Second World War era.

Judicial portraiture preferred symbols of justice. Richard Brathwaite's *Astraea's Teares* had mercy and justice surrounding Sir Richard Hutton's arms in 1641.[178] A mezzotint of Sir Thomas Jones of the King's Bench in the late 1670s included an alcoved justice, as did George Chinnery's portrait of early-nineteenth-century Indian judge Sir Henry Russell.[179] In the *London Magazine* of August 1780, Alexander Wedderburn, who claimed that 'in his majesty's breast there is a fountain of mercy which will be ready to make every allowance', was depicted with scales of justice and feather, and sword.[180] An engraving of Lord Eldon, for the frontispiece of a volume of the *Percy Anecdotes*, featured scales, fasces, and axe but no emblems of mercy. In the Victorian era Joseph Kirk's testimonial statue of the Irish Master of the Rolls Sir Michael O'Loghlen in the Court House at Ennis incorporated mercy and justice. A testimonial silver candelabra in 1854 for George Bankes, member of parliament (MP), as chairman of the Court of Quarter Sessions for Dorset, had 'four infantine figures … emblematic of Mercy, Justice, Wisdom and Truth': mercy fondled a dove and lamb.[181] Other memorials to judicial eminences might invoke mercy, whether in reality they were the 'furred homicides' of V.A.C. Gatrell's account. Thus the severe Lord Mansfield (see Figure 1.3), in a satirical inscription by Sir Herbert Croft, was praised for exemplary Candor and Moderation: 'In allowing the Sufferer to advance every Plea that might give Sanction to his Conduct he observed a nice and invariable Mean betwixt indiscriminate Mercy and rigid Justice.'[182]

Figure 1.3 Lord Mansfield, engraving by W. Holl after Joshua Reynolds, in H. Brougham, *Historical Sketches of Statesmen Who Flourished in the Time of George III* (London: Knight, 1839), 1st series, before p.101. Image courtesy of the University of Plymouth, Rare Books Collection.

Majesty was projected by the eighteenth-century Assize Court judges, ermine and scarlet clad; their Victorian successors still expected as representatives of the sovereign that officials who they encountered on circuit would 'dress as if in the royal presence'.[183] The sovereign's coronation oath to administer justice with mercy was compared with the judges' duty, since they represented the Crown.[184] The next chapter turns to the chief magistrate of the realm, the monarch, 'whose noble prerogatives are justice and mercy, and from whom all jurisdiction within the British dominions is derived', in the Lord Chancellor's words at the queen's opening of the Royal Courts of Justice in December 1882.[185] From the Hanoverian accession in 1714 to the death of William IV in 1837, Chapter 2 examines monarchs' association with mercy in public discourse, be it in newspaper accounts of the Recorder's reports and king-in-council, iconography, obituary eulogy, or historical anecdote. The statute book expanded to encompass such a variety of crimes against body and property as capital that it was described as the era of a 'Bloody Code' (though there was no single codified criminal law). The Reverend Schomberg's *Elements of the British Constitution* asserted in 1824 that the 'criminal law of England is not vindictive, but, on the contrary, merciful', seeing tenderness and compassion alongside its use of terror and 'awful example'. The sovereign had a central role in this mercy.[186]

2

Victoria's Merciful Predecessors

The Newspapers, which never fail to set forth with all historical exactness the virtues of the best of Kings, have often told us that for days before his Majesty receives the Recorder's report, he is moved to uneasiness, and full of anxiety from that period to the hour of doom.[1]

Let it be borne in mind that during three years and ten months of the good king William IV's reign not a single execution took place in the metropolis of Great Britain, and society, instead of being the worse in a moral point of view was the better for the absence of such revolting and brutalizing spectacles.[2]

Queen Victoria's grandfather George III and her 'royal uncles' George IV and William IV were associated with the operation of capital punishment for the reasons established in the previous chapter. One uncle, the Duke of Sussex, supported criminal-law reforms. This chapter explores public perceptions of Victoria's immediate and remoter Hanoverian and Stuart antecedents' mercy in capital cases, and the discourse in newspapers and periodicals developing around the prerogative. As the comments on George IV from the *Morning Chronicle* in 1828, and on his successor in the *Morning Herald* in 1840, quoted above, indicate, monarch and society were judged by their merciful disposition towards the death penalty.

The mercy of the Stuarts

The third mansion of hell in the Jacobite *Apotheosis Basilike* of 1708 was for courtiers and kings who abused justice and sold mercy, 'that jewel of the Crown'.[3] But the latter Stuarts distributed images of their mercy with William III commissioning a medal c.1692 of his co-ruler with the palm branch emblematic of her 'cheerful clemency'. In the context of their reign, as Kevin Sharpe notes, this went alongside images extolling William's martial achievements.[4]

William III's successor and the last Stuart monarch was praised by poets for her mercy and justice. At the start of her reign, artists were called by the poet Nahum Tate to represent Anne, with her virtues including mercy, as a new Astraea (goddess of justice).[5] Elijah Fenton despite being a non-juror, in 'An Ode to the Sun, for the

New Year, 1707', after the victory at Blenheim, commended 'the parent of her land who strove | T'exceed the transports of her people's zeal |With acts of mercy and majestic love'.[6] After her death, the praise continued. The diplomat and Tory Matthew Prior eulogized Anne in a ballad: 'Truth, mercy, justice did surround | Her awful judgment seat ... She held the sword and balance right | And sought her people's good | In clemency she did delight | Her reign not stain'd with blood.'[7] The Essex clergyman George Noone, admiring her in a memorial sermon, stated, 'what shall I say of those Godlike Virtues, which added the greatest Lustre to Her Crown, and were the brightest Jewels in Her Diadem. I mean Her Clemency and Mercy.'[8] The Anglican clergyman and antiquarian Francis Peck's *Sighs upon the Never Enough Lamented Death of Queen Anne* asserts, 'Sweet Truth | And Mercy kiss'd each others gracious Lips'.[9]

Tobias Smollet celebrated Anne's mercy in his history of England in the 1750s: 'a mild and merciful princess, during whose reign no subject's blood was shed for treason'.[10] Was Anne a merciful ruler? One finds contemporary printed evidence: thus 'Her Majesty has ordered us to direct that the Matter be prosecuted with the utmost Severity of Law and yet in the midst of Justice is pleased to think of Mercy by ordering only one of the Persons concerned to be prosecuted'.[11] Her offer of general indemnity for Jacobites in March 1703 triggered acclaim from the Scotsman David Symson. Praise for her clemency was also due to the dynasty's reputation for mercy as Symson gestured towards her 'God-like Grandsirs [Charles I's] Clemency'.[12] Joseph Gardner dedicated *The Glory of Her Sacred Majesty Queen Anne, in the Royal Navy* to one 'Boundless in acts of mercy by Descent' in 1703.[13] An amanuensis of the royalist Roger L'Estrange, Oswald Dykes, in *The Royal Marriage. King Lemuel's Lesson*, asserted in 1722, 'The forgiving Family of the gracious Stuarts were always reckon'd famous for Acts of Clemency, or Indemnity; and stand still so recorded in the truest Histories.'[14]

The parental care of subjects was a trope of iconography for the Stuarts and the succeeding dynasty.[15] Unsurprisingly, Hanoverian allegory used the figure of justice to emphasize a different legitimacy, though justice was a conventional element of European royal portraiture at the time.[16] Justice was invoked in expectations about the monarchy from political partisans (George Bubb Dodington in July 1762 hoped the sword was restored to 'national justice' by the king, against corruption and faction[17]). I have not found any visual representation of the first two Georges associated with mercy, although Smith suggests that the extensive prints of the dynasty 'might be scrutinised for signs of justice and benevolence in their physiognomies'.[18]

The education of a prince and heir involved discussion of historical acts of mercy and justice.[19] But as Hannah Smith notes, we lack the evidence for how the first two Georges saw their monarchy, either through surviving letters or political testament. The relationship of mercy to the early Georgian monarchy and monarchical culture in this chapter is here explored from sermons, pamphlets, newspaper comments, and later anecdotes. While the Court-Whig newspapers and official *London Gazette* presented kingship's benevolence and philanthropy, the early Georgian monarchy did not support an active and 'organised culture of monarchical representation'.[20]

The First Two Georges

The Hanoverians were presented by nineteenth-century historians as severe rulers. The later commentator Horace Bleackly referred to George II and his grandson as 'knowing their duty as public entertainers, seldom cheated the gallows of a victim of distinction'.[21] In a resume of English criminal law's development (at an abolitionist meeting in Coventry in 1849, chaired by the philosopher Charles Bray), a speaker noted, 'when the Brunswickers came to the Throne of England, death punishments were multiplied by the thousand'.[22] The dynasty had its apologists: Henry Ellis's collections of royal letters, published in 1827, asserted that when George the First acceded to the throne, 'a milder sway began than was known under the Plantagenets, the Tudors, or the Stuarts: the king was wise, benevolent, and merciful'.[23]

George I's clemency was bound up with rebellion and Jacobite propaganda about Hanoverian terror after 1715.[24] Pardons were part of the repertoire of responses to rebellion and mass protest.[25] The Jacobite threat involved a struggle over claims of mercy and justice between the competing dynasties: Charles Edward Stuart, appealing in print to 'nobility, gentry and freeborn subjects', referred to the authority and mercy of a young conqueror at Gladsmuir by contrast to that meted out by 'the German family' at Preston in 1715.[26] He also referenced the 'Mercy and Tenderness natural to Us, and the distinguishing Characteristick of our Family', in a general pardon issued at Holyroodhouse, 24 September 1745.[27] A Jacobite song anticipated the time when 'true greatness shine, | Justice and mercy join, | Restor'd by Stuart's line'.[28] In Scotland the swords of justice and mercy were carried before the Pretender (these ended up in the Tower of London, according to eighteenth- and nineteenth-century guides[29]).

Hanoverian supporters delivered and published sermons on the theme. Edward Lovell of St Mary, Rotherhithe, preached *Justice and Mercy Equal Supporters of the Throne* 'in vindication of his Majesty's most excellent administration from the unreasonable clamours of unruly and seditious men, for some seasonable instances of justice exercis'd on the rebels' in 1715.[30] The dynasty's defenders argued for the unparalleled mercy by which a greater number of rebels were merely transported to America. In the ballad 'Nobody Can Deny' the point is clear – there was no grounds for mercy: 'WHAT a pother is here what whining what crying | What bawling for mercy what raving what lying | Cause they had their deserts who spoke treason when dying | Which nobody can deny, deny, which nobody can deny.'[31] Richard Coleire's sermon at St. James's, Westminster, on 7 June 1716, the public thanksgiving for the rebellion's suppression, asked, concerning the king,

> can any one tell what inward Agonies and Bleedings he did not sustain, upon exercising this extreme part of the Regal Administration? Does not his known Character for Clemency make it reasonable to believe that it gave him Uneasinesses which are not to be express'd? What has been the Proportion of Executions … to the Number of the Guilty or of the Innocent Slain? Are there not many under the present Sentence of Death who have experienced his Unwillingness to let them feel the Weight of the most Just Laws, and who wait for the Consummation of Royal Mercy?[32]

Mercy was extolled by those lucky to escape execution. Thus John Paton of Grandham, at Carlisle in November 1716, 'made a famous Speech in Praise and Commendation of his Majesty King George's merciful Disposition, which he said, he had often time heard of but now felt to his utmost Joy and Gratitude; and that Eye had not seen, nor Ear heard the like before; but that he and other were living Witnesses thereof'.[33] The Irish House of Commons praised the king, casting the rebellion as the occasion for displaying his glory, 'by rendring your Justice and unparallel'd Mercy equally conspicuous'.[34] Yet to Parliament, closing the session in 1716, the king complained of the response of the Pretender's supporters to his gentle methods and 'numerous instances of mercy'.[35]

Reflecting on the aftermath, Oliver Goldsmith judged that the Hanoverians, 'brandishing the sword of justice to strike a vindictive blow', had retained social divisions: 'Clemency in the government at that time would probably have extinguished all that factious spirit which has since continued to disturb public tranquillity'.[36] It surprised a nineteenth-century historian of the rebellion that 'no publication of the time advocated the propriety of showing mercy … Almost the only remonstrance which appears to have been made, was the simple insertion in one or two of the Jacobite Journals, of the well known passage in *Measure for Measure*'.[37] In fact, it was discussed in pamphlets and periodicals. The anonymous tract *A Secret History of One Year* (of 1714) claimed the new king believed justice preferable to mercy in ruling the English temper.[38] Joseph Addison responded in the *Free-Holder*, 6 April 1716, to a pamphlet by Francis Atterbury on the people's affections being the best security of the government, about finding 'Room for Mercy'.[39] Another pamphlet noted that much was written on clemency: 'how eminent a part of the perfection of Majesty, this attribute of Clemency and Mercy is; how it illustrates the Crown; how it renders the Prince truly God-like; that Kings like Jehovah, should pity the miseries of their offending Subjects; and should shew themselves truly Fathers of their Country, by sparing their rebellious Children.'[40] The words are that of the Jacobite non-juror Mathias Earbery. The *History of Clemency of Our English Monarchs, from the Reformation, Down to the Present Time* addressed the controversy over mercy in rebellion's aftermath ('That King George has out-done in Clemency and Paternal Compassion, all the British or English Monarchs that ever went before him', or not). Earbery linked the Reformation, Protestantism, and a merciful nation and monarch. Edward VI was exemplary: 'the clemency and goodness of whose disposition was such, that he would always shed tears when he signed a Warrant for the Execution, even of common criminals.' Earbery was outlawed for seditious libel.[41]

Katherine Thomson, in *Memoirs of the Jacobites* of 1715 and 1745 (1845), regretted the absence of queen consorts in 1715 and 1745: 'a woman's heart would, one may trust, have pleaded for the young, gallant, and beloved [Earl of] Derwentwater.' Hannah Smith's study of the early Hanoverian monarchy briefly notes occasional efforts to 'plead for pardon from the king and try to persuade members of the royal family to intercede with him'. She cites an incident in 1716 when Caroline of Ansbach, the wife of the king's heir, was so disturbed at an attempt made in her drawing room on behalf of a Jacobite peer that she escaped to her own rooms and cried.[42] Thomson recalled the execution of the English James Radclyffe, Earl of Derwentwater. Related to this was the effort of another wife of a condemned Jacobite earl (Figure 2.1 depicts the execution

Figure 2.1 'A View of the Manner of Beheading the Rebel Lords in Tower Hill London, in the Reign of George II'. An engraving by John Goldar after the drawing by Robert Dodd and originally appearing in Barnard's *New Complete & Authentic History of England* (1781–83). Author's collection.

of the Jacobite peers, the Earl of Kilmarnock and Lord Balmerino in August 1746). The countess of Nithsdale threw herself at the king as he passed her in the palace. The episode appeared in many histories and became a lurid mid-nineteenth-century painting, *The Countess of Nithsdale petitioning George I on Behalf of Her Husband*, by the Scottish historical painter Robert Hannah. Hannah's complicated rendering depicted the countess's mourning-black form dragged by her hold on the royal coat along the floor, her right arm thrust out with a petition. A portrait of Henry VIII on the wall above a statue of Britannia made a symbolic point about state power and violence.[43] It was not easy, thought Sheffield Grace, publishing the countess's letter for mercy, in 1827, 'to conceive a being so rugged as to spurn a high born and lovely women who decked with a crown of imperishable virtue herself condescends even to implore the mercy of a mere thing of velvet and ermine'. Several works of fiction dramatized Winifred Nithsdale's efforts to save her husband – only successful through his escape in women's clothing from the Tower.[44]

Glimpses of public criticism appear on other occasions. In September 1716 there were 'offensive words' on 'an Example of Justice, unmix'd with Mercy' shown to the soldier Thomas Barron and sailor Edward Bourn. They were hanged for a robbery for three halfpence at York. The offending paper was the monthly *Mercurius Politicus* (which had promised to discuss the meting out of justice or mercy after the rebellion, without bias, in its first number).[45] For this, the Court of King's Bench, taking it as a reflection on the judges, imprisoned the publisher John Morphew.[46]

In 1726, a year before the king's death, in Swift's satire, Gulliver reported that nothing terrified Lilliputians more than 'those encomiums on his Majesty's mercy'.[47] While sermons and poems after his death in Hanover did not tend to mention his mercy, the poet laureate spoke of his 'Clemency … spread … Ev'n when the publick Weal sign'd Dooms demand, | The Father's Eyes weep o'er the Monarch's Hand'.[48]

The mercy of George II

George II had a reputation for clemency; certainly Horace Walpole thought his general disposition was merciful.[49] Another Jacobite rebellion renewed concern about the politics of mercy with discourse on the battle of Culloden in April 1746 debating unmerited mercy, merited punishment, and unnecessary severity.[50] The king's son, William, Duke of Cumberland, notoriously, failed in this.[51] The choice was offered visually by Jacobite and Hanoverian prints. One Jacobite engraving shows Britannia with scales, labelled 'Mercy' and 'Butchery', with a tartan-clothed Prince Charles on the side of the scales for mercy. An axe-wielding Cumberland is on the butchery side, with a three-sided gallows in the distance.[52] 'With George and Justice rules our British isles | No Popish Varlets shall our Rights defile' was the motto below one anti-Jacobite print in 1745 – depicting justice with scales and sword.[53] Ironically, John Gay's popular *Fables* (published 1727) was dedicated to the infant Cumberland, with the first fable, on a tiger, traveller, and lion, painting the moral that 'Cowards are cruel; but the brave | Love mercy, and delight to save', and 'Wise kings by love and mercy reign'.[54] In August 1746 the pamphlet *Mercy the Truest Heroism* was pointedly 'inscribed' to the Duke.[55] William Hogarth's unpublished comment on the Seven Years' War, 'The Times. Plate

Two' (1762), alludes, among many other matters, to Cumberland's butchery. A dog with 'Mercy' around its collar barks at a shrub entitled Culloden.[56]

Joseph Addison's essay of 1716 was reproduced in 1746 as 'Justice and Mercy to Rebels Considered', as 'nothing can set an Affair of this Nature in a better Light', when 'many of our Politicians both in Conversation and in publick Papers, have taken upon them to prescribe Methods in which the Government should proceed … some extolling Mercy to the Exclusion of Justice, and others Justice to the Exclusion of Mercy'.[57] 'Integritas', in *Truth, But No Treason*, spoke directly to the king about mercy.[58]

Efforts to establish George II's meritorious conduct included Henry Fielding's assertion in *The True Patriot*, in 1746, when discussing the king's justice: 'no Monarch, nay, no Man hath ever been more inflexibly just.' The king tempered 'the Rigour and Severity of Justice with Mercy', and in relation to military punishment, 'which in this kingdom can never be inflicted without the King's signing the Sentence, the Officers of the Army have been known to lament this merciful Disposition, that makes it always difficult to obtain the Royal Warrant for inflicting Death on Deserters'.[59] Given the military's significance in the first two Georges' self-images, the importance of the army's support for the new dynasty, and the role of the sovereign in army appointments after the 1720s, this martial mercy is important.[60] For Fielding, the quality of mercy was a branch of benevolence, 'or may be perhaps more properly called Benevolence in Authority'.[61]

Due to his absences in Hanover, George II's wife and regent faced the prospect of exercising mercy, or signing death warrants which, as one biographer states, she looked on with distaste.[62] Caroline granted temporary respite to Captain John Porteous when he killed rioters in Edinburgh in 1736; Walter Scott's *Heart of Midlothian* (1818) fictionalizes another event when Helen Walker walked to England to petition for mercy from the queen regent for her sister.[63] The mistress of the robes, Charlotte Clayton, was one channel for appeals to Caroline's mercy. The heir to the throne, Frederick Prince of Wales, was also associated with exercise of mercy before his untimely death. When the king was in Hanover, the Lords of the Regency were petitioned for mercy, for example in September 1750.[64] Frederick was eulogized as a lost prince of mercy perhaps in contrast to the 'tender mercies' of his brother Cumberland.[65] Who now, it was asked (by William Blackstone, pseudonymously), 'the vengeful sword of Justice wield, Or ope like him sweet Mercy's golden gate'?[66]

William Seward's collection of anecdotes gestured to George II's reluctance to sign the death warrant for the Jacobite Archibald Cameron of Lochiel, apprehended in 1753: 'he said, in the true spirit of mercy which has ever distinguished his illustrious family, "Surely there has been too much blood already spent upon this occasion."'[67] The king was a man of such 'humane and merciful Disposition' that should Cameron be executed, given the difficulty of gaining the royal ear, it was down to those who shut up the avenues to royal mercy, for he was a benevolent prince, 'ready to lay hold of any Pretence to administer any kind of Comfort to distress'd Criminal'.[68] The man's execution for high treason made Samuel Johnson extremely agitated.[69]

Another instance of the king deciding to let justice take its course, the execution of one of two officers who killed a postboy, was reported:

It having been intimated to a great King, that he would be most ardently importuned to pardon two Officers concerned in murdering a Post-Boy, his Majesty replied, that he should rejoice in every Opportunity to demonstrate that Mercy was the darling Passion of his Soul, yet Justice should controul his Conduct, being what he ever esteem'd the brightest Jewel in his Diadem.[70]

Later commentators recalled the legal murder of Admiral John Byng in 1757 after he was court-martialled following the battle of Minorca for failing to do his utmost, under the revised Articles of War. The leading politician Henry Fox turned 'mercy itself into an engine of faction', in Horace Walpole's words, to escape some of the blame for Minorca's loss.[71] Byng's fate excited public interest: for example, a 'young Lady of fifteen' urged, through poetry in the *Newcastle Courant*, 'tho' we've condemned him, for Mercy we pray, Lest his Case be our Case'.[72] Newspapers published variants on the vacillation parodying: 'Save him, great Sir, and royal mercy show; | Shoot him, dread Sir, let royal justice flow; | Regard your subjects with a pitying eye; | Contrive that he may neither live nor die.'[73]

Posthumous eulogies incorporated kingly mercy among George II's virtues.[74] In an obituary sermon the Baptist minister Samuel Stennett, of Little Wild Street off Lincoln's Inn Field, praised him as a merciful parent to the nation, 'and even those who had forfeited their lives to the laws of their country, were not beyond the reach of his compassion'. The king was reluctant to order executions and showed 'alacrity and pleasure' if mercy was consistent with the honour of the government or the people's safety.[75] The Jewish Isaac Mendes Belisario compared George II with David, in a funeral sermon at the synagogue of Portuguese Jews in London in November 1760. For both knew how to temper justice with mercy, and 'It cost our compassionate Monarch Tears, whenever he found himself obliged to confirm the Sentence of Death pronounced upon the meanest of his Subjects; whilst he punished the Crime, he at the same Time pitied the Criminal.'[76] The Irishman John Cunningham's ode described 'Mercy, co-partner of great George's throne', flying through the air to 'smooth his halcyon progress to the skies'.[77]

George III

The familiar praise for a merciful monarch was given to the young George III. The American poet Benjamin Church referred to him in 1765 as 'dread sovereign at whose sacred seat, | Justice and mercy, spotless maidens meet'.[78] 'As a proof of his sympathetic feelings', another poet, Robert Southey, recalled the following after his death in 1820: 'he never signed a death warrant without shedding a tear, indeed many an unfortunate delinquent would have met with royal clemency, had not the expediency of justice rendered it inadvisable.'[79] Ebenezer Sibly the astrologer claimed to see this disposition fated in his stars: 'no geniture in the world ever produced more evident proofs of that rectitude of principle, of that benevolence of heart and mind, of that regard to justice, mercy, and truth, which assimilates the human nature to the divine image of the Deity, and forms the interior of a patriot king.'[80]

The extant official correspondence suggests a king concerned like his contemporaries with the dangers of undue leniency. He was also confronted, as in the case of Thomas Chaffey and two other men in 1789, at the end of a decade which proved a high point for metropolitan executions, with instances where men and women *refused* the mercy of transportation.[81] Capital punishment impinged on the king right from the beginning of his reign, as Victorians recalled. The *New Monthly Belle Assemblée*, in 1857 saw 'no great straining of the "quality of mercy" … it is remarkable, and rather ominous, that on the day his Majesty came to the throne in 1760, a man was hanged at the end of Bow-street'.[82] The Victorian Erskine Neale recounted the respite for the murderer Thomas Daniel in 1761. The 'young king ever honoured be his merciful memory would hear of no such act as an execution on the morning of his coronation', despite pressure from judges and Home Secretary Egremont that the law required death within forty-eight hours after sentence. It turned out the man was innocent.[83] The anecdote was repeated in the 1860s during debate about capital-punishment abolition as a 'very curious instance of the kingly exercise of the prerogative of mercy'.[84]

In 1769 the press reproduced the pardon occasioned by doubts in the 'royal breast', as to the fatality of a blow to a bystander during electioneering at Brentford in Middlesex, by the coal-heaver Edward M'Quirk (or Kirk). It was an incident notable for its medical implications and discussed by 'Junius' (VIII, 18 March 1769).[85] As that suggests, the exercise of justice and politics of mercy figured in opposition to the king's government in the 1770s.[86] For his critics, the king's acts regarding the penalty of death were of a piece with other acts of 'tyranny'. His practice of mercy was biased in favour of the elite according to one sermonist, contrasting him with 'our late gracious SOVEREIGN, a Prince of great Mercy but at the same time of as great Justice'.[87] The Reverend John Horne Tooke, addressing Middlesex freeholders gathered in the Mile End Assembly Room in March 1770 to consider a petition to the king, against John Wilkes and others, decried the abuse of discretionary power in relation to justice and mercy. Yet Wilkes, returning from France an outlaw, supplicated for 'that mercy and clemency, which shine with such lustre among your many princely virtues' in March 1768.[88]

'A friend to constitutional liberty', writing in the *Oxford Magazine* in July 1771, condemned mercy's exercise without justice – with interest usurping power through the 'junto'.[89] A splendid cartoon followed this, later in the year, in which an angel (of mercy) proffered a sceptre adorned with the dove of mercy and advised, 'rule by this, thy enemies shall fear thee & thy subjects will love thee'; alas, there was a snake-headed daemon offering the sword and the words 'rule by this & thy – subjects will fear thee' (see Figure 2.2). The pictures behind the throne were of the phoenix-like patriot king, and the tyrant king as a lion killing a deer. The advertisement for this 'elegant engraving' offers the following gloss: the king being 'the father of his country, a friend to the distressed, a lover of justice, but more a lover of mercy; a pattern of piety and filial affection' yet misled by ministers.[90]

'Junius' in January 1772 highlighted abuse of royal mercy to save two 'labourers', Matthew and Patrick Kennedy (risen to 'something sufficiently like gentility'), after an 'appeal of blood' by Ann Bigby when her night-watchman husband died following their drunken assault on him with an iron poker. In this 'present gentle reign, we well know what uses has been made of the lenity of the Court and of the mercy of the

Figure 2.2 'Advice to a Great K–g', *Oxford Magazine*, December 1771, opposite p. 216. Image courtesy of the University of Michigan.

crown'. However, it was the influence of Polly, their sister, the 'pliancy of her virtue, that recommended her to the King'. Polly was a courtesan painted by Sir Joshua Reynolds, in whose circle she moved.⁹¹ She used connections to ensure the king and queen were petitioned and the Secretary of State 'besieged'. The case became 'a struggle between the City and the Bill of Rights Club to hang the men and the Court friends of their sister to save them'.⁹² John Horne Tooke was involved.⁹³ Accusations of royal absolutism were linked to the matter of justice and mercy.⁹⁴

Direct appeal was made to the king in an essay and accompanying verse on mercy that appeared in *The Fugitive Miscellany*, published by the radical publisher John Almon in 1775, about the 'frequency and cruelty of public executions', with inevitable quotation from Shakespeare, up-to-date allusion to the law reformer Beccaria, and suggestions for alternatives to the death penalty.⁹⁵ The king was addressed as 'one justly famed for the noblest of all virtues, Mercy … how would future historians celebrate the royal philosopher, who, instructed by Reason and Mercy, reformed a barbarous and sanguinary code of laws'. The verse imagined the young poet as the monarch, pausing over circumstances: 'ere I sign'd the law's word | That gave the victim to the law's sharp sword'. Would Albion, 'fam'd for Mercy', fail to follow where Naples and even Russia had ameliorated the capital code?

Forgery was a capital crime enjoying no royal mercy since it was the 'most dangerous crime in a commercial country'.⁹⁶ McGowen argues that there was no great complaint about this severity 'well into' the nineteenth century but also comments, 'forgery came to occupy an almost unique place in the minds of both those who demanded reform of the criminal law and those who defended the traditional legal order'.⁹⁷ In the case of the wealthy physician Robert Perreau (see Figure 2.3) and his twin Daniel, a merchant, the study by Andrew and McGowen shows the concern was with what would happen if 'powerful application' was perceived to be successful, for future forgery cases where the nobility were involved as supporters.⁹⁸ The Perreau case 'occupied the whole nation' for a season – stimulating a mass of tracts in 1776.

One of the most famous cases of forgery where royal mercy was withheld concerned the fashionable Anglican clergyman William Dodd in 1777. Radzinowicz's history of the criminal law judges it as a 'definitive stage in the crystallisation of public opinion on the subjects of capital punishment and the royal prerogative of mercy'.⁹⁹ Dodd's petitions included a skilfully illustrated and neatly calligraphed appeal with representations of mercy and justice on vellum. It was reported that he believed a pardon was granted through the Prince of Wales's intercession. This may be what is hoped, in the verse, 'On the melancholy Situation of a certain unfortunate divine', which used the figures of Mercy and Justice who 'On the same pillow both recline to rest, | Asunder, wretched! but together, blest!' The poem hoped that 'the Prince who's born a Briton's friend: | Self-judging, his prerogative extend! | And, if the Law should fatally prevail, | May he stern Justice weigh in Mercy's scale'.¹⁰⁰

The *Caledonian Mercury*, reporting the view that Dodd would be saved, thought that for 'political reasons, which appear obvious, this step is not to be taken too rashly'.¹⁰¹ Dodd's supporter Dr Johnson commented on the oddity of his composing a prayer to the king on the night before execution, when petitioning had failed.¹⁰² Dodd was concerned that friends should not complain of the lack of mercy of king and ministers:

Figure 2.3 Portrait of Robert Perreau. Engraving, *London Magazine; or, Gentleman's Monthly Intelligencer*, 1 July 1775. Author's collection.

'I love and honour the king; I doubt not his humanity: he and his councellors have acted according to justice, and his Majesty would have extended mercy, if he could have thought it consistent with the welfare of the nation.'[103] His posthumously published verse referred to friends' efforts to 'generous Pardon Royal Mercy move'.[104]

In 1783 newspapers recounted the efforts to win over the monarch for another celebrity forger, the king's engraver, William Wynne Ryland (who had successfully interceded when his brother was charged with a capital crime). Ryland engraved scenes of monarchical moment such as King John signing Magna Charta and Allan Ramsay's coronation portrait of the king.¹⁰⁵ His wife Henrietta and children petitioned for mercy, wearing deep mourning when they went to St James's palace and succeeded in moving Queen Charlotte by their account of his plight.¹⁰⁶ Ryland gave a paper to the Recorder to give to the king, and newspapers reported that the discussion of the petition in the Privy Council 'was carried on with greater warmth, and for a longer time, than perhaps any petition ever presented on a similar occasion'.¹⁰⁷ 'Persons of distinction' presented petitions to the king at St James's and Windsor (received 'most graciously').¹⁰⁸ Ryland was said to be 'borne up by the Idea, that he shall find Forgiveness from the Royal Clemency ... I yet think I perceive a Beam of Mercy!'¹⁰⁹ People did not expect execution since there was thought to be 'presumption alone' and admiration of a 'great Personage' for his engravings.¹¹⁰ One paper revealed that Lord North, and the Dukes of Portland and Rutland pleaded strongly for him, but that Lord Mansfield won the argument against mercy.¹¹¹

Ryland wrote from Newgate to a friend, admitting the seriousness of the crime which struck at the 'vital Part of Commerce, and carries with it Poison most deadly to public Credit'. He claimed never to have 'sought Mercy under the Idea of Court Interest', instead hoping for 'Royal Favour through these Circumstantials which indicated more the Probability of Innocence, than the Certainty of Guilt'. And he did 'not arraign the gracious Benevolence, that has so long dignified the Humanity of the British Crown. No – there Royalty receives constant Lustre from the Distribution of Mercy and there the Tears of the Sovereign have always accompanied the Warrant of Death'.¹¹² Ryland admitted the crime was 'unpardonable' but appealed at the bar to the king's mercy as he 'hitherto existed by his bounty'; others might draw the conclusion that this showed justice's impartiality.¹¹³ Anecdotes in his successor's reign suggested the king showed mercy in one case of forgery, where a personal channel, through a minister of religion (a Baptist) he approved of, was formed. So claimed one paper, reporting the instance of a clerk at a Leeds mercantile house, found guilty at York assizes in 1808.¹¹⁴

Other appeals to the king's mercy after sentence of death for other crimes were picked up by the press in the 1790s and early 1800s. The king bestowed mercy on the midshipman Peter Heywood – liable for death for unlucky association with the mutiny on the *Bounty* – while with his family at Weymouth in October 1792.¹¹⁵ Attempts on behalf of Major Henry Alexander Campbell, who had killed Captain Boyd in a duel, failed. He was executed at Armagh in August 1808 despite the efforts of his wife to seek an audience with the queen and royal princesses at Windsor, and an approach to the Prince of Wales at Brighton, who immediately wrote to the Duke of Portland on behalf of a man who was a first cousin of the Earl of Breadalbane.¹¹⁶

The claim to access channels of mercy at a price damaged trust in this 'most pleasant' of prerogatives. The Earl of Suffolk, Secretary of State for the Northern Department, was concerned about 'impositions on applications to the Crown for mercy' in the early 1770s.¹¹⁷ Then there was the trial of the sexagenarian Launcelot Knowles, an occasional gentleman and temporary sergeant in the city militia, at the Old Bailey in January 1797, for claiming to have 'great influence, credit and interest with the Duke of Portland, Sir Watkin Lewes and Mr Baldwin' to procure a felon's pardon. The case was reported in the London and provincial press. William Garrow was counsel for the prosecution and admitted he wished the accused could be hanged as it was vital that 'royal mercy should not be obstructed, or interrupted by the artifice of individuals making an impression against the propriety of applying for mercy' and that 'public opinion should be confirmed that the royal mercy flows in so pure a channel that nothing can corrupt or injure it'.[118] (Knowles, found guilty of the misdemeanour of obtaining money under false pretences, was transported to New South Wales abroad the *Lady Shore*, for seven years. With mutiny on board, the vessel went to Buenos Aires instead.[119]) Patrick Colquhoun's *Treatise on the Police of the Metropolis* (1796) – a presentation copy of the sixth edition was in George III's personal collection – claimed: 'PARDONS are applied for; and it is known that His Majesty's great goodness and love of mercy has been frequently abused by the tricks, devices, and frauds, too commonly resorted to, by the convicts and agents equally depraved as themselves.'[120] (The first edition of the work had 'his principal Secretary of State', as the figure deceived by the tricks, devices, and frauds[121].)

Presenting the British state as mildly ruled by 'another TITUS; whose days are numbered by acts of clemency and beneficence; whose love of justice and paternal affection for his people, are as conspicuous, as his exemplary private virtues', was necessary to legitimize the state.[122] As Henry Fielding commented of mercy in George II's reign, in 1751, 'in a Republic there is no such Power … it seems to our excellent Sovereign to be the most favourite Part of his prerogative, as it is the only one which hath been carried to its utmost Extent in the present Reign'.[123]

Mercy was also invoked when George III was spared assassination by 'Just Heav'n': 'The various virtues of his royal mind | His justice mercy piety combin'd'.[124] The print reproduced as Figure 2.4, with motto from Pope's *Essay on Man*, appeared on 6 August 1786, days after the assassination attempt by the deluded needle worker Margaret Nicholson. Sash of benevolence, star of virtue, and crown of mercy and justice make the message clear (representations of the episode depicted the king wearing a blue sash and the Garter star).[125]

The 'merciful' deliverance from illness is another area in which George III's reign can be linked with mercy discourse. Poetry on the king's recovery in the spring of 1789 from a first attack of what is thought to be porphyria invoked the 'Daughter of Mercy' descending from a throne in light to the relief of Britain.[126] The poet laureate imagined mercy, from the throne of God, waving a wreath to restore vigour to the royal sceptre.[127] In the public celebrations, a transparency from the Leadenhall Street synagogue appropriately presented a profile of the king under the words from the psalms: 'Mercy and Truth preserve the King for his throne is upholden by mercy'.

Colley sees this period as important in developing the political language of loyalist sentimentalism: the figuring of George's paternal rule and response by loyal subjects as the tender relations of parent to family members.[128] The mildness and mercifulness of the king were aspects of the British state used by loyalists and (employed strategically) by radicals in the 1790s.[129] Mary Robinson, for example, appealed to Queen Charlotte to exert her merciful influence in the case of the radicals William Skirving and Maurice Margarot, sentenced to transportation to New South Wales in 1794; and appeals to the king's mercy were made in an open-air meeting in Sheffield in April.[130] The queen was also appealed to on behalf of Thomas Palmer and Thomas Muir in Scotland in 1793.[131] Before that period, the queen's merciful propensities were extolled in Riley's *Historical*

Figure 2.4 Etching with aquatint of George III crowned by Mercy and Justice, with a sash of benevolence, published 6 August 1786, by W. Holland, Drury Lane, London. Royal Collection Trust/© Her Majesty Queen Elizabeth II 2020.

Pocket Library, where her 'humanity was … exerted in favour of the unhappy culprit sentenced to be shot for deserting the service of his king and country'.[132]

George III's posthumous reputation was partly linked to a record for mercy that was debatable. During the jubilee in 1808 the king was praised for 'liberating unfortunate debtors from the miseries of confinement' and exercising mercy where it was safe to do so, 'in entirely remitting, or commuting, capital punishments. Often has the broad shield of the prerogative been graciously interposed between the trembling culprit and the rigors of justice'.[133] In a review of a British work on capital punishment reform in 1807, readers were told that 'his present majesty has an almost invincible repugnance to capital executions, and that it is never without strong feelings of aversion and regret that he signs any warrant for the purpose'. Indeed, 'We think that this fact is highly creditable to the king, and we consider it with more pleasure, because it gives us assurance that he would readily assent to any bill for abolishing a practice which is at once opposite to scripture, to reason and humanity'.[134]

His death brought forth the traditional eulogies on clement rule, for instance in Taylor's memorial work: 'his extensive benevolence, – and his liberal exercise of that heavenly attribute *Mercy* ... volumes would be insufficient to enumerate.'[135] Beresford's loyal valedictory from Leicester claimed that responsibility for 'confirming the last dreadful sentence of the law' was 'deeply afflicting. Seldom except in the most flagrant cases did he sign that sentence and even then his mercy was at the bottom of his justice'.[136] In nothing, Heath sermonized, 'did our late most amiable Sovereign take more delight' than in mercy's exercise; 'If at any time he felt more than ordinary satisfaction it was when he was able without a violation of justice to grant pardon to the repentant criminal whose life had been forfeited to the injured laws of his country.'[137] Browne at the Court of Common Council in London Guildhall, voting an address of condolence, appealed 'to the Recorder whether the late King did not glory most in that prerogative' of mercy.[138]

One writer directly experienced the law's mercilessness. 'He who had signed more death warrants than any mortal that ever breathed, and who could kill or spare human beings by the mere dash of his pen', wrote the radical 'Orator' Henry Hunt, when the king was blind and, seemingly, insane, 'alas! alas! he once so powerful could not now even save the life of a poor mouse'.[139] Well might Hunt condemn the limited role of mercy when he was confined in Ilchester gaol in July 1821; quoting back at the king's successor the coronation oath's commitment to cause law and justice, in mercy, to be executed in all his judgments.[140]

George III's relationship with capital punishment was retrospected as part of the 'days of blood' when 'hanging was more in fashion'. Anecdotes about the king's role in the councils appeared; thus, Horace Twiss's life of the Lord Chancellor Eldon (1844) preserved a debate about hanging a robber for a crime in Bedford Square where Eldon lived.[141] Dodd's unhappy case, complete with his distraught wife begging mercy of the queen, was rewritten for the stage by William Wills and performed at the Royal Surrey Theatre in August 1837.[142] Literary fiction re-created this era. In Caroline White's 'My House in Cecil Street' in *Ainsworth's Magazine* in 1844, a reprieve was won from the king through Charlotte's agency (introducing the condemned man's wife into his closet to supplicate): 'till the resolution of the monarch merged in the compassion of the man and he granted to her persevering devotion the mercy that a strict sense of justice had hitherto denied'. The decision was too late to prevent the hideous execution in Edinburgh.[143] The queen's refusal to intercede when a stockbroker was sentenced to death for forgery features in Harvey's *London Scenes and London People*.[144] Douglas Jerrold's 'History of St Giles and St James', serialized in the abolitionist *Douglas Jerrold's*

Magazine in 1845, had a long paragraph on the king-in-council apportioning death through the hangman as the 'social physician': 'Yea it was with the hangman's fingers that the father of his people touched the People's Evil.'[145]

George IV

In Horace Bleackly's Edwardian account of capital punishment, George IV was equated with the penal reformers William Ewart, Sir James Mackintosh, and Samuel Romilly and described as 'the first humane monarch for more than a hundred years'.[146] This section studies his reputed acts of mercy. It begins by examining his official acts as Regent before 1820.

A merciful regent?

During the 'late royal indisposition' in 1789, execution of prisoners was delayed.[147] The Whig Samuel Whitbread asked the Commons in 1810, with news of George III's renewed indisposition, 'Is there in our Constitution any other seat of justice, or is there any fountain of mercy to supply the deficiency of the Kingly Power?'[148] It was not just capital convicts' fates at stake. In the case of Lovell the printer of the anti-ministerial *Statesman*, imprisoned for libel, it was argued in that year that there could be no justice while the prerogative of mercy was suspended. Sheridan, before Prime Minister Spencer Perceval brought in the Regency Bill in January 1811, aired concerns about this suspension: 'nothing more clearly shewed the present crippled state of the Monarchy, than that any individual should be obliged to assume the prerogative of mercy, and grant or withhold mercy according to the dictates of his own discretion.'[149] As well as mentioning Peter Ogilvie in Scotland, executed for uxoricide although the jury recommended mercy, Sheridan alluded to the execution of Antonio Cardoza, a Portuguese sailor, for murder and the 'considerable sensation respecting the alarming suspension' of the prerogative.[150] The case of Cardoza, who, at the behest of two insulted prostitutes, caused a scuffle which ended in a fatality, made a 'deep impression' on Sheridan and he wrote to Home Secretary Ryder on the subject. Perceval responded to Sheridan.[151]

The Prince of Wales's efforts after the Regency was established are documented in the press and Home Office files. He requested prisoners who were suitable to be released from prison in February 1811.[152] Efforts to secure mercy for the dressmaker Ann Walter, in that month, involved a royal chaplain and librarian (she was transported).[153] In April, there is a glimpse of the prince's attitude in the case of a burglar at Lancaster assizes, William Cunliffe. From Carlton House came the opinion that with no favourable circumstances, the death sentence must take its course.[154] The prince was reported to have admitted the father and brother of a man convicted at Hereford of uttering promissory notes to his audience in September 1811, 'and in the most feeling manner stated the impossibility of granting reprieve, and at the same time expressed the pleasure he should have had in extending mercy, if any feature of his case would justify such interference'.[155]

In the notorious case of Eliza Fenning in 1815, executed for the attempted murder of her employers by poisoning, appeals were made to the prince.[156] According to Samuel Romilly, in the Commons in 1816, the Recorder 'declared it to be the determination of the Prince Regent to execute the next boy who was convicted in order to give a check to youthful offences'.[157] The delay caused by the prince's 'indisposition' that year led to questions in the Commons.[158] Efforts to reach him through petition are preserved in the *Criminal Recorder*, where the fate of the attorney and forger Joseph Blackburn in 1816, despite his wife 'throwing herself at the feet of his Royal Highness to supplicate for the life of her unhappy husband', took its inevitable course at York castle.[159]

In October 1817 during the state trials associated with the Pentrich rising in Derby, reference was made to the king's mercy, to which a 'just appeal was never made in vain'.[160] In the case of George Matthews in February 1818, falsely charged with the capital crime of robbing his master, an appeal to the prince appeared in a tract. 'Equity ought to be made known to the public', the pamphleteer asserted, 'If a capital convict receives a free pardon from his Sovereign is it not necessary to show that such pardon was not capriciously granted?'[161] In April 1818 came an artful petition from the wife of William Gray, forger of bank notes: 'So may the petitions of your Royal Highness in that hour which equally waits the Prince and the Peasant, meet with a blessed answer form the KING of KINGS.'[162]

Executions for forgery were often unpopular by this period. A pamphlet by Charles Bowdler pointed out the prince's constrained constitutional power even if 'a petition, imploring mercy, and setting forth a detail of circumstances, such as command the feeling of every mind in which feeling lives', were to reach him. He was no absolute monarch and could not 'gratify his own wishes; he feels, pities, desires to save; he would rejoice to spare the life; but he cannot do it without the approbation of his ministers'. In such cases it was 'an invariable rule with them, never to listen to any recommendation of mercy, unsupported by the Bank of England'.[163] Mercy's exercise had descended from the Crown to mere solicitor's clerk, a commercial dictionary commented, as a result.[164] (A number of banks issued notes with Justice as the only figurative decoration.[165])

'It is time to pay some deference to the feelings of others', the *New Monthly Magazine* argued in October 1818, 'and not withhold from the Prince Regent the prerogative of extending mercy when his own benevolence would prompt him to do so'.[166] One case of capital sentence was reported by a London Sunday paper with a letter addressed to the prince pleading mercy, after the execution of three utterers of forged notes in Newgate in December 1818, with comment on the 'worthless regent' and the relentless Lord Sidmouth. The Home Secretary, so the radical *Black Dwarf* claimed (campaigning against the Bank of England's support of such executions), took upon himself the kingly function of exercising mercy.[167]

The king of kings was invoked in approval of the prince's reprieve for the butcher Henry Stent, convicted for the attempted murder of his wife for desertion and 'the guilty intercourse of a villain', at the Old Bailey in September 1819.[168] In that year, from Bristol, there appeared a petition to Parliament 'to take the Subject of Capital Punishments into its most serious Consideration and to make such Alterations in the Criminal Laws of these Realms as shall stamp them with that Character of Humanity which has so conspicuously and progressively marked the Exercise of the Royal Prerogative in the present Reign'.[169] A poem entitled 'The Regent's Song; or, the Song of the Regent' also took the conceit of the jewels of a crown to emphasize chastity and mercy: 'No dross adheres to cloud her ray; But beautiful, angelic, bright, She cheers and gladdens mortal sight!' It was the 'noblest jewel in a monarch's crown!'[170]

This was before Peterloo in August when state violence against political radicals implicated the prince. Thus John Crook's pamphlet against Peterloo referred to the prince being advised to give thanks to the yeomanry against his own sense of clemency in 1819 (*The Patriot* of Manchester defended the yeomanry and condemned clemency taken to an extreme).[171] The prince joked about his 'tyrannical self' with Walter Scott – swapping tales of the brutal humour of judges and quoting Thomas Moore: 'The table spread with tea and toast, | Death-warrants and the Morning Post.'[172]

A merciful king

The reputation for mercy at the start of the reign was exploited in Queen Caroline's trial for adultery. The defence in summing up spoke of 'this new reign in which even traitors were spared and felons pardoned by a lavish exertion of the royal prerogative of mercy'. If, the queen's defenders asked, 'mercy be the attribute of kings is it not physically impossible that an opposite principle should be the indurated habit of George IV'?[173] Henry Brougham's address to the House of Lords ended by appealing to the divine Throne of Mercy, in a lengthy speech that Queen Victoria will have read in Charlotte Bury's *The Murdered Queen!*[174] As part of the politics of Brandenburg House versus the king, Caroline unsuccessfully appealed to her husband for mercy for the forger Sarah Price in early December 1820, referring to the 'particular nature of the offence, and the very peculiar state of the law respecting it' – the letter appeared in the press.[175] The *Morning Post* commented,

> Faction pollutes every thing with its venom, at this moment, and we apprehend it could not have escaped those advisers of her majesty who have hitherto made her, at once, the idol and the puppet, of the mob, that an intercession for mercy (though with anticipated failure,) in behalf of a *Bank victim*, would add one more to the many merits she already possesses in their eyes.[176]

Emily Countess Cowper (the future Lady Palmerston) described Caroline's act as 'impudence'.[177]

George IV's reign saw organized efforts to ameliorate the capital code which necessarily touched on the sovereign's exercise of mercy. A meeting to consider petitioning Parliament in March 1821 heard Lord Ashtown discuss the deprivation of a royal prerogative 'that must be most grateful to his heart as a man of benevolence' and quoted from *Measure for Measure*, Isabella's lines.[178]

The most dramatic capital punishment of the reign was the execution of the Cato Street conspirators, whose plot to kill the Cabinet was triggered by George III's death. At least these would-be assassins were spared the horrors of drawing and quartering. The discourse of mercy was used by the council for the defence of John Harrison,

Richard Bradburn, John Shaw Strange, Charles Cooper, and John Gilchrist after the main conspirators were found guilty.[179] The tropes of mercy were mobilized not to *demand* mercy for 'they own they deserve none', but hope of mercy 'from the Crown where it is the brightest attribute even though the person of the Sovereign may have been menaced by their crimes'.[180] On retiring from the bar, Strange called, 'I beg to throw myself on the mercy of my Sovereign.' These conspirators were transported.

Reports of the new monarch's efforts to obtain mercy appear in the press in December 1820. The 'King would feel delighted', it was said by a 'gentleman at Carlton palace, holding a high and confidential situation in his majesty's Palace, if through the necessary course, the Secretary of State could recommend a respite', for the army officer Thomas Fuller Harnett, who forged an acceptance of a bill of exchange for £20.[181] The private efforts of a man 'entertaining the most enlarged ideas of the humanity, the soft-heartedness of his august Sovereign', failed despite a courtier passing a letter to the king. The writer, according to this account, 'was not mistaken in his estimate of his Sovereign's heart – of his genuine, his true character' with a letter to Sidmouth commanding the case be reconsidered, 'consistent with the Secretary of State's sense of duty'.

In September 1821 newspapers noted the Recorder in London's report to the king-in-council of capital convicts from the Old Bailey, when four were capitally condemned, the king 'immediately desired an interview with the Judges (who were then holding the assizes) which lasted for a considerable time, and the result of it was, his Majesty's most gracious respite of the sentences'. This meeting 'thus sought by himself', reported in the context of the king's return from his official visit to Ireland, 'was not the least of the happy moments he enjoyed'.[182] The newspapers assumed influence, in this case unsuccessfully, in November 1821, after Josiah Cadman was condemned to death for uttering forged £5 notes with his wife (who was spared). Cadman was a jobbing writer for the theatre; his execution at the Old Bailey alongside seven others was unpopular with the crowd, who cried 'murder' and 'shame, shame, no mercy; God bless you'. 'An oblique promise of powerful influence in my favour was held out at the time I made a free and candid confession', Cadman said on the scaffold, and even then 'expectations of mercy were again held out … The King has been advised to held me up as an example; but I do not wish to cast my reflections on him, for let it be known that I love and revere him in his station'.[183]

In the autumn of 1821, during George IV's visit to Hanover – where his power in mercy was so absolute that a mere wielding of the pen sufficed to grant pardon according to his private secretary William Knighton – the British operation of mercy was effected by a 'Commission of Lords Justices'.[184] *Leeds Mercury* commented that the king's return was a hoped-for opportunity 'for more than an ordinary display of the royal clemency, but unfortunately his Majesty has not the happiness to be served by ministers who possess either the inclination or the judgment to advise him to those acts which would confer a grace and dignity on royalty'.[185] The chaplain of Newgate sermonized in that year to convicts saying 'that although they had been selected for a public example, that the Sovereign (always gracious) would if it was consistent with the well-being of his subjects gladly hold out his sceptre of mercy to all'.[186]

Evidently responding to the current criticisms, a government pamphlet about the state of the nation at the start of 1822 spoke of the Home Department's record in relation to the 'most painful duties of the executive':

> But if mercy must always take the seat of justice at the side of royal power, mercy, like justice, has still the sword for her emblem. The guilty must suffer that the persons and properties of all may be safe. Mercy, therefore, herself, must appear with the appendages of justice, and must hence participate in the invidiousness accompanying the performance of her austere duties. What she spares, is too often forgotten in what she is seen to strike.[187]

Appeals were made from the city of Bristol in February 1823, when the Bristolian John Wait, convicted of forging a signature of a co-trustee to a deed, was executed at Newgate. Wait's wife and eldest daughter petitioned their 'Merciful King', expressing their belief that 'your Majesty's power of grace is unlimited, and none of your Majesty's subjects would dare to murmur should you, by the exercise of your Royal prerogative, achieve an act of clemency'.[188]

In June 1823 the artist George Cruikshank privately sketched 'The XEQtive – or a Cast Iron King signing death warrants by Steam dedicated to the admirers of new invention and old kings', but newspapers tried to correct the enduring popular error that death warrants were still signed by the monarch.[189] When Henry Fauntleroy the banker and forger was shown the warrant in 1824 (supposedly with black seal attached), 'some surprise was felt that the King's named was not signed thereto'.[190] *The Times* described this as perhaps the most erroneous of popular beliefs, in 1824. *The Times* claimed there were 'occasions wherein the personal feelings of the King would have inclined him to spare the life of an individual; but the general sentiment of the Privy Council has been so decidedly adverse, as to discourage the interposition of the Royal clemency'.[191] It was said that the Recorder's report was no longer 'delayed until the most daring criminal expected mercy, but on the contrary, is made with the most punctual and humane regularity'. The Home Secretary explained such delays as reflecting great honour on the king, whose 'abhorrence of signing death-warrants is so strong, that he trembles at the name of the Recorder'.[192]

In late 1828 the newspapers reported, of the king-in-council, 'it is no unusual matter in such a case for the King to find himself in a minority'.[193] At the same time, *The Examiner*, stimulated by the *Morning Chronicle*'s coverage of the case of the Quaker draper Joseph Hunton, described the king as suffering 'fits of the mercy'.[194] The king, in this case, was targeted by at least five petitions, including one from the foreman of the jury, which recommended mercy for the man who had uttered a forged bill of exchange.[195] The law said death; 'the whole country clamoured for mercy': was the diadem of mercy to be plucked from the crown? asked one outraged 'Justitia'.[196]

In discussing the metaphors of royal mercy, characterized as the 'truly British method of discussing questions of jurisprudence', Albany Fonblanque, anonymous author of an essay in *The Examiner* in December 1828, probably thought about the king's taste for jewel-encrusted *objets*:

The man who desired to vindicate to the King the prerogative of mercy in a popular manner, in The Quarterly Review, need only turn to the word mercy in Stockdale's 'Index of Shakespear,' and by merely stringing together all the fine things that have been said on the god-like attribute, he would compound an article perfectly convincing of the expediency and wisdom of continuing the prerogative in the Crown. By the mere force of calling mercy a jewel, the business might be accomplished. The idea of jewels is necessary to crowns. Of all the jewels, mercy is surely the brightest – 'Would you rob your Monarch, your own dear GEORGY, of his most precious stone?' At this appeal, John Bull fairly blubbers with tenderness for the Royal baubles.'[197]

This paper, facetiously, recommended to John Bull that the jewel of mercy in the king's case ('the best of Kings) be imagined 'in the tenderest part of his person, and as painful & troublesome to his feelings as a stone, like other bodies out of place'. Mercy for a king was less sweet than the more frequent distress of 'doubtingly withholding it'. The essayist suggested a tribunal to release the king from this role for 'mercy' had disguised unintelligible decisions. 'Vulgar' talk of the king's gracious acts confused the king's role in correcting 'too-heavy sentence of the Criminal Court' with mercy. For it was actually reducing 'to the standard of Justice'. It was a code under the stage directions of an old tragedy, 'as bloody as it may be', with the throne's correction of excess. The *Examiner*, concerned with the legal system's injustice, wished to discard the language of mercy as a jewel and improve the regular machinery. (In an essay on capital punishment in 1831, a writer described the jewel as 'set in laws offensive to reason and humanity. It is as the eye of the bloated and venomous toad.'[198])

The declining George IV failed, in the end, to save an Irish gentleman and sometime magistrate, Peter Comyn, of County Clare (connected to some of the leading families of Clare and Galway), from being hanged for arson, in late April 1830, after burning his own house in December 1829. Memorials were sent to the king from Ennis.[199] The reprieve through king's messenger (reported in the Irish press) delayed execution at Ennis gaol by weeks, and the affair involved the viceroy, the Duke of Northumberland, and Prime Minister Wellington.[200] The *Clare Sentinel* hoped that 'the brightest gem in the royal prerogative … may still be influenced to illumine his dungeon'.[201] It was not to be. Yet attendance despite the 'ardent curiosity of the lower classes of the people to witness fatal exhibitions of this kind, especially where the sufferer was far from the ordinary routine of such cases' was limited because of the general impression that Comyn would be spared. The junior sheriff even offered to delay the execution until 4 pm, to await any letter of respite.[202] The case for mercy on the basis of unsound intellect had not been demonstrated, although newspapers described Comyn as 'occasionally eccentric' or suffering from 'great mental aberration, amounting in many instances, to acts of insanity'. To use the *Limerick Evening Post*'s phrase when it appeared that Comyn would live, he was kept through George's mercy 'in a state of cruel vibration between life and death'.[203]

George IV's reputation, whatever the reality exposed by V.A.C. Gatrell, was promoted by loyal memorialists.[204] The late-Victorian publication of Sir Robert Peel's private papers made it possible to see the king pleading for forgers, desirous of reducing the numbers being executed, attempting to act mercifully under his mistress Lady Conyngham's influence, seeking to wield power of respite against Home Secretary Peel's wishes, and climbing down when a united Cabinet resisted. In one letter in 1824, George IV claimed mercy was a 'word more consoling to the King's mind than language can express', but Peel intended to resign if the king persisted and respited execution.[205] Peel's editor praised 'the firmness, promptitude, and tact … in restraining an attempt on the King's part to exercise the prerogative of mercy without responsible advice'.[206]

Memorial poetry touched on royal mercy, such as William Bowles's in July 1830: 'Meek mercy bless'd the Sceptre which he bore.'[207] A critical biography commented, 'let this pleasant trait be remembered to his honor, for there are few things in his life worthy of remembrance.'[208] 'We know that George IV was exceedingly averse to executions' – publicized the Society for Diffusing Information on Capital Punishments in 1835 – 'We have upon the best authority the fact … of his anxiety to save the life of a subject against the opinions of the Members of the Council, and his frequently endeavouring, by earnest and protracted argument, when the Recorder of London's report was under consideration, to induce them to change their minds'.[209] This claim derived from an anecdote in obituaries and biographies such as the Reverend George Croly's. While admitting that the story was embellished since surfacing in a monthly periodical, it was claimed to emanate from someone in the king's household who had witnessed the councils. The king appeared in his 'truly princely character' as the most powerful pleader for remission, a man 'whom the world, judging of uncharitably, though unwittingly, consider as too much absorbed in the pomp, and splendor and enjoyments, of royalty, to trouble himself with the miseries of his subjects'. Sometimes for nearly two hours the prince would 'plead thus … for those who had no other counsellor and his plea enforced by arguments not less just than wise has in many instances not been made in vain'.[210] This story appeared in an anonymous essay by the artist William Henry Pyne in *Fraser's Magazine* in 1841. Pyne was a watercolourist who published the unprofitable but superior *History of the Royal Residences*. Benjamin Jutsham, the king's comptroller and his informant, claimed the king urged mercy 'by the most eloquent appeal' and 'did not delight to punish, but, on the contrary, ever sought how he might spare'.[211]

Hopes of mercy? Princess Charlotte

A Princess who promised so fairly to rule with justice and mercy over our happy land so eminently entitled to our esteem and love…[212]

On many occasions, when pensioners of mercy waited upon her to solicit the intercession of her royal favour, in the midst of that affability and condescension which courted veneration while it commanded respect, what evident marks have been displayed of the contritions of piety, and the compassions of love. With alacrity she hastened to mediate the cause of others, not ashamed to own, that before a higher Tribunal she would stand in need of a mediator.[213]

In 1814 the estranged wife of the Prince of Wales, writing from Berne, expressed confidence in her daughter as an English princess who would one day rule and be 'admired for her merciful distribution of justice'.[214] When Charlotte married Prince Leopold of Saxe-Coburg-Saalfeld a few years later, it was publicly hoped that a reign of mercy would be ushered in after her father had died; in lines uttered at loyal Weymouth: 'Illustrious pair may Mercy sway | The sceptre of these realms to day' (see Figure 2.5).[215] This verse was reproduced in Robert Huish's eulogistic biography when she died in childbirth in 1818, a biography which reprinted a sermon by Reverend James Rudge of Limehouse that pointedly linked her supposed virtues with her 'grandsire ... our beloved and venerable Sovereign', our 'good and afflicted King after whose virtues she seems to have successfully copied'. Huish asked, 'how well the laws would have been administered and the rule of authority been tempered with the exercise of mercy' under her 'mild and maternal sway'. Verse by others also took the theme of mercy; thus a monody bore the lines, seemingly addressed to her parents: 'Mercy and Truth should still the Sceptre sway'.[216]

Actual instances of appeals to the princess include a case reported in the newspapers in 1812, re-appearing in the *Percy Anecdotes* (and anthologized elsewhere).[217] A man signing himself 'Joseph' was interested in the fate of Frances Sage, convicted of stealing seals and ring from a jeweller in The Strand. Sage, at seventeen, was the princess's age, as Joseph emphasized in writing to Charlotte, arguing also:

Figure 2.5 'Princess Charlotte of Wales and Prince Leopold of Saxe Coburg'. An engraving by Henry Meyer, after a design by Burney, published by Edward Baines of Leeds, 1 November 1816. Author's collection.

In such an effort, oh! royal lady, assist her; and let the harsh gratings of her prison hinge be drowned in the glad tidings of your father's mercy. The eloquence of a Trojan monarch gained, in a hostile camp, the body of his devoted Hector; and the force of royal advocacy was evinced at the memorable siege of Calais, when an enraged and stern king had firmly set his heart upon the execution of St. Pierre. Where then is the difficulty to be apprehended, when an only daughter, and a nation's hope, asks from a generous prince and an indulgent father, the life of a fallen but repenting woman.[218]

This was a successful appeal. The hack writer Huish, in his life of the princess, claimed that Joseph's petition was a treasured possession of the princess's, folded among her papers, and stimulated her to take up the petitions of female capital convicts in Newgate.[219] 'Immediately on being informed that any female was sentenced to die', he writes, 'her Royal Highness set on foot an inquiry not only into the circumstances of the case but also into the character which the unfortunate convict bore previously to her condemnation'. The princess 'was not one of those stiff starched moralists who turn away with abhorrence from a fallen one of their own sex and thereby close every avenue to repentance and reformation'.[220]

William IV

Strong links were fashioned in the public press between Victoria's immediate predecessor on the throne and the criminal code's amelioration. His was a reign of parliamentary and other reforms. Capital punishment was a major question for the press, as one provincial paper observed in 1831, the question 'almost divides the attention of the London press with that of [parliamentary] reform'.[221] William IV gave official sanction through the Commission on Criminal Law Reform in July 1833 to Henry Brougham's project of reform.[222] One *History of England* in 1856, in closing the account of his reign, summarized the great change: 'Crime and punishment became in a great measure equalized; treason and murder are now the only which render the perpetrator subject to the extreme penalty of the law'.[223]

As such, this matched the expectations of John Taylor's 'patriotic predictions', verse of 1830 which began with William's 'eager haste, at Mercy's sacred plea, | He joy'd to set the lesser guilty free – | Not those who, justly doom'd to forfeit life, | Drugg'd the dire bowl, or rais'd th'assassin's knife; | Mercy with justice thus his aim to blend'. 'Hence, Taylor predicted, 'we may now presage, throughout his reign | He Mercy's plea with justice will maintain'.[224] As in his brother's reign, newspapers informed of the council meetings attended by the Recorders of London and Middlesex. The results in the metropolis were extolled as signs of improvements in the law and a consequence of royal clemency. It was asserted the king possessed mercy, 'beyond any of his predecessors, even in his own family ... a merit which belongs to the King quite independent, as in other cases, of his constitutional advisers'.[225] A newspaper stated in 1835, 'to sanction the execution of a subject costs his present Majesty a great struggle and great pain; not only that, but he is accustomed to urge every point that can strike a considerate and humane mind in favour of the prisoner'.[226]

The radical Henry Hunt used the petitions for mercy for the Bristol rioters as a test of the king's commitment to parliamentary reform.[227] The rare critic who discerned a lack of royal mercy considered the treatment of the Tolpuddle martyrs. A woodcut series, 'The Political Drama', published by Drake of Clare Market, includes one image in 1834 of a king and queen with a minister, ignoring the Dorchester unionists' pleas: 'have Mercy upon us as you hope for Mercy hereafter. Remember Sire, your Coronation Oath strictly enjoins you to Temper Justice with Mercy.' '[L]et us do justice', wrote one newspaper during his reign, 'to the Supreme Magistrate, and separate the character and feelings of our august Sovereign from those of his constitutional advisers'.[228]

The former Indian missionary James Peggs's prize-winning abolitionist essay of 1839 stressed the king's humanitarianism. At that point royal mercy ensured that there were no metropolitan executions for three years.[229] The abolitionist *Morning Herald*'s documentation in the 1830s included such notes as 'Sept.30. Further proof of the clemency of William IV. Evinced by the reprieve of all the capital convicts mentioned in the Recorder of London's report'.[230] The verses of one ballad nodded towards the sailor king's clemency: 'Making justice and mercy prevail here; | With a hand that can guide and heart that can feel'.[231] His consort was also used as an intermediary for appeals to mercy in 1830.[232] His reputed last acts were merciful, for the business transacted with his private secretary Sir Herbert Taylor included remission of a court-martial, two appointments of colonial judges, and a free pardon to a condemned criminal, exemplifying, 'by an act of mercy, that spirit of benevolence and forgiveness which shone with such peculiar lustre in his Majesty's character'.[233] In the Commons, Lord John Russell mentioned the reprieve from execution of a convicted murderer as his last act before death.

The abolitionist John Sydney Taylor paid tribute to his clemency in an obituary essay.[234] The sermon of one of the king's chaplains in early July, reported in the *London Standard* and other journals, noted the 'distinguishing attribute' of William's clemency: 'the administration of the laws under his government was marked by an unceasing aversion to the dreadful extremity of punishment', influenced by his 'deep interest in the mitigation of the criminal code'. William IV's 'personal conduct materially contributed to the practical ameliorations in our laws for which his reign has been remarkable'.[235] The *Baptist Magazine*'s obituary prominently discussed this aspect of his reign: 'the distinguished humanity ... obvious in the amelioration of the penal code. While William the fourth occupied the throne of England few of our fellow creatures suffered the final penalty of the law'.[236] Huish's biography, published during Victoria's accession, ended with a reference to his clemency and reform of the criminal code.[237] Verse from 'R.S.', a poet of Camberwell, in the pages of a morning newspaper in 1837 gestured towards 'The culprit [who] doomed to die his mercy knows, | And lives to bless that pity which restored him'.[238] Similarly, Jesse Hammond eulogized the 'great Reformer' for that mercy which 'grac'd his royal diadem' in 'Britannia's Lament'.[239]

One of the king's brothers, Augustus Frederick, Duke of Sussex, patronized the society for reform of the capital code. In October 1831 he presented a petition to Parliament signed by foremen from seven successive Old Bailey grand juries, and merchants, traders, and others eligible to serve as jurors, for criminal code revision and amendment that distinguished between crimes against property and crimes of violence.[240] This appeared as No.5 of *Punishment of Death: a Series of Short Articles, to Appear Occasionally in Numbers Designed for General Circulation*. He presented a petition for abolition of capital punishment from Irish Quakers. According to the *Morning Herald*, a deputation visiting him at Kensington Palace in 1831 found a man with 'a knowledge of the subject which proved that a thorough reform of the Criminal Code had previously occupied his deep and serious attention'.[241]

The Duke of Kent's relation to reform of the capital code was mixed. One effort at association surfaced in the Reverend Erskine Neale's biography of Victoria's father in 1850. Neale stated that the Quaker reformer William Allen, an abolitionist, was a friend of the duke – the assertion in a passage of fervent abolitionist sentiment concerning the penal reformer Elizabeth Fry.[242] (Fry was described by one writer as a 'queenly quakeress'.[243]) Yet the duke was a punitive military officer, participating in the grotesque ritual of a death march and kneeling on the coffin following the sentence, by a soldier in Quebec in April 1793 – although the man, Joseph Draper, was reprieved.[244] Given his death shortly after Victoria's birth, the duke had no role in her education as one so close to the line of succession, in justice and mercy.

Victoria's inheritance of mercy

Hopes of mercy were reposed in Alexandrina Victoria of Kent. William Kennedy's address to the princess in 1828, in *The Atlas of New York*, stated: 'No breast imperial beats so lightly | As that where tender Mercy swells'. Thomas Dalling Barleé's 'Ode to the Princess Victoria' similarly offered advice on the merciful use of regal power in a poem 'intended for the Royal Esteddfodd [sic] held at Cardiff in August 1834 but by the forgetfulness of a Friend … delivered to the Committee too late for admission'. When she attained her majority in 1837, there appeared a birthday ode, with the line: 'Silence the voice of Mercy in thy breast | And let unbiass'd Justice do the rest'.[245]

This chapter surveyed the relationship between monarchy and acts of mercy from the last Stuart monarchs and after the Hanoverian accession. The monarchs of the eighteenth century were eulogized by official and unofficial laureates, as previous monarchs had been, for the princely virtues of mercy and justice. They were directly involved in the royal prerogative of mercy and might not avoid the opprobrium attaching to unpopular acts of mercy or justice carried out in their name. Printed news and anecdote circulated about royal acts of mercy in the context of the criminal code. But ideas about mercy must be seen in a wider context, including that involving rebellion and revolution, where the monarch, as father of a nation or empire, was invoked as wielder of a sceptre of mercy, or bearer of a crown of mercy. The next chapter examines the public mythology surrounding Victoria's mercifulness. Like a eulogy for a Tudor or Stuart queen regnant, Victoria's reign was hailed as *Aera Astraea, Or, The Age of Justice*.[246] How did poetic prophecy match the reality?

3

Public Views of Victoria's Mercy

Who sits on the throne of England?
A young and gentle queen;
Mercy's mild glow lights up her brow,
And hallows beauty's mien.[1]

a sovereign whose mild and gentle virtues speak to the heart and mind.[2]

It is the tendency of the time to make the Crown by far too ornamental in our Constitution. We, therefore, view with pleasure any opportunity where the SOVEREIGN can come into personal relation with the people – especially bestowing grace and mercy, and in return receiving treasures of love, deep, real, and abiding.[3]

The quotations introducing this chapter, from 1839, 1847, and 1859, represent sentiments expressed frequently in the first two decades of Victoria's reign: linking her gender and youth with hopes for merciful disposition and influence in mitigating punishment, whether in the case of the third commentator, mutinous sailors, or the most serious of domestic crimes, including homicide. The death penalty features in Victorian biographies of the queen, and a recent biographical companion to Victoria's life accurately notes in an entry on her personality that she adhered to established norms of law and morality and had no compunction in signing death warrants 'if she thought it was merited'.[4]

There was not just sincerity in the general gestures towards the queen being a 'generous-heart girl' but also relief that the new monarch was not Ernest Augustus, the reactionary Duke of Cumberland.[5] As *John Cassell's Illustrated History of England* later noted, the new queen had 'the advantage of a foil which with all the force of contrast placed her character as a constitutional sovereign in the best possible light'.[6] The *Public Ledger* of Newfoundland reported the following libel, a toast alleged to have been raised by Tories: 'Here's death to Queen Victoria! The Gallows to Lord Melbourne! The Gibbet to Earl Grey! And the Crown of England to the Duke of Cumberland!!!'[7] Partisan fears about the succession were expressed in an extraordinary passage from the *Eclectic Review*:

Victoria intervened as an angel of mercy to avert a degradation, which an indignant people would never have passively borne; and a man, if man he be, who would have been ferociously pleased to wear the British crown, and crush, if he could British liberty, passed away like another Vulcan to forge his chains in a foreign land.[8]

The *Stamford Mercury* spoke of the 'merciful interposition' bringing Victoria to the throne without mentioning Cumberland.[9] *Blackwood's Lady's Magazine* contrasted her youth with the aged state of her uncles: 'accustomed to connect the idea of infirmity with the person of the sovereign, there was something almost preternatural in the effect produced by the sudden apparition of youth and beauty on the throne. The guilty felt as if Mercy had appeared among them – the unhappy as if Peace.'[10]

If these references suggested her accession was a merciful deliverance, what training in mercy had she? One can suppose an awareness of her uncle William's reputation for mercy, from recurrent press coverage. Victoria's training under the 'Kensington system' involved chronology and history but nothing on her constitutional role in criminal law. Her husband was to ensure that the Prince of Wales's education familiarized him with criminal law, with Herbert Fisher teaching him.[11]

For penal reformers, the queen's reign dawned auspiciously. The abolitionist *Morning Herald* thought her speech in proroguing parliament, on 17 July 1838, 'derived its chief interest and lustre from the heart-touching sentiments of mercy with which that act of sovereignty was graced'.[12] Others hoped she expressed a fervent desire when from her throne in the Lords she delivered a widely reported speech worded in a 'tone of moderation and justice' (see Figure 3.1).[13] She regarded 'with peculiar interest the amendment of the criminal code, and the reduction of the number of capital punishments. I hail this mitigation of the severity of the law as an auspicious commencement of my reign'.[14]

The *Mirror of Parliament* reported her royal uncle, the Duke of Sussex (addressing peers after the queen's speech on 20 November 1837), noting those 'gracious expressions which were from the throne and which I shall never forget', concerning mitigation of the laws. Her manner 'must have convinced all those who heard her that the sentiments which she delivered were perfectly in accordance with her feelings'. The duke thought he had 'a fair right to hope that when the chroniclers of a future day shall have to record the annals of this reign … will not be written in letters of blood, but will commemorate the triumphs and glories of the strict observance of the law'.[15] Personal association between prominent abolitionists and Sussex allowed them to target the new monarch with gifts of literature. The Quaker philanthropist William Allen went to Kensington Palace with John Sydney Taylor's two volumes of essays on the death penalty from the *Morning Herald*, presents from the Quaker abolitionist John Thomas Barry, and asked the duke to give a copy to the queen and her mother.[16]

I turn now to the ritual of the coronation in 1838, to show how the ancient ceremony enshrined mercy as a royal attribute, as it had done for Victoria's Hanoverian and Stuart predecessors.

Figure 3.1 A late-Victorian rendition of Queen Victoria's first parliament from *Illustrated London News Record of the Glorious Reign of Queen Victoria*, p.4. Author's collection.

Crowned a queen of mercy

There is a pointless sword in our regalia, called Curtana, or the Sword of Mercy. A popular Government like ours, wants no sharper weapon to punish or restrain.[17]

No woman has yet perished on the scaffold under the reign of our maiden Queen, the clemency of whose disposition heightens the lustre of her other virtues ... May the eve of the Queen's coronation be stained with the blood of no such sacrifice.[18]

The association between the British monarch and justice is ritually made before peers and the nation, at the start of the reign. Even during the interregnum 'state pageantry' in 1657 brought out the role of justice and mercy in the nation's chief magistrate. The purple robe lined with ermine worn by Oliver Cromwell at his investiture, 'being the Habit antiently used at the solemn Investiture of Princes', represented the blending of justice and mercy.[19]

During the coronation Victoria received symbols of equity and mercy, swore to maintain the laws of God, and cause law and justice in mercy to be executed in all her judgements. Abolitionists and anti-abolitionists used this oath, as did campaigners in particular efforts for capital punishment reprieve.[20] (The oath was included by missionaries in the coronation rite developed for the short-lived child-king Pomare III in Papaoa in Tahiti, 21 April 1824; in Hawaii the kingship of Kalahaua in 1883 was inaugurated with a ceremony including an English-style sword symbolizing justice and mercy.[21]) The coronation sanctified the notion of a merciful ruler. (In another royal ritual, the Anglican Book of Common Prayer also emphasized mercy's role in a prayer composed for Maundy Day about 1850: 'Thou hast not only bestowed greatness and majesty upon our Sovereign Lady Queen Victoria, but hast given her a heart also to take compassion on them that are below her, and show mercy unto the poor and needy.'[22]

Detailed accounts of the coronation in newspapers and periodicals informed Britons of the part that the 'curtana' or sword of mercy had in the regalia.[23] A less spectacular element of the regalia than the crown and orb, it nevertheless had cultural prominence in coronation discourse, figuring in guides to the Tower of London and regalia in the eighteenth century. It featured in William Huntington's *Spoils Taken from the Tower of London*.[24] Eighteenth-century poets and moralists also alluded to it, thus the clergyman Augustus Toplady, author of the hymn 'Rock of Ages', used the curtana as an emblem for discussing divine mercy.[25])

The two preceding coronations of the nineteenth century saw the curtana's symbolism being raised. 'Monarchs frequently cut justice short,' wrote one commentator in the *New Monthly Magazine* in 1821, 'both in mercy and from less amiable impulses; and it is remarkable that this sword is pointless'.[26] *John Bull* informed readers that 'for the purpose of answering allegorically to its name, is made to appear as though its point were broken off'.[27] The ticket designs after Sir William Congreve, for admission to Westminster Hall and Abbey for George IV's coronation in June 1821, presented Britannia, justice, and mercy with her curtana, in attendance on the king (see Figure 3.2).[28]

Figure 3.2 Detail of the coronation admission ticket for George IV, 19 July 1820. Image courtesy of Toovey's Fine Art Auctioneers and Valuers.

The account in the *Saturday Magazine* for July 1838, described the sword of mercy as the 'principal in dignity of the three swords which are borne naked before the sovereign at the coronation'.[29] Representations of the 'pointless sword' appeared beside other elements of the regalia.[30] After the queen's ceremony the *Morning Chronicle* used the symbol of the sword in a critique of the Tory response to viceroy Mulgrave in Ireland, 'there is a party in the State that would point the sword with violence'.[31]

An early Victorian critic of poetry thought the notion of a *sword* of mercy – in a prize-winning poem for the Chancellor's medal for poetry entitled 'The Tower of

London' – as opposed to a *sceptre*, absurd.³² Much mediocre and bad poetry during the accession and coronation gestured to the sword and other emblems of royal mercy. In Margaret Richardson's stanza contrasting the sharp-edged sword of justice with mercy, the queen wields curtana when pity 'flutters, in her tender breast'.³³ There was the Cambridge graduate Charles Gregory Sharpley's six cantos, dedicated to the queen's mother:

> To Mercy's Queen bring Mercy's Sword,
> Low let the Curteyn before Her be laid:
> She will bid it await compassion's word,
> For blunted the point and minished the blade;
> This constantly near her alone will rest,
> For this is the weapon she'll love the best.³⁴

An alternative symbol of mercy was the sceptre. The 'sceptre in a maiden-hand', not 'by tyrant law' appeared in James Montgomery of Sheffield's 'Ode for Queen Victoria', in *Blackwood's Magazine* in July 1838.³⁵ The Conservative MP and littérateur Richard Monckton Milnes's 'Coronation Song' called on the people not to lament the sceptre of might in 'so tender a hand,' for, 'if strength can be gentle and mercy be just, | How well for the ruler, how well for the land!'³⁶ If not the sword or sceptre, poetry turned to the crown to examine the attributes of royalty. Thus the poet and playwright Margaret Cornwell Baron-Wilson, stimulated by witnessing the crown on show at the royal jewellers Rundell and Bridge's, selected its ermine as the symbol of mercy, as she worked through the regalia's constituent elements: 'View well thy Crown, it will impart | A lesson to thy Queenly heart'.³⁷

Other verse emphasized royal mercy's role, in expressing their authors' hopes about the new reign.³⁸ Evidently to the air of 'God save the Queen,' was the *Morning Post*'s 'Ever let mercy's ray, | Star-like, shed o'er her way | Its hallowed light.'³⁹ From Southampton came the poem, 'Who Sits on the Throne', similarly finding a 'young and gentle Queen, | mercy's mild glow lights up her brow'. The verse of the 'cottage girl' Elizabeth Brown of Woodend in Northamptonshire praised the queen's 'true mercy and justice oh, may she extend, | Her true royal clemency ever doth shine'. Her anthem extolled the queen's setting free of captives, 'she's granted prisoners sweet release'.⁴⁰ Women were fascinated with a queen regnant wielding this power (unexercised by a British woman since Queen Anne's death in 1714). The American actress and playwright Charlotte Barnes commented in verse in the *Southern Literary Messenger*, in the character of the queen, chief of all her sex in rank: 'When lives Thou gav'st | Are in my hand, let "mercy season justice," nor | Let misplaced clemency encourage vice.'⁴¹

Justice and mercy figured among the many illuminations for the coronation in June 1838 in a loyal London.⁴² Hawkins, an ironmonger in Bishopsgate Street, showed a full-length image of the queen with sword of justice and orb of mercy, painted by a window-blind maker.⁴³ Public imagery expressed no profound thought on the queen's role, but the monarch as fountain of justice and mercy proved to be a longstanding motif in the history of Victorian illuminations.⁴⁴

Tales of Victoria's mercy

> Doubtless the metropolitan philosopher imagines that her Majesty ought to do nothing else all the day long but sign death warrants and Commissions for Cornets in the Guards.[45]

This section studies three episodes linked to Victoria that represent vulgar error, public rumour and then 'tradition' about her handling of the royal prerogatives of mercy or pardon. The first took place at the start of her reign. The 'Chit-Chat' section to the metropolitan *Satirist*, imagined the following in 26 November 1837:

> 'How do they hang men?' asked the all gracious Queen of her royal mother, after executing the death warrant of the Scotch criminal. 'With a rope, my dear,' replied the Duchess. 'A rope!' exclaimed the maiden sovereign, 'do you mean a skipping-rope?' Lord Melbourne, who was present, as in duty bound, explained the mystery of criminal strangulation.[46]

Here, the Whig premier was the wise avuncular figure advising a childish monarch. The unfortunate Scotsman was the only man executed in Scotland that year, the tobacco spinner William Perrie, who stabbed his wife. He was executed despite petitions and efforts by John Sydney Taylor and the *Morning Herald* to 'prevent the commencement of the reign … presenting, in practice, a contradiction to the sentiments of clemency which hallowed the first great act of state under a maiden reign'.[47] In the previous chapter, detailing the change in arrangements in capital punishment in the metropolis after Victoria's accession, the reality according to Melbourne was cited, that 'she would [not] hesitate to sign a death warrant if the culprit deserved death'.[48] The *Satirist*'s fancy was stimulated by news circulating in this first year of the Victorian age. The London *John Bull*, rabidly anti-Whig, noticed a 'circular' in various papers in July and August 1837: 'On the first warrant for execution being presented to the QUEEN to sign, she burst into tears. Lord MELBOURNE said, "Your Majesty knows you have the prerogative of mercy." "Then", she replied, "let the sentence be changed to transportation for life."'[49]

John Bull corrected this misconception, for 'everybody who happens to know anything' knew this was not so – in the past it was only in London that the monarch was directly involved, it reminded its readers, when the king merely said to the Home Secretary, let the law take its course. The bill removing this role was introduced 'for some unknown reason' and thus 'a privilege taken away from the wretched culprits, who always looked up most justly and reasonably to the Royal mercy, or at least the royal investigation, of which the present Liberal Ministers have deprived them.' The 'poor young Queen' by *coup* was deprived of 'one of the blessed prerogatives of her station'. For *John Bull* in 1838 royal mercy reflected 'Liberal delicacy,' and also (in some strange association) tee-totallers and their twaddle.[50]

Angering the newspaper were two incidents. The first was the pardon for John Rickey, a thirty-year old soldier in the 12th regiment of Lancers. While drunk he shot Sergeant James Hamilton in the stomach at Hampton Court Palace barracks and was found guilty at the Central Criminal Court of wilful murder in June. The jury recommended mercy due to previous good character. A black-capped but tearful Justice Park, characterizing this as a 'false notion of compassion' the next day, did not pass sentence immediately as there were 'considerations' which were then found to be unfavourable to the prisoner.[51] Respite came, it was reported, through the Recorder of London's intercession and the sentence was commuted to transportation for life.[52]

The second event was the commutation of sentence on the youth Samuel Kirkby of Lincoln ('one of the most depraved wretches that ever disgraced humanity,' according to the *Lincolnshire Chronicle*) for fatally poisoning with arsenic his master, a butcher named John Bruce, for being thumped or flogged. In this case the newspaper referred the outcome to the queen herself.[53] Lest it appear seditious *John Bull* commented that 'as far as the law and the Constitution go, the QUEEN has of course the power of pardon; but with the signing of death warrants, and consequent weepings, the SOVEREIGN has no more to do than the Groom-Porter, or the Clerk Marshal'.[54]

The Conservative *Torch* also gave a partisan view of Melbourne's mercy in capital cases. 'Appius' complained of 'ill advised extensions of the Royal mercy' metamorphizing that 'once cherished boon into a curse and terror to your countrymen'.[55] Another Conservative newspaper published an anecdote of *weeping* royalty frustrated by the 'pseudo patriots' of the Whig government intent on stopping the 'fountain of mercy' in relation to the Imprisonment Abolition Bill, which the writer characterized as a system of 'slow murder'. 'Vindex', in the *Essex Standard* in July 1840, similarly identified abolitionism with the 'so-called Liberals of the age ... these are, almost to a man, the advocates of the total abolition of capital punishments ... [a] man ... has but to broach some novel and dangerous doctrine, and my Lord Melbourne will at once introduce him to the Queen'.[56] Concern about royal favourites was rhetorically linked to episodes in English history where impressionable monarchs were prevailed upon to sign death warrants.[57]

Party politics shaped how Victoria's early reputation for clemency was presented. From the opposite sides of the political divide, there might be approval. The London Whig *Globe* in 1838 discussed the widely reported clemency to two infanticides tried at Chester assizes, commenting, 'we are confident that our beloved and youthful Queen will exercise her darling attribute, and that her Ministers will advise its extension, if a sense of duty, imperious and painful, do not compel them to withhold it':

> The instances in which it has been extended during her short reign, even in cases of *murder*, and where the Judges who tried the case passed sentence without leaving a ray of hope, and the almost entire disuse of capital punishment during the time the present Ministry have held office, abundantly justify our opinion.[58]

When the sentence on the reprieved women was published, *The Times*'s correspondents were highly critical: 'A.B.' describing Lord John Russell's mercy from the Home Office as a 'scoff and mocker' of the word. 'E.W.', concerning the respite 'wrung from the framers of the Poor Law Bill,' hoped that as a young woman, the queen was 'full of mercy and compassion,' and that infanticide was one of all crimes which a female sovereign ought to deal with leniently.[59]

The paragraph about a tearful queen confronted with the decision of life or death, circulated rapidly in the provincial English and wider British press in 1837 and survived for many years.[60] Another early anecdote of royal clemency had more detail. On 17 May 1837 John Lowes, a dragoon in the Third or King's Own Light Dragoons stationed in Canterbury attempted to shoot his regimental sergeant major, during breakfast (the officer's wife and five children being present), his loaded pistol failing to go off.[61] The regiment was due to leave for India, and a court martial at Chatham on 27 May was organized instead of bringing the case before the civil court. Nevertheless the press reported it: 'a most diabolical attempt to commit murder'.[62] Lord Hill as Commander in Chief was forced to transmit the sentence to the consideration of Victoria in Council, but, so *Berrow's Worcester Journal* reported, 'The Royal mind of our youthful Sovereign showed that it was too much imbued with the sound principles of religious and humane feeling; tempering the sternness of justice, her Majesty declined to sign the death-warrant.'[63]

This very early act by Victoria, whose accession was in June, was interpreted hopefully, as doing 'a thousand times more service, in teaching mercy and forbearance to a people, than could the public execution of the miserable culprit.' Newspaper paragraphs appeared entitled 'her majesty's clemency'.[64] By chance, at the point at which her role in military mercy became apparent through such accounts, images of the queen in military costume after the review at Windsor in September, her first public ceremony as queen, circulated.[65] In 1839 James Peggs drew an optimistic conclusion from the queen's mercy in this case in an anti-capital punishment pamphlet.[66]

A similar early performance of royal mercy in a capital case of court martial, occurred in Dublin after the sentence passed on a soldier at the Royal barracks in 1839. A soldier of the 38th Regiment, William Page, for attempting to shoot colour-serjeant Michael Dolan, was read the sentence after marching behind the regimental band playing the Dead March in Handel's *Saul*. 'Every limb of the unfortunate man shook with his approaching fate, and his companions, who formed the firing party, were blanched with terror at the dread of the deed they were expected to carry into execution,' before the queen's pardon was read. Page was transported to New South Wales, becoming an anecdote in an Australian temperance journal.[67] One periodical described the whole ritual – with the queen's mercy some sort of *deus ex machina* – as an awful pantomime.[68]

Another military-related case of capital punishment provides the second significant mercy episode. 'How well known is the story of the young Queen saving a deserter,' said the *Poverty Bay Herald*, of New Zealand, in March 1901.[69] In what, from mid-century, became an oft-repeated and elaborated incident in royal biography, the new queen decided the fate of a deserter with a record for bravery on active service, court-martialled and sentenced to death after absconding a third time. The death warrant was presented to her – so readers were told – by Wellington. She pled for life and signed the word 'Pardoned' with a trembling hand. The anecdote first surfaced in 1838. The abolitionist *Morning Herald* in April alluded to the incident as proof of womanly gentleness coupled with the 'decision and firmness of a Queen' and in the context of her 'impressive and unaffected elocution' in parliament about mercy, which 'touched the hearts of a people more averse from the cold-blooded destruction of life than any perhaps, in the world'.[70]

Newspaper-circulated tales impressed upon the public the fact that their 'maiden queen' was merciful. A Sussex paper, in April – the month that news of the deserter's respite circulated – was relieved that the county was not shamed by an execution at Horsham Gaol following respite for Richard Standing. It credited the decision to 'petitions by the prosecutor and others,' the 'public press' and 'principally by the elevated and Christian principles of the Sovereign herself which teach her that – "Earthly power doth then show likest Gods | When mercy seasons justice."'[71]

In September 1838 the abolitionist *Sheffield Independent* printed verse entitled 'The White Rose of England' stimulated by the tale, and reputedly originating in the recounting of the incident by Wellington himself.[72] The same paper published another, 'Victoria's Victory,' in November, which included lines after 'hearing the popular report of the young Queen's very *popular* aversion to signing death warrants': 'A woman's heart may triumph more | Than ever sovereign did before, | By acts of clemency; | A woman's hand efface the stain | That Britain's laws too long retain; – | Victoria's victory!'[73] While the press took up the rumour of queenly unwillingness to sign death warrants, this misconception about the process was deplored by other papers.[74] If the 'senseless paragraph' went the rounds of the provincial press, 'happily in no case will the task of ordering a fellow-creature's death be cast on her'.[75]

In 1848 a correspondent in the abolitionist *Kendal Mercury* wrote that it had been Rowland Hill (Lord Hill) as Commander in Chief, at an audience on military affairs. This correction, ignored in all subsequent retellings, despite the obvious point that Hill *was* Commander in Chief until 1842, did not alter the details of the anecdote. The writer claimed Hill related the tale to a MP, and moreover that it went the round of newspapers and 'certainly did in Ireland, preparing that country to hope for a similar exercise of mercy on the present occasion' (this was uttered in the context of Smith O'Brien's plight, following his rebellion).[76] The liberal *Leinster Independent*, in May 1838, under the impression that several men found guilty of violent assaults at Clonaslee and condemned to transportation were released, spoke of a 'royal and vice regal prerogative of mercy … to whom the imploring cry of the injured does not rise in vain'.[77]

Victoria was a global icon and the anecdote crossed the Atlantic to appear for moral instruction in *Poughkeepsie Casket* (New York State) on 23 February 1839.[78] Canadians alluded to the incident – coupling it with a later example of the royal clemency towards a soldier in 1866 to show the 'queen's goodness of heart'.[79] Australian newspapers carried news of the incident in 1850 (subsequent versions elaborated details of Victoria's 'eyes flashing and her bosom heaving with strong emotion'). Later newspapers as diverse as the *Latter Day Saints Millennial Star* and the *Wairarapa Daily Times* of New Zealand circulated and enlarged the anecdote.[80] It appeared in improving mid-century texts as 'a beautiful incident'. A pacifist nonconformist minister sermonized on it in the context of the British decision to go to war in the Crimea in 1855.[81] The *Excellencies of Women*, a Scarborough publication of 1860 by a minister of the United Methodist Free Church, recounted the event, exemplifying the fact that women often chose mercy: 'Mercy with her drops as the rain, and her love is soft and gentle as the evening dew. Who that needs mercy would not wish their cause in the hands of Woman'.[82] Later religious texts such as encyclopedias of Christian illustration and anecdote, touched on it.[83]

In celebrations for royal marriage between the Marquess of Lorne and the queen's fourth daughter, Princess Louise, a clergyman trotted out the anecdote for public entertainment in 1871.[84] Late-Victorian and posthumous biographies mentioned it, including the Reverend Charles Bullock's bestselling *The Queen's Resolve* (1887); Robert Anderson's *Victorian Era* (1897) and the anonymous *Private Life of Queen Victoria by one of her Majesty's Servants* (1901). George Alfred Henty's *Queen Victoria. Scenes from her Life and Reign* (1901) noted 'The first death warrant', with an illustration (see Figure 3.3).[85] So too did Cassell's *Life and Times*, the picture (Figure 3.4) was described as 'striking' in one review.[86] The incident is recorded in Robert Wilson's *The Life and Times of Queen Victoria* – one provincial reviewer cited the handling of this incident as an example of Wilson's lack of power as a writer – 'all the aroma of the touching incident is lost for want of a little delicacy in the narrative'.[87] For the *Westminster Review*, reviewing a biography of Victoria and her grandson the Kaiser in 1896, the episode exemplified her 'great womanliness and a certain deep tenderness'.[88] Sermons after her death alluded to it. Sir Sidney Lee's biography also mentioned the event.

Figure 3.3 'The first death warrant', G.A. Henty, *Queen Victoria. Scenes from Her Life and Reign* (London: Blackie, 1901), p.33. Author's collection.

Figure 3.4 Illustration by Robert Barnes, in R. Wilson, *The Life and Times of Queen Victoria* (London: Cassell, 1893), p.249. Author's collection.

The illustrations represent a virginal young beauty deferring to the older male but also asserting her wish not simply to be good but merciful. There were other representations of her being instructed by Melbourne where less fateful paperwork is shown being signed by the queen. (Incidentally, David Wilkie's famous painting of the queen's first council elicited this comment from the *London and Paris Observer* in 1838: 'A stranger might take it to be a representation of an innocent girl under examination by a court martial, in the cabin of a ship, instead of a new-made sovereign, receiving the homage of recognition from the magnates of the land, in a palace.'[89])

The deserter's death warrant episode was evoked in verse by William Golder, author of the first English poetry collection in New Zealand, who published 'The Death Warrant' there in 1865. It imagined the 'virgin Queen', presiding over the imperial council, joyful and carefree, when stern Justice appeared: 'A convict's fate must settled be, | Her signature confirms his doom; | To which her thoughts could ill agree, | Which filled her peaceful mind with gloom.' Justice urges the duty, but 'sweet mercy' rises in her heart and 'pity made her bosom yearn | O'er the poor captive's fate undone!'

'Must such be so?' she sighed, when press'd,
(The law would not evaded be)
As stirr'd the emotions of her breast,
The tears bedew'd the sad decree![90]

For children, the anecdote surfaced in such works as the *Young People's Mirror* in 1850, in 'expository notes on scriptural lessons, on pardon', and in later biographies of the queen.[91] In 'Horrid Dates; or, Molly's Fairy History lesson' – a series in *Young Folks Paper* by Audrey Allen in 1889, the time-travelling Molly witnesses the sight of King Edward VI forced to sign the Duke of Somerset's death warrant (in 1552): 'And were the sovereigns of your time obliged to sign death warrants?' demands Molly, indignantly, 'I am sure that my Queen Victoria would not think of such a thing!'[92]

Her subjects *believed* in the incident – thus one pious lady (the New York-based British Baptist Mary Forbes Onslow), part of a circle of women praying for the young monarch, recounted the episode in a private letter published in 1860.[93] Yet the anecdote of 'Think again', while attaining the status of a tradition by the late nineteenth century, does not figure in modern accounts of her reign, their authors less eager to demonstrate that she was the 'good queen' of posthumous press eulogy. Reticence at the time also reflected doubt about whether the incident happened.[94] There is no mention in the queen's diary. The celebrated preacher Charles Spurgeon admitted in a sermon, 'I do not know whether the story is true.' The 'semi-official' biography by Richard Holmes, the royal librarian at Windsor (whose text was supposedly dictated, revised, and corrected by Victoria), left out the anecdote. Readers of the *St James Gazette* in 1897 were prepared by a note on Holmes's imminent book, for the explosion of pleasing myths such as the 'well-worn' story which had appeared in that year in the middle-class literary journal *Argosy* – it would be a shock to find these incidents 'relegated to the realm of fable; but *magna est veritas*'.[95]

Figure 3.5 'The Penge Mystery', *Illustrated Police News*, 1 December 1877, p.1. Newspaper image © The British Library Board. All rights reserved. With thanks to the British Newspaper Archive (www.britishnewspaperarchive.co.uk).

My final case study involves personal supplication before the throne of mercy. Like the tale of the deserter, its truth was embroidered. 'But all about the Queen sympathising with true womanly feeling is gammonish but will be handed down to posterity as an Anecdote of this reign.'[96] So commented a courtier in a private letter from Balmoral, 20 November 1877, referring to a 'roman fantastique' appearing in the Aberdeen paper. The incident involved the mother of the notorious 'Penge convicts', Louis Adolphus Staunton and Patrick Llewellyn Staunton, convicted of the murder by starvation of Mrs Louis Staunton. She attempted to intercede with the queen in person, reputedly arriving in a mail cart from Ballater, the nearest train station, and returning to Ballater thanks to royal kindness, in Her Majesty's carriage. There, since Home Secretary Assheton Cross's despatch recommending reprieve had by then reached the queen, the 'sister in sorrow' (as one newspaper styled the queen) was told of the good news.[97] As the courtier suggested, tales of mercy on the basis of the queen's gender had become the stuff of anecdote already.

Sure enough, newspapers and journals across and beyond Britain reported the incident of 'The Queen and Mrs Staunton'.[98] The weekly sensationalist paper *Illustrated Police News* provided three engravings on the subject on its front page (see Figure 3.5).[99] 'A writer in one of the weekly papers has questioned the truth of the above statement', it stated. 'Our artist has illustrated the account of the affair which appeared in *Touchstone* and another paper, and his treatment of the subject will be acknowledged to be at once graceful and felicitous.'

The incident suggested that the queen could set aside 'all etiquette and formality' in such cases and listen 'with a true Sovereign's and woman's heart' – and that even though the matter was 'entirely in the hands of her responsible Minister', her heart ached and she could think of the distressed mother's plight with a 'consideration so characteristic'. 'Such', the short-lived two-penny satirical paper *Touchstone, or The New Era* declared, 'is a simple account of an episode in the life of the Queen, well harmonising with all that her subjects already know of her'.[100] Other accounts, the tale being corrected at the request of Mrs Staunton, who was grieved at the misstatement, indicated the queen had *not* received her. She heard the narrative at second hand through the keeper of the Privy Purse, Sir Thomas Biddulph, and desired to express her deep sympathy, 'which she would have done personally, but that it might form a precedent in such cases'.[101]

'It is a pleasant story', another paper commented after recounting the queen's kindness in ordering a swift notification of the respite to be passed to Mrs Staunton as she returned to Brixton, 'and, if not true in all its details, as has since been hinted, at least deserves to be so'.[102] The ephemeral magazine *Mayfair* was more satirical, suspecting the 'touching story' was 'distant relative of the narrative we heard from Oban last summer about the sea serpent'. There was a 'suspicious evenness about its flow, an engaging dovetailing of incidents, which, on the whole, is suggestive of Effie Deans and three halfpence a line'. The writer could have accepted everything but the detail of Mrs Staunton driving to Balmoral 'seated on the mail-bags which contained the Home Secretary's recommendation for the reprieve'.[103]

J.H. Naylor of Staunton-on-Wye felt compelled to versify the recommendation to mercy, in poetry published in one Welsh-language newspaper: 'Justice uplifts the sword, | Above each victim's head; | But lo! The royal word, | On lightning wing hath sped.'[104] The queen's own diary confirms that she did *not* actually meet the poor woman; her great surprise at the incident is clear from the relative detail with which she noted Biddulph's role in talking with the 'very well spoken and respectable looking' mother: 'There has been great excitement & agitation about it, many people thinking that the case was not at all well proved'.[105]

Earlier, in 1837, the *Brighton Patriot* contrasted the personal approach adopted by the King of the French, meeting the aged mother of François Meunier, guilty of a regicidal attempt in December 1836, and sentenced to life imprisonment instead of death (he was actually sent to America), with the British monarchy:

> Divesting this account of the colouring so dexterously used, there is, we take it, no room to doubt of the facts. Such a scene could never have occurred in England. What mother of a criminal could have approached the 'fountain of mercy' in this country? Our customs admit of no such familiarity between the 'lower orders,' and our Kings and Queens as taking hands and raisings ups and sittings downs. The whole of this may be false in the French account, but we repeat it could 'never occur in England.'[106]

The Staunton episode was reported under the title of the 'Queen's Mercy'. In earlier cases of murder and attempted murder reported in the newspapers, appeals were made to the queen's mercy. The petition of one Suffolk farmer's wife surviving an unhusbandly dose of arsenic in 1852 was entitled 'A Wife's Love and the Queen's Mercy'.[107] The rumour of benevolence at the start of the reign and the prevailing conception of the mature queen as averse to signing death warrants echo the newspaper accounts of those earlier Hanoverians recounted in the previous chapter. The early nineteenth century saw the emergence of a capital-punishment abolitionist campaign in Britain presenting royal clemency as part of the argument for reform. The next section looks at the use made of Victoria by abolitionists.

The queen's mercy in capital-punishment abolition agitation and literature

'The brightest gem the Queen could add to her tiara would be that by which she should declare that henceforth no Englishman should suffer on the scaffold the death of a dog', commented an abolitionist agitator in 1847, applauded by his audience.[108] In *Victorians Against the Gallows* I briefly discussed the abolitionists' use of the female sovereign in their campaigns.[109] Abolitionists used their connections through the Duke of Sussex to approach her privately, but there were more public gestures. In 1838 the Sheffield silver-plate manufacturer and social reformer Samuel Roberts published *Queen's Coronation: An Address to the Females of Sheffield*, against capital punishment.[110] He wrote:

> England never but once before was governed by a Virgin Queen. Oh! what would not that Virgin Queen have given on her death-bed, had the females of Sheffield of those days been able, by any means, to have prevented her from ever during her life, signing the DEATH WARRANT of a human being whether subject or not, lover or not, relative or not, monarch or not, female or not! Whatever may constitute the glory of a King, the glory of a Queen, of a Virgin Queen, like yours, must be LOVE and MERCY. Beg of her, then with affectionate humility, to tell her Councillors that her hand, her pen, shall never be employed in a task, as abhorrent to her nature, as it is repugnant to Christianity, and opposed to the real welfare of States.[111]

In the same year the radical *Tait's Edinburgh Magazine* published 'Scroll of a Letter to the Queen, on the Punishment of Death', purporting to be the result of discussion by a 'few respectable women of the middle class' on death warrants. It was written by the Irish novelist Martha Macdonald Lamont, a correspondent of the Carlyles, and contrasted the queen's world of vanity, splendour, and comfort with her subjects' ignorance (Lamont published a pamphlet *The Mission of the Educator; an Appeal for the Education of All Classes in England* in 1840), degradation, and overwork. It pitied Victoria since 'imagination depicts you to us as signing a death warrant and we shudder as we contemplate the image even in fancy'.[112] Another approach in the form of an essay in a periodical appeared in the *Monthly Magazine* in May 1839. A loyal address from an 'aesthetic student', it hoped for a new regal dispensation of love rather than coercion, with the queen leading abolition of all cruel and uncivilized law, including those permitting corporal punishment (with recent scandals involving harsh martial punishment at Woolwich) and the death penalty. These were inconsistent with the merciful tone that ought to characterize the reign of a female:

> A queen should feel that a child of the Creator is in no case to be prohibited from making an earthly atonement for his offences. Conscience must show your Majesty that under our present penal laws contrasts may take place, the consideration of which you could hardly endure. A day, opening with a Newgate tragedy, and concluding with a Court ball, involves an antithesis – from the contemplation of which every finer sensibility revolts.

I have thus, Madam, endeavoured to draw your attention to two notorious evils, in the abrogation of which royal influence might aid. It is scarcely necessary to add that the feminine principle must be excited on all similar or analogous cases.[113]

There were more direct gestures than these literary appeals. The Society for the Abolition of Capital Punishment was inaugurated in 1846, at a meeting that agreed to petition the queen and Parliament. Enlightened royalty was invoked on this occasion since the audience heard of King Oscar of Sweden's abolitionist book *On Punishments and Prisons*. In Carlisle in late 1848, where there was an abolitionist society, a meeting with Lord Nugent, MP, for Aylesbury and a figure in the national movement, also raised the question of the queen's role. The *Carlisle Journal* reprinted Adkin of Drover's Lane's address to her, to present 'a small form of this petition to your presideing Ministery for them to form a bill in soport of your humble petitioners'. Nugent endorsed this, 'praying her royal sanction and sympathy with the wishes of her people, with the dictates of humanity, and with the soundest policy of national justice'.[114] Nugent argued, from her status as woman and mother, against infliction of the death penalty with the attendant scenes 'which there is not a mother in the empire who would not make her children shun as a moral pestilence and abomination'. Nugent debated the scriptural injunction 'Whose sheddeth man's blood by man's shall his blood be shed' in relation to the prerogative of mercy too; 'she must either be in obedience to God, or in rebellion against Him'.

The parliamentary leader of abolitionism, William Ewart, claimed at a meeting in Southwark in 1849, on the basis of the queen being relieved from the 'repugnant duty' of death warrants, that she 'shrunk from capital punishment'.[115] During a long speech, the Quaker Charles Gilpin, another abolitionist leaders, told a Sheffield audience in 1851 his memory of the 'petition of a poor man to the Queen'. The queen, being a mother, would have felt the appeal had it reached her, and Gilpin also implored her, as a mother, to remove the demoralizing gallows scenes from the sight of her subjects' children. Would the queen or those instructing the royal children allow them 'to see a poor fellow-creature strangling in the hands of the hangman for a moral example?'[116] Abolitionist propaganda, naturally, alluded to the incident of the deserter and the queen.[117] At Kendal, the secretary of the SACP, the Quaker Alfred Dymond, rehearsed the queen's refusal to sign the death warrant in 1855: 'at one moment the spirit of a queen and the nature of a woman rose up together, and to the eternal honour of her majesty, she exclaimed, "Then I will never sign it." (Applause.)'[118] Over a decade later, the SACP still exploited the dissonance between a female sovereign and the execution of women.[119]

In its abolitionist infancy the satirical magazine *Punch* linked the cause with the young queen. Thus in July 1843, in 'Punch's Labour of Hercules', the ninth labour involved the hero visiting Buckingham Palace, where he found the queen unknowingly wearing not the chivalric Garter but the hangman's halter. *The Times* – no supporter of complete abolition – made the association too, between mitigating the penal system and the 'presence of a maiden Queen upon the throne,' in 1846 when Victoria was no maiden.[120]

Others, through verse and prose, associated merciful queen and death penalty. A sermon by the Whig clergyman Sydney Smith in 1837 used the new queen's position 'with the fine feelings of youth, and with all the gentleness of her sex', confronted with a capital criminal, asking whether the malefactor had been educated or brought to a place of worship; 'am I, the fountain of mercy, the nursing-mother of my people, to send a forsaken wretch from the streets to the scaffold'. (Smith hoped that the Creator, 'in his mercy [had] placed in the heart of this royal woman the rudiments of wisdom and mercy'.) In 1859 a poem about a capital convict who is reprieved, exclaims, "'Twas well for me a female bosom reign'd, | Or else dear Mercy's suit had been disdain'd'.[121] A few works of fiction in the periodical press imagined the queen's exercise of mercy. In the same year as the report of the deserter's fate, the *New York Mirror* carried a story by the Anglo-American John St Hugh Mills in which the queen reprieved a young arsonist. Full of gaiety in Melbourne's company, when the Recorder appeared her 'girlish joyous expression vanished … a marble paleness spread over the features as she stood gazing on the fatal paper which was to confirm the sentence of hurrying a miserable being from earth'. She cannot sign it, and, 'tears swimming in her eyes', is relieved to be advised she can pardon the offence.[122] In the serial 'My College Friends' in *Blackwood's Edinburgh Magazine* (1844), a man intercedes for the life of another convicted of murder. The judge does not support this, but a 'private and personal interest' is at work, 'for once', more powerful than judges or Home Secretaries. A 'short but strong remonstrance' was sent directly to the queen and a letter 'accompanied a reprieve by return post', the letter being 'a few short lines dictated by a royal spirit and a woman's heart and signed "VICTORIA."'[123]

The radical journalist and anti-capital punishment propagandist George Reynolds's melodramatic *Mysteries of the Court of London* (1856) imagined the queen declaring abolitionist sentiments. But this was a serialized novel depicting a corrupt English aristocracy and establishment; the merciful queen was Indora of Inderabad, an independent kingdom in Hindostan.[124] Reynolds published a translation of Victor Hugo's abolitionist narrative, *Le Dernier Jour d'un Condamné*; another translation by Sir Peter Hesketh Fleetwood (who lived near Windsor) elicited royal permission for a dedication in 1840.[125] Fleetwood recorded 'a respectful appreciation of the mildness and clemency which has pervaded the administration of the laws during the present merciful reign'.[126] The dissonance between the royal gender and capital punishment also surfaced in the anonymous *How I Rose in the World* (1868), where a character faces execution despite the jury's recommendation of mercy and petitions: 'Women do not like to shed blood; and our royal lady has a true woman's heart.'[127] I now turn to those direct appeals to the woman's heart, through petitions addressed to the queen.

Petitioning and pressuring the queen in capital cases

A later chapter examines the Crown in relation to appeals to royal mercy in capital cases involving political crimes. Steve Poole examines the 'retreat from approachability' in the early years of the Victorian monarchy in studying the politics of regicide from the 1760s onwards: 'tolerance of individual intrusions into royal space was forcibly contracted', including the traditional attempt to petition the monarch informally or as an individual.[128] Yet the queen remained the target of memorials and petitions for mercy in many non-political capital cases, from famous murders to obscure infanticides where the woman's plight sparked organized campaigns.

The Swiss-born murderess Maria Manning appealed to the queen for mercy in 1849, for example.[129] In this notorious homicide, attracting the attention of celebrities such as Charles Dickens, a personal link was alleged since Maria had been frequently in the royal presence when she had been Lady Blantyre's personal maid. Blantyre's mother, the Duchess of Sutherland, was the medium by which Maria hoped to persuade the queen to use her influence. In the same year the equally notorious murderer James Bloomfield Rush wrote a letter to the queen, presumably to beg for mercy, but burned it, and said in parting to his family: 'I hope the Queen will not be in a hurry to hang me.'[130] Another high-profile murder led to pressure on the sovereign for Franz Müller, who killed the bank clerk Thomas Briggs in a railway carriage in 1864, when the German Protection Society and the King of Prussia attempted to save his life.

This section considers the strategic appeals to Victoria in less celebrated cases. At the start of her reign, newspapers related her commutation of sentence for two child murderers in Cheshire: Ann Byrom and Dinah Jones. Byrom strangled and then threw the corpse of her illegitimate baby into a river in Stockport. The Welsh farm servant Dinah Jones killed her infant daughter after complaining of the cost of upkeep and hid the body under a stone in a brook at Charley-bridge. Both were sentenced to death by Baron John Gurney on the same day at Chester Assizes. A newspaper reporter was 'favoured with a sight of her Majesty's sign manual, granting a conditional pardon'.[131] The women were told, 'this was not an absolute reprieve; that their lives were still in her hands and within her royal prerogative; that she might yet order them for execution, but that there was a hope that their lives would be spared'. The *Chester Chronicle*, in a column entitled 'The Condemned Females Respited', gave prominence to royal mercy ('above all, in gratitude to our most gracious Queen' in the exercise of the royal prerogative, that 'brightest jewel in the regalia of the sovereign') alongside local efforts to save Byrom and Jones. Women mobilized to address 'the Queen in affectionate and loyal language' in a petition of 700 inhabitants of Chester.[132] A former tutor to the queen, the Dean of Chester, George Davys, signed a petition.[133] A newspaper commented: 'It is generally expected that her Majesty will not turn a deaf ear to the appeal of reason and humanity.'[134] At St Martin-in-the-Fields inhabitants met in the vestry to petition the queen, the churchwardens ruling out discussion of the New Poor Law's bastardy clause, and declared 'the brightest ornament of the coronation of regalia was the curtana, or sword of mercy'.[135]

In 1844, a desperately poor forty-year-old seamstress Mary Furley drowned her child in Regent's Canal; she was condemned to be executed and *Punch* suggested that due to the Home Secretary Sir James Graham, Victoria now wore the 'dimmest of diadems' when it was revealed Furley would suffer transportation for seven years. Inhabitants of the Colonnade, Brunswick Square, appealed to the Commons to address the queen for mercy.[136] The *Satirist* depicted Graham pleading with the queen in a ballad of heavy irony entitled 'Modern "Mercy", or Sir James and the Convict': 'Oh! Who can tell what moving words, | There passed between those two, | Or count the tears of sympathy, | That fell, like Heaven's bright dew?'[137] The next chapter exposes the queen's views on infanticide as privately revealed to her Home Secretary.

Other cases had only the youth and sex of the culprit to commend themselves to royal attention. In 1846 the fate of Martha Browning, a twenty-year-old women who strangled an older woman in their shared lodgings in Westminster, for five pounds that proved to be a 'flash' note (from the 'Bank of Elegance' rather than Bank of England), also drew calls for female sympathy from the queen. 'Could we cause our voice to be heard within the walls of Windsor castle', wrote one, in the *Morning Advertiser*, 'we would supplicate her Majesty for her interposition on behalf of one of her own sex. It cannot but shock the better susceptibilities of her majesty's nature, to see a young female, untrodden in the paths of crime, publicly executed in the heart of the metropolis'.[138]

The Quaker Mary Howitt's petition for mercy for Mary Ann Hunt (who killed an elderly woman and was found to be pregnant despite a verdict to the contrary by a jury of matrons), published in *Howitt's Journal* and Chartist *Northern Star* in November 1847, argued that the queen could not be behind the greater portion of her female subjects in 'desiring to set aside the barbarism now impending over one of your own sex'.[139] The *Manchester Times*, too, stressed the 'death-warrant signed by a Queen and a mother'.[140] The Quaker Charles Gilpin publicly appealed to the women of England to seek a pardon for Hunt, 'now that one of their sex was on the throne'.[141] *The Satirist* appealed to her 'as a lady, and a mother' in an article entitled, 'Could the "Majesty of the Law" Be Maintained – Did Mary Hunt Not Suffer Execution?' It argued 'whether by reprieve, or a royal pardon, it will not reflect in future ages, brighter and more gloriously in her diadem, than the costliest jewel she ever wore, whether mercy and justice can here embrace, and the sword, that is now hanging over the wretched woman, cannot be sheathed'.[142] Hunt was transported.

In 1849 another woman-only petition was directed to the queen by a committee of Bristol women, headed by the temperance advocate Emma Matthews, to save the servant Sarah Harriett Thomas. She had brutally killed her aged employer in Bristol. The petition, signed by 3,500, included 'many of the most influential and enlightened ladies in the neighbourhood' but did not emphasize the queen's gender.[143] The effort was unsuccessful. Two other female murderers in that year attracted wide attention. Mary Howitt agitated for a reprieve for Charlotte Harris of Bath, who murdered her husband to marry an older and rich man, and was pregnant. One Scottish newspaper, in publicizing this appeal to the 'woman's and mother's heart' of the queen, claimed, 'If it were possible to collect the suffrages of the women of England and Scotland, we feel persuaded that the petitioners for mercy would be as a million to one.' The queen was appealed to not simply as monarch 'and the first woman in this great empire' but as 'reverencing in your person the virtues which, whilst they belong to our common nature, grace your Majesty in a peculiar manner – pity and maternal love'.[144] Verse in *Punch* in late October ended thus: 'mother and queen, forget not | Pardon is in thine hand; | For woman's pity, let not | This hanging shame our land; | But cause the mob ferocious | The spectacle to miss, | Inhuman and atrocious, | Of butcher-work like this!'[145] Another female petition addressed to the queen via the freethought journal *The Reasoner* argued that 'the hanging of women is calculated to produce moral effects the contrary of those designed by the law'.[146] The woman was transported after two years in Westminster Bridewell.[147]

Other petitions to the queen in that year were assembled for Annette Meyers, who shot her soldier lover – with similar reprieve as a result. Verse directed the attention of the queen to this woman's sentence, in a poem in *Punch* which was reproduced in the newspapers, in the closing stanza: 'VICTORIA, in thy courtly train | The duellist goes free: | One hast thou pardon'd in thy reign, | Spite of the law's decree; | Pity and precedent may strive, | To save this erring soul alive.'[148]

It was claimed that when agitating for another 'mother-murderess' Mary Ann Newell, in 1859, the queen was 'never deaf to the appeals of her own sex' in the exercise of mercy.[149] The queen's attitude to male murderers is shown in the next chapter. The campaigners for the working-class Samuel Wright in 1864 (who murdered a woman he cohabited with, in a lodging-house on the Waterloo Road, in December 1863) organized a deputation to Windsor received by her private secretary, Sir Charles Phillips. There they learned that the queen, though she deeply regretted the unfortunate man's position, could not constitutionally interfere with the Home Secretary's decision.[150] As the bearer of one petition (a surgeon, Alfred Ebsworth of Newington) presented it to General Knollys, the queen passed up the stairs, and he saw Knollys 'deliver it into the Queen's hands, but the answer he received to it was that the Queen could not undertake to advise her advisers'.[151] A provincial newspaper correspondent took the queen and Grey to task: the 'prerogative of mercy, the brightest jewel in the crown' was a farce. The statement that the queen 'could not advise her advisers' in translation meant that she could not commute Wright's sentence; that is, she 'had not the prerogative that all the world supposed she had'. But the writer reflected that she 'might have commuted the sentence if she would'. To ask for mercy on the basis of the birth of Prince Albert Victor was an 'absurd plea … simply a piece of genuine flunkeyism'; nevertheless the Prince of Wales had 'lost a good chance of adding to his popularity by not saying a word to his royal mother in favour of commutation'.[152]

Prince Albert had died in 1861, and the republican *Reynolds's Newspaper* said that the 'womanly tenderness of Queen Victoria is absorbed in the tomb otherwise the womanly heart would have felt compassion for Wright's motherless child'.[153] Constitutionally the monarch could do no wrong, so that 'Queen Victoria is perfectly innocent of the foul judicial murder which her pious and piteous Secretary has caused to be perpetrated in her name'. This account left no doubt that such events led to the toppling of palaces.[154]

The Home Office files preserve poetry linking the appeal to the birth of Albert Victor, petitions to his father, and pointed comments on the queen building a semi-Popish mausoleum to her husband while Wright faced death.[155] The deputation – 'ignorant, unconstitutional, and cowardly' – was deplored by one commentator for putting the queen in a cruel position. But the abolitionist journal *Morning Star* queried the decision not to permit the memorialists to meet her. The *Bath Chronicle*'s London correspondent thought it showed the ignorance of the leaders of this agitation: clinging to the belief that the queen signed death warrants and did so with red ink.[156] One of the agitators himself criticized the refusal at one meeting to play the national anthem the evening before the execution on 12 January 1864 and defended the queen – whatever her private impulses she could not save the life of 'Convict 1' without being criticized for the death of 'Convict 2'.[157]

The phenomenon of the poetic call for mercy in newspapers during high-profile capital cases continued into the 1890s. 'She Shall Not Die!' was asserted by one unnamed poet, of the infanticide Fanny Gane in Winchester gaol, hoping that a 'tender Queenly heart' would respond to the shout that ascended to the 'very Throne': and that 'the regal part | Of clemency our Sovereign make her own'.[158] At the same time, others decried the relevance of the royal clemency. In the 1890s, in the Australian colonies, critics of interference from the mother country treated the royal prerogative as 'fossil as that of the mastodon'.[159] By 1900, the power of granting mercy was presented as a mere shadow with the rest of the queen's political powers, exercised only by the Home Secretary's approval. For the radical journalist W.T. Stead, it was part of a process whereby royalty's political power declined while its influence increased.[160]

Victoria and her gallows: abolitionism and interference?

The radical *London Pioneer* imagined, in the year that the SACP was launched, that the royal couple discussed the 'great effort in the country to effect the abolition of capital punishment', with Albert having abolitionist sympathies.[161] In 1863 it was said, by one former member of the royal household, T.H. Siddons, claiming to be one of her gentleman at arms before 1859, that it was 'always a subject of deep sorrow to the Queen when the Home Secretary does not see reason for recommending her to exercise the royal prerogative of mercy'. Capital punishment revolted her 'Christian spirit and especially when that fellow creature is a woman'. Siddons claimed, in fact, that 'since the last paroxysm of anguish which the Queen endured on this account it has been customary to assume that a murderess is a lunatic and to confine her for life'.[162]

Both instances of imputed abolitionism are doubtful. It is unclear what Albert thought, but his advisor Baron Stockmar held clear views on the imprudence of total abolition.[163] *Trewman's Exeter Flying Post* said Siddons's role in the household was analogous to the 'Boy Jones', who sneaked into Buckingham Palace, and highlighted the misconception about the death warrants as an example of his twaddle.[164] Yet rumours of Victoria's abolitionist sympathies persisted. There was the 'very odd rumour' in the *Illustrated London News* in 1867 that the queen, 'having come round to the view of the capital punishment abolitionists, has determined henceforward to use her Royal prerogative ... and to allow no criminal to be executed'.[165] A hopeful abolitionist claim was proposed by one radical newspaper from the north of England in the golden jubilee year, and similar views were expressed in the United States in the 1890s. Victoria was far from being abolitionist.[166] She was interested in a reform of public executions in the mid-1840s, to the extent of requesting the Home Secretary's view, but saw a place for capital punishment in dealing with murder, whether acts of terrorism or domestic violence.[167]

One can find public criticism of mercy in cases of homicide and other crimes, linked to Victoria's name directly or by hints. Reprieve for William Stolzer, who murdered his fellow German bootmaker Peter Keim by stabbing him after being refused financial assistance, was rumoured to be the result, *The Examiner* reported in 1843, of his nationality, 'a fact which moved an interest in his behalf in a high quarter'.[168] Unsurprisingly criticism came most prominently from republicans. There was the deliberate slip in 1856 in Gracchus's article on 'The Gallows' in the abolitionist and republican-democratic *Reynolds's Newspaper* in August 1856, in discussing capital punishment: 'the eccentric manner in which the Queen, or rather Sir G. Grey, hangs and pardons' in the context of a case where it was rumoured the murdered child was the offspring of 'some "great man," whose influence saved the wretched mother's life'.[169] A few years later, when mercy was exercised to release a banker and MP, Humphrey Brown (who swindled the Royal British Bank), the paper referred to the 'prostituted mercy of the British monarch'.[170] 'Northumbrian' in *Reynolds's Newspaper* in 1863 claimed that 'The older the reign of Queen Victoria goes, the more it resembles the reign of her pious grandfather … of bigoted and bloody memory' and also equated it with the bloody kings of Dahomey.[171] Over a decade later the paper pounced upon the rumours of royal interference in justice over an illegitimate member of the house of Brunswick, calling herself the Comtesse de Civry.[172] The Tichbornite journal *The Englishman* hinted in 1879 that the queen granted a free pardon to the infanticide by Alice Wilson because of her first name (as her recently deceased daughter was Princess Alice).[173] Jubilee celebrations were looked on with a critical eye by *Reynolds's Newspaper*, especially when the number executed in England seemed unusually high, the 'antiquarian of the future' would 'see the year of the Queen's Jubilee decorated by a row of executed convicts dangling at the end of the fatal rope'.[174]

The reality of the queen's sympathies, knowledge of capital cases, and attitude towards murders, whether domestic or political, can be explored through the surviving documents in the Royal Archives. These range from the material generated by remissions or execution of sentence to the private thoughts of the queen in her correspondence and diaries. Interest in the law was no abstract or distant concern: involved as she was with the security of her 'faithful and loyal subjects'. She was also the repeated target of assassins and acutely aware of similar threats to other heads of state and monarchs. The following chapters move away from public campaigns, public anecdote, and myth-making to interrogate some of the actual operation of mercy in relation to the queen in capital cases.

4

Victoria's Mercy in the Archives

The previous chapter was concerned with the imagined powers and fantasized mercies of the monarch. In their irate letters to the Home Secretary when men and women were not saved, members of the public and abolitionists contrasted the heartless functionary with the 'merciful mistress' or declared the minister more suited to serve that symbol of cruelty, the 'king of Dahomey'.[1] The reality can be uncovered through studying the treatment of crimes, including murder, in the queen's diaries and the official communication between the queen and her Home Secretary.[2] The correspondence with Home Secretaries and others (either personally or via the queen's private secretaries such as General Charles Grey) is preserved in the Royal Archives. Reginald Brett, Viscount Esher, who did so much to shape the posthumous legacy of Victoria through publication of her letters, commented in an essay on the monarchy after the Great War, on the records accumulated through the commitment to writing ministerial policy in correspondence with the sovereign. He asserted that the 'Royal Archives at Windsor are a mine of wealth in a country like ours, where precedent is honoured as a counterpoise to ill-considered action and jobbery'.[3]

As Esher noted, this was 'intimate communion'.[4] Naturally, even if she thought reprieve was 'a mistaken mercy', Victoria eschewed public association with unpopular decisions in capital cases.[5] Sidney Lee's biography of the queen (published in 1904) spoke of her 'tenderness of feeling and breadth of sympathy with mankind', coupled with no lenity 'in the punishment of those guilty of cruel acts':

> In many instances she expressed disapproval of remissions of punishment which her Home Secretaries, acting according to statute in her name, but really on their own responsibilities, granted persons convicted of criminal offences against women and children. She paid scant attention to the provocative circumstances which attended the crime and justified the interference of the Home Office. Wife-murder and child desertion were outrages which in her eyes always demanded the severest penalties known to the law.[6]

The Queen's relationship with her Home Secretaries: Some general points

Early entries in her journals show that Prime Minister Lord Melbourne and courtiers discussed prominent murders with her. In March 1838 the Home Secretary Lord John Russell spoke of the two young men, George Fletcher and William Roach, condemned to be hanged for killing an old army pensioner at Hertford, on the Whig Peer Lord Cowper's estate. Melbourne told the queen that the unhappy men should be executed, and she showed petitions she had received.[7] Russell's uncle was murdered by his valet François Courvoisier in May 1840, and naturally the matter – murder and chief suspect – was discussed by the queen and the prime minister.[8] The president of the Board of Trade, Sir John Hobhouse, reported in his diary that Russell 'looks very much worn and affected' by the murder – the Cabinet had 'much conversation' on Fitzroy Kelly's House of Commons motion on abolition of capital punishment except for murder and high treason, 'a disagreeable subject for Lord John'.[9]

Later Home Secretaries' conversations about murder cases were referred to less frequently and never in detail in the queen's journals as they now survive. Notable crimes such as the Earl of Cardigan's duel on Wimbledon Common and trial in the Lords for felonious wounding (it was 'no murder', she reported Melbourne as saying in October 1840), the murders by the burglar Charles Peace (a horrid hypocrite who delivered a speech full of religion on the scaffold, she noted, in February 1879), and seemingly endemic 'horrid murders' in Ireland were noted in her diary.[10] Conversation with her Home Secretary Sir William Vernon Harcourt, recorded in her diary in November 1881, covered vivisection (which she opposed) and the 'dreadful case' of the railway murderer Percy Lefroy.[11]

Details of the relationships with the responsible ministers are found in the Royal Archives and Home Office archives: what follows is an overview of cases involving the royal prerogative (as remissions, conditional pardons, and free pardons) examined through the former archives, organized by the periods of office of particular ministers. This is an incomplete survey – passing over a number of brief Home Secretaryships, though undoubtedly the surviving correspondence contains forthright comments from the queen – and there is less to uncover in the Royal Archives in relation to one important Home Secretary, the Whig Sir George Grey. We have encountered, too, the odium heaped on the Tory Home Secretary Sir James Graham over the infanticide mother Mary Furley in 1844.[12]

Before this survey of the interactions between the queen and her ministers, I focus on the matter of female infanticide. This is an area where the queen sympathized with lenient responses to desperate women who killed their illegitimate infants. Yet at a time of moral panic about rising levels of infanticide linked to financial gain, according to 'experts' such as Dr Edwin Lankester, in the 1860s, the queen's gender was linked to the national shame. 'It is not a pleasant subject for reflection', commented a leader in *Reynolds's Newspaper* in 1865, 'that in the reign of Queen Victoria the murder of infant children should have grown into a regular profession'.[13]

There was a connection between the queen and this crime because her son and heir, the Prince of Wales, was wet-nursed by a woman who went on to kill her children. This was 'the Esher tragedy' of June 1854, when six children had their throats cut by Mary Ann Brough, former royal nurse and part of the royal establishment at Claremont. Found not guilty due to insanity, Brough was sent by the Home Secretary, Lord Palmerston, to Bethlehem Hospital. Some speculated there was royal pressure (street ballads noted the royal connection but were not explicit about the role this played).[14] The queen was opening the re-located Crystal Palace on the day of the murder as one commentator noted; her diary refers to being haunted by news of the 'horrid tragedy'.[15] The murder scene was apparently re-created in a waxwork at Birmingham's Bull Ring with the label on the figure of Brough: 'this woman was nurse to his Royal Highness the Prince of Wales'.[16]

Victoria asserted to Sir William Vernon Harcourt, Liberal Home Secretary from 1880 to 1885, that she argued strongly for poor women sentenced to death for killing their illegitimate children. It was, she claimed in November 1880, 'only in minor cases that the Queen is anxious there should not be too much laxity as also in this case of gt brutality & murders of a different nature to those above mentioned'.[17] Victoria's diary supports this claim with expressions of pity for women moved by a sense of shame to commit this act. She read Frederick Robinson's *Female Life in Prison* (originally published, in 1862, anonymously as the work of a 'prison matron') before visiting Parkhurst gaol on the Isle of Wight in 1864.[18] There she was pointed out at least one of the 'poor young girls' who destroyed their babies after desertion. Her ministers informed her of legal reforms which removed the capital penalty from cases so often actuated by 'despair'.[19] She also commissioned the watercolourist Edward Corbould's rendering of 'Hetty Sorrel and Captain Donnithorne in Mrs Poyser's dairy' (1861), a scene from George Eliot's *Adam Bede* (which she read in 1859), depicting the girl who would commit infanticide.[20]

The era of Sir George Grey, 1846–1852; 1855–1858; 1861–1866

Her Parkhurst visit took place during the last of the three periods in office of the Whig Sir George Grey (see Figure 4.1 for *Punch*'s satirical comment on him in this period). His controversial decisions in capital punishment included commuting the sentence of the murderer George Townley in 1864, noted in the previous chapter.[21] The Capital Punishment Commission also reported in that period, leading to the abolition of public hanging in 1868. In this minister's first period, a letter in the Royal Archives indicates her advisors' roles: with reference to Charles Phipps, the keeper of the Privy Purse to Prince Albert. It was sent to Catherine, Countess of Dunmore, a former lady-in-waiting, after intercession by her in late 1855 (it was not a capital case but seems to have involved two cousins in the private bank Strahan, Paul and Bates, which failed in that year[22]):

> The perusal of it has caused me much pain, for I do feel deeply for the unhappy wife whose husband is thus taken from her in the most distressing manner imaginable.

Figure 4.1 John Tenniel, 'The garotter's friend. "Let go, Bill, can't yer – it's our kind non-interfering friend, Sir George Grey !!!"', *Punch*, 29 November 1862, p.221. Author's collection.

But it w^d have been better not to forward this letter to me but to send it to Sir G. Grey for it w^d never do were it to be supposed (& it w^d not long remain unknown) that there were private Channels by w^h means my feelings w^d be influenced.

The Administration of Justice is perhaps the most sacred duty entrusted to a Sovereign & were private intercession or personal motives to have the slightest influence on the infliction or modification of punishment, it appears to Col. Phipps & the award of sentences w^d become perfectly unjustifiable. Punishment belongs to the Office not to the Individual, & it w^d be dreadful if the gentleman Banker surrounded with every comfort & brought up in religious & moral culture were to possess a Channel thro' w^hc my feelings of compassion w^d be assailed, whilst the wretched outcast [?] with want & education in Sin sh^d suffer his punishment unheard of & unpitied.

This is alas! The truth & I fear I can do nothing to release the 2 poor Cousins whom I so well remember in former times.[23]

In the case of the railway murderer Franz Müller in 1864, the queen's journal shows that she felt harassed by efforts to secure a reprieve. She was targeted by royalty ('Ernest C telegraphed for a German "Protection Society" & George of Meiningen wrote, making out the man was innocent, also others applied. It quite agitated me, as I can do nothing in the matter & the man's guilt seems absolutely clear'[24]). She was interested in how the young man behaved on the scaffold and what his statement was. Grey spoke a 'good deal about Müller and how clear the case was, but that a change ought to be made to prevent these frightful public executions, which are so brutalizing and demoralizing for the people'.[25] The change would come in 1868.

The Queen and Sir William Vernon Harcourt, 1880–1885

As the son and biographer of the queen's Private Secretary Sir Henry Ponsonby notes, Sir William Harcourt was 'unfortunate in seldom pleasing the Queen' (see Figure 4.2).[26] One of the reasons was the critical view the queen took of the handling of wife murder, telling Ponsonby that men were 'lenient to criminals who murder their wives'.[27] The queen was reluctant to agree to remission or commutation of sentence for this crime and at least had the capacity to divert Home Secretaries (and, at times, prime ministers) from other duties by requesting information about decisions in particular cases where the royal prerogative of mercy was exercised in remission of sentences.[28] Ponsonby agreed with Harcourt that the question was better not touched but that the queen had a right to know the reasons.[29]

Harcourt was sceptical about capital punishment as a deterrent for murder before becoming Home Secretary and critical about severe punishment for youthful offenders.[30] In November 1880 the queen contrasting him with Assheton Cross, his predecessor, wrote that 'Harcourt is become very lax'. She disapproved of the remission from their full punishment, of several militia men for desertion.[31] She inquired, 'What can be the reason of this immense number of "Remissions"? The queen had 18 the other day & this has never happened before! 3 or 4 at a time occasionally'.[32] After a request for an explanation via Ponsonby, Harcourt sent detailed analyses, explaining how these related to evolving Home Office precepts and in some cases had therefore not even been presented to him for minuting. He also expressed humane feeling (in the case of female infanticides and juvenile offenders, for example) and proposed sending her all the paper work whenever there were cases to be remitted.[33] 'The notion that I am

Figure 4.2 Sir William Vernon Harcourt MP. Steel engraving by W. Roffe after the photograph by Elliott and Fry, and published by William Mackenzie. Author's collection.

letting felons out of prison right and left out of pure *gaiete de coeur* is quite unfounded', he told Ponsonby. The long letters and memoranda on the remissions led the queen to reply – perhaps chastened: 'The Queen is quite satisfied about these remissions. It was only her fear that as many Ticket of leave people do get abt & do gt harm'.

Thereafter, as the evidence of the Royal Archive suggests, short memoranda were sent to the queen, identifying reasons for remission in capital and other cases – from murder to assault.[34] There was the particularly contentious case of the young dock labourer John Richmond in Durham in 1881, who killed his estranged wife with a poker, when the queen communicated her dissatisfaction with Harcourt's advice via Ponsonby. 'The responsibility of advising Your Majesty in questions of Life and death is at all times a heavy and painful duty even where the Secretary of State has reason to hope that his recommendations will meet Your Majesty's approval', he wrote. He pointed out that it would be unparalleled to act against the judgement and representations of judge and jury as in this case.[35] Ponsonby's handling of the irate minister in their correspondence persuaded the minister not to offer his resignation. Harcourt made the same point about going against the expressed recommendation of mercy from the judge and jury – '[if] such a thing was done capital punishment would come to an end' – in 1883.[36] The queen's reply was that the case was 'just one w^h. ought to have been punished by death, for the poor wife lived happily with him, & if drunkenness leads to such things as murder, & if people are to be pardoned "because it was not premeditated" who will be safe'.[37]

When the Staffordshire farmer and stonemason Isaac Brooks's false evidence was revealed by his death-bed confession in January 1882, Harcourt no doubt took satisfaction from the following observation to the queen concerning two men unjustly imprisoned for his attempted castration: 'Heart rending to think what they and their families have suffered during these two years of penal servitude – These are the things which make the decision in capital case where there can be no remedy so terribly anxious'.[38]

There was the case of the young factory worker and former domestic servant Emily Wilcox of Bath. Wilcox was sentenced to death for killing Mercy Ellen, her illegitimate two-year-old-child, in 1884, when she was unable to afford a charwoman's nursing of the infant.[39] The queen queried commutation, as this was the third or fourth case in which murder conviction was commuted, she thought. Then, Harcourt emphasized to the queen that many were opposed to capital punishment and that the Home Secretary needed to avoid shocking public opinion when it was opposed to execution. He also referred to the innocent who had, from time to time, been sentenced to death. The queen's reply showed her depth of feeling.[40] His letter had pained her,

> as it gives her the impression that Sir Wm Harcourt thinks she wishes to be harsh & cruel & to insist on the Extreme penalty of the Law being carried out in cases wh. above all commend themselves to mercy – especially when poor young creatures have been driven from despair to destroy newly born infants. On this particular crime the queen herself spoke to some of his predecessors arguing strongly they poor criminals sh^d not be executed.[41]

She claimed her observation concerned remissions for the murder of 'wives ... which had struck her as very bad cases & the commutation for w^h she hardly c^{ld} understand'. But picking up his observation on the punishment of innocent people, she wrote this was 'terrible to contemplate'.[42] The conditional pardon followed when Harcourt detailed the reason for commutation.

Another case in which the queen intervened was that of John Lee, condemned to death for brutally killing his employer Ellen Keyse, once a maid of honour to the queen, at Babbacombe in Devon, in November 1884. The hangman notoriously failed at his work. By cipher telegram to Harcourt in February 1885, the queen expressed her horror at the 'disgraceful Scene at Exeter, at Lee's execution'. Surely, she asked, after the third attempt by James Berry to hang him, he could not be executed; it would be 'too cruel. Imprisonment for Life seems the only alternative' (he would be released in 1907).⁴³

The queen and her last Home Secretaries

In the Conservative Home Secretary Henry Matthews's time (1886–1892), a similar practice of sending details of the cases for remission was observed (see Figure 4.3) – even for offences such as horse stealing, bigamy, vagrancy, drunkenness, and disorderliness.⁴⁴ Salisbury was compelled to interview his Home Secretary after a Cabinet meeting in June 1888 when the queen desired information about capital sentences (he concurred with her about mercy for the domestic servant Mary Holliday, who drowned her illegitimate nine-year-old daughter and was found to be pregnant

Figure 4.3 Wood engraving of Henry Matthews Q.C., the new Home Secretary, *Illustrated London News*, 14 August 1886. Author's collection.

after sentence). He informed her that he 'did his best to leave on Mr Matthews' mind the impression that his discretion in making recommendations of this kind ought to be guarded with great jealousy'.⁴⁵

When a reprieve for the Polish Jew Israel Lipski in 1887 after his conviction for the murder of a woman with nitric acid in the East End of London was refused, his solicitor sent a telegram to Osborne House: 'Innocent man to be hanged on Tuesday.'⁴⁶ The queen's diary recorded the many appeals to her, the 'violent effort' to save the man, and his subsequent confession and admission of the justice of his sentence.⁴⁷ The queen's concern about the Whitechapel murders in 1888 has also been documented (one leaves to one side the alarming flights of Ripperology connecting the crimes to her grandson, the Duke of Clarence). She recorded these 'Dreadful murders of unfortunate women of a bad class in London' in her diary in early October 1888. She was associated through a memorial from Samuel Barnett with efforts to deal with the 'moral disorders' of the East End. She was informed of such actions as a Cabinet discussion of a possible pardon for information leading to the apprehension of the murderer. She sent to Salisbury and Matthews her own thoughts about what the detectives should do in Whitechapel in November 1888 after reading 'the accounts of those horrible crimes': a study of single men occupying rooms to themselves, enhanced surveillance at night, investigation of cattle boats, and alertness for blood-soaked clothing.⁴⁸

In the notorious case of Florence Maybrick in 1889, the queen's belief in the American's guilt (for the death of her English husband by arsenic) sustained the Home Office's resolve (see Figure 4.4).⁴⁹ It was a controversial trial because of the prejudicial behaviour of the judge Fitzjames Stephen and the general conduct of the Crown was condemned in the barrister Alexander MacDougall's account of the case, in which the queen shared the blame for the failure to employ the prerogative of mercy.⁵⁰ A presentation cartoon for *St Stephen's Review*, 17 August 1889, has no less a figure than Jack the Ripper pressing for execution, while Justice presents Matthews with a pardon.⁵¹ In reality, Matthews explained to the queen that Maybrick's death sentence had to be commuted to penal servitude for life because of the doubt that the arsenic in the body was sufficient to kill James Maybrick and since he was in the habit of taking arsenic.⁵² The queen was outraged, as she told her private secretary to tell Matthews that 'so wicked a woman, shd escape by a mere legal quibble! The law is not a moral profession she must say. But her sentence must never be further commuted'.⁵³ The queen 'entirely agreed' with Matthews, in a letter from Balmoral in October 1891. The Home Secretary was clear in his advice that there were no grounds for 'further exercise of Your Majesty's gracious clemency'.⁵⁴

The columnist 'Northumbrian', in *Reynolds's Newspaper* in April 1890, did not exculpate the queen, since telegrams addressed her and she should have influenced her Home Secretary.⁵⁵ Newspapers reported the procedure whereby petitions sent to the queen (and other members of the royal family) were 'returned with suitable replies'.⁵⁶ British petitioners in subsequent years had a similar response to direct appeals to the queen, through Whitehall.⁵⁷

Given Florence Maybrick's nationality, it was a transatlantic *cause célèbre*. British readers learnt that American newspapers, after the queen's death, declared that the

Figure 4.4 'The Trial of Mrs Maybrick at Liverpool. Mrs Maybrick making her statement to the court'. *The Graphic*, 17 August 1889. Author's collection.

several Home Secretaries favoured her release 'but Queen Victoria was against it'.[58] American papers, unsurprisingly, covered the case extensively. One reported that the 'good Queen does not propose to have the closing years of her reign disturbed'.[59] The *Illustrated American* titled one article discussing Maybrick in the context of 'reflections upon the prosecution of judgment and justice in the realms of her Majesty', as 'English Brutality' in 1892. A petition signed by the wives of President Harrison, the Secretary of State, the Secretary of the Treasury, and the Secretary of Agriculture was sent to Salisbury for passing to the queen in 1891, 'confiding in the power of your majesty and in the power of your goodness'. There was 'rumor that your Majesty received the petition graciously', but there was no official reply and Sir Henry Ponsonby was next addressed. Mary Dodge (a writer under the *nom de plume* Gail Hamilton), founder of the International Maybrick Society, published an open letter to the queen in the *North American Review* the next year.[60] It ended: 'if your Majesty must be set upon the mercy-seat before all England and the world, yet be forbidden to show mercy, I beg to offer you the homage of a profound regret.'

President McKinley also appealed to the queen for pardon and release, through the American ambassador in June 1897, but (as the *New York Times* claimed) 'probably on account of the course of the Irish in refusing to participate in the Jubilee, no pardons were given'.[61] The Florence Maybrick Club of Chicago and Victoria Club of Toronto celebrated the queen's eightieth birthday in 1898, by jointly sending a cablegram of congratulations, but the Maybrick Club's president also sent a letter on Maybrick's behalf to Princess Henry of Battenberg to influence the queen to secure a release.[62] Other addresses to the queen came from America in 1899 as the *American Lawyer* reported.[63] That journal discussed the reality of the queen's power in this case: 'the real power behind the throne is not even the Home Secretary, but the under officials of the Home Secretary's office who have hitherto been successful in preventing Mrs. Maybrick's release.'[64] Later, in January 1900, the Cabinet resolved that Maybrick's sentence could be commuted.[65] Her autobiography would not mention the queen except to note that the lowering of the prison flag conveyed the news of her death.[66]

Telegrams in the case of the 'Crewe tragedy', a murder which revealed a 'Zola-like tragedy of tyranny and selfishness' within a middle-class home,[67] were sent to the queen at Aix le Bains, to try and save one of the two parricidal Davies brothers in 1890. (Mathews told Victoria that commutation could not be done, as her diary recorded, 7 April 1890.) The mother appealed, 'Queen of England, my boy Richard Davies, whom the jury recommended to mercy, is to be executed on Tuesday. I beseech you to respite him for a week for further inquiry: Mary Davies.'[68] The *Saturday Review* in this case complained of the 'unmanly, unconstitutional, and indecent practice of addressing letters and telegrams directly to the queen, when comparatively legitimate efforts to prevent the execution of convicted criminal seem likely to fail'. If they reached the queen, constitutionally she could do nothing.[69] They would just 'give pain and anxiety to an August Lady, whom every one of her subjects ought to be anxious to save from both'. The queen could not override her ministers' advice, another provincial paper pointed out, but 'the anguished appeals of an agonised mother must have wrung her heart, and sorely tempted her to exercise her prerogative as the Plantagenets might have done'.[70]

In March 1892 the queen asked that the upper-class Ethel Osborne, imprisoned for larceny and perjury after stealing jewellery from her cousin and host at Torquay, be exempted from hard labour on account of her condition (she was pregnant); 'it might have such very serious consequences', she asked Salisbury to be informed.[71] Agitators for Maybrick drew the contrast. But the Irish woman Anne Margaret Montague, wife of a Londonderry Justice of the Peace, was 'more like a fiend than a woman', when her three-year-old died through harsh discipline (the jury accepted the argument that the girl was accidentally hanged) and the queen thought that Matthews would not recommend mercy. She was far more to blame than Osborne; the torment and cruelty inflicted on the children 'are really dreadful instances'.[72] Interestingly the queen's note referred to press complaints about the leniency of sentence (Montague was sentenced to a year's imprisonment with 'suitable labour').

The queen also marked her displeasure at commutation of sentence on a sixteen-year-old cooper, William Willan, who stabbed another youth in a 'scuttling' gang conflict in Manchester in 1892. She did so 'not without 1st strongly protesting ... It was deliberate & premeditated murder. VRI'.[73] In this case, a copy of a letter from the Home Office to the Mayor of Manchester was sent to the queen. The new Liberal Home Secretary Herbert Asquith had to explain to her the decision to remit the death sentence on the sixteen-year-old Arthur Shaw in 1893, who had killed an elderly woman in Halifax, on the grounds of his age and mental derangement (he had also assaulted a girl).[74]

And still the telegrams and appeals against sentences of death were addressed directly to the aged monarch. 'Sweetheart's appeal to the queen', was one headline when the policeman George Samuel Cooke was executed for murdering a woman in Wormwood Scrubs in July 1893.[75] Telegrams sent to the queen were reprinted by the press on behalf of the married dockyard clerk James Canham Read, who killed a woman pregnant with his child, at Southend in 1894. 'May it please your Majesty to exercise your gracious clemency behalf of my brother ... as I do not think my brother could have committed the crime, and as it does not appear to have been proved against my brother beyond reasonable possibility of doubt. – Your loyal subject, Harry Victor Read'.[76] The press reported the telegram imploring mercy in 1896, 'Mother to Queen', for the uxoricide James Bate: 'The mother of James Bate, lying under sentence of death, beseeches mercy for her only son, who was recommended to mercy by twelve of his countrymen.'[77] Appeals were sent on behalf of Alfred Chipperfield, who killed his wife at Linslade in Buckinghamshire, to the Prince of Wales and the queen in 1896.[78]

A paragraph from *The Spectator* was read to the queen by one of her ladies-in-waiting, to ease her mind over Mary Ann Ansell's fate in July 1899.[79] A domestic servant, she sent her sister, a patient in a lunatic asylum, a phosphorus-poisoned cake. The Central News Agency reported that the attempt to organize a deputation on the subject of a reprieve was rebuffed by the queen through her secretary Sir Arthur Bigge, referring the memorialists to the Home Secretary, who declined to intervene without the queen's command. A group of MPs and others sent the queen a long telegram praying for 'direct intervention'.[80] In the Royal Archives there is a minute from her Conservative Home Secretary Sir Matthew White Ridley, who had seen the judge and medical experts and concluded it was a cold-blooded and premeditated murder 'committed for the sake of the insurance money on the life of the deceased whom the prisoner insured for the very purpose'. Since there was 'no grounds for mercy on age (though comparatively youthful at 22) or sanity, the plea of sex would create a dangerous precedent, and would practically amount to abolition of capital punishment in the case of women'.[81] Her fate was raised in the House of Commons, and when she was hanged at St Albans, the journalist Charles Laurent in *Le Matin* in July suggested the queen should hang.[82] 'Une Femme Pendue en Angleterre. Execution de l'empoisonneuse Mary Ansell' appeared as one of the lurid covers of the sensationalist daily *Le Petit Parisien*.[83]

The reform removing the prerogative of mercy from the monarch's direct involvement and placing it with the Home Secretary was initiated because of the queen's youthfulness and gender, so various authorities asserted, wrongly, as I have shown. Some scholars view Victoria's accession as providing, by chance, 'leverage' for reform of the reprieve system.[84] Although Britons were informed that their new monarch could pardon any prisoner, the situation that developed under Victoria, where the monarch did not do anything on her own initiative but left the matters to be decided by the Home Secretary, would continue.[85]

I have shown in the previous chapter how the myth of Victoria's fraught and tearful response to signing death warrants developed. The only civilian 'death warrant' she *was* closely involved with was due to the different constitutional arrangements in the Isle of Man, the parricide John Kewish in 1872. She was not pleased, unsurprisingly, to be drawn in (the warrant was actually signed by the Lord Lieutenant Sir Henry Loch).[86]

Newspapers informed their readers about the extent of the queen's involvement in the punishment of death. The *Hereford Journal* in 1842 – for example – (prematurely) commenting on the execution of women as 'virtually abolished', accepted that 'the credit of acting upon motives of humanity must be conceded to her Majesty's Ministers, who doubtless also consulted the feelings and wishes of their Royal Mistress. The prerogative of mercy is indeed a heavenly one, and becomes no person so well as the wearer of a queenly diadem'.[87] A female petitioner for mercy, Hester Banks, in the case of the murderer Townley, hoped that the queen participated in his reprieve in 1864 (even though aware she 'was not suffered to peruse trials of life and death') as it was the 'only real power left to Royalty'.[88] But even so, into the 1880s the queen confidently intervened by criticizing Home Secretaries and proffering advice on investigations in notorious cases. Her prejudices were clear in correspondence with ministers. Harcourt felt impelled in June 1884 to end his lengthy response to her criticism of remissions by pointing out that the Home Office's conduct did not vary 'according to the caprice of the particular Home Secretary ... the decisions are guided by fixed principles, which would lead any holder of the Office to very nearly if not exactly the same conclusions in each case'.[89] Personal rule was replaced by almost impersonal 'bureaucratic mercy'. But sometimes a case gave the minister 'sleepless nights in the anxiety it causes' so that Harcourt was anxious that the queen was spared any share in 'this painful deliberation'.

The files preserved in the Royal Archives do not show the queen, except in the case of women convicted of the infanticide of their children through despair and shame at illegitimacy, to be a supporter of capital-punishment abolition. The *Northern Echo*'s assertion in 1886 that the queen sympathized with the abolitionist cause was far from the mark. Like the petitioners in capital cases at the start of her reign, late-Victorian abolitionists sought to exploit the idea of a merciful queen.[90] The execution of the Oldham hospital nurse Elizabeth Berry for the poisoning of her eleven-year-old daughter was said to be likely to be respited because of the jubilee in 1887. The woman had killed her relations for the insurance and was hanged.[91] Nevertheless, late-Victorian Home Secretaries did worry that shocking and unpopular capital sentences would encourage abolitionism. Harcourt told the queen when he believed her to be pressing for the execution of someone recommended to mercy by the judge and jury in 1884: 'There are considerable number of people in this Country who are altogether adverse to Capital Punishment. It can only be maintained by so guarding it that executions shall carry with them the general support of public opinion.'[92]

Focusing principally on the Home Secretaries Harcourt and Matthews, this chapter demonstrated the queen's involvement in the operation of royal mercy through interactions with her responsible ministers, and her awareness through the newspaper press and her courtiers, of sensational or controversial cases, and press attitudes towards sentencing. I offer a similar study through the Royal Archives and press coverage in the next chapter's exploration of the exercise of Victoria's royal mercy and justice against other delinquents. The crimes meriting severe punishment, including potentially the full rigour of the laws against treason, were political crimes such as rebellion (rebellious Ireland's rich history of mercy appealed to and withheld, I leave to my larger study of British mercy), and attempts at assassination. Chapter 5 begins by considering the queen's association with appeals to mercy in British North America at the start of her reign.

5

Victoria's Mercy: Rebellion and Attempted Assassination

> *IT was the peculiar felicity of Queen Anne, a happiness communicated to none of her predecessors, that during her reign of twelve years no traitor suffered death. Our present sovereign has held the sceptre with as gentle hand for a still longer period, and first of the House of Brunswick, has been blest with the same good fortune. The clemency which softens the councils of Queen Victoria deserves the more especial comment, as the attainted assailants of her throne have been more criminal and daring than those who threatened the supremacy of the Stuart.*[1]

So William Townsend, the Recorder of Macclesfield, claimed in a collection of modern trials in 1850. Early Victorian radicals included a reluctance to endorse the capital sentence among the sympathies which the queen supposedly harboured. Thus John Dobson Collet, in the free-thought *Reasoner* in 1848, argued that the nation 'seldom had so good a sovereign', on the basis of her attitude to bishops, corn laws, and the fact that she never signed a death warrant, 'preferring to submit to a diminution of the royal prerogative rather than to be responsible for the legal murder of a subject'.[2] The previous chapters looked at the queen's response to 'ordinary' acts of murder in the British Isles. While tales of her mercy at home in relation to individual military deserters, or infanticidal women, circulated in the late 1830s and early 1840s, there were other prominent appeals for royal mercy. This chapter studies the ways she was presented in relation to mercy in the aftermath of rebellion or acts of terrorism, and, in more direct acts of treason, in the treatment of would-be assassins. How she responded to her ministers and how the public perceived these acts of mercy are examined. I begin with rebellion in British North America in 1837–1838, 'the first great historical event in the reign', to quote *The Life and Times of Queen Victoria*, before turning to rebellious Chartists at home.[3] Two decades after her accession, came the largest-scale challenge to British imperial rule in her reign with the Indian rebellion, and I briefly explore how the monarchy was related to mercy claims in its aftermath, in the sub-continent. The chapter ends by looking at her response, and those of her ministers, to frequent assassination attempts on her royal person.

The Canadian Rebellion, 1837–1838

as I judged it becoming that the extraordinary legislature of Lower Canada should take upon itself all measures of vigorous precaution and leave to her majesty the congenial office of using her royal prerogative for the sole purpose of pardon and mercy the proclamation contained an entire amnesty qualified only by the exceptions specified in the ordinance.[4]

So commented John George Lambton, Earl of Durham, as governor-general with extraordinary prerogative powers to deal with the British North America rebellions, in the proclamation issued on 9 October 1838 to explain his actions and resignation. Amnesty was deliberately declared by him on Victoria's coronation day, 28 June 1838, to associate the queen's name with clemency, and on that day he informed his sovereign of the justice received by the guilty and mercy given to the 'misguided'.[5] This was an 'irrevocable pledge', which would create difficulties once the ordinance 'to provide for the security of the province of Lower Canada', which he also issued, was disallowed by the British Parliament.[6] To particular Canadian groups begging for mercy and justice, a similar message of royal mercy was conveyed, that on his sovereign's behalf he 'exercised … one of Her Majesty's most glorious prerogatives that of mercy'.[7]

From the largely French province of Lower Canada, the leaders of Louis-Joseph Papineau's *Patriotes* rebellion were exiled by Lord Durham to Bermuda. They would not 'propitiate unworthily to conciliate your favour', they told him: 'We implore no mercy'.[8] Greer cites vulgar misogynistic comments against the young queen in Lower Canada; in Upper Canada, the Scotsman William Lyon Mackenzie's rebellion also drew on republicanism.[9] The new lieutenant governor of Upper Canada, Sir George Arthur, was appealed to for mercy from communities and publicly rejected this as inappropriate as he meted out punishment in the aftermath. Two of the leaders, the blacksmith Samuel Lount and the farmer Peter Matthews, were executed for high treason in Toronto.[10] The inhabitants of West Flamborough, petitioning for mercy for those convicted, learnt that 'however grateful to his feelings the universal exercise of mercy would be, an imperative, but very painful sense of public duty, forces him to draw a line, beyond which interference with the course of Justice, cannot properly be carried.'[11] Similar positions were made by a local militia leader faced by American invaders: 'British Law repudiates all mawkish sympathy, miscalled "conciliation"', Colonel John Prince said, 'in all its native majesty as the avenger of the Briton's wrongs; and in tempering justice with mercy it proclaims to all who touch the sacred soil of Britain or her colonies and seek protection from her laws, "Fiat Justitia, ruat Coelum!" [Let justice be done though the heavens fall]'.[12]

American responses to those convicted of treason examined the claims of justice and mercy. Thus the *Niagara Reporter*, on the fate of three men involved in Mackenzie's rebellion in Upper Canada in 1837 – John Montgomery, Gilbert Morden, and John Anderson (respited for forty days) – thought more was gained by clemency than a 'too scrupulous adherence to the demands of justice, now that the majesty of the law has on one occasion been asserted'. The godlike attribute accorded with the 'spirit of the British monarchy … we should rejoice for the sake of humanity, if the extension of it to those unhappy men shall be an inducement to others who have hitherto been disloyal with impunity'. Allegiance would be given 'to a power which forgets not that "To err is human – to forgive divine"'. The newspaper imagined Victoria's natural disposition was merciful. For 'were it otherwise she would dishonour her sex, which we are sure the young and virtuous Monarch of the British Empire never will do'.[13] The involvement of Americans in the Upper Canadian rebellion and their treatment by loyalists brought to the fore claims for clemency on the prisoners' behalf and gestures to the mercy-in-victory 'which adorns the British name' (in the words of the province's governor).[14] When an appeal to the queen by the American ambassador to reprieve the youth David Deal of Shippensburg was reported in the *Extra Globe* of Washington, the 'great lustre of the benignity of the British Queen' was emphasized.[15]

Critics of Durham saw excessive mercy. The phrase 'tempering justice with mercy' was 'a passport to guilt and the surest guarantee that crimes may be committed with impunity'.[16] For the *Western Herald* (of Sandwich, Ontario), inconsistent punishment and mercy were a 'living memento of British PARTIALITY and DAMNING INJUSTICE', and a 'hateful monument of British "MERCY"'.[17] In Britain the *Examiner*, in August 1838, scorning Henry Brougham's critique of his fellow Whig-Liberal Durham, deprecated the punishment of death in the ordinances. The true object of Durham's proclamation was mercy, not the 'very last rigour of the justice'.[18] In public, bringing the Canadian Indemnity Bill to the Commons in August 1838, Lord John Russell stood by Durham's 'wise and statesmanlike policy'. It 'reconciled the ways of mercy with all that the safety of the province and the interests of the Queen's subjects really demanded', rather than, as British Lower Canadian critics alleged, representing 'over generous and mistaken lenity'.[19]

The debates in the new Province of Canada's Legislative Assembly about extending the royal pardon in 1841 saw the 'spontaneous exercise of the Royal clemency' idealized in contrast to the proposal for a formal address to the queen which would effect mercy by parliamentary interference.[20] Yet 'Her Majesty delights in the twice blessed exercise of mercy', the new governor-general of Canada, Lord Metcalfe, told the township of Scarborough in 1844.[21] By 1849, the Legislative Council (the upper chamber) recorded the queen's merciful intentions towards those still liable to punishment for offences arising from the events between 1837 and 1838.[22]

The Canadian rebellions led to Victoria's personal association with violent repression. Her diary recorded her delight at the quelling of rebellion in a part of her empire, which, as Paula Bartley notes, for family reasons she had a great interest in.[23] The republican Englishman, George Merryweather, in *Kings, the Devil's Viceroys*, published in New York in 1838, was acerbic about the rebellion's handling: 'We are called upon to admire the mildness of the British government for the merciful exercise of such clemency.'[24] William Lyon Mackenzie, now in Rochester in the United States, wrote in his *Caroline Almanack* (1840) of 'Victoria Guelph, the bloody Queen of England', 'Victoria Melbourne's bloody divan', and 'as keen for spilling Canadian blood as her mad old grandfather Geo. 3d'.[25] The *Almanack*'s engraving by John Orr showed two gallows-hanged martyrs (representing, as the reader chose, any number of Canadian martyrs), with an explanation including the ironic 'ROYAL MERCY!' and quotation from the coronation oath to cause 'law and justice, in mercy to be executed' (see Figure 5.1).²⁶ The meaning of the 'Indian savage' wielding a tomahawk, as part of the gallows guards, derives from the 'patriot' discourse against British use of Native American troops in the war of independence.

These rebellions at the start of Victoria's reign expose the imperial dimension to the exercise of royal mercy and to the appeals made to her personally, as well as the strategic need to demonstrate moderation and display the '"mildness and beneficence of her Majesty's Government' to rebels.²⁷ Political disorder represented wilful rejection

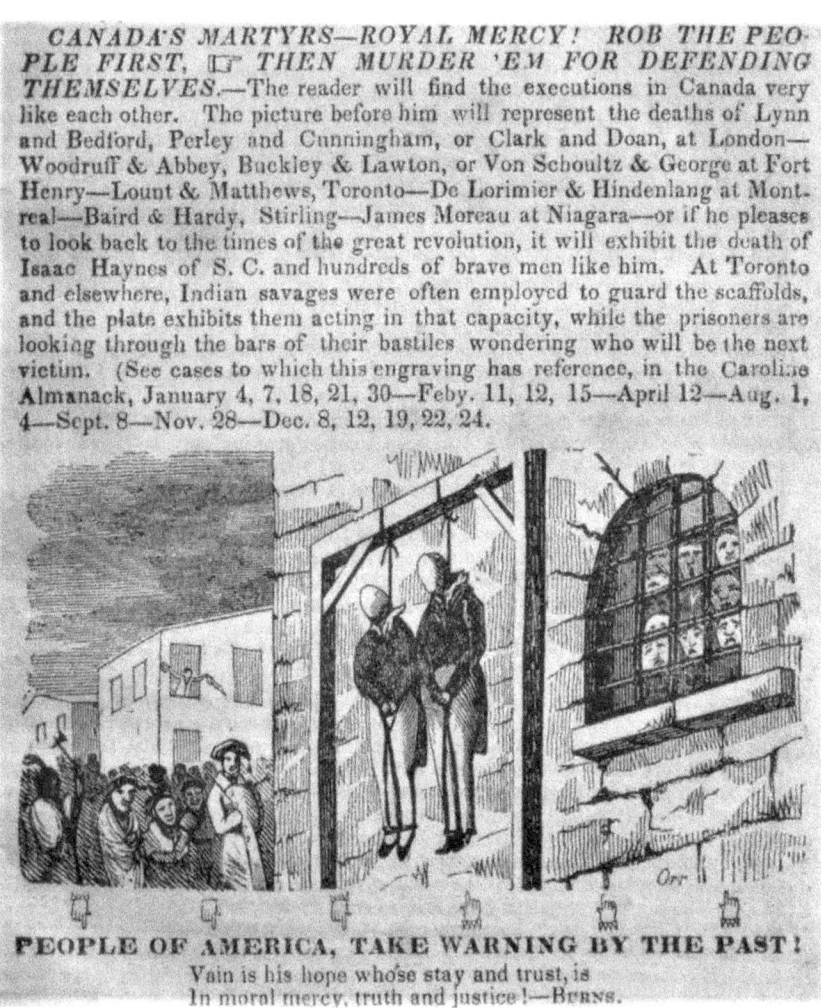

Figure 5.1 Engraving by J.W. Orr, in *Caroline Almanack and Freeman's Chronicle for 1840* (Rochester, NY: Mackenzie Gazette Office, 1840), p.3. Image courtesy of Lande Canadiana Collection, Rare Books and Special Collections, McGill University Library.

of British forbearance, regard for justice, 'and the love of mercy, which is inherent in the British character', according to Sir Francis Bond Head's memorandum submitted to the Colonial Secretary Lord Glenelg in October 1836.[28] Nineteenth-century writers reflected on the sovereign's fountain of mercy and how the representatives in Canada had ignored this appeal to the 'kingly virtue'.[29] As Barry Wright notes, appeals to the queen's clemency did not hide the political and administrative realities, so that one of those who enjoyed the royal mercy in Van Diemen's Land spoke of the hyperbolic language of this clemency, doubting texts addressing her 'ever meet the eyes of majesty'.[30] Later risings in Canada also stimulated appeals beyond the colonial authorities, to the British Crown. Petitions and appeals referred to the queen's 'high prerogative', after Louis Riel's conviction for high treason in the North West rebellion in 1885 (he was executed on 16 November 1885).[31]

Mackenzie's *Caroline Almanack*, as well as rehearsing the British state and crown's mercilessness, linked the Canadian cause with British political struggle: 'O, that chartism may flourish and deserve to put down the bloody and cruel Guelphs!'[32] Chartists and radicals in Britain failed to create a stir at home about distant colonial rebellion, but I turn now to the sustained appeals for mercy made to the queen by Chartists in the 1840s.[33]

The Queen's mercy towards Chartists

How sad would the historic page
Hand down to distant years,
Youth, innocence, disdain'd t'assuage
A nation's burning tears.
Let 'Mercy temper Justice' – Love
The boon shall fond repay:
And bright thy spirit soar above,
To realms of endless day.[34]

Blessing attend her for the pardon she gave,
The sceptre of mercy she extended to save,
The Chartist from death & an untimely grave
Did the mercyfull Queen of Old England,
Old England's Victorious Queen.
Of that pious deed after ages will tell,
And each loyal bosom with gratitude swell
As the fame of her virtues with rapture they dwell,
And revere the great name of Victoria,
The glory of England the Queen.[35]

So went Drapier's 'Chartists' Appeal to the Queen', in the Chartist *Northern Star* in late 1839 and a street ballad from Spitalfields to the air of 'The Roast Beef of Old England' in 1840 at the time of Victoria's marriage. Chartists appealed to the queen for commutation of capital punishment for high treason after the riots in Birmingham and the rising in Newport in Wales in 1839 and invoked that familiar language of diadem and jewel of mercy in appeals for non-capital prisoners such as William Lovett, John Collins, and Henry Vincent. The relationship between the Chartists and the young queen in the late 1830s–1840s expressed a populist interpretation of the monarchy, in which the right to petition her was part of a strategy to present the cause as a constitutional struggle, as well as an expression (in John Plunkett's words) of the 'idealization of the Queen's femininity'. Paul Pickering argues for the lack of cynicism in which many Chartists organized their campaign for democratic reform 'around the person of the monarch'.[36]

The solicitor general told John Frost's jury at Monmouth in January 1840 that 'Mercy is a delightful attribute, but God forbid we should forget Justice, for if we abandon Justice, mercy must soon flee'.[37] One Chartist petition for clemency for Frost and fellow Newport leaders, Zephaniah Williams and William Jones, from memorialists in Dewsbury in Yorkshire in early 1840 emphasized that mercy tended to 'establish your Throne in the hearts of the people' and accord with the 'gracious and benevolent nature of her majesty's character'.[38] A petition to the queen from Glasgow in January, arguing that the shedding of blood 'ill accords with female purity', refused to believe 'that "Victoria" will ever be adhibited to the death-warrant of men whose sole crime was an infatuated attempt to confer natural rights upon their fellows; or that she will stain her bridal wreath with the blood of patriots'.[39]

A London petition reported in February spoke of royal mercy affording 'proof to your people of your just and humane disposition' – imagined dashing aside the halter, axe, and ripping-knife with the sceptre of mercy; and juxtaposed nuptial day and bridal vestments with bloodshed.[40] Another metropolitan petition, from St Martin-in-the-Fields, from parochial authorities and inhabitant householders, argued that the 'exercise of clemency would prove the goodness of your Majesty'.[41] From Coventry, in the same month, a handbill commanded the men of the city to 'meet, meet in thousands this Evening, at the large room at the George Inn, Little Parkstreet, Coventry, to memorialize the Throne to remit the cruel and barbarous sentence which has been passed upon them'.[42] From Hull, also in February, Chartists led by the cabinetmaker John Peck, hoping to add a request for mercy to a loyal address congratulating the queen on her impending marriage, contrasted labourers' rough hands with the 'brightest gem'. Thomas Wilde observed, 'The meeting would find that most of the crowned heads in Europe granted a general amnesty to political offenders in the event of the marriage of the Sovereign.' The queen should show mercy, 'as her father in heaven was merciful to her'.[43] A petition in December stressed the fact that this was the 'year of your majesty's Royal nuptials and maternity', maintaining that 'we are twice blessed in this our timely application, inasmuch as since the above-named Frost, Williams, and Jones were tried, condemned, and sentenced to death for the crime of high treason, your majesty has become a wife and mother'.[44]

The *Northern Star*, imagining that like Louis Philippe (pardoning a man implicated in an assassination plot), personal imploring by a convict's relations could effect a pardon, suggested that Frost's wife see Victoria:

Our Monarch is called gracious; is a female, imbued with all the soft and kindly feelings of her sex; and could she, upon the day after her marriage, refuse the application of Mrs. FROST and her lovely daughters, when imploring pardon for husbands and fathers? No! we will not believe it, until the experiment has been tried, and shall have failed … This, we expect, would do more than all the memorials which meet the Royal ear through the tainted channel of palace mediation. What the eye sees not, the heart feels not for. The Queen has already felt the bitterness of parting from a father by the ordinary course of nature: let her be taught to think how fearfully the bereavement must be augmented in its poignancy by circumstances like those in which Mrs. FROST's daughters are placed![45]

The *Northern Star* returned to the contrast between British and French monarchs in 1844 when it compared the 'lovely and beautiful' queen's lack of mercy in the impersonal form of printed responses from her Home Secretary to appeals for the 'Welsh martyrs' unfavourably with Louis Philippe.[46] For while the death sentences were commuted to transportation in early February 1840, personal entreaty for pardons was a strategy that Chartists continued to put their hopes in, through the 1840s. The Executive Committee, addressing members of the National Charter association, explained this in January 1846. According to the constitution, 'the Queen is the fountain of mercy. She alone has the power of annulling or commuting a sentence pronounced by judicial authority.' So the course was clear, 'to snap the chains of captive patriots, we must work upon the royal sympathy; we must strive by every available means to direct the current of royal clemency to Frost, Williams, and Jones'.[47] The Irishman Thomas Clark, on the Chartist Executive, at a meeting on capital punishment in the South London Chartist Hall in March 1846, thought she must feel acutely the signing of a death warrant, 'surely, as a mother, as the head of the church, as the sovereign'.[48]

Given the failure to secure a rapid release of Frost and others, an association between Whigs, the queen, and mercy withheld, in the mind of some Chartists, led to criticism of Victoria. A critical correspondent in the *Northern Star* condemned her as a Whig tool signing 'death warrants of criminals whose crime were caused by mal-administration'.[49] An essay in the *Chartist Circular* in 1841 on the Protestant reformer John Knox occasioned a swipe at queens regnant: 'the bold Chartist who would dare to write as much evil of Queens in the present day; we fear the Queenly-loving-Whigs would have very little pity on his poor carcase.'[50] John Watkins's play *John Frost* criticized royal mercy in its concluding scene of Frost receiving news of the death sentence's commutation to transportation.[51] Criticism also appears in a report of Chartist prayers at a meeting in Clerkenwell Green in 1840, asking the 'king of kings' to have 'mercy on the queen; shew unto her the error of her ways … that she receives too much money for merely living in a large house, and signing acts of parliament for oppressing the people, Thy servants'.[52]

As Dorothy Thompson suggests, though addresses and petitions directed at the queen 'probably had in the end very little effect on the final decision to commute', street ballads and other evidence indicate people believed otherwise. Later press commentary on Frost's fate related the nature of British government to the exercise of mercy towards Chartists and others: 'There is a pointless sword in our regalia, called Curtana, or the Sword of Mercy. A popular Government like ours wants no sharper weapon to punish or restrain.'[53] That was in the *Examiner* in 1856; other mainstream newspapers had commented on mercy for Chartists in the late 1830s and 1840s. One provincial newspaper, advocating petitioning to prevent 'judicial murder', expressed revulsion: the 'reign of a maiden Queen is to witness the horrible and revolting scene of the public strangulation of three men for rioting at Birmingham, unless the voice of the people be loudly and promptly expressed in deprecation of it'.[54] For an 'Observer', in the anti-Whig *Era*, although the failure to show mercy would leave a bloodstain on royal ermine and dim the imperial diadem, the appeal ought to go to Lord John Russell as the queen was merely an 'automaton in your hands in this affair'.[55] *Lloyd's Weekly Newspaper* compared the treatment of the Chartists with the mercy bestowed on Canadian rebels, in early March 1846, seeing a partiality in the empire: 'The heart of the monarch will gladly respond to the entreaties of her people; and by the merciful exercise of her royal prerogative, restore the husband to his long sorrowing wife, the father to his child.'[56] Britons in Australia, fearing a similar prospect of grisly punishment for rebellion, also appealed in 1855 following the 'Eureka' rising: 'The disembowelings and burnings, the drawings and quarterings of the days of former Queens, are unsuited, and indeed hateful to our present Queen Victoria.'[57]

Royal mercy and the Indian rebellion, 1857–1901

White female victimhood was central to the British narrative of the Indian rebellion. At the same time female clemency – whether queenly mercy or the emotions ascribed to native British women in general – had a muted presence in the discursive response before 1858. Christopher Herbert argues for the trauma inflicted on the British middle class by their own pitiless response to the uprising – seeing it as the recrudescence of Puritan harshness that went counter to 'sentimentalized humanitarianism' and the ideals of pity and mercy.[58]

As a striking contrast to the massacre of women and children at Cawnpore, in the visual commentary that followed news of this in 1857, *Punch* depicted justice as a female warrior (Figure 5.2). Mercy-imploring native women cower under her shield's protection, her sword wielded against their guilty menfolk, in the famous cartoon by John Tenniel, published on 12 September 1857. In the distance, behind the advancing line of bayoneting British soldiers, their faces impassive, can be glimpsed a row of cannons upon which the distorted bodies of Indian men – about to be blown to smithereens – can be glimpsed.[59] The shield's decoration of justice's scales is obscured. The cartoon was linked, in the same issue, to the anonymous, bloodthirsty, verse by the journalist Shirley Brooks, 'Liberavimus Animam', which began, 'Who pules about mercy? … Our swords come for slaughter: they come in the name | of Justice', reproduced in *The Times* and elsewhere. *Punch's* Victoria was now mother protector, eyes raised to heaven as she knelt, cradling an apparently sleeping child whilst surrounded by similarly kneeling widows, and a group of orphaned children dressed in white, in another full-page cartoon by Tenniel in October 1857, with the king's lines

Figure 5.2 John Tenniel, 'Justice', *Punch*, 12 September 1857, p.109. Author's collection.

before Agincourt from Shakespeare's *Henry V*, 'O God of Battles! Steel my Soldiers' Hearts' (see Figure 5.3). This was apparently the first image of the queen by Tenniel to appear in *Punch*. The same issue scorned pity for the 'poor sepoy' and attacked twaddlers wishing to 'blend mercy with justice'.[60] Unsurprisingly, in looking at the

Figure 5.3 'O God of Battles! Steel My Soldiers' Hearts, *Punch*, 10 October 1857, p.151. Author's collection.

'British Temper towards India', seven years later, the Indian civil servant George Otto Trevelyan recalled of the 1857 volume of the 'good natured and sensible periodical', the images marked with Justice or Nemesis, 'a big female, with a helmet and a long sword, knocking about a black man'.[61]

The *Lady's Newspaper*, in October 1857, spoke of a cry of 'heart-curses' from 'the very island where the Queen of such vast dominions sits enthroned' to India but also called for mercy as something natural in women, 'especially the women in England'.[62] The queen privately wrote to the governor-general's wife (a former lady-in-waiting), in sympathy as woman, wife, and mother, in the agonies of the British in India.[63] But she was notably merciful in her language, in response to wholesale reprisals following the 'mutiny' and sensible to the 'great mercy' that the loyalty of her godson, the Sikh maharaja Dhuleep Singh, was untried in India during the rebellion. Naturally Governor-General Lord Canning wrote to his sovereign about his policy of clemency. His sovereign urged mercy towards women, children, and elderly men through Lady Canning – and 'great forebearance' on the basis of Christian values and the need to secure respect and esteem after the mutiny was over.[64] Prince Albert recorded in a memorandum, from copies of the governor-general's letters, Canning's self-perception of 'a most merciful course'. Contrasting with the queen's sense of the 'strange' nature of the British blood thirst, the outrage of Anglo-Indians and Britons who perceived his proclamation in July 1857 as excessive leniency (or what the English-language *Bengal Hurkaru* called 'morbid conscientiousness') is a well-known episode in the historiography of the rebellion.[65]

The royal proclamation announcing Victoria as the ruler of India in November 1858 was described by *Blackwood's Magazine* as heralding the reign of *Victoria Beatrix* after *Victoria Vindex* and sovereignty 'befitting a Christian monarch' – 'righteousness and justice, with mercy and toleration'.[66] The evangelical Anglican *Christian Observer* emphasized the coronation oath and her role as Christ's representative through commitment to rule with justice and mercy.[67] It was 'quite impossible to overrate the momentous nature of such a document', wrote the Christian Socialist J.M. Ludlow (born in India), who described it as British India's Magna Carta.[68] Ludlow's critique contrasted the message of mercy of the 'Queen's sway' with cruel British reprisals, but the transition from East India Company to a 'living personage' was praised as an astute measure to ensure loyalty or confidence through a figure 'inspired by sentiments of justice, and prompt to exercise the grand prerogative of mercy'.[69] The queen would rule with kindness and mercy, 'Meerbanee Warahum', reported *Allen's Indian Mail* in February 1859.[70] The civilian government in India was praised in the British press in the late 1850s for 'making the best use of the promises of mercy which that proclamation set forth'.[71] Indian groups who publicly showed their appreciation for the queen's clemency in 1859 included the community of the Muslim reformer Sayyid Ammad Khan, but as Miles Taylor notes, at least one prominent native voice disputed the proclamation's claims to clemency and forgiveness: Hazrat Mahal, the begum of Awadh (Oudh).[72]

Looking back at the event from the perspective of 1896 during the Indian National Congress's twelfth congress, Rahimtulla Sayani commented:

> It was granted by the free will and pleasure of the Sovereign, and truly displays the generosity of the Royal nature ... and is a remarkable proof of the clemency of the British Crown. It is characteristic of the Noble Lady, the Mother of her Subjects, whose reign has been an epoch in the history of the world. Deep reliance on merciful Providence and true sincerity pervade the document.[73]

Such was the rhetorical use made of the royal proclamation by Congress nationalists – linking the queen's 'sagacious clemency' (and racial and religious tolerance) with aspirations for 'liberal reform', in India.[74]

One early-twentieth-century apologist for British rule contrasted what he saw as the British conception of justice ('tempered as it is with Mercy') with a 'Hindu' concept of the justice of kings ('not modern justice' and a 'merciless type of Justice').[75] And the unjust or merciless character of native sovereigns had political significance, to provide a 'fair pretext for seizing upon their possessions', as the Indian (and British) politician Dadabhai Naoroji commented.[76] Yet queenly acts of clemency were part of Indian culture: Asoka's pillar edicts referred to 'queens with queenly mercy', helping the poor.[77] Moreover, Mithi Mukherjee has argued, with British rule, the language of justice and mercy in the Indian sub-continent was related to the English tradition of equity. Appeals were to the law and the mercy of a monarch rather than to the universality of impersonal law: a 'discursive change from justice under natural law to justice as equity', which linked justice to royal mercy and benevolence.[78]

The 'stream of benevolence' was deliberately turned on during Anglo-Indian royal celebration. In 1876 (which saw the start of widespread Indian famine), with the proclamation of the imperial title, good-conduct prisoners were released in Poona and neighbouring Yerrowda (Pune and Yerawada), Bombay, and the other presidency gaols. However, twenty-two prisoners escaped from Hooghly gaol 'from an impression among the convicts that it was the intention of Government that the clemency of the Crown on the occasion of the declaration of the empire should be extended to them all, and that they were detained wrongfully'.[79] In 1887 the British press complacently reported the 'right royal and gracious act of clemency', performed in India in that year, while noting that the release of prisoners in 1876 had not resulted in many repeat offenders: '[i]t was necessary of course that the celebration should be calculated to impress the Oriental with a befitting sense of the power, the magnificence, and the clemency of the Empress of INDIA'.[80] The Bengali weekly *Burdwan Sanjibani* argued in 1887, 'we have on many occasions felt the mercy of Her Majesty ... Her Majesty ought to show us some favour and thereby commemorate Her name'.[81]

The queen-empress's character was linked to the empire's zenith: 'the most benevolent and constitutional monarch', the Anglican clergyman Bourchier Savile eulogized in *How India Was Won by England Under Clive and Hastings* in 1881.[82] In Britain just before diamond jubilee celebrations, the queen was associated iconographically with justice and mercy in India.[83] David Mclaren Morrison (Austro-Hungarian consul at Calcutta) eulogized in a work on Indian and imperial federation published in 1902 thus: 'In a time of darkness and travail she stood forth in the midst of her Indian people as the incarnation of mercy and clemency'.[84]

The British queen's mercy as a trope in 'native' Indian literature has also been noted.[85] An example is reference to 'Mother Victoria! The very embodiment of mercy and kindness', in Sanskrit set to 'Hindu music' by the pro-empire Sourindro Tagore, president of the Bengal Music School, and published in 1875. Mother Victoria is implored to 'diffuse thy mercy alike on the noble and the ignoble – thy mercy from which flow all our blessings'.[86] On the other hand, the Indian press, but especially the English newspapers in Bengal, showed 'intolerable' licence in attacking Canning in the 1850s.[87] How did vernacular and English-language Indian-owned newspapers understand imperial, viceregal, and gubernatorial exercises of mercy? Native papers certainly used the language of British mercy: the Persian Bombay weekly *Pandit*'s editor protesting in 1893 it 'always places before [sepoys] instances of mercy and justice' by the government, when it made the complaint that native officers were barring subscription to the paper.[88] They critiqued British justice in terms of the mercy prerogative after controversial sentences. *Bhárat Sanghsarak* of Calcutta in 'The Lieutenant-Governor and official mercy', in December 1877 characterized the prerogative as the means by which the 'severity of the despotism, which the Government of India would otherwise be', ought to be mitigated.[89]

The subject of bureaucratically administered royal mercy in India surfaced occasionally in the British press, and there is some slight evidence of interest, in the queen's published letters. In 1891 she was keen to save the Senapati (commander of the army) of the princely state of Manipur from execution after the political agent Frank St Clair Grimwood was murdered.[90] Readers of British newspapers learnt of a 'death sentence revoked by the Queen' from the *Bombay Gazette* in 1893: on a Mahar at Sattara who appealed to the governor and viceroy, it was stated, '[t]he point having been established that appeals to the Queen lie, there is apparently nothing now to prevent any convict from appealing from any sentence in India'. The report referred to Section 401 of the criminal procedure code – the power to suspend or remit sentences – where an amendment of 1874 had inserted a proviso about the royal prerogative and the right of her Majesty to grant pardons, reprieves, remissions, and respites, 'though this has hitherto been rare'.[91] Viceregal exercise of mercy, of 'going personally into petitions', was noted of the queen's last viceroy, Lord Curzon.[92]

Mercy for assassins

It is especially worthy of remark, that, although the intention of the criminals could not be mistaken, and England's majesty was well beloved by all, mercy in each case tempered justice. In the old time attempts upon the life of the sovereign brought down swift destruction on the offender … though there could be no doubt at all about the murderous intentions of those misguided men, in the case of Queen Victoria no blood was shed. Surely this clemency tends highly to enhance the love of the people for her majesty.[93]

The mercy shown by her Gracious Majesty the Queen in pleading the cause of those who have attempted her life is an ever memorable example to the world at large of womanly benignity and great souled-ness. By no other monarch has such clemency been shown.[94]

As these quotations indicate, the first from a collection of lives of illustrious women published in 1861, the other the words of a colonial governor interviewed late in her reign, encounters with would-be assassins were repeated moments to balance justice and mercy in a personal context and contributed to Victoria's reputation for clemency. Chartist and Canadian rebels had not planned the assassination of political leaders or their monarch: in this final section I turn to these objects of royal mercy and begin with the queen's participation in the notorious McNaghten case in 1843.

A Glaswegian shopkeeper, Daniel McNaghten, labouring under a persecution mania involving the Tories, killed the secretary Edward Drummond in attempting to assassinate Sir Robert Peel, the prime minister, in January 1843. The royal couple – shocked at the potential loss of their respected premier – was alarmed at the prospect that the man responsible might escape punishment: 'no one's life would be safe, if people were continuously being let off on the plea of insanity', Victoria wrote in her diary.[95] The queen was prepared for capital punishment even before Drummond died, being informed on 24 January 1843: 'Sir Robert Peel humbly concurs in Your Majesty's opinion that it should be unfortunate, if any circumstances whatever should occur, to prevent the infliction of Capital Punishment for this most atrocious crime.'[96] Peel 'frequently [wrote] to your Majesty on the painful subject in respect to which your Majesty has manifested so deep an interest'.

The queen evidently felt the danger of an insanity plea, and the Home Secretary referred to the prisoner's 'collected and intelligent' demeanour.[97] Preparing the queen for the plea, Peel told her that the Home Secretary had news that 'McNaghten is a Chartist, that he has attended political meetings at Glasgow, and that he has taken a violent part in Politics'. Peel thought that the doctrines laid down after Prime Minister Spencer Perceval's assassination in 1812, as to the 'just responsibility of parties who may be labouring under delusion', ought to have been followed in the case of Edward Oxford (on whom more, shortly).[98] Reporting Peel's conversation in early February, her diary stated, 'if he were not hanged, there would be no more security'.[99] The charge by the Lord Chief Justice, Lord Denman, in Oxford's case, 'which I know shocked everyone at the time, had done more harm than anything'. The prime minister also corresponded with the queen about McNaghten, after his acquittal on the grounds of insanity, at the beginning of March.[100] As the queen told uncle Leopold of Belgium, the trial was '(as usual) badly conducted, & his acquittal – lamentable. I have very strongly urged some improvement in the Law, but they all say the Law is so perfect, – yet that no one is safe & still are too frightened to do anything; but it is being considered & at any rate people are become very vigilant about Madness'.[101] In her diary she noted that she had 'written very strongly to Sir Robert on the subject'.[102] Peel, sending her the news of the acquittal and a newspaper account, found it 'a lamentable Reflection that a man may be at the same time so insane as to be reckless of his own Life and the Life of others – and to be pronounced free from moral Responsibility – and yet capable of preparing for the Commission of murder with the utmost Caution and deliberation – and of taking every step which shall enable him to Commit it with certainty'.[103]

The reference to Oxford in the discussion of the case, which famously laid down rules, known as the 'McNaghten rules', for subsequent criminal trials involving insanity, was to the pot-boy Edward Oxford and one of the queen's early would-be regicides. In June 1840 he shot at the queen and Prince Albert with two pistols as they rode up Constitution Hill and (defended by the capital-punishment reformer John Sydney Taylor) was ruled at the trial 'guilty … at the time insane'. 'How badly the Trial of Oxford seems to have been managed', the queen wrote in her diary, berating the Jury as 'very stupid … This is too absurd! I will never believe the man is in the least mad'.[104] The queen was reported as instrumental in ensuring that Oxford was not executed but incarcerated (by her 'special wish and influence'): though Melbourne told her Oxford had 'quite sense enough to merit the punishment of death'.[105] He featured in Tussauds Chamber of Horrors.

Another attempt came from John Francis, a journeyman carpenter, found guilty of high treason and sentenced to death in June 1842 after shooting at the queen in Hyde Park in 30 May (see Figure 5.4). The queen was also said to strongly express the wish that the sentence be commuted to transportation. She recorded in her diary for 17 June that his death sentence while desired and 'most necessary, yet the feeling he is to be executed is very painful to me', and a day later wrote in a letter:

Figure 5.4 Wood engraving showing John Francis aiming a pistol at the queen's carriage, as it passes Constitution Hill, 30 May 1842, *Illustrated London News*, 4 June 1842, p.49. Author's collection.

The Verdict of Guilty has been pronounced agst the unfortunate Francis; the Queen feels, – & she believes every body else does, that he had ought to be made an example of – still it is a painful feeling for her, herself, that this poor Wretch sh^d be hung for her sake! She pities his poor Father – much.[106]

The Prince Consort's handling of the case was cited as an instance of his calm and wise manner.[107] Albert's interest in improving his wife's security is preserved in his dossier: 'Attempts on the Queen | by | Francis & Bean | 1842 | their Trial | & | Consequent alteration of the Law'. It contained correspondence with Sir Robert Peel and the Home Secretary Sir James Graham, reports of witnesses' evidence and the trials, and correspondence from Victoria, including one to Albert in German, which, significantly, Albert docketed 'Scruples'.[108]

This must have been the decisive factor, although the Lord Chancellor, Lord Chief Justice, and the judge involved in the trial discussed the implications of Francis's use of wadding and gunpowder, which they saw as showing there was no intention to kill, and remittance, 'provided signal Punishment, next in severity to Death, were inflicted', as Sir James Graham wrote.[109] Albert communicated the queen's sanctioning of this advice.[110] Albert's Memorandum for the Cabinet set out the problem. The life of the sovereign was 'the most important in the Kingdom' and the most exposed. The liability was increased (so he thought) when the sovereign was female, and the 'proneness of the People to commit attempts upon the person of the Sovereign is increased in our times by the increase of democratical & republican Notions & the Licentiousness of the Press'.[111]

Peel's letter to Albert, as politicians were amending the law (through what would be the Royal Protection Act, enacted in July 1842), set out the problem:

> It is important on the one hand to take as effectual a precaution as possible against the Risk of injury of any description to the Person of the Sovereign – and at the same time not to run counter to the public feeling and temper of the Times in respect to penal inflictions. If the Law were in public opinion one of undue severity – it would have less effect in deterring from the Commission of the Crime against which it was directed – than if it had the moral weight and authority of that opinion in its favour.[112]

The public papers had their views on appropriate responses. *John Bull* believed that those who in the past 'loudly declaimed against capital punishment, have declined to interfere, lest they may be charged with a want of loyalty. Whether praying for the exercise of the prerogative of mercy (which attribute is possessed by our gracious Queen to an eminent degree) be an act which can be construed into disloyalty must be left to those who have doubts about the matter'.[113]

A day after Francis's sentence was commuted 'in contemptuous clemency to the worthless offender and in deference to the humane feelings of her Majesty', as Samuel Warren, in *Blackwood's Edinburgh Magazine* in 1850, characterized what he viewed as a 'questionable act of mercy', there came William Bean's attempt.[114] The queen, thinking it right that Francis's death sentence was commuted, now trusted that Bean would be severely punished.[115] As Sir Theodore Martin's official life of the Prince Consort stated, Victoria was 'most anxious that the sentence of death should not be carried into effect, although fully conscious of the encouragement to similar attempts which might follow from such leniency', adding that the prerogative of mercy was not exercised 'except under the direction of the Government'.[116] The *Court Magazine* ended its account of the outrage by recording the queen's 'gracious kindness in *sparing the life* of Francis tho' sending him for life, by way of *painful* example, to one of the most penal of her Majesty's settlements'.[117] Quickly drafted legislation was designed to prevent attempts to hurt or alarm the sovereign.[118]

The Spectator, in 1842, observed of the state of criminal jurisprudence: 'there appears practically to be a positive premium on shooting the Queen.'[119] Responses to attempted assassinations of the sovereign were in the context of general qualms about the efficacy of the gallows, and doubts about alternatives, such as the pillory that had been 'unanimously condemned to the social lumber room with other antiquated and more powerful instruments of torture'.[120] But whipping, proposed for those who attempted to harm the sovereign from no apparently rational motive, seemed to equate an attempt to shoot the queen with mere apple stealing. Mercy had been outraged by its abuse, thought the *Pictorial Times*.[121]

There was a respite of seven years before the 'insufferable annoyance', of another attempt.[122] This was on 19 May 1849, by the Irish bricklayer William Hamilton. A year later in May 1850 there was an attempt by the ex-officer Robert Pate. In February 1872 there was Arthur O'Connor, nephew of the Chartist leader Fergus O'Connor. A decade later it was Roderick MacLean in March 1882 (see Figure 5.5). Unsurprising, given the

Figure 5.5 'Roderick Maclean, after his attempt to shoot the Queen at Windsor, taken to the police station', *Extra Supplement to the Illustrated London News*, 11 March 1882. Author's collection.

number of assaults and attempts on her life by this period (listed in a document in the Royal Archives[123]), the queen was concerned that 'stringent measures' must be taken against MacLean, a grocer's assistant from Portsmouth. She was more annoyed and amazed that no one was hurt when he fired at her as she left her train at Windsor, she wrote.[124] Some example ought to be made of him apart from merely shutting him up for life – she contrasted this 'horrid creature' with Oxford, who was 'very repentant' and settled in Australia after being released.[125]

But she was faced with a premier (Gladstone) who wished to avoid giving these 'weak and morbid minds' the notoriety they craved through loyal addresses which fed their 'vain imaginations'. Gladstone told the queen it was considered 'whether means should be adopted to ensure the trial of the cause by a strong Judge' and he knew her concerns about MacLean becoming at liberty.[126] Victoria wrote, 'The not doing it now will the Queen fears be put down to the radical tendencies of the Govt'.[127] She was 'greatly surprised & shocked at this Verdict': she would be forever exposed to horrible attacks 'till I am wounded or killed'. How was Maclean not even punished, she asked Gladstone and Granville? She thought the judge's reference to MacNaghten was a mistake.[128]

> She thinks it simply Unaccountable – if every Eccentric person who is not considered mad enough to be locked up is not to be considered responsible for his actions – then indeed no one is safe any longer! It is awful! Severe punishment they ought to have. And the Law ought really to be amended or crime will be on the increase & all criminals escape.[129]

She gathered that there was no intention to have any cross-examination. The verdict made her feel inclined 'to shut herself quite up'. Another letter made her displeasure more explicit: 'And this always happens when a Liberal Govt, is in!'[130] Ponsonby told his royal mistress that if MacLean was sentenced to death, the likelihood was that this would be commuted to imprisonment and there would be continual efforts to get a further commutation.[131] Others expressed the view that the case demonstrated that no sane person would think to attack the queen.

In the year that MacLean struck, the telegraph clerk Albert Young of Doncaster was punished with ten years' penal servitude for a letter threatening the queen with murder (the letter was read by Henry Ponsonby) unless money was paid to him. The seventeen-year-old was impersonating a Catholic priest and spun a story about evicted Irishmen. The queen was pleased with the severe punishment as a check on a system of threatening letters to frighten people.[132]

Correspondence in the Royal Archives reveals, unsurprisingly, the queen's views on capital and corporal punishment as protection from assassination. Many may have thought her life endangered because unsuccessful assassins, even the insane, were unhanged or leniently punished. Oxford, following the attempts by Francis and Bean, reputedly observed, 'If they had hung me there would have been no more madmen firing at the queen' – and it was certainly a comment that the queen knew about.[133] The *Dublin University Magazine* agreed, in 1863: 'Hang a so called madman and murders by lunatics will speedily disappear from the criminal records.'[134] Sir Henry Ponsonby took a similar line, writing to the queen after the Maclean trial.[135] The incident made prominent the problem of acquittal due to insanity in cases of attempted homicide by 'eccentric individuals'.[136] As Ponsonby told Gladstone, in conveying the queen's views: 'Punishment deters not only sane men but also eccentric men, whose supposed involuntary acts are really produced by a diseased brain capable of being acted upon by external influence.'[137]

Other instances of merciful providence and appeals to the queen's mercy involved attempts on the Prince of Wales, thus in 1900 the young Belgian anarchist Jean Baptiste Sipido's parents sent appeals to the queen and the prince, which were reported in the newspaper press around the world, after his assassination attempt in early April.[138] The *Pall Mall Gazette* reported the family had on six occasions written to Edward VII for mercy and received no reply, after the youth's imprisonment in the École de Bienfaisance in Ghent. It was a crime linked to the imperial war in South Africa, for which the youth blamed the prince, and amid a wave of anarchist attempts on heads of state and monarchs. The 'insulting leniency' was associated with the successful attempt on King Umberto of Italy shortly afterwards. Monarchical mercy remained risky.[139] In the next chapter the perspective on royal mercy is opened up further, to consider transatlantic perspectives from American slavery abolitionists, and the imperial sphere in the queen's relationship to the claims of mercy in the Australian colonies.

6

Victoria Beatrix: Victoria's Empire of Mercy

To her protection, multitudinous nations, provinces, and tribes, of every hue and creed, from 'The gorgeous East' to those primeval forests of the Western world

'Where the poor Indian whose untutored mind
Sees God in clouds or hears him in the wind,'

all look up with hope; and think that, while the diadem of England sits on so fair a brow, and its sceptre is wielded by so gentle a hand, they may count on seeing Mercy,

'The brightest jewel that adorns the crown,'

so tempering Justice in its administration as to make the condition of themselves and all their children more happy than under any previous reign.[1]

In this study of Victoria's monarchy through the perspective of its role as a throne of mercy, the imperial dimension must be attended to. It has already been touched on in relation to British North American and Indian rebellions. As the quotation (a royal dedication from the writer and former MP James Silk Buckingham in 1841) that begins this chapter indicates, the way royal power was gendered in her reign made rhetorical associations between mercifulness and imperial rule tempting. Humanitarians involved in a variety of campaigns added royal reputation to their arsenal of arguments. The Quaker Samuel Gurney may be unsurprising to us in dramatizing what he saw as the British guilt against 'Caffres' in the Cape of Good Hope colony, when he privately hoped in 1851 that 'the history of the happy reign under which we live should not be tarnished with so foul a blot, but that the crown of our beloved Queen should be adorned with the bright jewels of justice, mercy, and righteousness'.

At the end of her long reign, stage shows to glorify the British Empire connected the queen empress with mercy and other qualities. 'Might with mercy constant blended', sang the chorus surrounding her image in *India*, performed in London in 1895–1896.[2] But starkly contrasted is the association of monarch with slavery as Victoria's reign began, explored in the first part of this chapter. A similar appeal was made to the queen in capital cases in the Antipodes – sometimes related, as at 'home', to capital-punishment abolitionism, but also making calls for fairness and mercy in treating indigenous peoples using a language of mercy recognizable from the British press. The second chapter showed that tales of the queen's personal mercy circulated across the empire. This chapter concludes with some brief commentary on entreaties for clemency from outside the empire, involving the mercy of a monarch, whether Christian or non-Christian.

The reproach of being crowned a queen of slaves

A further stage in the emancipation of former slaves in the British Empire became related to the accession of a monarch in 1837. For as the second edition of Esther Copley's history of abolition noted in 1839, some West Indies colonies planned to emancipate 'apprentices' (the former slave population who were supposedly being prepared through education, to be freemen), on 21 June, six weeks earlier than the date assigned by legislation. This honoured Victoria's coronation, with some proprietors, through acts of liberation, 'rescu[ing] their amiable young sovereign from the reproach of being crowned the Queen of slaves'.[3]

The association of the new monarch with further amelioration was an explicit strategy for slavery abolitionists. As Clare Midgley notes, a 'double opportunity' appeared with her accession and the parliamentary election ensuing from William IV's demise.[4] Arguably, by this point, with a large measure of 'emancipation' achieved, the respectability of the cause now accepted, royalty could afford to be more closely associated with anti-slavery as a philanthropic act, the queen's uncle the Duke of Sussex chairing the Anti-Slavery Society meeting at Exeter Hall on 13 July 1837 (leaving under the excuse of pressure of other business but endorsing the meeting).[5]

The early months of the reign demonstrated the evolving approach of shaming a female court. In Birmingham, the *Philanthropist*, reporting an anti-slavery meeting to hear the accounts of atrocities reported by the Quaker abolitionist Joseph Sturge, returned from the West Indies, commented, 'Would that the young Queen had heard the address. She could not have resisted his appeal to her young and gentle womanhood.'

> Now is a most favourable opportunity for such a scheme. An election is at hand, and all will be in motion. Levees and court movements will be frequent. The young Queen will have to be crowned, and probably married. Into the midst of all this, let the case of the slaves be thrust, as a dark shadow – an appalling apparition. Let such a statement of the wrongs and woes of the wretched slaves be pictured to the Queen and to her female Court, as shall make them miserable, until they have done what they are perfectly able to do – Justice to the Slave.[6]

This account was reproduced in *Leicester Chronicle*, which published a letter linking the effort with the pioneering work of its townswoman, Elizabeth Heyrick, and the desire to make emancipation a 'peculiar glory' of the reign.[7] Angell James of Birmingham also entreated the queen in July 1837, at a meeting at Livery Street chapel: 'we have our young, our noble-minded, our tender-hearted Queen – (loud cheers) – may God bless her … She cannot; she will not resist the appeal of her afflicted subjects, and, ere long, slavery shall cease'.[8] Advice from the *Monthly Magazine* in November 1837 included 'the serious consideration of your Majesty [to] the necessity of devising further means to prevent the bill for the Abolition of Slavery in the West Indies from being infringed alike by chicanery and fraud, or by violence and outrage'.[9]

The abolitionist George Thompson's speech at Salem Chapel in Newcastle in late January 1838 linked the queen to the *beginning* of the transatlantic slave trade by referring to the 'time when another Queen swayed the sceptre over these realms' and regretting that down to the present day and the 'reign of our virgin Queen, Victoria the First' there was a 'reign of terror and blood'.[10] The prospect opened up by a young woman on the throne, 'holding the sword of justice with the hand of mercy', was hopeful. So Brougham addressed the queen in the Lords on 20 February 1838, in a widely regarded speech: 'To the merciful Sovereign of a free people I call aloud for mercy to the hundreds of thousands in whose behalf half a million of her Christian sisters have cried aloud that their cry may not have risen in vain.'[11] (Brougham, in the context of criminal law, saw the prerogative of mercy as an illicit source of favourable opinion towards sovereign or government.[12])

There was a transatlantic fascination with the new monarch. The American abolitionists Sarah Grimké and Angelina Grimké addressed the queen in October 1837 about lending her power to the apprenticeship cause: contrasting the republic's boasted humanity with the reality, noting that a queen had legalized the American slave trade, and hoping a '*Queen* may burst the bonds of every slave over whom her sovereignty extends'. The sisters hoped that a 'crown of glory' would encircle her and that she would seek a wisdom that was gentle, 'easy to be entreated, full of mercy and good fruits'.[13]

The constitutional role as the target of petitions ensured abolitionists' efforts were directed at the new monarch. 'Illustrious and amiable Queen!' said the nonconformist minister William Bevan of Liverpool in 1837, 'your mandate is invincible. It is but to determine, to declare'.[14] Ladies' emancipation committees were established. Female addresses for abolition of apprenticeships presented to Victoria, according to the *Friends' Intelligencer*, 'contain 692,000 signatures of women – the English address 450,000, the Irish 77,000, the Scotch 130,000, the Manchester 25,000, and the Carlisle 10,000' (Midgley states the total signatories were over 700, 000).[15] The language of petitions associated the queen's gender with the female efforts. '[W]e fervently pray', went one petition from ladies of Glasgow and the vicinity, in August 1837, 'that the commencement of your Majesty's reign may be distinguished by an act of justice and benevolence, which would be a bright example to other nations, and shed a hallowed lustre around our beloved sovereign's name'.[16]

As ever with such pleas, the idea of sparkling mercy attracted many a public speaker. The combination of 'brilliants', a 'virgin crown', and manumission of 100,000 subjects led one orator, the Quaker banker William Henry Leatham at Wakefield (to cheers from his audience), to imagine the 'most engaging and lovely being that ever ascended the British throne', obtaining imperishable glory.[17] In appealing to the queen, George Thompson (who linked the efforts of female abolitionists to the 'petticoat government' under which they lived 'entirely') asked: would a 'young and amiable Queen' wish to keep in her crown a single gem, 'however brilliant, stained with the blood of any portion of her subjects?'[18]

From Carlisle, after a meeting at the chapel of the Wesleyan Methodists, in May 1838, came a petition, praying that her throne would 'shine with some reflection of the mercy of the Heavenly Throne', that at the coronation she would be proclaimed ruler over a free people and 'that the brightest ornaments of the British [was] rendered most resplendent by your Majesty's special interference as the advocate of humanity and justice'.[19] In Birmingham abolitionists heard from Joseph Sturge: 'If her countenance is a transcript of her feelings, she is not callous to the sufferings of her sex, and if the miseries of the negro mother under this accursed system could be but faintly pictured to her view, I feel persuaded her heart would beat in unison with yours.' Unhappily, however, the queen's ministers seemed to defy the 'people's prayer' and Sturge saw the prospect that she should be 'crowned a Queen of slaves':

> May He by whom 'kings reign and princes decree justice,' who has the hearts of all at his disposal, and whose loveliest attribute is mercy, yet grant that ere the diadem descends upon your monarch's brow, the fiat may be given that the sun shall rise no more upon a single slave of any colour or of any clime in her extended empire.[20]

The sense of stigma linked to the impending coronation appeared in comments at other meetings. In Bradford in January 1838, one speaker suggested that the queen boycott her coronation until slavery was abolished![21] Dr Williamson, at a meeting convened in the Brunswick Street Wesleyan chapel in Leeds in April, was applauded when he spoke of the damage to royal reputation if she was crowned a queen of slaves.[22] Another meeting of Methodists at Bristol hoped repeal coincided with the coronation 'and the name of Victoria shall be written on the heart of every child of Africa'.[23] Chairing a civic meeting, Exeter's mayor, William Wilkinson, was applauded for suggesting it was fated 'that this great act of mercy should flow from a woman, and that woman our youthful and beloved Queen … This would, indeed, be a wreath around the royal brow, brighter and more glorious than any crown or jewel that would adorn her Majesty's head on the day of her Coronation'.[24] The Reverend Thornton of Darlington, at a meeting in Stockton in April, suggested that they introduce a 'black slave in fetters, with a bleeding bosom, and placing himself at the step of the throne, say to the queen "Behold one of your subjects a bleeding slave!" (Applause)', during the coronation.[25] In the capital an 'extensively posted and circulated' placard depicting the iconic kneeling African asked, 'Will her Majesty consent to become a *Queen of Slaves?*'[26] The visual propaganda otherwise seems limited: a coronation transparency presented 'two negroes kneeling to receive the cap of liberty' from the queen, at the Essex town of Halsted.[27]

Verse on the coronation made the association. The 'bard of Sheffield', James Montgomery's widely circulated *Coronation Ode* stressed, 'No Slaves within thine empire breathe'.[28] In *The Sun* 'The Coronation Day' similarly linked African joy with the queen's reign over the free.[29] To the tune of 'God save the Queen', readers of the *Sheffield Independent* were told: 'No wretch on Britain's soil, | Can e'er degraded toil | In slavery's gloom. | Mercy his chains would break, | Vengeance fresh fury take, | The tyrant's throne to shake – | And seal its doom'.[30] Another of those coronation odes to Victoria preserved in the local press imagined the refrain 'Rule Victoria! Victoria rules the free', crossing the Atlantic: 'On mercy's wings the theme flown; | And soon the suffering, toil worn, slave. | Shall back resound a kindred tone. | Rule Victoria! Victoria we are free, | The enfranchise'd Negro still shall bless and pray for thee.'[31] Expressive of that anticipation of the agency of female sovereignty in the cause, the English-born Frances Elizabeth Browne in a volume published in Massachusetts in 1846, asked: 'Shall the sceptre of Britain by woman be grasped, | Nor the fetters which bind the poor negro unclasped? | Shall the voice of her people ascend to her throne, | Nor Victoria the claims of humanity own?'[32]

'Hurrah for Jin-Jin Lick an Lock-up Done Wid, Hurray fuh Jin-Jin' is the faulty folkloric memory of the personal link between abolition of apprenticeship and Queen Victoria.[33] 'Of their young Queen', according to one account of St Kitts, 'they are very proud and the name Victoria is quite a fashionable one among them insomuch so that some have wished us to baptize their daughters Queen Victoria'.[34] This association by the emancipated (and the missionaries who wrote letters to the queen and governor of Jamaica, which expressed these sentiments) with the monarchy was politically astute, as Demetrius Eudell notes.[35] In Jamaica, the queen figured alongside icons of abolition like Wilberforce, at one emancipation celebration, and there was talk of a 'jubilee'.[36]

At the private dinner of Liverpool worthies presided over by the mayor, William Rathbone, to celebrate emancipation day, it was declared that Victoria was the first English sovereign 'who could say that all her subjects were free'.[37] The publisher Egerton Smith's poem was sung here: 'This day, 'mongst the gems that bedeck the fair brow | Of our fair Queen, – a new jewel we see, | At its lustre so bright – tyrants crouch in affright, | And the negro erect stands, and FREE!' The empire now offered refuge from the violence of slavery, under Victoria's benevolent rule.[38] The General Anti-slavery Convention in London in June 1840 (American female abolitionists sought to be present and consequently the role of Victoria as monarch was alluded to[39]) heard moving testimony about finding freedom in Canada: 'Ah! Sir, I wish she could be our QUEEN too, long enough to make our subjects free', and 'wherever the flag of our gracious Queen floats upon the breeze, there is glorious freedom'.[40] This view is expressed in the American John Pierpont's 'Star of the North' (1839), with its lines: 'The Lion at the Virgin's feet, | Couches, and lays his mighty paw, | Into her lap! – an emblem meet | Of England's Queen and English law: – | Queen, that hath made her Islands free! | Law that holds out its shield to me!'[41] Fugitive American slaves associated Canada with the queen's merciful disposition. Organizations capitalizing on the association between merciful or benevolent queen and the plight of former slaves included a Queen Victoria Benevolent Society established in Canada by the wife of the ex-Virginian apprentice and black entrepreneur Wilson Abbott, in 1840, to aid poor black women.[42]

What did the monarch actually feel about this act of mercy? Victoria, in her speech to Parliament, 5 February 1839, spoke of 'great satisfaction' in emancipation being 'anticipated' by colonial legislatures and effected without public disorder.[43] American journals such as the Quaker *Friend* quoted this as if it revealed her feelings.[44] Her childhood reading included Maria Budden's *True Stories of Modern History*, with its quotation from William Cowper about British power and mercy, and dismay that the act of abolition was delayed until 1806. An American eulogist, seeking to enrol her in the abolitionist cause, asserted he had heard from an 'English gentleman' that 'reading, when a child, a passage in Cowper's Works, describing the horrors of Slavery, she exclaimed with tears in her eyes, that if she ever came to the throne, it should be her first care and chief concern that no slave should be found in her dominions'.[45]

In Victoria's diary, slavery was alluded to as a non-partisan parliamentary effort. Melbourne schooled her in the stance to take with one of her foreign uncles, in May 1818: 'it would be well, if I were to state to Ferdinand that the feeling was so strong in this country about Slavery, and we were so pressed about it, that it is impossible for us to do otherwise, &c., &c.'[46] We know, from the same record, that Victoria was advised to avoid a group of Protestant Dissenter women, who had given her a fine Bible in 1838, they being women 'who of late had put themselves so forward, about this Slavery, would not do'. Victoria read Wilberforce's *Life* and a work by the abolitionist Thomas Fowell Buxton and discussed slavery with Melbourne, who thought much 'must be exaggerated' and the proposed measures 'very wild'.[47] From Melbourne, Victoria heard that anti-slavery was 'so much stronger in this country than in any other,' that the women of England were for abolition, and that antislavery petitions were signed by 'many thousands' of them.[48] Prince Albert associated the monarchy with the anti-slavery cause on 1 June 1840 by addressing the new African Civilization Society in his first role as public speaker – he was the society's president ('induced to preside', he said – the words were not his but Anson's and his mentor Baron Stockmar's – from a conviction of its 'paramount importance to the great interests of humanity and justice').[49] He acquired Henry le Jeune's depiction of biblical liberation of slaves in 1847 and the royal couple read *Uncle Tom's Cabin* in the early 1850s.[50] As efforts to eradicate slavery in Africa followed, Victoria was associated with such declarations as those to the kings and chiefs of the Gold Coast in 1874, noted in the British press: her determination to 'put a stop at once to the buying and selling of slaves. This thing is against a law which no King or Queen of England can ever change'.[51] Victoria's opposition to slavery in the United States was signalled, it was reported, by refusing a dedication for a work expressing pro-slavery sentiments by her lady-in-waiting Amelia Murray in 1856.[52]

Australian appeal to the queen's mercy

> When the history of Queen Victoria is written, the manner in which she has tempered judgement with mercy will be dwelt on with approval. In these distant colonies the prerogative is a second-hand affair and has been often discharged in a manner which has not commended itself to the judgement of reflecting men. Still, on the whole, few would desire to see any limitation imposed on the representatives of Her Most Gracious Majesty. The prerogative of pardon has as a whole been fairly exercised. These remarks are applicable to all the colonies.

So commented the Hobart *Mercury* in 1876. Appeal to royal mercy in capital cases was an aspect of imperial rule – as seen in post-Mutiny India, in the previous chapter. The early Australian colonies had marked royal birthdays with acts of clemency.[53] This section briefly uncovers some associations between the royal mercy and these colonies. I have already indicated a wider Anglophone interest in Victoria's youthful mercy, through the verse on the 'death warrant' story emanating from New Zealand: tales circulated rapidly about royal mercifulness in the empire.

From the early years of the reign, there were capital-punishment abolitionists in Australian colonies, with one petitioning effort directed at the queen. The civil engineer and surveyor Nathaniel Lipscomb Kentish organized a petition in 1844, from Van

Diemen's Land: expressing anxiety that her reign 'should, and that without delay, be distinguished as an epoch of wisdom, of mercy, and of Christianity – of enlightened, humane, and religious legislation, which shall be more glorious to your Majesty in life than the diadem of the imperial crown'. Kentish spoke of a ministerial and royal disposition to mercy ('the maternal bosom of your Majesty'). The petition, laying at a stationer's for signature, referred 'to the gratifying relief ... of your Majesty's mind and conscience from the awfully responsible duty of the sovereign under the penal code as at present established ... and immortalising the fame of your Majesty's reign as greater not only than that of any of your royal predecessors, monarchs of the British realm; but as the most mercifully wise and Christian that the world has known'.[54]

The *Argus* of Melbourne referred appreciatively to Victoria's reign of royal mercy in the face of insurrection and attempted assassination in an editorial pointed at Governor Sir Charles Hotham in 1857, during state trials after the Ballarat rising.[55] By the 1870s a republican and anti-monarchist movement existed in the Australian states. Scandals such as the mercy shown to the bushranger, Francis Gardiner, stimulated public criticism of the governor's exercise of the prerogative in New South Wales. The counter-assertion, against the setting up of the 'standard of Republicanism', was that the governor Sir Hercules Robinson acted as the Crown's agent and was not beholden to any colonial parliament. The Parkes government fell as a result of the Gardiner case in early 1875.[56]

I have shown the interest in the Penge homicide case in the British press in Chapter 3: reports of royal compassion shown to Mrs Staunton appeared in the wider British world. The incident was employed in appeals for mercy in New South Wales in 1879: when 'coloured citizens of Sydney' asked for mercy for an aboriginal youth, Alfred, condemned to death for rape. They appealed to the lieutenant governor (Sir Alfred Stephen), during a public meeting of the Knights of Sheba Club (an organization for aboriginal mutual aid) in the corner of George and Park Streets: a 'reverential conclave ... stalwart, intelligent fellows, quiet and respectful in demeanour'. At the same time there were two whites awaiting sentence of death at Bathurst Gaol. The audience was asked to pray for mercy for the aborigine and the white youths, with one of the speakers referring to the Penge case which had taken place while he was in England: 'the petition for mercy presented by his mother alone was accepted by the Queen in person, and a reprieve granted.' 'Sir Alfred ought to strive', another argued, 'to imitate his noble Queen, from whom mercy flowed like a river'. The petition to Sir Alfred included an appeal to the queen's reputation for justice and mercy: 'We desire to respectfully remind your Executive that our gracious Sovereign, who is the fountain of mercy, is Empress of many millions of dark men, to whom she has ever extended her protection, and to whom she has meted out equal justice.'[57] The man was executed at Mudgee.[58]

At the time of her golden jubilee in 1887, the Howard Association, inheriting the abolitionist mantle of the Society for the Abolition of Capital Punishment, claimed it was 'hoped by many persons that the Jubilee year of Queen Victoria's reign might have been kept from such disgusting scenes' as the execution of women.[59] Australian campaigners acted similarly, *Queensland Figaro and Punch*, to secure the release of the first woman condemned to be hanged in Brisbane in Queensland, linking Ellen Thompson's plight with the jubilee: 'Shall this womanly year of the Queen's Jubilee be the first to mark the hanging of a woman?' The bracketing of the extremes of a female hanged one week and the jubilee of another was deliberate.⁶⁰

In the same year, the question of the governor's role in the operation of mercy was raised after multiple death sentences for a gang rape at Mount Rennie in New South Wales in 1886, with a similar campaign for clemency linking the condemned men's fate to the queen's jubilee. Rape was a capital crime in the colony, unlike Britain. Sir Henry Parkes, the premier of New South Wales, in asking the governor, the Liberal politician Lord Carrington, for clemency, linked the aspirations of the young colony with the celebrations to demonstrate the 'loyal attachment' to the queen.⁶¹ As the *Westminster Review* commented in 1894, 'it was the demonstrated uselessness of reposing the prerogative of mercy in Governor Carrington's hands which led to its being taken away from Australian Governors altogether.' While the focus was on the governor, appeals for mercy and commentary on the governor's predicament referred to Victoria: a letter to the *Launceston Examiner* in December 1886 gestured towards her 'beneficent and vigorous reign' in contrasting the capital code in the 'mother country' with the situation in New South Wales.⁶²

In Queensland the prospect of prisoner release as part of jubilee celebrations received a tart response from the *Maryborough Chronicle*'s leader-writer in June 1887: 'another of those delicious farces which ultra-jingo minded persons rejoice to play off, and like most of the old fashioned modes of displaying the largeheartedness of royalty, the idea will not suffer being inquired into with the matter of fact reasoning used these times.' The best that could be done, with this 'clemency business', given the horrific gallows scenes already that year, was if the 'royal clemency ... do away with capital punishment as one of the monstrous outgrowths of old time barbarity'.⁶³

Yet the fact that royal phraseology hedged the prison and legal system in the colonies allowed reformers to continue their calls for prisoners to be released, a decade later, when celebrations of the diamond jubilee or 'record reign' were planned. At a time when loyal subjects showed 'their affection for her person, by works of mercy, such as please best the Sovereign's heart', it was natural to present the idea of prisoners' release for attention. 'Caritas', writing to the *Sydney Morning Herald* and *Australian Star*, argued, 'it would be peculiarly appropriate were some abbreviation of existing sentences granted as a mark of Royal clemency in commemoration of the record reign', and thus exhibiting the Crown 'in the light of a source of mercy and fountain of pardon'.⁶⁴ Another aspect of the Australian clemency debate in relation to the jubilee was the fate of Irish political prisoners, which naturally exercised Irish emigrants.⁶⁵ Back in the 'old country', however, the royal clemency formed part of the complacent reporting of 'rejoicings in the colonies' and celebratory measures such as 'special rations and clothing' for '[t]he aborigines'.⁶⁶

By the 1880s, Australian public discourse on the royal prerogative of mercy was shaped by attitudes towards independence from gubernatorial control; it had earlier been complicated by the status of the territories as penal colonies. In the 1850s the passing in the State of Victoria of the Convicts Prevention Act (with a moral panic about the convicts from Van Diemen's Land – Tasmania) stimulated discussion about the royal prerogative's relationship to the 'dignity and independence worthy of the representative legislature of a free people'. There was a collision between Legislative

Council and the British Crown. According to the Colonial Secretary, the Council 'asked the Queen to concede to the colony of Victoria what she had refused to give up to any other portion of the empire, and had not even granted to the House of Commons'. This was disputed by the Melbourne *Argus*, leading the campaign against convicts: despite the 'holy writ' of Shakespeare on royal prerogative, John Bull and Mr A' Beckett (Chief Justice William à Beckett, knighted by the queen) had syllogized that 'Jewels are necessary to Crowns; of all jewels, mercy is the brightest: ergo, the prerogative of mercy is the brightest jewel in the Crown'. What, the paper asked, 'after all, is this royal prerogative of mercy but a remnant of feudal folly and injustice?'[67]

Colonial newspapers pondered the prerogative's place in the colonies and mother country through the 1890s. One writer, keen to see it abolished in line with 'complete self-government in colonial matters', argued that 'untrammelled by tradition' the question could be looked at clearly in 'these young countries'.[68] Still, the radical *Truth* of Brisbane used the tradition of mercy bestowed in jubilee, royal births and marriages, to lambast New South Wales's prime minister in 1900 in the case of the condemned man John Sleigh, believed to be insane, at Goulburn gaol, against the backdrop of the inauguration of the federal commonwealth.[69]

Mercy, monarchy, and empire

My earlier chapters focused on the queen's symbolic role as source of justice and mercy in the domestic or 'metropolitan' arena. This chapter was interested in how the monarchy was appealed to as symbol or source of justice and clemency in the colonies whether these were white settlers or non-European subjects. According to Millicent Fawcett's biography of the queen, she used the 'weight of her influence and authority in the scale of mercy', in India.[70] We will see in the clemency called for by Lajput Rai in 1910, discussed in the concluding chapter, the use by the colonized of this figurehead of mercy in political struggles against the post-Victorian imperial state.

The constitutional authority Arthur Keith described the prerogative in 1912 as 'an essential part of the working of the executive government of a British Dominion'.[71] More research could be done on this imperial dimension by examining in detail the discourse in the colonies of South Africa, New Zealand, and Canada. I look in *Mercy and British Culture, 1760–1960* at the associations made between the British monarchy, mercy, and unmercy, in Ireland. Antony Taylor's *Down with the Crown* reproduces a striking *Weekly Freeman* cartoon of June 1887: in the year of jubilee, the artist John Fergus O'Hea depicted a shackled Miss Erin glancing defiantly at an obese and complacent Victoria in the form of a marble bust bearing the ironic legend, '50 Years of Prosperity and Gentle Rule'.[72]

This examination of the meaning and use of mercy in the era of British domination is not intended to suggest that the empire was a site of unusual mercy. 'Cruel Britannia' is not whitewashed through rehearsing tales of clemency to 'political offenders' and others.[73] Sometimes this was acknowledged. Robert Seeley pointedly referred to the 'gentle and merciful reign of Queen Victoria', when noting the killing of several of the king of Delhi's sons after rebellion in 1857.[74] Sir William Denison, governor-general in

Australia and governor of Madras, who admitting in a private letter in 1862 that British rule had been obtained sometimes 'between you and me, by very dirty processes', advised on the response to a resurgence of unrest in Hyderabad:

> We must not expect gratitude or affection from them, and must be prepared to deal with them, should they be foolish enough to break out a second time, just as their native rulers would do; that is to show but little mercy, to act thoroughly upon their fears. Leniency, they, as well as other savage or semi-civilised nations, regard as a proof of weakness.[75]

Mercy beyond the empire

As a great power, Britain could assist subjects and fellow Christians outside the British imperium, appealing in the language of royal mercy. Thus Victoria's merciful interventions were noted, outside the formal empire, in Madagascar, whose ruler, Ranavalona I, was notorious in early-Victorian missionary discourse as a merciless lioness.[76] One account, in the *Christian World Magazine*, in 1866, describes the 'memorable plea' to one of her successors, Rasoherina, 'a plea that thrilled from woman's heart to woman's'.[77] The queen also intervened by telegraphing 'a request for mercy direct to the Empress Dowager in China through Sir Thomas Wade' to ensure a pardon for the ambassador Chung How in 1879. As an aside, Cixi found it calming to dress as the goddess of mercy Guanyin, according to her lady-in-waiting, Der Ling.[78]

A personal appeal by telegraph came to the queen from the Prussian king, for Franz Müller, convicted of murder on the North London railway line in 1864. Victoria was reputed to be among those who feared it would be judicial murder if the German was executed.[79] She was relieved to have doubts quelled when he confessed on the scaffold and after reading about him in *The Globe*, as her diary noted: although horrified at the German press claiming that his execution was revenge for the second Schleswig-Holstein war.[80] She avoided giving any support to the king of Portugal's call for mercy in the case of a murder by one Portuguese man of another in Hong Kong in 1898; telegrams from Carlos begged his dear aunt to commute the punishment 'in remembrance of the memorable date when we came to celebrate your nephew who you kissed on the hand'.[81] The ambassador, prime minister, and Colonial Office were all involved; the queen advised to argue that 'she had delegated the prerogative of dealing with death sentences entirely to Governors of various Colonies and regrets she cannot interfere with regard to sentence'. As Lord Salisbury told the queen's Private Secretary Sir Arthur Bigge in a ciphered telegram in late June, 'Whenever a Portuguese is condemned to death for murder in any part of her Majesty's Dominions, the Government of the King of Portugal makes the utmost possible effort to prevent his being punished according to law' – clemency that caused resentment in the British community. It should not be the case that 'a Portuguese subject committing murder is quite safe from the ordinary punishment', simply as result of the Portuguese government's 'strong opinions against Capital Punishment'.[82]

In other cases, appeals by non-European monarchs to Victoria demonstrated the royal pattern of mercy. In Ethiopia, according to Major William Harris in 1844, King Sahle Selassie of Shewa, releasing long-imprisoned royal relations who were, by tradition, kept in prison, instructed the British representatives to tell Victoria, 'that though far behind the nations of the white men from whom the nation of Ethiopia first received her religion there yet remains a spark of Christian love in the breast of the King of Shoa'.[83] Readers might encounter other instances of regal mercy: it would be an interesting task to uncover tales of non-European princely mercy as reported in the British press in the Victorian era and consider what these meant (extolling the benevolence of heathen princes by way of contrast with the violence of Christians?). Sarah Lushington's account of the ambitious, Westernizing Ottoman vassal, Mehmet Ali of Egypt, in 1829, spoke of the sultana's benign influence:

> That such an arbitrary ruler should be in a great measure governed by a woman, could not have been expected: yet he suffered his late wife to infuse even a tincture of clemency into his administration ... esteemed beloved by the people; for her influence was ever employed on the side of justice and mercy. Much of her time was occupied in receiving petitions.[84]

John Caunter's *India* in 1836 had a character, begging mercy of a new monarch, comment, 'I need not tell you that mercy is the brightest jewel in the regal sceptre. It is the axiom of every country where sovereigns reign and people are obedient.'[85]

7

Victoria Humana: Representing Victoria as Merciful

> *She is, one may fearlessly say without danger of being accused of exaggeration or flattery, the model of a constitutional sovereign. Her influence, the extent of which can hardly be over-estimated, has always been exerted on the side of justice, mercy, and humanity.*[1]

This study has examined royal mercy in British culture from the start of the eighteenth century to the close of the Victorian era, exploring the reality and perception of this mercy from the reign of the Georges to the death of Victoria, in response to sedition, rebellion, and capital crimes such as murder and forgery. Regal mercy supposedly followed the divine pattern and figured as an intelligible simile for conveying the subtleties or majesty of Christian redemption. It was an instrument of colonial rule. Acts of royal mercy could be related to gendered moral attributes or disposition in the reign of a queen regnant and helped elaborate or dramatize female power and characteristics.

This brief chapter returns to artistic treatment of the sovereign's performance of mercy briefly touched on in the book's Introduction, firstly by examining the neo-classical sculptor John Gibson's commission to depict the queen in the rebuilt Palace of Westminster. I then study associations made between a female monarch represented as compassionate or sympathetic and the many 'little wars' waged in her name. To do this, I examine three artefacts: beginning with another statuary group (a famous depiction of Boudicca) that could be said to invoke Victoria, turning to a campaign medal linking vengeance with the queen, and a private royal commemorative gift which praised female acts of mercy in the context of war. Despite sustained aggression, Victoria's era was assessed by Britons as merciful in spirit and practice, its mercy claims associated with the queen. The opening quotation of this chapter is one such estimation, from the *Boys' Journal* in 1867.

Depicting contemporary and historic royal mercy

The queen's exercise of mercy was presented as natural in a woman, for a host of nineteenth-century writers. The art critic and social commentator John Ruskin's *Sesame and Lilies* (1864) famously called for women to wield queen-like powers of redemption and mercy. The throne of female power was founded on justice and ascended only on steps of mercy, he stated.[2] Taking its cue from Ruskin's imagery, this section explores representations of the merciful queen in works of art, such as sculpture, and visual sources, such as engravings.

The idea of the virtues enthroned took three-dimensional form in a seven-foot-high Carrara marble Victoria sat between embodiments of justice and clemency (those 'two best prerogatives of the British crown'[3]) within the heart of the parliamentary complex. This group was created by John Gibson of Rome for the Prince's Chamber in the Houses of Parliament and news of its creation was reported from late 1852. It was intended as instruction to monarchs, following advice to the Fine Arts commissioners in 1844: 'That, if allegorical figures should be excluded from the halls and galleries of the Houses of Parliament, yet it might not be improper that in the Queen's Porch, the eyes of the Sovereign should first be met by statues emblematic of Religion, Justice, Mercy, and Fortitude.'[4] Recent commentary makes the group emblematic of the 'Albertine' project, linking the monarch with the technological and commercial progress of the age through Gibson's sculptural relief decoration of the plinth (commerce and industry are just visible in Figure 7.1, underneath the throne); or sees in the figures and their positioning in the antechamber to the Lords a symbolic expression of the constitution, the very 'model of a constitutional sovereign', to refer back to this chapter's opening epigraph.[5] Representations of Gibson's work appeared in illustrated newspapers in early 1857, after the queen and various courtiers were shown round the Prince's Chamber with Gibson's figures in situ. Engravings and photographs of the statuary appeared in guides to Westminster and Victorian jubilee books.[6]

The queen referred to it as her 'colossal statue … The conception is fine, but I do not like the likeness'.[7] Prince Albert had proposed two accompanying allegorical figures and suggested the emblematic subjects 'as the sovereign is a lady'. Gibson wrote for the benefit of visitors: 'The expression of Justice is inflexible, whilst that of clemency is full of sympathy and sadness – sad for the constant sins which come to her knowledge, but with lenity she keeps the sword sheathed, and offers the olive branch, the sign of peace.'[8] *The Land We Live In*, an illustrated historical guide to the British Isles, commented of the statuary in the mid-1850s,

> a true thought to be suggested at a good time when the sovereign is passing beneath; but which loses much of its force, when we reflect how little personal influence or responsibility remains to our sovereigns, in matters of state justice and state mercy: her ministers are the men who should take the lesson to heart: we hope they will.[9]

The plaster statues of clemency and justice were among Gibson's bequest to the Royal Academy.[10] George Cruchley's guide to London described it as 'the famous group in marble' in the 1860s, but for decades in the twentieth century, the flanking personifications were separated from the royal figure.[11]

This exile echoed the contemporary embarrassment with the execution of the allegory, and perhaps the claims of the allegory itself. If unsurprisingly, given Prince

Figure 7.1 'Marble group in the Prince's Chamber, House of Lords. Her Majesty Queen Victoria. Supported by Justice and Clemency. John Gibson, R.A., Sculptor', *Illustrated London News*, 7 March 1857, p.207. Wood engraving. Author's collection. (The engraving was reproduced, *Illustrated Weekly News*, 12 December 1863, p.409. A version by Loudan appeared also in *Illustrated Times*, 18 April 1857, p.249.)

Albert's presidency, the eleventh report of the Fine Arts Commission claimed the group 'deserved and received general approbation', art critics in the public journals were unconvinced.[12] They were critical of the group's scale and the mismatch between the relative simplicity of Gibson's neo-classical design and the chamber's ornamentation. Several focused positive comments on the figure of clemency: 'stamped by that thoughtful but passionless melancholy that best suits the allegoric impersonation of a great principle', for *The Critic*, 'tender and almost divine expression ... is such as to defend this group', for the *Art-Journal*.[13] The *Athenaeum* was unimpressed by the symbolism of the sheathed sword as a 'presentiment of Clemency' and was later snide about this 'least fortunate production ... a composition upon which other generations will look with amazement'.[14] Not everyone was clear about what was allegorized: the queen herself called the figure 'mercy' in her journal, Augustus Hare thought it was judgement and mercy in his *Walks in London* and during the international exhibition in London in 1862 Gibson's grouping was misidentified as representing justice and peace.[15]

The queen's underwhelmed response to Gibson's work matched uninterest in extending the representation of clemency in royal residences. The royal residences were unadorned by mercy's representation, although Buckingham Palace had statues of the virtues and possibly Baron Carlo Marochetti was commissioned to produce a statue of Victoria later described as 'La Reine de la Paix' at the time of the Crimean war: wielding royal sceptre and olive branch from her throne and supposed to embody (in the words of a French critic) 'le genie de la Paix et de l'Abondance'.[16] Yet the presentation of the queen surrounded by embodiments of justice and mercy (and thus, in a sense, being the balance of these two qualities) exists within a larger visual history of monarchical mercy and the monarch supported by mercy.

The frontispiece of the 1569 edition of the 'Bishops' Bible', for instance, displayed Elizabeth crowned by 'mercie' and 'iustice' and similarly classical embodiments of fortitude and prudence. In our period a European genre of historical art showed the ruler bestowing or withholding mercy. One wonders what the impact of imagery of monarchs reluctantly signing death warrants (Mary I, Elizabeth, and Charles I) was on the popular misconception of Victoria's death warrants.[17] There were also images of monarchs implored for clemency, as in the case of Hannah's lurid rendition of the Countess of Nithsdale's desperate act, mentioned in an earlier chapter, or the women clasping a king in the 'rude times of early Scotch history' in John Faed's 'The Justice of the King'.[18]

Other instances, with a similar theme of the intercessory queen consort, from earlier English history and engraved on several occasions in the eighteenth and nineteenth centuries, included Richard II's queen Anne of Bohemia entreating the Duke of Gloucester for Sir Simon Burley's life in 1388. The most prominent was Philippa of Hainault imploring Edward III for mercy towards the Calais burghers in 1347, as recounted by the chronicler Jean le Bel. Eighteenth-century students of English history could see renderings such as the American-born artist Benjamin West's in 1788 and engravings in Russell's *History of England*. The artist Richard Westall – the princess Victoria's drawing master – sketched the scene.

It was a familiar episode for Victorians. The Victoria Lobby of the new House of Lords depicted the scene of intercession in plaster over the fireplace.[19] Victoria dressed as Philippa for a court ball in May 1842 in which Albert naturally appeared as Edward and Edwin Landseer depicted the couple in these roles in a splendid painting. Prints reproduced the dramatic event in Calais: the Art Union's engraving of the queen's intercession appeared in the *Illustrated London News* (Figure 7.2; with a poem following, 28 February 1846).[20] John Leech rendered it as a comic scene in a series of historical pictures. Marcus Stone's painting of Philippa's intervention was reproduced by the wood engraver Dalziel in 1862. Sir John Gilbert's version also appeared as engraving.[21] New technologies presented the scene when Julia Margaret Cameron depicted the event in photographic tableau in 1860 and in 1911 when Pathé filmed *Le Siege de Calais*.[22]

Gibson's group was placed in an anteroom to the Lords with a series of architectonic portraits of the Tudors: the viewer of his colossal representation of the monarch might have contrasted her with the merciless Henry VIII, whose spousal victims were among those depicted. Historical royal contrasts, male and female, also sprang to the minds of critics of capital punishment. Thus the non-conformist minister George Murphy, in the republican *Reynolds's Newspaper* in 1864 after Samuel Wright's execution, wondered if he was living 'in the time of the Tudors or of the Stuarts, or indeed in

Figure 7.2 'The Art-Union Prize Cartoon, by Mr Selous. – "Queen Philippa Interceding for the Burgesses of Calais"', wood engraving of prize-winning design by H.C. Selous in *Illustrated London News*, 7 February 1846, p.96. Author's collection.

the reign of some monarch of times gone by'.[23] For others, the record in capital cases signified a 'good queen's reign' by contrast with Bloody Mary, Elizabeth I, or Victoria's male Hanoverian forbears, and was matched with the record of Queen Anne.[24] The Chartist *Northern Star* charted 'progress' in jurisprudence from the age of Queen Bess in an essay 'Past and Present Aspect of the Criminal Code' in January 1845.[25] Douglas Jerrold contrasted Victoria and Elizabeth in the *Illuminated Magazine*'s first (May 1843) number (see Figure 7.3). The present age of maudlin sensibility lacked such wholesome monitors of morality as the rotting cadavers of the executed, he ironized. Why the Elizabethan royal prerogative was more awful was plain: the king of beasts was a carnivore; the queen's prerogative 'was for the most part fed upon flesh'. It would be instructive to try and calculate how many 'noses, and arms, and hands, and human heads, and quarters of human carcases, which – during the merry, golden reign of Elizabeth, of those days we shall never see again – were required by law to keep strong and lusty the prerogative of the Virgin Queen!'[26] The radical George Reynolds's *Canonbury House, or the Queen's Prophecy* (1858) criticized the Tudor queen's claim to mercy in the midst of anti-Catholic oppression.[27] Victoria herself passed judgement, it being reported that as a child she 'pronounced Elizabeth a bad queen'.[28]

Americans discoursing on female power in the 1860s also made a contrast, which touched on mercifulness or otherwise, between the politically impotent Victoria, Mary Tudor, and her sister Elizabeth, a 'most merciless, capricious and unjust tyrant'.[29] Comparisons closer in time might be odious. For Christopher Wordsworth, nephew of the poet who published sonnets on the death penalty, writing in the late 1840s,

Figure 7.3 John Leech, 'Elizabeth and Victoria', *The Illuminated Magazine*, May 1843, p.3. Image courtesy the University of Plymouth, Rare Books Collection.

'Queen Victoria, by not condemning people to death for those offenses whose penalty was death in the reign of George III, condemns her grandfather as a murderer of his subjects.'[30] In 1853 in *Woman's Record or Sketches of All Distinguished Women*, the New England writer Sarah Josepha Hale compared Victoria with George III: 'vaunted as the good king … It is notorious that he delighted in signing death-warrants, and never would grant a pardon to the condemned unless driven by the greatest importunities.' By contrast Victoria pardoned 'even against the remonstrances of her advisers and so painful to her is the signature of her name to the death penalty that she has been relieved from the duty though the delight of the pardoning power'.[31] The 'lone and widow'd one', in verse of 1862, was praised as the 'monarch mild and merciful as nation e'er hath known'.[32] The Quaker 'T.F.' in the *British Friend* in 1864, in discussing capital punishment, gestured towards the 'good reign of Queen Victoria'.

Figure 7.4 'Mercy v Justice'. A commentary on the reprieve for Thomas Burke, in *Judy, or the London Serio-Comic Journal*, 5 June 1867. © The British Library Board. General Reference Collection P.P.5270.c.

Although I leave discussion of Britain's relationship to Ireland in the discourse of mercy to my wider study, it would be remiss of me to ignore the compelling image of Victoria mercifully deciding the fate of an American Fenian terrorist, Thomas Burke, in *Judy*, the new and cheaper satirical rival to *Punch*, 5 June 1867 (see Figure 7.4). Not at all like the idealized queen of Gibson's neo-classical masterpiece, in her widow's weeds, Victoria stays the hand of a blind Justice ready to execute the prostrate, noose-haltered, and hand-shackled 'general' Burke. The accompanying verse contrasts the monarch's awful authority with 'Woman's pity'.[33] Coupled with the cartoon's title, the artist (Matt Morgan) presents the queen as mercy herself, her black-silk clothing offering an appropriate background to the naked sword and a contrast with the white-clothed virtue.

The idea of a merciful queenship may be linked with the trope of the tearful new monarch, as expressed in Elizabeth Barrett Browning's 'Victoria's tears' of 1838. As the British capital-punishment abolitionist Susannah Beedle wrote, 'Our beloved Queen wept when she became Queen, and well she might with this subject before her.'[34] The queen's more mature maternal sensitivities were also stressed – many references to the queen's motherhood in petitions for mercy have been cited in this study. For the Whig politician and memoirist George Russell, in retrospect, the queen's motherly heart was in 'keen sympathy' with various reforms (he listed restriction of capital punishment alongside reform of penal code, abolition of duels, prohibition of brutal, and degrading sports).[35] This was also in keeping with that treatment of the queen as 'gentle', from her accession to her demise.[36]

Mercy and queenship at war

The selection of clemency, rather than wisdom, as the second attribute to associate with the monarch in Gibson's commission, was suggested by Prince Albert because of the queen's gender.[37] One verse allusion to the Gibson sculpture, by the hymnist Elizabeth Colling ('Well was the Sculptor skilled to trace | Thy fairest friends thy fitting place'), came during the Indian rebellion.[38] The monarch's feminine attributes – for 'Pardon and Peace' in Colling's words, were complicated by her role as head of the army. This chapter on the artistic representation of the monarch concludes with the competing representations of mercy and vengeance in the context of queenship in war. I begin with the figure of Boudicea (Boudicca), ruler of the Iceni people.

In the early-seventeenth-century tragedy by Francis Beaumont and John Fletcher, *Bonduca*, the ancient Briton scorned mercy and love as 'sins in Rome and Hell', and she was a challenge to dramatists of female nature in the eighteenth century.[39] Victoria, whose name was seen as the Latin equivalent of the Celtic Boudicca, was compared to her advantage before and after her accession with her vengeful regal forbear.[40] There is no evidence from her diary that she felt an association: though the inspection of a coin of the Iceni queen by the princess on her tour of York was noted in 1835 and a cartoonist early in her reign had her leading Daniel O'Connell and Lord John Russell captive, as the 'modern queen Boadicea'.[41] For George Jones in 1843, Boadicea acted as a model for Elizabeth, but Victoria outstripped these queens' heroism when faced by regicide, 'for its true Courage and Patriotism, – Religious dependence, – pure Heroism, and her royal Mercy to the convicted regicide, – will bear a triumphant comparison with any renowned record in the Annals of Antiquity'.[42]

Samuel Maunder's biographical dictionary of 1839 encapsulated the sense of contrast in its subtitle, *From the Rude and Warlike Days of Boadicea to the Victorian Era*.[43] In 1854 one writer claimed never to pass the 'classic and unsavoury district of Battle Bridge', where Boudicea was supposed to have been finally defeated, 'without feeling gratefully assured that it is better to live under the constitutional sway of Victoria even with the double income tax annexed than to have been subject to her namesake ... with double scythes upon her chariot wheels'.[44] Dialogue between child and father compared the queens in the Reverend Giles's *Story Book of English History* ('*Papa*. There is no one for her to fight with now, my dear, it is peace all over the world', was the assertion in this work published in the year of the Great Exhibition).[45]

Boadicea's plight attracted many artists, including competitors designing frescos for the rebuilt Houses of Parliament, such as Henry Selous (in 1843), whose rendering of the intercessory Philippa is reproduced above. The group modelled in the 1850s by Thomas Thornycroft became the lasting Victorian representation of Boadicea. One commentator thought the subject was fitting for he was 'the sculptor of Victoria the Great', creating an equestrian statue for the Great Exhibition, reproduced in reduced scale for the Art Union of London. A colossal version for Liverpool in 1869 showed the queen 'in half-military costume, such as she used to wear when visiting the [army] camp at Chobham'.[46] Victoria's features, idealized, are perhaps echoed in Boudicca, but the artist resisted close parallels between the two queens. This was unsurprising given the Celtic warrior queen was hardly a pattern of Christian submission or, in the conduct of her revolt, a figure of humanity and mercy.

The figures of the 'British Queen' and her daughters were admired in Thornycroft's studio by Prince Albert, who sent horses to be modelled for the group and tried to interfere in the design (as with the Gibson statuary).[47] After a trial display in plaster at the meeting place of the Victoria Embankment and Westminster Bridge, from late 1897 (see Figure 7.5), the colossal group was erected outside Parliament shortly after the queen-empress's death and in the context of the Boer War in 1902. Among the subscribers for the bronze casting was Frances Power Cobbe the feminist, who pointed out the Latin version of the Celtic queen's name. The Welsh folklorist Marie Trevelyan's *Britain's Greatness Foretold*, published during the war and featuring Thornycroft's group as frontispiece, also noted the 'coincidence of the two imperial names'.[48] The *Woman's Signal* bewailed the London County Council's apparent reluctance to memorialize 'one of our British heroines', while *Fun* imagined that contemporary figure of the 'new woman' would use the site as a feminist rallying point.[49]

As the Thornycroft statuary suggested, Victoria was also a 'warrior queen', closely involved with military affairs. During the Crimean War, one observer described her as gripped by military mania.[50] This conflict mobilized ideas about British justice and mercy under the monarch's command: as Eleanora Hervey claimed in a poem reproduced in many newspapers in 1854: 'She heard, and bade her legions go | At Mercy's tender pleading'.[51] True, she was represented in art performing such traditional female roles as visiting wounded soldiers and performed other acts of mercy towards

Figure 7.5 'The Statue of Queen Boadicea, to be placed on the Thames Embankment', *The Sketch*, 28 January 1898, p.9. Author's collection.

those injured in war. She demonstrated esteem for Florence Nightingale by presenting a brooch designed by Prince Albert and made by the royal jewellers Garrard, with the 'feeling' legend, 'blessed are the merciful' in 1855 (see Figure 7.6).[52]

Press accounts of this artefact were in keeping with the royal effort to capture some of the attention attracted to Nightingale during the conflict, by showing that Nightingale's sympathy was 'also that of the highest person of this realm'. 'NO ONE', a letter from her own hand, leaked to the press, asserted, '*takes* a warmer interest, or feels *more* for their sufferings ... than their Queen'.[53] The press recorded that the jewel was 'worn not as a brooch ... but rather as the badge of an Order'. Indeed, patronage of

Figure 7.6 'The Nightingale Jewel', *Illustrated London News*, 2 February 1856, p.109. Author's collection. The accompanying text explains, 'in diamonds are the letters "V.R" and the Royal crown; from the centre issue gold rays, implying Heavenly sympathy'.

the Royal Red Cross for ladies, an order founded in 1883 whose cross had the words 'faith', 'hope', and 'charity', brought to the sovereign's notice 'acts of mercy in attending to the sick or wounded in time of war'.[54] Appropriately, although Nightingale may have preferred a more practical gift for Scutari, when she was memorialized after her death in 1910, the same beatitude appeared above her low-relief representation in St Paul's cathedral.[55]

While there was 'Victoria Beatrix' and 'Victoria humana', there was also 'Victoria vindex', the avenger, the title appearing on the Afghan campaign medal of 1842 (Figure 7.7). David Urquhart, critic of Britain's foreign policy, thought its inscription was 'painful and humiliating … The Sovereign of England an avenger on brave men of the crime of defending their homes and hearths', and a lecturer, the former Chartist Christian and now Baptist, Arthur O'Neill of Birmingham, deplored the 'gentle and noble queen' being associated with the campaign, in a lecture on the bombardment of Canton and war with Persia in 1857.[56] Later, about the same medal, O'Neill commented, 'the Queen's name was used, although she was a most kind-hearted creature, and had a most tender regard for human life'. But as Miles Taylor comments, 'No British monarch before or since has been so indelibly linked to the representation of war in the colonial theatre'.[57] The queen's early gift of mercy towards a military deserter was one of the

Figure 7.7 Obverse of the second form of the Afghanistan medal in bronze, designed by William Wyon (1842). Metropolitan Museum of Art, accession X.14.23. Image assigned public domain status. https://www.metmuseum.org/art/collection/search/208753.

reign's anecdotes: one rare instance of Victoria's appeal for mercy in the punishment of male offenders came in the context of a recipient of the Victoria Cross.[58]

The Gibson sculptural group, the *Judy* representation, and the artefacts of queenly vengeance entailed the wielding, sheathing, or turning away of the sword. When G.K. Chesterton argued for the continuing importance of symbols of mercy in 1913, he observed of the coronation ritual that the blunted sword of mercy, however we might judge its human bearer, remained relevant.[59] The concluding chapter looks at Victoria's two successors as participants in the ritual of coronation, in rounding off this study of the throne of mercy.

Conclusion

> *We know how painful and impossible Queen Victoria felt it to be to sign the official document that condemned a murderer to death. That is the true woman's view, though women may theoretically agree that capital punishment is a necessity.*[1]
>
> *I think Queen Victoria would have been yet more popular and satisfying if she had never signed a death warrant.*[2]

Royal mercy in the age of Edward VII and George V

The two comments beginning this concluding chapter represent assessments in the year of George V's accession, when the coronation ritual that established a reign in mercy and justice was enacted. The first is from that curiously entitled periodical *The Nineteenth Century and After* in an essay on suffragettes by the positivist Frederic Harrison's wife. The second was by G.K. Chesterton, in a short essay against enfranchising women, entitled 'The Queen and the Suffragettes'. The wisdom of the monarch's removal from the death penalty's operation through king-in-council examined in Chapter 1 was recognized by early Victorian statesmen: removing the sovereign from personal implication in unpopular decisions.[3] Despite this, those fables about the queen's involvement in acts of mercy in criminal cases had 'gone the rounds of most of the pulpits of the country for the last half century', a newspaper correspondent noted in 1899.[4] The possibility that the queen *was* still involved fascinated newspaper inquirers. That Chesterton laboured under this misapprehension of personal involvement in the death penalty merely indicates the long survival of this public error.

Eulogies to the dead monarch across the British Empire asserted her mercifulness.[5] A reign of self-devotion made true Isaiah's prophecy: 'In mercy, shall this throne be established.'[6] Loyal addresses to the new king gestured towards the legislative reforms of the Victorian era, 'all of which have tended to clemency, combined with justice'.[7] Edward VII celebrated the replacement of a 'barbarous penal code', in 1907 when opening the new Central Criminal Court, Old Bailey: 'a more humane spirit … [u]nder the present laws the mercy shown to first offenders is, I am well assured, often the means of re-shaping their lives'.[8]

Sidney Lee's biography of the king (1927) noted the concern which he shared with his mother about royal prerogatives. Recalling the doodle by George Cruikshank from

1823, it is noteworthy that he resented being conceived as a 'mere signing machine' and was 'keenly interested in the prerogative of mercy, and examined with care the manner in which it had lately been exercised'.[9] Nowell-Smith states that 'he interfered much more vigorously than had his mother over the reprieve of criminals', but constitutional commentary considered it 'improbable ... that any Sovereign would now exercise the prerogative of mercy without having first taken his Ministers into his confidence and obtained their approval'.[10] The Home Secretary Aretas Akers-Douglas told him in September 1903, given Edward VII's interest in the 'maintenance or rehabilitation of all ancient royal prerogatives', that the partisan and radical press whipped up criticism of the Home Secretary in his mother's reign (as in the case of the Polish Jewish immigrant Israel Lipski, in 1887).[11] With 'yellow journalism' increasing, the monarchy was better out of the limelight in this sphere; the Home Secretary's duty was to receive the opprobrium.[12] The royal prerogative 'had thus become merely a royal interest', Lee wrote, but the royal interest was 'in no uncertain or spasmodic manner'.[13]

Even so, as the quotation from Chesterton shows, old errors lingered. A newspaper reported, when a murderer was not reprieved in February 1901, that this was the king's first death warrant.[14] Others, more knowing, admitted a merely nominal role and scorned such 'royal watching' as the Press Association's belief that hours spent with the Home Secretary during the Adolf Beck inquiry in 1904 showed the king's interest in this Norwegian who was wrongly sentenced to seven years' penal servitude in England due to mistaken identity in 1896.[15] The following comment appeared in the press:

> Only those who are about the Court know the desperate effort, which are made to get the Sovereign's influence for the revision of sentences alike by the high and low. Some of the petitions addressed to his Majesty at Windsor Castle are in illiterate characters, and would in their clumsy terms of courtesy be amusing if they were not pathetic. The King would be able to do nothing else were he to give time and attention to these things, and so to constitute himself a court of criminal appeal.[16]

As Herman Cohen's *The Spirit of Our Laws* suggested in 1906, the mercy prerogative, though a 'happy survival from primitive times', was now as 'highly organised as the machinery of punishment', from the same Home Office.[17] I have shown how the tradition of mercy at the time of coronations and anniversaries continued – so that in 1908 the king-emperor's name was associated with the release of prisoners to mark the fiftieth year of rule in India by the Crown.[18]

Royal mercy was reported in the form of pardons for Cape rebels after the Boer War, such as Colonel Arthur Lynch of the 'Irish Brigade', and bestowed on a German in Johannesburg when the Home Office refused to intervene.[19] But his inability to resist the claim of Cabinet collective responsibility prevented the king's pardoning power in the case of a young officer cashiered for cowardice.[20] There was the 'singular but delightful departure from established practice' when the remainder of a sentence was remitted on a prisoner, James Mannion, as a result of Queen Alexandra being implored by his elderly wife at Recess in Connemara, during a highly successful royal tour of Ireland in 1903.[21] Alexandra's role as 'angel-princess' on daily errands of mercy figured in public lore and royal biography: the Yale-educated former West Indies banker William Trowbridge's study of the queen emphasized the value of the quality of mercy and the right of personal appeal to the sovereign.[22] If royalty's right to exercise the prerogative was no longer as free, 'disuse had not yet atrophied its sense of pity'.[23] Edward VII's letters to his Home Secretaries in the cases of George Edalji, convicted of mutilating horses in Staffordshire – a notorious miscarriage of justice which interested Conan Doyle – and Horace Rayner, who was convicted of the murder of the founder of Whiteley's store in 1907 but reprieved on the grounds of insanity in 1907, are reprinted in Lee's biography. The king was critical of sentimental agitation to save criminals, identifying these with the agitations of the 'halfpenny press'.[24]

On the other hand, when mercy was denied, critics of unpopular death sentences (or opponents of capital punishment) still found mileage in shaming the state (whether British or colonial) by linking execution to royal mercy withheld. Thus the cattle duffer Patrick Kenniff, executed at Boggo Road Gaol in Brisbane in 1903 for the wilful murder of two policemen, was launched into eternity in clothes 'bearing the broad arrow of His Most Gracious Majesty King Edward VII … It was queer satire that the condemned man, who had fruitlessly appealed to his King to respite his execution, should be hanged in a gaol uniform the property of that king who knew not that HIS CLEMENCY HAD BEEN ASKED!'[25]

A new class of recipient for royal mercy appeared during Edward VII's reign: at least it was debated whether suffragettes were appropriate subjects of royal mercy as a category of prisoners.[26] When he died in 1910, there was the usual attempt to present the king as merciful, for instance the eulogy by a nonconformist minister in Truro reported, in the *Royal Cornwall Gazette*, that, every inch the king, beneath the robes of the ruler, 'there beat a heart in which the quality of mercy was enthroned'.[27] The courtier Lord Esher's character sketch of the late king in the *Quarterly Review* emphasized an innate kindness and forgiving disposition; tales of the king's humanity would circulate years after.[28] The *Saturday Review* praised his 'catholic humanity … Forgiveness is the prerogative of princes'.[29].

With the accession of George V (see Figure C.1), a new opportunity to display royal clemency appeared, since '[n]ot forgetting that mercy may season justice, he has extended a measure of reprieve to those who are in prison for offences against the law'. It was commented that this accession clemency was 'an echo of earlier days and other conditions, but it is nevertheless a happy thought which does his personal feelings all honour'.[30] The newspapers duly reported later instances – in the case of manslaughter and murder, exercised by the king or in Ireland by the Lord Lieutenant, in the era before the Great War. In the Staffordshire town of Walsall, the majestic language of a free royal pardon for a woman charged with petty larceny, dated 29 November 1913, was reported complete with reference to Blackstone's *Commentaries* and thoughts on the necessary role of the monarch in pardoning.[31] When the driver Samuel Caudle was given a free pardon in the same year, after conviction for manslaughter in a railway accident that claimed the lives of sixteen people, newspapers explained, in the altered circumstances of the creation of the Court of Criminal Appeal in 1908, what this meant.[32]

'The King … one may be sure, has … his father's leaning towards clemency', an editorial on British rule in India in the *London Daily News* suggested in May 1910,

Figure C.1 'The Sword of Mercy. Coronation 1911'. Cigarette card in 'Coronation Series 1911. Published by Salmon and Gluckstein of London. Author's collection.

stimulated by a suggestion for release of political prisoners such as Bal Gangadhar Tilak and Aurobindo Ghosh sent by the nationalist Lajput Rai, who emphasized the connection between 'kingship with unbounded mercy and unsurpassable generosity'.[33] The defence of British rule was seen in the 'comprehensible fact' of a king, 'vivid embodiment of righteousness in high places', for the 'eastern mind'. Rai asserted: 'Orientals always connect kingship with unbounded mercy and unsurpassable generosity. It is customary for kings to signalise their accession to the throne by acts of clemency.' 'Would not the present be a singularly well-chosen occasion to make generous bid for the hearts of the people of India?' the London newspaper asked.[34]

Imperial acts of mercy by colonial governments *were* related to the accession and reported as 'the first official act' of the reign. In India 'national work of mercy' by the princely rulers had already been praised by the king when as Prince of Wales he toured India during the famine in 1905.[35] The king-emperor's visit was also praised by the Indian National Congress president, for acts of 'clemency and generosity' in 1911. 'The Indian people', said Bishan Narayan Dar, 'have seen their Sovereign, and have been touched to appreciate his boundless generosity, his deep and touching regard for their true welfare, his great justice, and his mercy, which is even greater'.[36]

The appeal to the king during and after the First World War is a topic for another study.[37] Contrast was made with the Kaiser's mercilessness: the 'Hohenzollern throne will totter and fall, if for no other reason, because its strength is never tempered with mercy … It is as true today as when Isaiah said it that in mercy shall the throne be established'.[38]

Mercy and British culture: concluding remarks

This book studied mercy in its British monarchical associations, operations, and usages over the 'long nineteenth century', with some necessary glances back to earlier periods. Monarchy's centrality as a symbol is further demonstrated when turning to other challenges to mercy's exercise in the British state and British world. The monarchy was present in the discussion involving viceroys and royal proclamations of mercy and pardon in rebellion in Ireland. The king was mobilized in the patriotic struggle in the era of revolution and Napoleon, when mercy figured as a powerful element of British propaganda. The royal family played a significant part in the war effort during twentieth-century conflicts.[39] My larger study of mercy examines these theatres for 'large-scale' mercy: moving from Ireland, through the wider history of empire, and encompassing British warfare and global conflict from the American and French revolutions to the atomic age. *Mercy and British Culture, 1760–1960* ends in post–Second World War Britain, with a culture that displayed continuities in the way mercy was presented with earlier eras. Kingship's religious element, the bearing of 'Christian witness' which Philip Williamson stresses in studying the twentieth-century monarchy's relationship to public values, was one reason why mercy remained part of public discourse – if only in the hushed tones of commentators on coronation ritual.[40] One royal biographer, writing in 1921, was convinced that the mercy of the state 'is purely mechanical and impersonal … no longer a case of some wretched, powerless individual appealing to the clemency of some other all-powerful individual'.[41] Personal pity was replaced by the machinery of the democratic state. And yet for monarchists, a status as moral touchstone remained evident in the latter years of George V's reign: explained by Shakespeare's 'king-becoming graces', which included mercy.[42]

Notes

Introduction

1. My second book on mercy explores the historiography and scholarship on mercy, in the context of associated historical, literary, and philosophical studies of emotions and virtues (such as *pity*) in more detail, but see M.B. Dowling, *Clemency and Cruelty in the Roman World* (Ann Arbor, MI: University of Michigan Press, 2006); D. Quint, *Montaigne and the Quality of Mercy: Ethical and Political Themes in the 'Essais'* (Princeton, NJ: Princeton University Press, 1998); D. Punter, *Literature of Pity* (Edinburgh: Edinburgh University Press, 2014); A. Tuckness and J.M. Parrish, *The Decline of Mercy in Public Life* (New York: Cambridge University Press, 2014), G. Sanchez, *Pity in Fin-de-Siècle French Culture: 'Liberté, Égalité, Pitié'* (Westport, CN: Praeger, 2004). A recent work is M. Bull, *On Mercy* (Princeton: Princeton University Press, 2019).
2. E. Smedley, H.J. Rose, and H.J. Rose, eds, *Encyclopaedia Metropolitana, or, Universal Dictionary of Knowledge* (London: Fellowes, 1845), vol.22, p.104; and *Encyclopaedia Perthensis; Or Universal Dictionary of the Arts, Sciences and Literature* (2nd edition; Edinburgh: Brown, 1816), vol.14, p.459, 'Tenderness; goodness; pity; willingness to spare and save; clemency; mildness; unwillingness to punish' and 'a virtue that inspires us with compassion for our brethren, and inclines us to give them assistance in their necessities. Mercy is also taken for those favours and benefits that we receive either from God or man, particularly in the way of forgiveness of injuries or of debts'. For the second definition, J. Ogilvie, *The Imperial Dictionary, English, Technological, and Scientific* (London: Blackie, 1871), vol.2, p.154, 'there is perhaps no word in our language precisely synonymous with mercy'.
3. The phrase 'mercy's sway' is in numerous poems, e.g. J. Beattie, *The Minstrel; or, The Progress of Genius. Book II* (London: Dilly, 1774), p.11 – with love; C.A.B. Bruce, *Poems* (Calcutta: privately printed, 1846), p.81; J. Green, *Claverton Church-yard, and Other Poems* (Bath: Hayward, 1851), p.29; R.B. Beverley, *The Redan, a Poem* (2nd edition: London: Hamilton Adams, 1856), p.51; R. Young, *Poetical Works: Comprising Historical, Agricultural, and Miscellaneous Poems* (Londonderry: for the author, 1863), p.172. The phrase 'mercy's reign' appears in H. More, *Slavery, A Poem* (London: Cadell, 1787), p.14; M.C. Hume, *The Bridesmaid, Count Stephen and Other Poems* (London: Chapman, 1853), p.127; E.L. Edmunds, ed., *The Life and Memorials of the Late W.R. Baker* (London: Tweedie, 1865), p.112.
4. R. Pearsall, *Night's Black Angels: The Forms and Faces of Victorian Cruelty* (London: Hodder and Stoughton, 1975). For a transatlantic perspective, see M. Abruzzo, *Polemical Pain: Slavery, Cruelty, and the Rise of Humanitarianism* (Baltimore: Johns Hopkins University Press, 2011) and her review, 'The Rights of Dependents and The Wrongs of Cruelty: Animals, Children, and the Sympathetic State', *Reviews in American History* 40: 4 (December 2012), pp.617–22. For earlier history, see J.A. Steintrager, *Cruel Delight: Enlightenment Culture and the Inhuman* (Bloomington:

Indian University Press, 2004); D. Baraz, *Medieval Cruelty: Changing Perceptions, Late Antiquity to the Early Modern Period* (Ithaca: Cornell University Press, 2003).

5   E.g. S. Butler, *The Mercy of God; Especially Considered with Reference to Our Present Situation. A Sermon Preached at St. Julian's, Shrewsbury. Sept. 14, 1800* (Shrewsbury: Eddowes, 1800); C. Lawson, *Sermons Delivered in the Chapel of the Foundling Hospital, London* (London: Parker, 1834), sermon on Micah vi.8.

6   D. Hay, 'Property, Authority and the Criminal Law', in D. Hay, P. Linebaugh, J.G. Rule, E.P. Thompson, and C. Winslow, *Albion's Fatal Tree: Crime and Society in Eighteenth-Century England* (London: Allen Lane, 1975), pp.17–63 [p.63]. For recent critique, see R.R. Sullivan, 'The Warwick School's Challenge and the Rule of Law', in *Liberalism and Crime: The British Experience* (Lanham: Rowman & Littlefield, 2000), ch.8.

7   S. Smiles, *Self Help; with Illustrations of Character and Conduct* (London: Murray, 1859), p.333 refers to gentlemen merciful to their animals; *Character* (1872; London: Murray, 1876), p.165, on women as merciful, while p.14 characterizes the energetic but noble man as merciful. On mercy's absence from 'Victorian values' debate, see e.g. J. Walvin, *Victorian Values* (London: Deutsch, 1987).

8   See J. Gregory, D.J.R. Grey, and A. Bautz, eds, *Judgment in the Victorian Age* (Abingdon: Routledge, 2019), pp.3–39.

9   L. Throness, *A Protestant Purgatory: Theological Origins of the Penitentiary Act, 1779* (Aldershot: Ashgate, 2008), discusses 'godlike' attributes of the monarchy in English justice and theology, noting, p.96, that the 'royal pardon held clear spiritual overtones'.

10 'Law and Gospel', *On and Off Duty*, October 1886, p.156. Other Victorian-era examples of this simile include: A.N. Beamish, *The Christian Visitor's Companion* (London: Wertheim, Macintosh and Hunt, 1858), p.34; W. Fetherston H., *Primeval symbols, or The Analogy of Creation and New-Creation* (Dublin: Hodges, Smith, 1862), p.356. The philosopher Martha Nussbaum's *Anger and Forgiveness: Resentment, Generosity, Justice* (New York: Oxford University Press, 2016), characterizes one Western conception of mercy as 'monarchical', p.206.

11 *The Examiner*, 30 December 1838, p.3.

12 W.M. Punshon, *The New Handbook of Illustration; or, Treasury of Themes, Meditations* (London: Eliot Stock, 1874), pp.272–6.

13 R. Philip, ed., *The Works of John Bunyan: With an Introduction to Each Treatise, Notes, and a Sketch of His Life, Times, and Contemporaries* (3 vols; Glasgow: Blackie, 1850), vol.1, p.642.

14 G. Stevenson, *A Dissertation on the Atonement. In Three Parts* (Philadelphia: Towar, 1832), p.113.

15 For other references to the phrase 'mercy is the brightest jewel in the diadem of God', see O. Winslow, *The Lord's Prayer: Its Spirit and Its Teaching* (London: Shaw, 1866), p.265, W.B. Cadogan, 'God's Mercy to the Fatherless. A Sermon' (1786), reprinted in *Discourses of the Honourable and Reverend W. B. Cadogan. To Which Are Now Added Short Observations on the Lord's Prayer, and Letters to Several of His Friends* (London: Rivington, 1798).

16 *Blackburn Standard*, 5 January 1895, p.8.

17 Praise for Tsar Alexander's mercy refers to Pity or an angel's tear as the brightest gem in his diadem, W-T. FitzGerald, 'The Tyrant's Downfall', *Gentleman's Magazine*, May 1814, p.487. For references to non-European monarchs' mercy, see F. Gladwin,

'Description of the Time and Manner in which Justice is administered by the upright Monarch', in *The Persian Moonshee* (London: Wilson, 1801), p.54.

18 See J. Forster, *Eminent British Statesmen*. vol.6 *Oliver Cromwell* (London: Longman, Rees, Orme, Brown, and Green, 1847), p.304.

19 A. Munich, 'Dressing the Body Politics', ch.3 in *Queen Victoria's Secrets* (New York: Columbia University Press, 1996), p.74; A. Ponsonby, *Henry Ponsonby. Queen Victoria's Private Secretary* (London: Macmillan, 1942), p.79.

20 Based on works read to her thirteenth year, in G.T. Houston, 'Reading and writing Victoria: The Conduct Book and the Legal Constitution of Female Sovereignty', ch.9 in M. Homans and A. Munich, eds, *Remaking Queen Victoria* (Cambridge: Cambridge University Press, 1997), pp.177–81. Thus [Mary Hughs] *Aunt Mary's Tales* (London: Darton, Harvey and Darton, 1819) used the analogy of human 'condescension to notice or show mercy to these little animals', p.40; *Claudine: Or Humility the Basis of All Virtues*, with its several references to 'God of Mercy' and the merciful Power, who 'wounds in mercy'; E. Helme, *Maternal Instruction; or, Family Conversations, on Moral and Entertaining Subjects, Interspersed with History, Biography, and Original Stories… The Second Edition* (London: Longman and Rees, 1810), on mercy not shown by Edward at his deathbed, p.252; Mary Tudor and the mercy of her short reign, pp.137–8; and the show of mercy by canons of Rouen Cathedral, p.211; S. Trimmer, *A Description of a Set of Prints of English History: Contained in a Set of Easy Lessons, Part 2* (London: Baldwin, Cradock and Joy, 1817), pp.40–1 on Essex's execution and the queen's vacillation about mercy; and p.187 on Anne, 'a pattern of domestic virtues and a mild and merciful princess during whose reign no subject's blood was shed for treason'; E. Ward, *The Reciter: A Work Particularly Adapted to the Use of Schools; Consisting of Pieces Moral, Religious and Sacred, in Verse and Prose* (London: Hatchard, 1812), various references to mercy, e.g. Earl of Cromertie in 1746, pleading for mercy to George II, and Cowper on mercy in his poem on Alexander Selkirk. On Victoria and religion, W.L. Arnstein, 'Queen Victoria and Religion', in G. Malmgreen, ed., *Religion in the Lives of English Women, 1760–1930* (London: Croom Helm, 1986).

21 The sovereign is asked whether he or she will 'cause law and justice in mercy to be executed in all your judgements', see ch.1, endnote 25. Guides include *The Coronation of Victoria, Queen of England, In Westminster Abbey, June 28, 1838: A Historical Chronicle of the Inaugural Rites, State Pageantry, Regalia, Solemn Services, Religious Ceremonies, &c.* (London: Painter, 1838). For early-nineteenth-century interpretations of regalia and coronation, see J. Dennis, *A Key to the Regalia; or, The Emblematic Design of the Various Forms Observed in the Ceremonial of a Coronation* (London: Hatchard, 1820); A. Taylor, *The Glory of Regality. An Historical Treatise on the Anointing and Crowning of the Kings and Queens of England* (London: Taylor 1820). For a recent study, see R. Strong, *Coronation: A History of Kingship and the British Monarchy* (London: HarperCollins, 2005).

22 RA VIC/MAIN/QVJ (W), 28 June 1838, Princess Beatrice's copy, has no mention of mercy.

23 R.B. Brett, ed., *The Training of a Sovereign. An Abridged Selection from 'The Girlhood of Queen Victoria', Being Her Majesty's Diaries Between the Years 1832 and 1840* (New York: Longmans, Green, 1914), p.175.

24 See G.E. Buckle, ed., *The Letters of Queen Victoria. Second Series. A Selection from Her Majesty's Correspondence and Journal Between the Years 1862 and 1885. In Three Volumes. Vol. 2. 1870–1878* (London: Murray, 1926), p.101, p.198, p.582; *More Leaves*

from the Journal of a Life in the Highlands, from 1862 to 1882 (5th edition; London: Smith, Elder, 1884), p.401.
25 *Brighton Gazette*, 18 December 1862, p.8; *Werner's Magazine* 29/30:1 (1902), p.713 (phonographic recording) and C. Mahajan, *Intermediate Poetry Selections* (Lahore: Uttar Chand Kapur, 1944). The art historian Anna Jameson's treatment of Portia (published in 1832) was a significant intervention: J. Hankey, 'Victorian Portias: Shakespeare's Borderline Heroine', *Shakespeare Quarterly* 45: 4 (Winter, 1994), pp.426–48.
26 RA VIC/MAIN/QVJ (W), Prince Beatrice's copy, 5 January 1877.
27 *Sheffield Independent*, 31 May 1889, p.2. Her diary for 26 April 1889 does not mention the incident in her account.
28 *Morning Chronicle*, 1 July 1845, p.5.
29 William Riviere's 'Act of Mercy', *Civil Engineer and Architect's Journal*, July 1844, p.257; *A Critical Examination of the Cartoons, Frescos, and Sculpture, exhibited in Westminster Hall. To Which Is Added the History and Practice of Fresco Painting. By Henry G. Clarke, Assisted by Eminent Artists* (London: Clarke, 1844), p.15.
30 *Art Journal*, August 1844, p.238.
31 *Illustrated London News*, 21 August 1847, p.117.
32 On this fresco, and the competition, see R. Simpson, *Sir John Tenniel. Aspects of His Work* (Rutherford, NJ: Fairleigh Dickinson University Press, 1994), p.38, which also discusses his design 'Spirit of Justice', 1845. Other fresco designs included William Thomas's 'Justice', see F. Summerly, *A Handbook for the Architecture, Tapestries, Paintings, Gardens, and Grounds of Hampton Court… New Edition* (London: Bell and Daldy, 1862), p.115: Justice sat between Moses, with the 'Laws of Condemnation', and the Baptist, with the New Testament of mercy.
33 *Art Journal*, 1 November 1865, p.334.
34 'Robert Browning's Poems', *English Review* 11 (March–June 1846), pp.354–86 [p.370]. The play was performed at the Haymarket in April 1853.
35 J-L-H. Campan, *Memoirs of the Private Life of Marie Antoinette, Queen of France and Navarre: To Which Are Added, Recollections, Sketches and Anecdotes, Illustrative of the Reigns of Louis XIV, Louis XV, and Louis XVI* (London: Colburn, 1823), vol.1, p.439.
36 J. Plunkett, *Queen Victoria: First Media Monarch* (Oxford: Oxford University Press, 2003), p.35.
37 See *Friends' Intelligencer*, 1861, p.182; see also 'E.A.S.', speaking of a woman's 'tearful eye' in verse, 'To Queen Victoria', *Southern Literary Messenger* (Richmond, VA), June 1839, p.369; for a later reference, see J. Campbell, *V.R.I. Queen Victoria: Her Life and Empire* (London: Eyre and Spottiswoode, 1901), p.73. Reviews of Victoria's writings such as *Journal of Our Life in the Highlands* noted the 'woman's heart' revealed, e.g. *Literary World* 15 (1884), p.58.
38 *Leeds Mercury*, 13 February 1866, p.7: a letter defending Baptist missionaries there from blame for the rebellion. The Reverend George William Gordon's letter before execution contrasted his hopes for the justice of the 'righteous and merciful Queen' with that of slave owners and planters, *Leeds Mercury*, 4 December 1865, p.4. The Royal Proclamation of general amnesty and pardon, issued 'in our Royal clemency and mercy', was prepared by the attorney general in Victoria's name, 30 October 1865. The 'Queen's Advice', 30 June 1865, issued by the Colonial Office, was one of the expressions of support for planters, which contributed to the rebellion.
39 *Bath Chronicle and Weekly Gazette*, 7 June 1832, p.4.
40 Review of Caroline H. Spear, *A Brief Essay on the Position of Women* (London: Trübner, 1866) in *Victoria Magazine* 7, August 1866, p.373.

41 See K.T. Brown, *Mary of Mercy in Medieval and Renaissance Italian Art: Devotional Image and Civic Emblem* (London: Routledge, 2017).
42 'A Tale', *Cambridge University Magazine* 1: 3, November 1839, pp.165-74 [p.173].
43 J. Ruskin, *Sesame and Lilies. Two Lectures Delivered at Manchester in 1864* (London: Smith Elder, 1865), pp.180-1; see also 'Mr Ruskin on Books and Women. Part II', *Victoria Magazine* 6, December 1865, p.136.
44 M. Greenwood, 'Degrees of Guilt', *Woman's Herald*, 7 January 1893, p.2; H. McIlquham, 'Women in Local Administration', *Woman's Herald*, 23 March 1893, p.74; 'A Female Freeholder', *The Lady Overseer: A Pamphlet with Notes on Country Life, Natural History, and Women's Rights* (London: Richardson, 1874); 'The Duties of Matron and Schoolmistress', *Women and Work*, 7 November 1874, p. 3 (from *Labour News*).
45 Debate on London Government Bill, House of Lords, see *Morning Post*, 27 June 1899, p.2.
46 'A Voice from the Jewel Cage in the Crystal palace', *Punch*, 14 June 1851, p.254. Verse in *Leicester Journal*, 4 April 1873, p.3, the diamond in Victoria's diadem glitters with her people's love, surpassing the Koh-i-noor; *John O' Groat's Journal*, 26 July 1877, p.6, describes her as 'Britain's Koh-i-noor'.
47 M. Taylor, *Empress: Queen Victoria and India* (New Haven: Yale University Press, 2018), p.7;
48 S.M. Latif, *History of the Punjab from the Remotest Antiquity to the Present Time* (Calcutta: Calcutta Central Press, 1891), p.629.
49 W. Somervile, *The Chace, a Poem* (3rd edition: London: Hawkins, 1735), pp.95-6.
50 *Globe*, 5 July 1887, p.7. On royal mercy noted in the context of animal welfare, in support of RSPCA, see 'The Queen on Cruelty to Animals', *John o' Groats Journal*, 2 July 1874, p.4.
51 Letter XVI, 'Of Public Education irrespective of Class-distinction', 30 March 1867, *Time and Tide, by Weare and Tyne: Twenty-five Letters to a Working Man of Sunderland on the Laws of Work* (London: Allen and Unwin, 1867), p.110
52 W. Allingham, *Day and Night Songs* (London: Routledge, 1854), p.71.
53 *It Is Never Too Late to Mend*, quoted in N. Rance, *Wilkie Collins, and Other Sensation Novelists: Walking the Moral Hospital* (Rutherford: Fairleigh Dickinson University Press, 1994), p.78.
54 Reported in *London Evening Standard*, 7 March 1876, p.3.
55 *The Referee*, 26 June 1887, p.1.
56 *Baptist Magazine*, September 1837, p.400, excerpting pamphlet by C. Stovil, *National Bereavement Improved a Sermon Occasioned by the Death of His Most Gracious Majesty King William the Fourth* (London: Jackson and Walford, 1837).
57 [J. Lhotsky] *Era Victoriae Humanae. The Era of 'Queen Victoria the Humane': A Narrative and Philosophical Retrospect of the Earlier Years of Her Majesty's Life and Her Reign, etc. By a German Metaphysician* (London: privately printed, 1847), p.12.
58 F. Mason, *The Story of a Workingman's Life: With Sketches of Travel in Europe, Asia, Africa, and America, as Related by Himself* (New York: Oakley, Mason, 1870), p.320, also quoted in *The Friend, or, Advocate of Truth*, September 1874, p.75.
59 *The Spectator*, 22 July 1843, p.683.
60 E.g. *Yorkshire Evening Post*, 12 August 1896, p.2.
61 *Huddersfield Chronicle*, 9 September 1880, p.3.
62 'A Royal Pattern', *Sunday Magazine*, 1 November 1866, pp.127-8. For images, see *Down with the Crown*, p.45, Fig. 8, 'The Queen Visiting Her Poorer Neighbours', on

her visit to Kitty Kear on the Balmoral estate. See T.F. Ball, *Queen Victoria: Scenes and Incidents of Her Life and Reign* (Toronto: Willard Tract, 1888), p.131, on visiting the poor; Wilson, *Life and Times of Queen Victoria*, vol.2, p.413, Mary Lightbody Gow's 'At Balmoral: A Morning Call'.

63 *Belfast Newsletter*, 27 December 1897, p.8. See also R. Temple, 'The Reign of Queen Victoria', *Cosmopolis*, June 1897, pp.621–36 [p.632].
64 F.G.V. Lawford, *Our Queen, and Other poems* (London: Digby, Long, 1895), p.2.
65 *Reynolds's Newspaper*, 2 September 1855, p.8.
66 *Reynolds's Newspaper*, 8 December 1889, p.4.
67 'The Queen's Love of Animals', *The Mercury* (Hobart), 30 June 1883 [p.2].
68 *Pall Mall Gazette*, 1 February 1901, p.2.
69 D. Thompson, Queen Victoria (1990; London: Virago, 2001), p.134.
70 C. Badger, *Friendly Admonitions to Parents, and the Female Sex in General; with Reflections on Moral and Religious Subjects; Intended for the Benefit of the Rising Generation* (London: Cadell and Davies, 1803), p.122.
71 'O.B.' *The Times*, 10 May 1842, p.6.
72 'Mercy's Reign', *Ballymena Observer*, 30 July 1864, p.1; *Banner of Ulster*, 30 July 1864, p.4.
73 F.W. Farrar, *Mercy and Judgment: A Few Last Words on Christian Eschatology, with Reference to Dr. Pusey's 'What Is of Faith?'* (London: Macmillan, 1881), p.130.
74 L.C. Berry, *The Child, the State and the Victorian Novel* (Charlottesville/London: University Press of Virginia, 1999), p.133, on J. Brownlow, *History and Objects of the Foundling Hospital* (London: Warr, 1858); and K. Ledbetter, on Hope and Mercy in the iconography of *Magdalen's Friend*, in *British Victorian Women's Periodicals: Beauty, Civilization and Poetry* (New York: Palgrave Macmillan, 2009), p.88.
75 T.E. Jordan, *Victorian Childhood: Themes and Variations* (Albany, NY: SUNY Press, 1987), p.145, the legislation was passed in 1840.
76 F.K. Brown, *Fathers of the Victorians: The Age of Wilberforce* (Cambridge: Cambridge University Press, 1961), p.323; *Literary Panorama*, December 1812, col.1021; *Fund of Mercy: Or an Institution for the Relief and Employment of Destitute and Forlorn Females* (London: Philanthropic Society, 1813).
77 A.W. Barber, 'The European Law of Torture', *Popular Science*, March 1894, pp.648–60 [p.660].
78 R. Percy and S. Percy, *Percy Anecdotes. Anecdotes of Crime and Punishment* (London: Boys, 1822), p.5.
79 T.B. Macaulay, *The History of England: From the Accession of James the Second* (1848; Philadelphia: Butler, 1849), ch.3, 'State of England in 1685', p.290.
80 J. Kirkpatrick, 'The Victorian Era. (First Half: 1837–65)', *Atalanta* vol.5 (1891), pp.173–7 [p.174].
81 *Belfast Newsletter*, 19 September 1848, p.1, reprinting from *Britannia*. See use of 'mercy' in *Humane Review*, e.g. C. Heath, 'Blake as Humanitarian', *Humane Review* 7 (April 1906 – January 1907), pp.73 [p.77].
82 [G.W. Steevens], 'The New Humanitarianism', *Blackwood's Edinburgh Magazine* 163: 987 (January 1898), pp.98–106 [p.104].
83 G.K. Chesterton, *The Napoleon of Notting Hill* (London: Bodley Head, 1904), p.16.
84 [T. Hughes] *Tom Brown's Schooldays, by an Old Boy* (3rd edition, Cambridge: Macmillan, 1857), p.25.
85 C. Dickens, *The Life and Adventures of Martin Chuzzlewhit* (London: Chapman and Hall, 1844), p.10; 'oh, what a charming name of such a pure-souled being as the youngest Miss Pecksniff!'

86 Listed in census returns for 1851, registration district Stockport, HO/107/2154 (this and trends estimated from census data accessed via ancestry.co.uk).
87 RA VIC/MAIN/QVJ (W), Princess Beatrice's copy, 7 June 1839.
88 See H. Lacey, *The Royal Pardon: Access to Mercy in Fourteenth-Century England* (York: York Medieval Press, 2009). For earlier reference to kingship, mercy, and 'Christianisation of the royal duty', see W.A. Chaney, *The Cult of Kingship in Anglo-Saxon England: The Transition from Paganism to Christianity* (Berkeley: University of California Press, 1970), p.256
89 M. Villeponteaux, *The Queen's Mercy: Gender and Judgment in Representations of Elizabeth I* (New York: Palgrave Macmillan, 2014), pp.3–6; on Gloriana's face, A. Riehl, *The Face of Queenship: Early Modern Representations of Elizabeth I* (Palgrave Macmillan, 2010), p.115
90 C. Herrup, 'The King's Two Genders', *Journal of British Studies* 45: 3 (July 2006), pp.493–510 (p.506).
91 K.J. Kesselring, *Mercy and Authority in the Tudor State* (Cambridge: Cambridge University Press, 2003). See p.20, for critics such as Sir John Elyot, *The Boke of the Governour* (1531), influenced by Seneca's *Clemency*. For mercy in Mary's reign, see S. Duncan, '"Most Godly Heart Fraught with al Mercie": Queens' Mercy During the Reigns of Mary I and Elizabeth I' ch.3 in C. Levin and R. Bucholz, eds, *Queens and Power in Medieval and Early Modern England* (Lincoln: University of Nebraska Press, 2009), pp.31–50 and S. Duncan, *Mary I: Gender, Power and Ceremony* (New York: Palgrave Macmillan, 2012).
92 Kesselring, *Mercy and Authority*, p.20. For Puritan ideas on mercy and justice, see W. Perkins, *Epieikeia, or a Treatise of Christian Equity and Moderation* (Cambridge: Legat, 1604); and the English-born American Puritan, Edward Taylor's *Gods Determination Touching His Elect* (c.1680), which figures a dialogue between mercy and justice.
93 The Roman ideal of clemency and moderation in victory is extolled in *The Method of Teaching and Studying the Belles Lettres* (Edinburgh: Drummond, Donaldson, Bell, Eliot, 1773), p.88.
94 E.H. Shagan, *The Rule of Moderation: Violence, Religion and the Politics of Restraint in Early Modern England* (Cambridge: Cambridge University Press, 2011). J. Grose, *Ethics, Rational and Theological: With Cursory Reflections on the General Principles of Deism* (London: the Author, 1782), p.138 on moderation as 'the refinement of wisdom, – the quintessence of policy, the ornament of truth, – the laurels of unequalled honour, – the throne of justice, – and the seat of mercy'. See 'Moderation in Judging and Punishing', *London Magazine Appendix to 1754*, pp.585–6.
95 Shagan, *Rule of Moderation*, p.7, p.9.
96 For European perspective, see M. de Waele, 'Conflict Resolution Under the First Bourbons', in A. Forrestal and E. Nelson, eds, *Politics and Religion in Early Bourbon France* (Basingstoke: Palgrave Macmillan, 2009), pp.142–53.
97 K. Sharpe, *Rebranding Rule: The Restoration and Revolution Monarchy, 1660–1714* (New Haven, CT: Yale University Press, 2013), p.473, see also p.173 on justice as the 'principal royal virtue', damaged by civil war. This work comments on mercy in Restoration politics, e.g. pardon for Cromwellian George Downing, p.151; and Declaration 'to All His Loving Subjects', 26 December 1662, p.30.
98 Herrup, 'The King's Two Genders', p.509.
99 Sharpe, *Rebranding Rule*, p.220.
100 Ibid., p.239, p.254.
101 Ibid., p.259.

102 D. Hay, 'Property, Authority and the Criminal Law', in *Albion's Fatal Tree*, pp.17-63. See also L. Sebba, 'Clemency in Perspective', in S.F. Landau and L. Sebba, eds, *Criminology in Perspective: Essays in Honor of Israel Drapkin* (Lexington, MA: Lexington Books, 1977).
103 Hay, 'Property, Authority and the Criminal Law', p.54
104 Ibid., p.39, p.49.
105 Ibid., p.45. For discourse associating mercy with royal paternalism, see *Philomathic Journal* 4:2 (1826), p.323, on 'mitigation or a remission of the penalties of the law when it would ill become the sovereign, as the father of his people, to close his ears against the voice of one of his children imploring for mercy'.
106 Hay, 'Property, Authority and the Criminal Law', p.47.
107 Ibid., p.52: C. Jenkinson to the Recorder of London, 22 May 1761, from the National Archives (hereafter TNA), State Papers 44/87, fos.19 and 20.
108 Hay, 'Property, Authority and the Criminal Law', p.62.
109 Ibid., p.40.
110 Ibid., p.42.
111 Ibid., p.51.
112 J.M. Beattie, *Crime and the Courts in England, 1660-1800* (Oxford: Oxford University Press, 1986); and 'The Royal Pardon and Criminal Procedure in Early Modern England', *Historical papers/Communications historiques* 22: 1 (1987), pp.9-22; 'The Cabinet and the Management of Death at Tyburn after the Revolution of 1688-1689', ch.12 in L.G. Schwoerer, ed., *The Revolution of 1688-89: Changing Perspectives* (Cambridge: Cambridge University Press, 1992).
113 R.M. Andrews, *Law, Magistracy, and Crime in Old Regime Paris, 1735-1789*, vol.1 (Cambridge: Cambridge University Press, 1994), p.408.
114 E. Giloi, *Monarchy, Myth, and Material Culture in Germany, 1750-1950* (Cambridge: Cambridge University Press, 2011), p.17. On royal mercy in a Spanish imperial context, see V. Uribe-Uran, *Fatal Love: Spousal Killers, Law, and Punishment in the Late Colonial Spanish Atlantic* (Stanford: California: Stanford University Press, 2015), ch.5.
115 D.T. Andrew and R. McGowen, *The Perreaus and Mrs. Rudd. Forgery and Betrayal in Eighteenth-Century London* (Berkeley, CA: University of California Press, 2001).
116 See R. Shoemaker, *The London Mob: Violence and Disorder in Eighteenth-century England* (London: Hambledon and London, 2004), p.267, for the Old Bailey proceedings, tracts, and newspaper accounts of cases and trials.
117 C. Strange, ed., *Qualities of Mercy: Justice, Punishment, and Discretion* (Vancouver: University of British Columbia Press, 1996), p.3.
118 E. Cobden, *The Blessedness of the Merciful: A Sermon Preached Before the Sons of the Clergy at Their Anniversary Meeting in the Cathedral-Church of St Paul, April 14, 1743* (London: Cooper, 1743), p.27.
119 F. Prochaska, *Royal Bounty: The Making of a Welfare Monarchy* (New Haven: Yale University Press, 1995).
120 M.B. Lowndes, *His Most Gracious Majesty King Edward VII* (London: Grant Richards, 1901), p.291.
121 R. Williams, *The Contentious Crown: Public Discussion of the British Monarchy in the Reign of Queen Victoria* (Aldershot: Ashgate, 1997); A. Taylor, '*Down with the Crown': British Anti-Monarchism and Debates About Royalty Since 1790* (London: Reaktion, 1999).

122 Williams, *The Contentious Crown*, ch.7.
123 On Alfred, see eulogy in S. Warren, *The Lily and the Bee: An Apologue of the Crystal Palace* (London: Blackwood, 1851), p.130: in which 'I see upon thy brow a jewelled crown, with Mercy, Justice, Valour, Wisdom, Truth and Piety, so richly studded'. See also S. Keynes, 'The Cult of King Alfred the Great', *Anglo-Saxon England* 28 (1999), pp. 225–356.
124 Taylor, *Down with the Crown*, pp.41–5, p.83. For response to male homicide in this period, see M.J. Wiener, 'The Sad Story of George Hall: Adultery, Murder, and the Politics of Mercy in Mid-Victorian England', *Social History* 24: 2 (1998), pp.174–95, which focuses on another case in 1864 where reprieve was granted after mass campaigning.
125 J. Vernon, *Politics and the People: A Study in English Political Culture, c.1815–1867* (Cambridge: Cambridge University Press, 1993).
126 P.T. Murphy, *Shooting Victoria: Madness, Mayhem, and the Rebirth of the British Monarchy* (New York: Pegasus Books, 2012).
127 Plunkett, *Queen Victoria*, p.2.
128 Ibid., p.7.
129 M. Taylor, 'The British Royal family and the Colonial Empire', in R. Aldrich and C. McCreery, eds, *Crowns and Colonies: European Monarchies and Overseas Empires* (Manchester: Manchester University Press, 2016), pp.27–50 [p.30]; Taylor, *Empress*.
130 See S. Carter and M. Nugent, ed., *Mistress of Everything: Queen Victoria in Indigenous Worlds* (Manchester: Manchester University Press, 2016), p.4; H. Sapire, '"We Have Seen the Son of Heaven? We Have Seen the Son of Our Queen": African Encounters with Prince Alfred on His Royal Tour, 1860', ch.1 in the collection, referring to memories in the 1947 royal tour, p.25; S. Rosenberg, '"The Justice of Queen Victoria": Boer Oppression, and the Emergence of a National Identity in Lesotho', *National Identities* 3: 2 (2001), pp.133–53 (p.136).
131 B. Meyler, *Theaters of Pardoning: Sovereignty and Judgment from Shakespeare to Kant* (Ithaca: Cornell University Press, 2019).
132 T. McGeary, *The Politics of Opera in Handel's Britain* (Cambridge: Cambridge University Press, 2013), p.244.
133 Joseph Reed's 'Mercy', in *Tom Jones, a Comic Opera: As It Is Performed at the Theatre-Royal in Covent-Garden* (London: Becket and De Hondt, 1769), p.54, asserts 'Sweet Mercy is the loveliest flower'.
134 See J. Reddington, ed., *Calendar of Home Office Papers of the Reign of George III: 1760–1775; Preserved in Her Majesty's Public Record Office* (London: Longman, and Trübner, 1878), on dissatisfaction at royal mercy, see letter of the home secretary Halifax to the former MP for Hampshire and Winchester, Paulet St John, 31 March 1764, p.399; and his successor, Earl of Sandwich to the same, in the case of James Heathwood, 18 August 1764, p.439. The case of Richard Williams and William Pearse is discussed in *Calendar of Home Office Papers of the Reign of George III. 1766–1769, Preserved in her Majesty's Record Office* (London: Longman, and Trübner, 1879), pp.187–8 in a letter from the Earl of Shelburne to Humphry Morice, 30 September 1767, setting out the king's position in relation to judge's reports in cases outside the capital.
135 Petitions for mercy, addressed to the monarch or Home Secretary for exercise of the royal prerogative, are in TNA, Criminal Petitions, HO17, covering England and London in 1819–1858. Appeals to, recommendations for, and judgements on their status as deserving of royal mercy are part of the phraseology of some petitions and

their official processing. I studied these via digitized copies through findmypast.co.uk, e.g. HO17/126/2, John Owen of Colchester, sentenced to transportation for larceny, gestured to 'Royal Clemency which is so inate [sic] in your Majesty'; and reference to the 'infancy of a New Reign... the pardon of our Youthful and most Generous Queen', HO17/126/3, in petition from the wife of a fraudster Richard Charles Claremont Smythe Parker (23 August 1837). The HO17/3/130 catalogue description indicates in the case of Samuel Taylor, sentence commuted to transportation for burglary, the monarch's mercifulness was one of the grounds pled. Digitization makes accessible other sources for clemency in criminal cases: judges' reports on criminals HO47 (1784–1830).

136 The Georgian Papers include essays or notes on the law, extracted from his reading of William Eden and others, by George III (RA GEO/ADD/32/1040, *c*.1771–1805).

137 *Kentish Gazette*, 24 March 1812 [p.3]. *Hull Packet*, 24 March 1812, p.4. Skene was married to the widow of the Earl of Fife.

138 On earlier petitions, F. Dabhoiwala, 'Writing Petitions in Early Modern England', ch.6 in M.J. Braddick and J. Innes, eds, *Suffering and Happiness in England 1550–1850: Narratives and Representations; A Collection to Honour Paul Slack* (Oxford: Oxford University Press, 2017), pp.145–7.

139 *Lincolnshire Chronicle*, 17 August 1838, p.2.

140 *Universal Magazine of Knowledge and Pleasure*, May 1761, p.273; see *Old Bailey Proceedings Online* (www.oldbaileyonline.org, version 8.0, 7 September 2019), *Ordinary of Newgate's Account*, April 1761 (OA17610420), for transcript of the Ordinary's Account, 20 April 1761.

141 In literature memorializing Elizabeth, e.g. *England's Mourning Garment; Worn Here by Plain Shepherds, in Memory of Their Sacred Mistress, Elizabeth; Queen of Virtue, While She Lived; and Theme of Sorrow, Being Dead* (London, by V.S. for Thomas Millington [1603]).

142 J. Bowles, *Thoughts on the Late General Election as Demonstrative of the Progress of Jacobinism* (3rd edition; London: Rivington, 1802), p.75.

143 *Monmouthshire Merlin*, 27 October 1838, p.1.

144 *Rural Repository*, 9 May 1846, p.137: 'Where for a thousand years is a Howard among her kings, or an Elizabeth Fry her queens?' This was reprinted from *Christian Parlor Magazine*, January 1845.

145 C. Jerrold, *The Early Court of Queen Victoria* (New York: Putnam, 1912), p.vi.

146 R. Finnegan, *Why Do We Quote?: The Culture and History of Quotation* (Cambridge: Open Book Publishers, 2011), p.261; W. Benjamin, fragment in *Das Passagen Werk*, cited in H.D. Harootunian, 'The Benjamin Effect: Modernism, Repetition, and the Path to Different Cultural Imaginaries', ch.4 in M.P. Steinberg, ed., *Walter Benjamin and the Demands of History* (Ithaca: Cornell University Press, 1996), p.76.

147 The paraphrastic mode is queried in M. Jay's semi-critical defence, 'Two Cheers for Paraphrase: The Confessions of a Synoptic Intellectual Historian' reprinted in *Fin-de-siècle Socialism and Other Essays* (New York: Routledge, 1988). On quoting, the 'quotingful' and 'citation-imbued' writing of academia, R. Finnegan, *Why Do We Quote?* appendix 1, p.280. In relation to 'historiographic narratology', A. Munslow, *The Future of History* (Basingstoke: Palgrave Macmillan, 2010), p.195 describes extensive direct quotation as a 'buoyancy aid' for historical meaning, 'deployed as a means to directly connect the interpretation to the source'.

148 G. Clark, review of K. Thomas, *The Ends of Life: Roads to Fulfillment in Early Modern England* (2009), *Journal of Economic History* 71: 1 (March 2011), pp.236–7; and also

review of same by V. Evener, *Journal of Religion* 91: 4 (October 2011), pp.548–50 [p.549]. See also the penetrating review by L. Jordanova of *Man and the Natural World: Changing Attitudes in England 1500–1800*, in *Comparative Studies in Society and History* 29: 1 (January 1987), pp.195–200; T. Harris, reviewing *The Ends of Life* in *Journal of Interdisciplinary History* 41: 3 (Winter 2011), pp. 421–33 [p.423, p.430]; and R. Porter, reviewing Thomas's *Man and the Natural World*, in *Historical Journal* 28: 1 (March 1985), pp.225–9 [p.228]. Thomas defends his method in *The Ends of Life* and 'Diary', *London Review of Books*, 32: 11, 10 June 2010, pp.36–7. I am stimulated to make these reflections by the observations of my publisher's anonymous reader.

149 Williams's definition of keywords in *Keywords: A Vocabulary of Culture and Society* as 'significant, binding… in certain activities and their interpretation' is therefore relevant to the chapters that follow on the language of mercy in the exercise or advocacy of royal (and for example, judicial or juror) mercy.

150 J. Ree notes the tendency to consensus from 'thousands of particulars', in Thomas's methodology: 'Civilizing Efforts', *History Workshop Journal* 87 (2019), pp.294–300 [p.296].

151 D.T. Rodgers, 'Keywords: A Reply', *Journal of the History of Ideas* 49: 4 (October – December 1988), pp.669–76 [p.669]; M. Leja, 'Keyword', *American Art* 23: 1 (Spring 2009), pp.34–5, notes that in the digital era the keyword is 'fundamental to our very processes of formulating questions', p.34.

152 Rodgers's definition in 'Keywords: A Reply', of 'keyword' is helpful: a word mattering enough for it to be the subject of conflict to control it, 'for the power to redefine, redeploy, and gain possession,' and containing 'profound ambiguities, possibilities, and antagonism'. In the ideal of mercifulness, the wielding of power which renders another at one's mercy, in the operation of mercy in criminal and social justice, and in imperial and military propaganda, the word fulfils Rodgers's threshold of 'burdens, transformations and conflict', p.672.

153 J.G.A. Pocock, 'Concepts and Discourses: A Difference in Culture? Comment on a Paper by Melvin Richter', in H. Lehmann and M. Richter, eds, *The Meaning of Historical Terms and Concepts. New Studies on Begriffsgeschichte* (Washington, DC: German Historical Institute, Occasional Paper No.15, 1996), p.53: concept history will be 'a diversity of synchronic histories of the ways in which [cognates of a word for a concept] have been used and made to perform a diversity of linguistic and other historical contexts'.

154 'Justice' appears in T. Bennett, L. Grossberg, and M. Morris, eds, *New Keywords: A Revised Vocabulary of Culture and Society* (Oxford: Blackwell, 2005), but not mercy, and B. Parekh's entry makes no reference to it.

155 Q. Skinner, 'The Idea of a Cultural Lexicon', revised as ch.9 in *Visions of Politics*, vol. 1 *Regarding Method* (Cambridge: Cambridge University Press, 2002), p.159 notes a concept may appear in texts that do not employ the word. Skinner argues a 'pre-existing language of moral principles' (p.174) exerts force: 'It is true that our social practices help to bestow meaning on our social vocabulary. But it is equally true that our social vocabulary helps to constitute the character of those practices.'

156 Methodological discussions of this approach in studies of single words include T. Dixon, *The Invention of Altruism: Making Moral Meanings in Victorian Britain* (Oxford: Oxford University Press for the British Academy, 2008), pp.38–9.

157 Rodgers calls this meaning found in 'verbal action', 'Keywords: A Reply', p.676.

158 M. Fortier, *The Culture of Equity in Restoration and Eighteenth-Century Britain and America* (Routledge, 2016), 'Introduction: Equity as a Keyword'. An appreciative review of Fortier's early study notes that even when such an exercise generates a 'catalogue-like' result, they are helpful for future scholars, B.J. Sokol, reviewing *The Culture of Equity in Early Modern England*, in *Notes and Queries* 54: 1 (March 2007), pp.99–102.

Chapter 1

1. Engraving by W.S. Leney after 'Northcoat', of the king with aureate crown surmounting the oval portrait; and design for *Royal Lady's Magazine and Archives of the Court of St James's* of 1832. L. Colley, *Britons: Forging The Nation, 1707–1837* (1992; New Haven: Yale University Press, 2005), p.223, reproduces one such mass-produced engraving.
2. Print based on Russell's portrait engraved by Joseph Collyer, published 4 June 1791, British Museum, Q, 2.7; mezzotints by John Fairburn, 'His Most Excellent Majesty Charlotte, Queen of Great Britain, &c. &c', British Museum, 2010, 7081.776 and companion piece of king, 1800, British Museum, 2010, 7081.775. (Queen Charlotte is an illustration for 'charity', A. Berquin, *L'amico dei fanciulli* (London: 1788–89), see British Museum, S,7.2.).
3. Engraving in *The Life of Princess Charlotte* (London: Kinnersley, 1818), before p.505.
4. Title-page engraving by James Johnstone of Edinburgh, to T. Stephens, *The Book of the Constitution of Great Britain* (Glasgow: Blackie, 1835).
5. The anti-radical *Palace of John Bull, Contrasted with the Poor 'House That Jack Built'*(London: Greenland, 1820) includes title page with balance, sword of justice, and constitutional texts; and justice in the temple of the constitution; see title-page image in *The House That Jack Built*; *The Real or Constitutional House That Jack Built* (London: Asperne, 1819); *The Loyalist's House That Jack Built* (9th edition; London: S. Knights, n.d.).
6. From Henry Brougham's account, *Historical Sketches of Statesmen Who Flourished in the Time of George III: To Which Is Added Remarks on Party and an Appendix* (Paris: Baudry, 1839), p.25, of George III's dealing with the 'Great Commoner' through pension and peerage – and from Brougham's quotation from Chatham's effusive description of the king's benevolence, 'the tone of feeling and even the style of diction in which a condemned felon having sued for mercy returns thanks when his life has been spared'.
7. T. Mortimer, *Lectures on the Elements of Commerce, Politics, and Finances: Intended as a Companion to Blackstone's Commentaries on the Laws of England* (London: Longman and Rees, 1801), p.288.
8. T. Hobbes, *Leviathan or the Matter, Forme, and Power of a Commonwealth Ecclesiastical and Civil* (London: Crooke, 1651), Part 2, ch.17, p.85: on 'Lawes of Nature (*as Justice, Equity, Modesty, Mercy*, and (in summe) *doing to others, as wee would be done to*) of themselves, without the terrour of some Power, to cause them to be observed, are contrary to our naturall Passions'.
9. 'Discourse 10. On the power of God', in S. Charnock, *Discourses upon the Existence and Attributes of God* (London: H.G. Bohn, 1853), p.396 [p.404].
10. L. Mercier, *Mon Bonnet De Nuit* (1784–5), translated as *The Night Cap* (London: Hookham, 1785), 2 vols, p.80, quoted in 'On Good Kings. From the French', *The*

       Times, 28 August 1789, p.1; *Universal Magazine of Knowledge and Pleasure* 81.567 (December 1787), p.363.
11   Tuckness and Parrish, *The Decline of Mercy in Public Life*, p.259.
12   *The Works of Jeremy Bentham. Published Under the Superintendence of His Executor, John Bowring* (Edinburgh: Tait, 1843), vol.9, pp.36–7.
13   P.B. Shelley, *Essay on Christianity*, published in *Memorials: From Authentic Sources Ed. by Lady Shelley. To Which Is Added an Essay on Christianity* (2nd edition; London: Smith, Elder, 1859), p.263.
14   'Of Mercy', *The Art of Knowing Mankind* (London: Wilkie, 1766), pp.204–13 [p.209].
15   *Family Expositor, or, a Paraphrase and Version of the New Testament* (1739; London: F. Westley and A.H. Davis, 1831), p.539, an observation quoted in other nineteenth-century works of exposition.
16   Henry Christmas, in letter read at an abolitionist meeting, *Worcestershire Chronicle*, 11 April 1849, p.3.
17   *Solicitors' Journal and Reporter*, 20 June 1857, p.564.
18   Modern histories include L. Radzinowicz, 'Commutation of Death Sentences Through the Exercise of the Royal Prerogative of Mercy', in *A History of English Criminal Law and Its Administration from 1750: The Movement for Reform, 1750–1833*, vol.1 (London: Stevens, 1948), ch.4. The chapter focuses on judges' roles and outlines the trends of thought about the royal prerogative by contrasting Beccaria (anti) with Blackstone (pro), and through a consideration of the penal reformers William Eden and Patrick Colquhoun. Radzinowicz concluded that 'George III paid great personal attention to many cases brought before him, often desiring to acquaint himself with all the circumstances which could bear upon his decision' (p.121). His prejudice in favour of capital punishment for forgery is made clear (p.122), citing J. Reddington, *Calendar of Home Office Papers of the Reign of George III. 1766–1769, Preserved in Her Majesty's Record Office* (London: Longman, and Trübner, 1879), p.326, letter of Lord Weymouth to John Calcraft, 14 April 1768.
19   N. Johnston, *The Excellency of Monarchical Government, Especially of the English Monarchy: Wherein Is Largely Treated of the Several Benefits of Kingly Government, and the Inconvenience of Commonwealths* (London: Clavel, 1686), p.91.
20   [C. Leslie], *A View of the Times, Their Principles and Practices* (London: 1708), from *The Rehearsal* (1707) and reprinted as 'Philalethes', in *A View of the Times. Their Principles and Practices: In the Rehearsals* (London: Bowen, 1750); it is quoted in T. Rennell, *The Ruinous Effects of Faction, Discord and Mutiny* (London: Rivington, 1797), p.23, p.25.
21   K. Digby, *Mores Catholici: Or, Ages of Faith* (London: Dolman, 1846), vol. 2, p.307, 'the simple symbolic forms of government, whether monarchical or republican, which prevailed during ages of faith, were more favourable to the development of mercy in public measures, than the complicated oligarchical constitutions'.
22   R. Acherley, *The Britannic Constitution: Or, The Fundamental Form of Government in Britain* (London: A. Bettesworth, 1727), pp.59–60.
23   *A Report of Some Proceedings on the Commission for the Trial of the Rebels in the Year 1746, in the County of Surry: And of Other Crown Cases: To Which Are Added Discourses upon a Few Branches of the Crown Law* (London: Brooke, 1792), p.284.
24   L. Vallone, *Becoming Victoria* (New Haven: Yale University Press, 2001), p.166.
25   W. Blackstone, *Commentaries on the Laws of England. Book the fourth. By William Blackstone, Esq. Solicitor General to Her Majesty* (Oxford: Clarendon Press, 1769), p.389. W.R. Prest, *William Blackstone: Law and Letters in the Eighteenth Century* (Oxford:

Oxford University Press, 2012); on Blackstone's clemency, see p.266. For the medieval oath in relation to mercy, see A. Spencer, 'The Coronation Oath in English Politics, 1272–1399', in B. Thompson and J. Watts, eds, *Political Society in Later Medieval England: A Festschrift for Christine Carpenter* (Woodbridge: Boydell and Brewer, 2015); E. Powell, *Kingship, Law and Society: Criminal Justice in the Reign of Henry V* (Oxford: Clarendon Press, 1989), pp.127–9, discussing Thomas Hoccleve's *Regement of Princes*. For reflections in the context of Catholic emancipationism, see J.J. Dillon, *An Essay on the History and Effect of the Coronation Oath: Including Observations on a Bill Recently Submitted to the Consideration of the House of Commons* (London: Collins, 1807). See J.B. Collins, *The State in Early Modern France* (Cambridge: Cambridge University Press, 1995), p.80, for the oath in French coronations.
26 Blackstone, *Commentaries.... Book the Fourth*, p.389.
27 Ibid., p.390.
28 Ibid., p.391.
29 A statue by J.F. Moore of 1777 on which porcelain figurines such as British Museum 1887, 0307, II.301, are based.
30 H. Arnot, *The History of Edinburgh, from the Earliest Accounts to the Present Time* (Edinburgh: Creech, 1779), p.486.
31 E. Nelson, *The Royalist Revolution: Monarchy and the American Founding* (Cambridge, MA: Harvard University Press, 2014), argues for some at least – 'patriot Royalists', imagining the new republic as headed by a strong chief magistrate who wielded the prerogative of mercy among other powers, rather than parliamentary supremacy, p.1, p.187. Alexander Hamilton discussed the 'Pardoning Power of the Executive', *New York Packet*, 25 March 1788: 'Humanity and good policy conspire to dictate, that the benign prerogative of pardoning should be as little as possible fettered or embarrassed', reprinted in *The Federalist. On the New Constitution* (2 vols; New York: Hopkins, 1802), vol.2, p.187. See J. Kent, *Commentaries on American Law* (8th edition; New York: Kent, 1848), vol.1, p.283. Blackstone, *Commentaries*, argued that 'in democracies, however, this point of pardon can never subsist'.
32 *The Looker On*, 35, 29 December 1792, p.277.
33 *The Duty of Submission to Magistrates, Recommended in a Sermon, Preached at the Assizes at Reading, before the Honorable Mr Justice Wilson and Mr Justice Grose, March 5, 1793* (Reading: Smart and Cowslade, 1793), p.84.
34 John Taylor's Prologue to the 'World in a Village', *Ipswich Journal*, 14 December 1793, p.4.
35 'Pardon', *Encyclopædia Britannica*, vol.13 (Dublin: Moore, 1795), pp.736–8, quoting *An Enquiry Concerning Political Justice* (1793) [p.737]. The entry on pardon in Dobson's Philadelphia edition (1798), vol.13, pp.736–8, makes no changes.
36 *The Tomahawk! Or, Censor General*, 25 December 1795, p.204.
37 'Farther proceedings respecting libels', *The Monthly Mirror of the Times* (August 1811), p.64.
38 'Republican Versus Royal Humanity', *Reynolds's Newspaper*, 29 August 1858, p.1.
39 *Illustrated London News*, 8 December 1849, p.379.
40 For 'reform era' defence of mercy as one of the 'great advantages and blessings of monarchy', see Stephen, *The Book of the Constitution of Great Britain*, p.231.
41 F. Hardie, *The Political Influence of Queen Victoria, 1861–1901* (London: Oxford University Press, 1935). On royal prerogative of mercy, R. Chadwick, *Bureaucratic Mercy: The Home Office and the Treatment of Capital Cases in Victorian Britain* (New York: Garland, 1992). On Victoria's political status in her era's imaginary, see G.T. Houston,

Royalties: The Queen and Victorian Writers (Charlottesville, VA: University Press of Virginia, 1999): 'her position as a high-profile anomaly brought constitutional notions of sovereignty into question' (p.23). On George IV, J.D. Potter, *The Fatal Gallows Tree. An Account of the British Habit of Hanging* (London: Elek, 1965), p.160 and – as a corrective – Gatrell, *The Hanging Tree*, pp.550 ff., the spectacular and successful attempt to secure a royal pardon, reported in *Law Times* 7 (1846), p.98, of a barrister John Sargent, under sentence of death in 1821 and thus left for execution for the crime of forgery.

42 *The Speeches of the Right Honourable William Huskisson, with a Biographical Memoir* (3 vols; London: Murray, 1831), vol.3, p.636.
43 'Art.10. The New Reign', *London Quarterly Review*, June 1837, pp.137–55 [p.154].
44 E.A. Smith, *George IV* (London: Yale University Press, 1999), p.211.
45 J.Q. Whitman, *Harsh Justice: Criminal Punishment and the Widening Divide Between America and Europe* (New York: Oxford University Press, 2003), p.165.
46 'The Prerogative of Pardon and the Punishment of Death', *Westminster Review*, April 1864, pp.185–95 [p.187].
47 'Home Office Inspiration', *All the Year Round*, 24 January 1863, p.467.
48 Ball, *Queen Victoria: Scenes and Incidents*, p.60; and A.E. Knight, *Victoria: Her Life and Reign* (London: Partridge, 1896), pp.78–9: 'if we may whisper a little secret, the Queen's tender heart is not to be trusted in such an awful business.'
49 Inicidentally *Death Warrant: A Reprinted Record of Facts* (London: F.A. Walker), a periodical published in 1844, later styled *The Death Warrant, or Guide to Life*, was intended to convey to readers the 'Grand Moral lesson' that in the midst of life we are in death; it campaigned for burial reform in London.
50 *An Essay on Crimes and Punishments: By the Marquis Beccaria of Milan. With a Commentary by M. de Voltaire* (Edinburgh: Donaldson, 1788), p.204.
51 V.A.C. Gatrell, *The Hanging Tree*, p.545; for Recorders (John Silvester, Newman Knowlys, Charles Ewan Law), see A.N. May, *The Bar and Old Bailey, 1750–1850* (Chapel Hill: University of North Carolina Press, 2003), p.150. See *John Bull*, 10 November 1828, p.356, on reports 'presented to the KING in the county of Middlesex – why such as exclusive clog upon the Royal prerogative of mercy should be inflicted either by law or custom it would indeed be difficult to determine'.
52 T.B. Howell, *A complete collection of state trials and proceedings for high treason and other crimes and misdemeanors : from the earliest period to the year present time*, (London: Hansard, 1812), vol.13, col.772, 'The court of England hath the least regard to petitions of any court in Europe'.
53 *Derby Mercury*, 9 July 1779, p.1.
54 *Sussex Advertiser*, 16 February 1829, p.2.
55 *Bristol Journal*, reported in *Salisbury and Winchester Journal*, 2 May 1825, p.2; and *Bristol Mirror*, in *Oxford Journal*, 30 April 1825, p.1.
56 See G.F. Rudé, *Hanoverian London, 1714–1818* (Berkeley: University of California Press, 1971), p.200, for background; *Annual Register*, and *Gentleman's Magazine* (Dublin: Exshaw 1770), April 1770 had notes relative to the executions of John Doyle and John Valline and quoted from *Genuine Copies of All the Letters Which Passed Between the Rt Hon the Lord Chancellor and the Sheriffs of London and Middlesex, and Between the Sheriffs and the Secretary of State Relative to the Execution of Doyle and Valline* (London: Davis: 1770), see p.239: 'In London and Middlesex where the King is resident it is usual not to proceed to execution but to wait for the declaration of the King's pleasure.'
57 A. Stephens, *Memoirs of John Horne Tooke, Interspersed with Original Documents* (2 vols; London: Johnson, 1813), vol.1, p.109.

58 [M. Madan] *Thoughts on Executive Justice with Respect to Our Criminal Laws Particularly on the Circuits* (London: Dodsley, 1785), pp.98–9, reviewed in *The County Magazine* 1: 2, February 1786, p.27.
59 Published in *The Meteor*, 1 April 1814. *Gentleman's Magazine* 133 (1823) p.652 – see for the Lord Chancellor's tearful encomium on Silvester when he died.
60 E.G. Wakefield, *Facts Relating to the Punishment of Death in the Metropolis* (London: Ridgway, 1831); see for critique of Wakefield on the process in London, *London Quarterly Review* 17: 93 (1832), pp.170–216 [pp.203–4].
61 *John Bull*, 30 April 1837, p.207.
62 *Recorder's report fate of Greenacre decided* (1837), Bodleian Library, John Johnson Collection, Crime 1 (78) in *The John Johnson Collection: An Archive of Printed Ephemera* http://johnjohnson.chadwyck.com.plymouth.idm.oclc.org (accessed 7 July 2019).
63 *Morning Herald*, as quoted in *Sherborne Mercury*, 6 October 1834, p.2.
64 7 Will IV & 1 Vict c 77, 'An Act to assimilate the Practice of the Central Criminal Court to other Courts of Criminal Judicature within the Kingdom of England and Wales with respect to Offenders liable to the Punishment of Death'. See J.C. Hobhouse, *Recollections of a Long Life. Vol.5. 1834–1840* (London: Murray, 1911), p.5.
65 Hobhouse, *Recollections of Long Life*, vol.5, p.81.
66 RA VIC/MAIN/QVJ (W), Lord Esher's typescript, 20 March 1839. The Recorder's role fascinated contemporaries: advert in *Figaro in London*, 22 August 1835, p.142, serial, *Crimes of London in the Nineteenth Century*, 'an interesting description of the interior of the Condemned Cells of Newgate with a highly impressive account of the Recorder's reading the Warrant for the Execution'.
67 *London Standard*, 23 October 1837, p.2; *Morning Chronicle*, 24 October 1837, p.4.
68 For instance *The Examiner*, 23 July 1837, p.7. The *London Evening Standard* noted the proposal earlier and reported, 6 July 1837, on hurrying this bill through Parliament as threatening to rob Victoria's reign of the clemency of William IV.
69 *Cheltenham Looker-On*, 15 July 1837, pp.451–2 [p.452].
70 *Bell's Weekly Messenger*, 25 June 1837, p.204.
71 'The Central Criminal Court', *London Saturday Journal*, May 1839, p.282.
72 *The Era*, 15 December 1839, p.10.
73 *Morning Post*, 22 June 1842, p.7.
74 C.P. Cooper, *The House of Lords as a Court of Appeal* (London: Stevens and Norton, 1850), p.92.
75 A. Todd, *On Parliamentary Government in England* (2 vols; London: Longmans, Green, and Company, 1867), vol.1, p.344.
76 C. Philipps, *Vacation Thoughts on Capital Punishment* (London: Cash, 1857), p.83.
77 A.H. Dymond, *The Law on Its Trial: Or, Personal Recollections of the Death Penalty and Its Opponents* (London: Bennett, 1865), p.65.
78 *The Spectator*, 12 April 1890, p.503.
79 S. Lee, *Queen Victoria. A Biography* (London: Smith, Elder, 1904), pp.57–8.
80 Gatrell, *The Hanging Tree: Execution and the English People 1770–1868* (Oxford: Oxford University Press, 1994), p.565.
81 J. Pellew, *The Home Office, 1848–1914, from Clerks to Bureaucrats* (London: Heinemann, 1982), p.8. Memorials were sent to other members of the royal family e.g. poisoner Dr Thomas Smethurst to Prince Albert in 1859. On the Secretary for Scotland, *London Standard*, 7 February 1888, p.5; *Sheffield Evening Telegraph*, 8 February 1888, p.3.

82 Hacket was treasurer of the Glasgow Operative Cotton-Spinners association. *Northern Star*, 10 February 1838, p.8. See *Report of the Trial of Thomas Hunter, Peter Hacket, Richard M'Neil, James Gibb, and William M'Lean: Operative Cotton-spinners in Glasgow, before the High Court of Justiciary, at Edinburgh, on Wednesday, January 3, 1838, and Seven Following Days, for the Crimes of Illegal Conspiracy and Murder* (Edinburgh: Clark, 1838).

83 'The Comic Blackstone', ch.7, *Punch*, 16 December 1843, p.266.

84 *Jerrold's Weekly Newspaper*, quoted in *The Friend* (Philadelphia), 13 February 1847, p.162.

85 'Muzzy Notions of Mercy', *Punch*, 17 September 1859, p.113.

86 The gallows victims were Wilmot Buckley and Betty Eccles, executed for murder, *Morning Chronicle*, 10 June 1843, p.3.

87 'The Condemned Woman at Dumfries', *Carlisle Journal*, 15 April 1862, p.3. *Paisley Herald*, 26 April 1862, p.6, for details of the male, female, and 'influential inhabitants' petitioning from Dumfries, Maxwelltown, and Annan and other places.

88 *Newcastle Daily Journal*, 5 January 1864, p.2.

89 *Morning Post*, 2 January 1864, p.4.

90 See M. Eder, *Crime and Punishment in the Royal Navy of the Seven Years' War, 1755–1763* (Aldershot: Ashgate, 2004); see the chapter 'The Use of Mercy in the Royal Navy', in R.V. Hamilton, ed., *Letters and Papers of Admiral of the Fleet Sir Thos. Byam Martin, G.C.B.* (3 vols; [London]: Navy Records Society, 1903), vol.1, p.130, for George III's response to a suggestion about extending mercy in a court-martial on the charge of false muster, and Lord Howe's desire to have every member of the court-martial struck off the navy list, p.130: 'The King was a great stickler for the prerogatives of the crown but would never lend himself to a misuse of his powers.' H. Reeve, ed., *The Greville Memoirs: A Journal of the Reigns of King George IV and King William IV* (3 vols; London: Longmans, Green, 1874), vol.2, p.85, includes gossip on mercy in cases involving king-in-council following reflections on hearing reports in Admiralty cases in 1830, after Lady Burghersh's reprieve for a good-looking forger.

91 E.g. Liberal Home Secretary H.A. Bruce, lambasted in a pro-Conservative satirical rival to *Punch*, 'The Quality of Mercy!!' *Will o the Wisp*, 1 May 1869, p.90.

92 *The Manual of Rank and Nobility, or Key to the Peerage* (London: Saunders and Otley, 1828), p.423.

93 For association between jubilee and mercy in 'that painful exercise of that branch' of royal power, J. Hewlett, *The Jubilee; or, Motives for Thanksgiving Derived from a Consideration of the Character and Conduct of King George the Third, a Sermon* (London: Rivington and Johnson, 1809), p.12.

94 *Morning Post*, 22 October 1810, p.3; 'Long Live the King! Long may he reign!' in *The Roundelay; a Selection of Comic, Martial, Naval and Sentimental Songs* (Doncaster: Thomas and Hunsley, 1815), p.64. The association between mercy and release of debtors is captured in a medal commemorating John Howard; on the reverse, mercy bids the debtor 'Go Forth'. Shakespeare's quality of mercy speech prefaces 'The Insolvent Debtor, a Pathetic Narrative, Founded on Facts', J.C. Cross, *Parnassian Bagatelles: Being a Miscellaneous Collection of Poetical Attempts* (London: Burton: 1796), p.41. On the general role of royal anniversary in linking king with benevolence and generosity, see M. Morris, *The British Monarchy and the French Revolution* (New York: Yale University Press, 1998), p.149. George III's royal act of beneficence paying for a debtor's release in Dorchester in 1793 was depicted: British Museum 2003, 1031.4, mezzotint after Thomas Stothard.

95 W.L. Brown, *On the Character and Influence of a Virtuous King* (Aberdeen: Chalmers, 1810), p.19.
96 Leopold Louis Lamb, *South London Press*, 15 January 1887, p.10.
97 *Parliamentary Debates*, 3rd series, vol.331, House of Lords, 22 February 1887, cols.280–286. For release of prisoners, see *Narrative of the Celebration of the Jubilee of Her Most Gracious Majesty Queen Victoria, Empress of India in the Presidency of Madras* (2nd edition; London: Macmillan, 1887), p.231.
98 Lord Lytton, House of Lords, 22 February 1887, reported *Kentish Independent*, 26 February 1887, p.7.
99 *The Globe*, 16 February 1887, p.4.
100 H. Day's final stanza to 'A Jubilee Ode', *Kentish Independent*, 7 May 1887, p.4; *Commonweal*, 26 February 1887 cited in E.P. Thompson, *William Morris: Romantic to Revolutionary* (1955; London: Merlin, 1996), p.480.
101 *Morning Post*, 19 February 1887, p.5.
102 *Nottinghamshire Guardian*, 26 May 1876, p.12.
103 *South Australian Register*, 21 June 1897, p.4. See *London Evening Standard*, 12 January 1897, p.4, *Pall Mall Gazette*, 12 January 1897, p.2.
104 *Chester Courant*, 28 October 1817, p.2.
105 'The Majesty of Mercy', *Truth*, 20 May 1894, p.4.
106 See TNA, HO17/34/11, August 1821.
107 See Lord Brougham, *Southern Reporter and Cork Commercial Courier*, 10 August 1839 [p.1]; the phrase is not in *Parliamentary Debates*, 3rd series, vol.49, House of Lords, 6 August 1839, cols.1275–1325 [col.1311].
108 *Western Morning News*, 23 May 1910, p.5. See *Dublin Daily Express*, 23 May 1910, p.5 for the Lord Lieutenant's intentions.
109 In the case of Thomas Coleman, 'The Mabbot Street Murder', *Dublin Daily Express*, 11 May 1910, p.5; 'Prerogative of Mercy. Exercised by Lord Aberdeen', *Weekly Freeman's Journal*, 14 May 1910, p.1. *Coventry Evening Telegraph* reported this as the 'first reprieve by King George', 12 May 1910, p.3.
110 See Churchill Archive, CHAR 12/10/36-37, 20 June 1911 (digitized version accessed); A.S. Baxendale, *Winston Leonard Spencer-Churchill: Penal Reformer* (Oxford: Peter Lang, 2010).
111 E.g. TNA, HO42/34/10; HO42/34/13; HO42/34/21.
112 Letter of 'Hope', *London Daily News*, 5 February 1858, which cited the Spanish monarchy's pardoning of criminals.
113 G.B. Smith, *Life of Her Majesty the Queen Compiled from All Available Sources* ('People's Edition', London: Routledge, 1887), p.166; 'G. Greenwood', *Queen Victoria, her Girlhood and Womanhood* (Montreal: Dawson, 1883), p.209.
114 See TNA, HO17/5/36.
115 *A Diary of Royal Movements and of Personal Events and Incidents in the Life and Reign of Her Most Gracious Majesty Queen Victoria* (London: Elliot Stock, 1883), vol.1, p.164.
116 Sir Robert Peel, *Parliamentary Debates*, 3rd series, vol. 36, 8 February 1837, col.396.
117 Captain Bernard Trench RMLI, Lieutenant Vivian Brandon RN, and Bertrand Stewart, a solicitor and member of West Kent Yeomanry, *Pall Mall Gazette*, 19 May 1913, p.1.
118 *Morning Herald*, reported with title, 'Generous Act of Royal Mercy', *Kentish Gazette*, 13 May 1856, p.3.
119 E.g. 'Halifax', *Northern Star*, 15 February 1840, p.8; 'Brighton', *Southern Star*, 16 February 1840, p.4; 'Trades Political Union', *Limerick Reporter*, 17 January 1840, p.2.

120 R. Heathcote, *The Irenarch; or, the Justice of the Peace's Manual. II. Miscellaneous Reflections upon Laws, Policy, Manners, Etc. III. An Assize-Sermon [on Mic. Vi. 8] Preached at Leicester. 12 Aug. 1756* (London, n.p., 1781), p.242.
121 Heathcote, *The Irenarch*, p.247. C. Strange, *Qualities of Mercy* and C. Strange, 'The Royal Prerogative and Executive Pardoning', in P. Knepper and A. Johansen, eds, *The Oxford Handbook of the History of Crime and Criminal Justice* (New York: Oxford University Press, 2016), pp.575–8; M. Fortier, *The Culture of Equity in Early Modern England* (Aldershot: Ashgate, 2005); and Fortier, *The Culture of Equity in Restoration and Eighteenth-Century Britain and America* (Aldershot: Ashgate, 2015).
122 *Parliamentary Debates*, 3rd series, vol.156, House of Commons, 1 February 1860, col. 419.
123 For toasts, alongside 'May justice and mercy for ever entwine', W.T. Moncrieff's 'Chapter of Toasts and Songs of Sentiments', in *An Original Collection of Songs* (London: Duncombe, 1850), p.97.
124 *The Trial of Joseph Gerrald, Before the High Court of Justiciary, at Edinburgh, on the 13th and 14h of March, 1794, for Sedition: With an Original Memoir, and Notes* (Glasgow: Muir, Gowan, 1835), p.100.
125 J.L. De Lolme, *The Constitution of England, or an Account of the English Government: In Which It Is Compared with the Republican Form of Government, and Occasionally with the Other Monarchies in Europe* (first published in French, 1771; London: Spilsbury, 1775), p.160; See De Lolme, p.379, noting mercifulness contained in the Bill of Rights and revised coronation oath, on 'justice executed with mercy'.
126 On the significant variation from the centre, and role of jury decision-making in relation to property offences in periphery, see P. King, and R. Ward, 'Rethinking the Bloody Code in Eighteenth-Century Britain: Capital Punishment at the Centre and on the Periphery', *Past & Present* 228: 1 (1 August 2015), pp.159–205. See essays in J.S. Cockburn and T.A. Green, eds, *Twelve Good Men and True: The Criminal Trial Jury in England, 1200–1800* (Princeton, NJ: Princeton University Press, 2014), for juror behaviour; T.A. Green, *Verdict According to Conscience: Perspectives on the English Criminal Trial Jury, 1200–1800* (Chicago: University of Chicago Press, 1985), and as survey, J.A. Hochstetler, *Criminal Jury Old and New: Jury Power from Early Times to the Present Day* (Winchester: Waterside Press, 2004). For eighteenth-century juries, see G.J. Durston, *Fields, Fens and Felonies: Crime and Justice in Eighteenth-Century East Anglia* (Hook: Waterside Press, 2016), 'Jury Trial'; for compassion in juries, see D. Rabin, *Identity, Crime and Legal Responsibility in Eighteenth-Century England* (Basingstoke: Palgrave Macmillan, 2004).
127 'Our Jury System', *Dublin University Magazine*, December 1848, pp.717–28 [p.718].
128 *Bolton Chronicle*, 5 October 1839 [p.3].
129 'Trial by Judge and Trial by Jury', *Westminster Review*, April 1872, pp.289–324 [p.315].
130 'Declaration of the London Jury', *The Calcutta Journal* 4: 136 (16 July 1819), p.120.
131 Alderman Harmer, before Commissioners of Criminal Law, cited in 'Our Jury System', *Dublin University Magazine* 32: 192 (December 1848), pp.717–28 [p.718].
132 'Juries as They Were and Are', *Chambers's Journal* 153 (6 December 1856), pp.355–8; 'Revolting Leniency to Criminals', *Examiner*, 6 November 1847, pp.705–6; 'Capricious Leniency and Rigour', *Examiner*, 10 January 1852, p.18.
133 For appeals to mercy made by defendants, see *Bell's New Weekly Messenger*, 5 December 1841, p.5: the appeal made by Edward Beaumont Smith, who pleaded guilty to forging a £1000 exchequer bill, previously a capital offence.

134 The query (4 December 2017, and repeated in September 2019) was to search for all texts where the transcription matched '+mercy +tempered' (all words present), between 1800 and 1913, and then the fifty hits were checked and reduced to the following that matched the meaning: January 1813, Joseph Milton Green (t18130113-81); April 1821, John Snape (t18210411-72): ('I trust that your verdict of this day, will be tempered with that humanity, which is so predominant in the breast of every English judge and juryman'); 'written defence' September 1828, Peter Fenn (t18280911-6); October 1830, James Monds (t18301028-5). For instances where 'justice and mercy' were appealed to by the defendant, see April 1802, Elizabeth Hall (t18020428-92); September 1807, John Green (t18070916-26); October 1810, Anthony Fisher (t18101031-91); December 1912, Gertrude Williams (27) (t19121201-35). I have not studied the use of appeals to be 'merciful' in the database, nor studied written appeals to mercy, examples of which are: February 1810, Eliza Iredale (t18100221-106) and April 1807, Dennis Dempsey (t18070408-81) (appealing for merciful compassion). There is one reference to 'divine mercy', April 1828, Hambry Price and Mary Price (t18280410-29).

135 For felonious stealing of two knives, see October 1783, trial of John Coltman (t17831029-71).

136 'Marlborough-Street – A Modern Orator', *Morning Post*, 16 November 1836 [p.4].

137 *Leamington Advertiser*, 28 April 1870, p.5.

138 *Wicklow News-Letter*, 5 April 1913 [p.12].

139 'Court Ceremony. New Falkirk Bailie Introduced', *Falkirk Herald*, 9 December 1942, p.1.

140 J. Campbell, *The Lives of the Lord Chancellors and Keepers of the Great Seal of England: From the Earliest Times Till the Reign of King George IV* (8 vols, London: Murray, 1869), vol.8.

141 E. Foss, *The Judges of England* (London: Murray, 1864), vol.9, p.237.

142 W.C. Townsend, *The Lives of Twelve Eminent Judges of the Last and of the Present Century* (2 vols; London: Longmans, 1846), vol.1, pp.18–19.

143 F.E. Smith, *Fourteen English Judges* (London: Cassell, 1925), p.256.

144 Judge Garrow, a 'hanging judge', in tears after a tale of poverty from someone fined for petty theft, 'Fashionable Chit-Chat', *The Satirist*, 7 August 1831, p.141; T. Dixon, 'The Tears of Mr Justice Willes', *Journal of Victorian Culture* 17 (2012), pp.1–23 and *Weeping Britannia: Portrait of a Nation in Tears* (Oxford: Oxford University Press, 2012), ch.12. 'Damp Justice'.

145 See F. Watt, *Terrors of the Law* (London: Lane, 1902).

146 On Jefferys, see 'The Mercy of Judge Jefferies', *London Saturday Journal* 3: 61 (29 February 1840), pp.139–40. On Page, see Pope's words, quoted e.g. *Saunders's News-Letter*, 9 March 1811, p.1, 'Hard words and hanging if your Judge be Page!' On Page in Victorian texts, see 'A Fly in Amber: Or, Some Account of The 'Hanging Judge' of the Eighteenth Century', *All the Year Round*, 5 May 1888, pp.421–5; J.C. Jeaffreson, *A Book About Lawyers* (2 vols; London: Hurst and Blackett, 1867), vol.2. For magazine anecdotes, see 'Some Judges', *Temple Bar* 107 (February 1896), pp.269–81.

147 'C. M. B,' 'Irish Sketches – Lord Norbury – No. 2'. *The Penny Satirist*, 18 September 18, 1841, p.1; *The Georgian Era: Military and Naval Commanders. Judges and Barristers. Physicians and Surgeons* (4 vols; London: Vizetelly, Branston, 1833) vol.2, p.307; *Dublin Monitor*, 8 July 1842. See also chapter on him, R.L. Shiel, *Sketches of the Irish Bar* (2 vols; London: Colburn, 1855), vol.2, originally in *New Monthly Magazine*; and 'Moran-Of-The-Collar', 'Some Loose Thoughts on Hanging', *Tait's Edinburgh*

Magazine 8: 89 (May 1841), pp.314–17; 'The Late Dr Radcliffe', *Dublin Weekly Register*, 22 July 1843, p.4; 'Irish Politeness', *Northern Star*, 30 November 1844, p.7; 'A Hanging Judge and His Solitary Tear', *Salisbury and Winchester Journal*, 21 August 1847 [p.3]. See W. Andrews, 'Gibbet Lore: Remarkable Chapters in the Annals of Great Britain and Ireland, IX. Hanging Judges', in *Newcastle Courant*, 7 September 1883, p.2; and J. Larwood, *Forensic Anecdotes: Or, Humour and Curiosities of the Law and of the Men of Law* (London: Chatto and Windus, 1882).

148 'Black Sheep of The Law', *The Satirist*, 17 August 17 1834, p.259. On Furley case, see 'Modern "Mercy;" Or, Sir James and The Convict', *The Satirist*; 26 May 1844, p.162; 'Judges' Sentences', *Punch*, 15 June 1844, p.249; 'Severity and Leniency', *Examitner* (1844), pp.258–9.

149 See the colourful and frank report of Jessie McLachlan's trial, *Falkirk Herald*, 2 October 1862 [p.2], where Deas's bitter nature is conveyed.

150 On Hawkins, 'E.', 'Her Majesty's Judges', *Strand Magazine* 11 (January 1896), pp.455–65 [p.460]; and J. Corlett, 'Personal Recollections of Lord Brampton', *Sporting Times*, 12 October 1907, p.3.

151 *Daily Telegraph*, 7 May 1892, p.5. 'Judges were not necessarily blind to the hardships, the inequalities, and the necessary imperfections of every human system under which men live', they were told.

152 *The Miscellaneous Works of the Right Honourable Sir James Mackintosh: Complete in One Volume* (London: Longman, Brown, Green and Longmans, 1851), pp.290–2; [T.B. Macaulay] 'Mackintosh's *History of the Revolution in England*', *Edinburgh Review*, July 1835, pp.265–322 [p.270], the inscription on his memorial at Westminster Abbey includes the claim he was 'merciful' as a judge; E.B. Bowen-Rowlands, 'Great Criminal Judges', *Pall Mall Magazine* 29:120 (April 1903), pp.519–27 [p.524].

153 Account of *The Hanging Judge*, *Hull Daily Mail*, 15 April 1919 [p.2]. On ghost stories, see Sheridan le Fanu's 'An Account of Some Strange Disturbances in an Old House in Aungier-Street'. For melodrama in literature, see W. Westall, 'Birch Dene; or, Sentenced to Death', *Daily Gazette for Middlesbrough*, 6 May 1889 [p.4]. Stevenson's *Weir of Hermiston* is based on Macqueen, Lord Braxfield. H.L. Adam, in *The Story of Crime: From the Cradle to the Grave* (London: T. Werner Laurie, 1908), refers, pp.53–4, to judges seeking to sway jurors away from mercy.

154 'Letters to the Editor. The New Avatar', *The Irishman*, 28 February 1885, p.556. On images incorporating Norbury, see National Library of Ireland's digital collection: 'Speech of Robert Emmet, Esq.' Schnabel and Finkeldey, Lithographers, Philadelphia: W.M. Smith, 706 South Third Street, n.d., post 20 September 1803; 'Robert Emmet and Norbury'.

155 On the role of the chancellor, linked to appeals to mercy, see [W.J. Fox] 'Publicola', 'Letter VII. Liberty of Conscience', *Weekly Despatch*, reprinted in *Letters of Publicola. First Series* (London: Cunningham, 1840), p.37 (17 February 1833).

156 J.J. Schomberg, *Elements of the British Constitution: Containing a Comprehensive View of the Monarchy and Government of England* (2nd edition, London: Painter, 1824), p.128.

157 See Judge George Hardinge on infanticide of Mary Morgan (1805), on the 'merciful terror' of her example, and merciful juries, rules, and judges, see *The Miscellaneous Works, in Prose and Verse, of George Hardinge, Esq* 3 vols (London: Nichols, 1818), vol.1, p.63 and his various other mercy-related comments, e.g. in a charge to the Grand Jury, *c*.1813, p.139; vol.2, p.172, the verse 'Mercy'; and vol.3, p.262 for

Christianity's elevation of mercy as moral principle; *An Elegy, Written in the Church Yard of Presteign, Radnorshire; with Admonitory Reflections on the Grave of Mary Morgan, Etc* (Leominster: F. Went, 1818), p.11: 'Thy case alas his anxious bosom mov'd | For though to justice dear he mercy lov'd | Strove all his power thy acquittal to obtain | But Oh sad truth alas he strove in vain.'
158 *Justice of the Peace*, 19 January 1856, p.33.
159 *Universal Magazine* (1793), p.248.
160 E.g. 'Scandal to Justice and Humanity', *Examiner*, 1 October 1842, pp.626–7; 'The Inverse Rule of Justices' Justice', *Examiner*, 21 August 1847, p.530.
161 'Mad Miss Mercy', *Fun* 45: 1136, 16 February 1887, p. 70.
162 'The Inequality of Judicial Sentences', *Reynolds's Newspaper*, 5 August 1888, p.4. Also 'Judges and Justice', *The Speaker*, 19 April 1890, pp.416–17; 'The Book of Sentences', *The Speaker*, 2 October 1897, p.369.
163 Bowen-Rowlands, 'Great Criminal Judges', p.522.
164 *A Sermon; Preached at the Assizes Held at Guildford, July the 30th, 1798, before the Right Honourable Lord Chief Justice Kenyon, and the Honourable Sir Francis Buller, Bart* (London: Clarke, 1798), reviewed in *Anti-Jacobin Review*, p.547.
165 E.g. A. Hammond, *Scheme for a Digest of the Laws of England, with Introductory Essays on the Science of Natural Jurisprudence* (London, 1820), as cited in B. Hilton, 'The Gallows and Mr Peel', in T.C.W. Blanning and D. Cannadine, eds, *History and Biography: Essays in Honour of Derek Beales* (Cambridge: Cambridge University Press, 1996), pp.88–112; also George Ollyffe in D. Lemmings, *Law and Government in England During the Long Eighteenth Century* (Basingstoke: Palgrave Macmillan, 2011), p.96. The penal reformer William Tallack presented the 'mercy of moderate corporal punishment', *Penological and Preventive Principles, with Special Reference to Europe and America* (London: Wertheimer, Lea, 1889), pp.292–4.
166 K. Fry and F. Cresswell, eds, *Memoir of the Life of Elizabeth Fry with Extracts from Her Journal and Letters. Edited by Two of Her Daughters* (2 vols; London: Gilpin/Hatchard, 1847), vol.2, p.431.
167 *Leicester Chronicle*, 17 September 1881, p.6.
168 'Clerical Magistrates', *Examiner*, 10 October 1819, pp.641–2. See also 'Clerical magistrates', *Northern Liberator*, 2 May 1840, p.4; and (for later radical newspaper coverage, on controversy of clerical magistrates at Chipping Norton), *Reynolds's Newspaper*, 1 June 1873, p.5; 'A Reverend Rhadamanthus', *Reynolds's Newspaper*, 18 December 1881, p.4. For an essayist seeing no inherent demerit, see 'Clerical Magistrates', *Saturday Review*, 6 October 1866, pp.416–17.
169 *Morning Advertiser*, 13 October 1855, p.4.
170 'Clerical Magistrates', *Examiner*, 28 January 1865, p.49. Also 'Clerical Justice', *Examiner*, 23 April 1864, p.258. *Western Daily Press*, 19 February 1868 [p.3] and 21 February 1868 [p.3], published 'Why are clergymen less merciful as magistrates than laymen?' and (21 February) explained it as the result of an exaggerated estimate of crime and warped nature.
171 [E.P. Hood] 'VI. Measure without Measure', *The Eclectic Review* 14 (March 1868), pp.271–4 [p.272]; the theme of clerical inhumanity continued in 'V. Inasmuch As Ye Did It Unto One of The Least of These', *Eclectic Review* 15 (September 1868), pp.231–4.
172 'Clerical Magistrates', *Chester Chronicle*, 13 October 1855, p.6.
173 'A Clergyman and the Cat o' Nine Tails', *Reynolds's Newspaper*, 19 June 1870, quoting *Newcastle Daily Chronicle*; see also 'The Durham Flogging Case', *Newcastle Journal*,

14 June 1870 for discussion between Lord Chief Justice and Solicitor General; and 'Clerical Magistrates', *London Review*, 31 March 1866, pp.358–9 [p.358]. Clerical magistrates allegedly had a penchant for birching children, 'Whipping at Police-Stations', *London Review*, 8 April 1865, pp.371–2. On clerical corporal punishment, J. Gay, *The Cultivation of Hatred. The Bourgeois Experience. Victoria to Freud* (1993; New York: Norton, 1994), p.187, citing Gibson, *The English Vice* (1978), p.73.

174 'A Clergyman', *The Times*, 27 October 1855, p.10; report of *Diocesan Gazette* discussion, 'Clerical Magistrates', *Norfolk Chronicle*, 8 October 1898, p.7.

175 J. Rowbotham, K. Stevenson, and S. Pegg, *Crime News in Modern Britain: Press Reporting and Responsibility, 1820–2010* (Basingstoke: Palgrave Macmillan, 2013).

176 They are legion, but see that for John Stagg of Stockton, *Durham Chronicle*, 8 March 1844; John Thornely of Barnesley, *Leeds Intelligencer*, 30 June 1849; E.J. Lloyd, Esq of Oldfield Hall, *Manchester Courier*, 6 July 1850; Sir John Nelthorpe, Bt, of Brigg, *Stamford Mercury* 1 December 1865, W.D. Lucas-Shadwell, *Hastings and St Leonard's Observer*, 23 January 1875; J.S. Stephenson, County Derry, *Belfast Weekly News*, 7 July 1888.

177 'Our Dialect Corner', *Preston Herald*, 10 May 1913, p.2; 'Justice and Mercy', *Sunderland Daily Echo*, 1 April 1939, p.2.

178 R. Percy and S. Percy, *Percy Anecdotes. Anecdotes of Justice* (London: Cumberland, 1826), vol.8, frontispiece; R. Brathwaite, *Astraea's Teares: An Elegie upon the Death of That Reverend, Learned and Honest Judge, Sir Richard Hutton, Knight* (London: Nevil, 1641).

179 Mezzotint, British Museum 1854, 1113.138, Thomas Jones of the King's Bench; Scottish Natural Portrait Gallery, SPL 167.1, Samuel Reynold's mezzotint of Russell after the portrait by Chinnery in Calcutta.

180 *London Magazine*, August 1780, p.322.

181 *The Builder* 8, 31 August 1850, p.416; *Illustrated London News*, 4 February 1854, p.97.

182 H. Croft, *The Abbey of Kilhampton. An Improved Edition* (London: Kearsley, 1778), p.26. His severity is commented on in N.S. Poser, *Lord Mansfield: Justice in the Age of Reason* (Montreal: McGill-Queen's University Press, 2013). The title of ch.18, Gatrell's *Hanging Tree*, derives from Dr Samuel Parr.

183 Lord Hawkins, reported in *The Law Journal*, 10 August 1878, p.491. On majesty in the eighteenth-century Assize, see Hay, 'Property, Authority and the Criminal Law'.

184 Thus Lord Chief Justice Kenyon's summing up, trial of Vint, Ross, Parry, for libelling Tsar Paul of Russia, 4 March 1799, in T.B. Howell and T.J. Howell, *A Complete Collection of State Trials* (London: Longman, Hurst, Rees, Orme and Brown, 1820), vol.27, col.639. Thomas Hobbes, *Leviathan*, states, 'For in their seats of justice they represent the person of the sovereign; and their sentence, is his sentence'.

185 *Morning Post*, 5 December 1882, p.6.

186 Schomberg, *Elements of the British Constitution*, p.198.

Chapter 2

1 *Morning Chronicle*, 19 December 1828, p.3.
2 *Morning Herald*, 12 March 1840, quoted in *Law Reporter* (Boston, 1840), 2, p.62.
3 *Apotheosis Basilike; or, a Pindarick Ode, upon the Pious and Blessed Transit of That Most Excellent Prince James the II. King of Great Britain* (n.p. 1708), p.8.

4   Sharpe, *Rebranding Rule*, pp.438–9.
5   Ibid., p.584, the verse by Tate reflecting on the royal portrait by Closterman, *c*.1702. On the theme, 'Queen Elizabeth I as Astraea', in F.A. Yates, ed., *Astraea. The Imperial Theme in the Sixteenth Century* (London: Routledge and Kegan Paul, 1975).
6   *The Poetical Works of Elijah Fenton* (London: Cooke, 1796), p.70; and p.25, 'Verses on the Union': 'Thy mercy cures the wound thy justice gave, | For 'tis thy lov'd prerogative to save'.
7   A. Drift, ed., *Miscellaneous Works of His Late Excellency Matthew Prior, Esq* (London: for the editor, 1740), vol.2, pp.40–58 [p.53].On Anne's reputation, Sharpe, *Rebranding Rule*, ch.15; A. Strickland, *Lives of the Queens of England* (revised edition, 8 vols; London: Colburn, 1852), vol.8, pp.159–60, quoting her memoranda on mercy for deserters sentenced to death; *Gentleman's Magazine* 120, August 1816, p.136: on notes regarding respite for Jeffries.
8   *A Sermon upon the Death of Queen Anne: Of Blessed Memory, Who Departed This Life Aug. 1. 1714. Preached at Chelmsford in Essex, August 15. 1714. By George Noon* (London: Keble, 1714), p.16.
9   [F. Peck] *Sighs upon the Never Enough Lamented Death of Queen Anne* (London: Clements, 1719), p.47.
10 T. Smollett, *A Complete History of England: From the Descent of Julius Caesar, to the Treaty of Aix la Chapelle, 1748* (3rd edition; London: Rivington and Fletcher, 1759), vol.10, p.151.
11 [A. Boyer] *Quadriennium Annae Postremum, or, The Political State of Great Britain, with the Most Material Occurrences in Europe. For the Month of December, 1713* (London: Baker, 1713), p.485.
12 J.A. Winn, *Queen Anne: Patroness of Arts* (Oxford: Oxford University Press, 2014), pp.346–7 citing David Symson's *A Poem on Her Sacred Majesty*.
13 J. Gardner, *The Glory of Her Sacred Majesty Queen Anne, in the Royal Navy, and Her Absolute Sovereignty as Empress of the Sea, Asserted and Vindicated* (London, for the author, 1703), dedication [p.ii]. See also the comment, apropos of refusal to be 'teazed into an ill-timed Act of Mercy', 'tho' like all her Family, most tender in her own Nature', J. Campbell, *Lives of the Admirals and Other Eminent British Seamen* (London: Applebee, 1744), vol.4, p.280 (on Admiral Benbow's reputation). See also [C. Leslie] *The Church of England's Advice to Her Children and to All Kings, Princes, and Potentates* (London, n.p., 1721), p.31, 'The Breast of every Branch of it that God had given to you, has been replenish'd with *Mercy*'.
14 O. Dykes, *The Royal Marriage. King Lemuel's Lesson* (London: for the author, 1722), p.106.
15 J. Bailey, *Parenting in England 1760–1830. Emotion, Identity and Generation* (Oxford: Oxford University Press, 2012), p.119.
16 S. Wale, *King George I and the Line of Succession*, *c*.1748 and reissued 1752, which includes the figure of justice. The famous example of justice in a royal portrait is Rigaud's portrait of Louis XIV of 1701; from Portugal, attributed to Francisco Lusitano, *Allegory of the Acclamation of Dom José I*, *c*.1750.
17 J. Black, *George III: America's Last King* (New Haven, CT: Yale University Press, 2006), p.12.
18 H. Smith, *Georgian Monarchy: Politics and Culture, 1714–1760* (Cambridge: Cambridge University Press, 2006), p.138.
19 RA, GEO/Add.32, cited in Black, p.13, and P.D.G. Thomas, 'Thoughts on the British Constitution by George in 1760', *Bulletin of the Institute of Historical Research* 60: 143

(October 1987), pp.361–3, also cited in Black, p.13. The role of mercy and justice is emphasized, in relation to Princess Charlotte of Wales, at the conclusion of a work dedicated to the 'learned prelate who had the care of her education', H. More, *Hints towards Forming the Character of a Young Princess* (London: Cadell and Davies, 1805), see Z. Leader and I. Haywood, eds, *Romantic Period Writings 1798–1832: An Anthology* (1998; London: Routledge, 2005), p.168; and Vallone, *Becoming Victoria*, pp.40–3.

20 Smith, *Georgian Monarchy*, p.62. On the role of the press, pp.80–1, with quotation on the organized culture at p.81. See also Colley, *Britons*, p.201.
21 H. Bleackley, *Some Distinguished Victims of the Scaffold* (London: Kegan Paul, Trench, Trübner, 1905), p.29.
22 Reverend A. O'Neill, *Coventry Herald*, 11 May 1849, p.4.
23 H. Ellis, *Original Letters, Illustrative of English History*, series 2, vol.4 (London: Harding and Shepard, 1827), preface to *Letters of the Reign of King George the First* [p.284].
24 I. Higgins, *Swift's Politics: A Study in Disaffection* (Cambridge: Cambridge University Press, 1994), p.176; M.D. Sankey, *Jacobite Prisoners of the 1715 Rebellion: Preventing and Punishing Insurrection in Early Hanoverian Britain* (Aldershot: Ashgate, 2005) details the strategy of 'retribution tempered with clemency'.
25 See Kesselring, *Mercy and Authority*, ch.6, on the theme of 'Protest and Pardons'.
26 Printed address, TNA, SP54/26/72D, p.2. See G.G. Plank, *Rebellion and Savagery: The Jacobite Rising of 1745 and the British Empire* (Philadelphia: University of Pennsylvania Press, 2006). For contemporary argument on mercy abused by rebels, see C.L., *The Advantages of the Success of the House of Stewart to the Crown of Great Britain Demonstrated* (London: Noble, 1747), pp.59, 65.
27 A. Henderson, *The History of the Rebellion: 1745 and 1746. Containing, a Full Account of Its Rise, Progress and Extinction;… by an Impartial Hand, Who Was an Eye-witness to Most of the Facts*, (reprinted from Edinburgh edition, sold by R. Griffiths, 1748), vol. 7, p.35.
28 *Jacobite Minstrelsy* (Glasgow: Griffin, 1829), p.148.
29 *A New and Complete History and Survey of the Cities of London and Westminster, the Borough of Southwark, and Parts Adjacent: From the Earliest Accounts, to the Beginning of the Year 1770* (London: J. Cooke), p.100; *A Companion to All the Principal Places of Curiosity and Entertainment in and about London and Westminster* (London: Drew, 1797), p.30.
30 E. Lovell, *Justice and Mercy Equal Supporters of the Throne; or, The Duty of the Magistrate to Employ His Sword Against the Stubborn and Rebellious* (London: Corbett, 1716); T. Pyle, *The Wisdom of a Government in Distributing Punishment or Mercy to State-criminals. A Sermon Preached at the Lent-assizes Holden at Thetford in Norfolk, on March 23 1715* (London: J. Wyat, 1716).
31 J. Hogg, *The Jacobite Relics of Scotland: Being the Songs, Airs, and Legends, of the Adherents to the House of Stuart* (2 vols; Edinburgh: Blackwood, 1819–1821), vol.2, appendix, p.456.
32 *A Sermon Preach'd at St. James's Church, Westminster, on June the 7th, 1716: Being the Day of Publick Thanksgiving to Almighty God for the Suppression of the Late Unnatural Rebellion* (London: J. Tonson, 1716), p.12.
33 P. Rae, *The History of The Rebellion Rais'd Against His Majesty King George I. By the Friends of the Popish Pretender… To Which Is Now Added, A Collection of Original Letters, and Authentic Papers, Relating to That Rebellion* (London: Millar, 1746), p.388.

Essays on mercy in princes include 'The Excellence of Virtue Appearing a Publick Character', in *The Occasional Paper* (London: Burleigh, 1716), no.v, p.24. For a discussion of justice and mercy in the legal system, see *Georgicum: or, a Supplement to the Mirror of Justice* (London, 1716), p.31, cited in R. McGowen, '"Making Examples" and the Crisis of Punishment in Mid-Eighteenth-Century England', in D. Lemmings, ed., *The British and Their Laws in the Eighteenth Century* (Woodbridge: Boydell, 2005), p.186.

34 *Mercurius Politicus*, June 1716, p.13.
35 Ibid., p.55.
36 O. Goldsmith, *History of England from the Earliest Times to the Death of George II* (4 vols; London: Davies, 1771), vol.4, p.228. John Almon judged George II, in disposition merciful, 'not remarkable for either severity or clemency' in the rebellion, *A Review of the Reign of George II* (2nd edition, London: Wilkie, 1762), p.255.
37 R. Chambers, *History of the Rebellion in Scotland in 1745, 1746* (Edinburgh: Constable, 1827), vol.2, p.255.
38 *A Secret History of One Year* (London: Dodd, 1714), p.9; see also pp.12–13 for arguments against mercy.
39 J. Addison, *The Free-Holder*, 6 April 1716, pp.166–88; F. Atterbury, *An Argument to Prove the Affections of the People of England to be the Best Security of the Government, Humbly Offered to the Consideration of the Patrons of Severity, and Applied to the Present Juncture of Affairs* (London: W. Jones, 1716; reprinted London, 1746), p.4.
40 *A History of the Clemency of Our English Monarchs: From the Reformation, Down to the Present Time. With Some Comparisons* (London: N. Mist, 1717), pp.23–4.
41 This text is cited in R.J. Merrett, *Daniel Defoe: Contrarian* (Toronto: Toronto University Press, 2013), p.158 as an instance of 'generic ambivalence'. On Defoe and royal mercy, see 'Colonel Jack and the Perils of Delusion' in S.H. Gregg, *Defoe's Writings and Manliness: Contrary Men* (Farnham: Ashgate, 2009), pp.136–7. On Earbery, see A. Pettit, *Illusory Consensus: Bolingbroke and the Polemical Response to Walpole, 1730–1737* (Newark, DEL: University of Delaware Press, 1997), pp.106–8.
42 Smith, *Georgian Monarchy*, pp.214–15 (also involving George I returning from chapel).
43 Descriptions and criticism in *The Art-Journal*, 1 June 1854, p.167; *The Works of Eminent Masters: In Painting, Sculpture, Architecture, and Decorative Art* (London: Cassell, 1854), p.411; *The Athenaeum*, 6 May 1854, p.560; *The Critic*, 15 May 1854, p.275.
44 *A Letter from the Countess of Nithsdale with Remarks by Sheffield Grace* (London: n.p., 1827); B. Dacre, *Winifred, Countess of Nithsdale: A Tale of the Jacobite Wars* (New York: Sadleir, 1869), p.127; B. Hutton, *Tales of the White Cockade* (London: Griffith and Farran, 1870). On the Nithsdale episode, J.W. Bayley, *The History and Antiquities of the Tower of London* (London: Cadell, 1830), p.606; *John Cassell's Illustrated History of England* (London: Cassell, Petter and Galpin, 1860), vol.4, p.351.
45 *Mercurius Politicus*, Introduction, [p.ii]; *Mercurius Politicus*, September 1716, p.261.
46 W. Lee, 'Daniel Defoe and "The London Review"', *Notes and Queries*, 3rd series 8, 21 January 1865, pp.58–61 [p.59]; P.R. Backscheider, *Daniel Defoe: His Life* (Baltimore: Johns Hopkins University Press, 1989), p.432.
47 [J. Swift], *Travels into Several Remote Nations of the World. In Four Parts* (London: Motte, 1726), vol.1, p.129. See note 65 in edition by Claude Rawson with notes by Ian Higgins (Oxford: Oxford University Press, 2005), pp.299–300; and Swift's

letter to Robert Cope, 9 October 1722, for Whig praise of George I's mercy during controversy over Jacobite Francis Atterbury, Bishop of Rochester.
48 L. Eusden, *Three Poems; the First, Sacred to the Immortal Memory of the Late King; the Second, on the Happy Succession, and Coronation of His Present Majesty* (London: Roberts, 1727), p.7.
49 H. Walpole, *Memoirs of the Reign of George the Second* ed., Lord Holland (2nd edition; London: Colburn, 1846), vol.1, p.176.
50 See *Culloden Papers: Comprising an Extensive and Interesting Correspondence from the Year 1625 to 1748* (London: Cadell and Davies, 1815), p.284, on severity and pity.
51 See P.K. Monod, *Jacobitism and the English People, 1688–1788* (Cambridge: Cambridge University Press, 1989), p.60, for Cumberland's unmerciful reputation.
52 National Library of Scotland, Blaikie. SNPG.1.16, 'Britannia sitting between Prince Charles and Cumberland weighing Mercy and Butchery', via 'Jacobite prints and broadsides' digital collection, digital.nls.uk; J.H. Jesse, *Memoirs of the Pretenders and Their Adherents* (2 vols; London: Bentley, 1845), vol.2, p.250. See also Monod, *Jacobitism and the English People*, p.85; and p.70, which refers to lines attached to a print of the 1745 medal of Charles Edward Stuart, 'Courage with mercy, Wit with Virtue join'd'.
53 Blaikie. SNPG.18.6; see Blaikie. SNPG.19.10, 'Fate of Rebellion or a Monumental Warning to Rebels' for explicitly representing prudence and justice but not mercy. Blaikie. SNPG.19.5, 'Rebellion Displayed Most humbly Inscribed to his Sacred Majesty King George' has the king lead sea power, justice, religion, mercy (or it may be *order* – symbolized by sceptre), and liberty, to safety.
54 *Fables in Two Parts. Wrote for the Amusement of His Royal Highness William Duke of Cumberland, by the Late Mr. John Gay* (Glasgow: Foulis, 1761). See D. Dugaw, *'Deep Play': John Gay and the Invention of Modernity* (Newark: University of Delaware Press, 2001), pp.260–1 for changing imagery associated with this work. Mercy appeared in *A Collection of Poems in Three Volumes by several Hands* (London: Hughs, 1748), for 'The Trophy, being Six Cantatas to the Honour of his Royal Highness William Duke of Cumberland', as 'crown'd; soft-smiling'.
55 *Mercy the Truest Heroism: Display'd in the Conduct of Some of the Most Famous Conquerors and Heroes of Antiquity; viz. Cyrus, Alexander, Julius Cæsar, Augustus, Flavius Vespasianus* (London: Cooper, 1746). See M. Pittock, *Culloden* (Oxford: Oxford University Press, 2016), p.102.
56 S. Shesgreen, *Engravings by Hogarth* (New York: Dover, 1973), p.97; R. Paulson, *Hogarth: Art and Politics, 1750–1764* (Cambridge: Lutterworth, 1993), p.30.
57 *London Magazine and Monthly Chronologer*, September 1746, pp.453–7.
58 'Integritas', in *Truth, but No Treason: Or, Oppression Often the Cause of Rebellion. Being a Necessary Caution to the People of Great Britain, That They Do Not, whilst They Are Laudably Endeavouring to Keep Out the One, Widen the Door for the Other,... Humbly Dedicated to the King, by an Englishman* (London: Wood, 1748), dedication.
59 H. Fielding, *The True Patriot*, 29 April to 6 May 1746, no.27; reprinted in W.B. Coley, ed., *The True Patriot and Related Writings* (Oxford: Oxford University Press, 1987), pp.277–84. Fielding's defence of justice rather than mercy, for deterrence, is noted in P. King, *Crime, Justice and Discretion in England* (Oxford: Oxford University Press, 2000), using Fielding's *An Enquiry* to consider the 'compassion, sympathy and pity of the good mind' (p.329). For Fielding's intervention in the case of Bosavern Penlez and other rioters convicted in 1749, see *Gentleman's Magazine*, November 1749,

pp.561–3. Mercy as against justice figures in *The History of Tom Jones, a Foundling* (London: A Millar, 1749), vol.1, book 18, ch.12; p.328, Squire Allworthy, apropos of Blifil, tells his nephew of the danger of mistaken mercy: 'not only Weakness, but borders on Injustice, and is very pernicious to Society as it encourages Vice'.

60 On the military aspect to George I and George II, see Smith, *Georgian Monarchy*, pp.108–9.
61 Fielding, *True Patriot*, 27, in Coley, p.279.
62 W.H. Wilkins, *Caroline, the Illustrious Queen-consort of George II, and Sometime Queen-regent; a Study of Her Life and Time* (London: Longmans, Green, 1901), vol.2, p.184.
63 K. Thomson, *Memoirs of Viscountess Sundon, Mistress of the Robes to Queen Caroline, Consort of George II* (2 vols; London: Colburn, 1847), vol.1, p.345. On petition from John Porteous, see T.B. Howell, *A Complete Collection of State Trials and Proceedings for High Treason and Other Crimes and Misdemeanors from the Earliest Period to the Year 1783, with Notes and Other Illustrations* (21 vols; London: Longman, Hurst, Rees, Orme and Brown, 1816), vol.17, col.989. *The Life of the Most Illustrious Prince, John, Duke of Argyle and Greenwich* (Belfast: Foy, 1745), p.316, 'tho her natural Disposition was all Mercy, yet would not rashly pardon the Criminal but was graciously pleased to grant a Reprieve for six weeks'. Caroline's mercy figures in S. Johnson, *An Account of the Life of Mr Richard Savage, Son of the Earl Rivers* (1744; London: Newbery, 1777), pp.40–1. The encounter with Jeanie Deans was engraved and painted by C.R. Leslie.
64 *Newcastle Courant*, 22 September 1750 [p.2]. *The Grand Magazine of Magazines*, October 1750, pp.251–4, prints William Smith's appeals for mercy to the Regency when sentenced to execution for forgery.
65 Charles Knight's comment, *The Popular History of England: An Illustrated History* (6 vols; London: Bradbury and Evans, 1860), vol.6, p.170.
66 See 'By Mr James Clitherow of All Soul's College' [Blackstone's brother-in-law], 'On Prince Frederic's Death', in *The Union* (London: Baldwin, 1759), p.76; *Scots Magazine*, August 1781, p.432.
67 W. Seward, *Anecdotes of Some Distinguished Persons, Chiefly of the Present and Two Preceding Centuries* (3rd edition; London: Cadell and Davies, 1796), vol. 2, p.354.
68 *Oxford Journal*, 2 June 1753 [p.4]. Carlyle's *History of Friedrich II of Prussia, called Frederick the Great* (4 vols; London: Chapman, Hall, 1858), vol.4, p.468 comments on his wife's efforts to supplicate 'Royal George… who had to turn a deaf ear… I hope not without pain'.
69 G. Birkbeck Hill, ed., *Boswell's Life of Johnson* (6 vols; New York: Harper and Brothers, 1889), vol.1, pp.168–9.
70 *Derby Mercury*, 23 April 1756, p.4, referring to the killing of a post boy at Shooter's Hill by Brown and Lauder, 12 April 1756.
71 H. Walpole, *Memoirs of the Reign of King George the Second*, vol.2, p.310; *United Services Magazine*, August 1835, p.463.
72 *Newcastle Courant*, 12 February 1757. *Derby Mercury*, 16 July 1756, published a poem about the execution of a woman, contrasting her voice with Byng (unnamed): 'My King, (I tremble at thy Name) "Tho" Mercy guides his Throne, Must punish for his People's Shame, But scorns me for my own.' See queries in *Miscellaneous Correspondence in Prose and Verse*, February 1757, p.492.
73 *London Chronicle for 1757*, 1–3 March, p.216.
74 Thus *Gentleman's Magazine*, January 1761, p.39: 'Large was his soul, his mercy unconfin'd', the sixth stanza of J. Cowper's 'On the King's Death'.

75 Sermon of 2 November 1760: S. Stennett, *The Works of Samuel Stennett, D.D.* (London: Tegg, 1824), vol.3, p.193.
76 *A Sermon Occasioned by the Death of His Late Majesty: Preached on Saturday the 29th of November, 1760, in the Synagogue of the Portuguese Jews in London. By Isaac Mendes Belisario ... Translated from the Spanish* (London: Brotherton, 1760), p.9.
77 'An elegiac ode on the death of his late Majesty', *The Poetical Works of John Cunningham* in *The Works of the British Poets* (Edinburgh: Mundell, 1794), p.739.
78 *The Times: A Poem* (Boston: T. and J. Fleet, 1765), reprinted in S. Kettell, *Specimens of American Poetry* (3 vols; Boston: Goodrich, 1829), vol.1, p.156.
79 R. Southey, *Authentic Memoirs of Our Late Venerable and Beloved Monarch, George the Third* (London: Jones, 1820), p.99. By contrast, J. Duncan, 'the late King [who] entertained such laudable scruples about signing death-warrants, violated the positive command, "Thou shalt not kill" in wider extent than any of his predecessors', *Remarks on the Legality and Expediency of Prosecutions for Religious Opinion. To Which Is Annexed an Apology for the Vices of the Lower Orders* (London: Hunt, 1825), p.99.
80 E. Sibly, *A New and Complete Illustration of the Celestial Science* (12th edition, 2 vols: London: Lewis, 1822), vol.2, p.891.
81 See TNA HO47/2/59: the Earl of Mansfield on Molyneux case, 3 August 1785; on Chaffey, see TNA HO42/15/56, where at the king's request, the Home Secretary sought the Lord Chancellor's advice, 21 September 1789. See S. Devereaux, 'Imposing the Royal Pardon: Execution, Transportation, and Convict Resistance in London, 1789', *Law and History Review* 25: 1 (Spring 2007), pp. 101–38; L. MacKay, 'Refusing the Royal Pardon: London Capital Convicts and the Reactions of the Courts and Press, 1789', *The London Journal* 28: 2 (2003), pp.21–40.
82 *The New Monthly Belle Assemblée*, January 1857, p.20. On Patrick M'Carty's execution for killing Marshalsea Court officer William Talbot, see *Oxford Journal*, 25 October 1760, p.3. John Fielding committed him to Newgate, *The London Magazine*, October 1760, p.553.
83 [E. Neale] *Dark Deeds. By the Author of 'The Gaol Chaplain'* (London: Vickers, 1857), p.79. See *London Magazine*, September 1761, p.503; and *Dodley's Annual Register* (London: 1762), p.171. Thomas Daniel, a boxmaker, was accused of throwing his wife naked from a window.
84 'Punishment of Death', *Church and State Review*, 1 October 1864, p.110.
85 *Annual Register* 1770, p.228. Also, 'Some Reflexions upon the Pardon of M'Quirk; as whether such a Person could be a proper Object of Mercy; or whether it proceeded from some other Motives', pp.34–7 in J. Free, *Common Safety: The Cause and Foundation of Human Society* (2nd edition; London: for the author, 1769). For the medical side, J. Foot, *An Appeal to the Public, Touching the Death of Mr. George Clarke, Who Received a Blow at Brentford on Thursday the Eighth of December Last, of Which He Languished and Died on Wednesday the Fourteenth of the Same Month* (London: Davis, 1769).
86 F. McLynn, *Crime and Punishment in Eighteenth Century England* (1989; London: Routledge, 2013), briefly comments on suspicion and fear of the royal exercise of prerogative.
87 Free, *Common Safety the Cause and Foundation of Human Society*, p.vii.
88 *London Magazine*, April 1768, p.219.
89 'On the Nature and Institution of Government', Oxford Magazine, July 1771, pp.21–24 [p.22].
90 'B.C.' *Oxford Magazine*, December 1771, p.216.

91 *Public Advertiser*, 21 January 1772 [p.1].
92 C.R. Leslie, T. Taylor, *Life and Times of Sir Joshua Reynolds* (2 vols; London: Murray, 1865), vol.1, p.396.
93 *Memoirs of John Horne Tooke*, vol.1, p.105. The case stimulated lamentation that 'a national misfortune that mercy has been once misplaced', in J. Shebbeare's *An Answer to the Queries, Contained in a Letter to Dr. Shebbeare... Together with Animadversions on Two Speeches... The First Pronounced by the Right Hon. Thomas Townshend... The Second by the Right Learned Counsellor Lee, Etc* (Dublin: Wogan, 1775), p.82. See J. Brewer, 'The Wilkites and the Law, 1763-74: A Study of Radical Notions of Governance', ch.4 in J. Brewer and J. Styles eds, *An Ungovernable People: The English and Their Law in the Seventeenth and Eighteenth Centuries* (Brunswick, NJ: Rutgers University Press, 1980); F. McLynn, *Crime and Punishment* (1989; Abingdon: Routledge, 2013), p.45.
94 'Justice, with Mercy join'd, the throne maintains; | And in his People's HEARTS OUR MONARCH reigns', in prologue (1759) to A. Murphy, *The Orphan of China: A Tragedy* (3rd edition, London: Vaillant, 1772), p.vi, by William Whitehead, poet-laureate, correcting Murphy's overzealous defence of a monarch's cause. See R.C. Taylor, *Goldsmith as Journalist* (Rutherford, NJ: Fairleigh Dickinson University Press, 1993), p.147.
95 *The Fugitive Miscellany. Being a Collection of Such Fugitive Pieces, in Prose and Verse, as Are Not in Any Other Collection* (3 vols; London: J. Almon, 1775), vol.2, pp.153–62; reprinted, *The New Foundling Hospital for Wit* (6 vols; London: Debrett, 1784), vol.5, pp.189–200.
96 J. Boswell, *The Life of Samuel Johnson, LL. D.* (2 vols; London: Baldwin, 1791), vol.2, p.136.
97 R. McGowen, 'From Pillory to Gallows: The Punishment of Forgery in the Age of the Financial Revolution', *Past & Present* 165 (November 1999), pp. 107–40 [p.109, p.137].
98 D.T. Andrew and R. McGowen, *The Perreaus and Mrs. Rudd. Forgery and Betrayal in Eighteenth-Century London* (Berkeley: University of California Press, 2001), p.261; see P. Baines, *The House of Forgery in Eighteenth-Century Britain* (Aldershot: Ashgate, 1999) for the wider cultural context for forgery cases such as Perreau and Dodd.
99 L. Radzinowicz, *A History of English Criminal Law and Its Administration*, vol.1, p.451; p.463 (footnote 44), quoting Sir Nathaniel Wraxall, 'If it could have been extended to him without producing by the precedent incalculable injury to society his majesty would undoubtedly have exercised in his case the prerogative of mercy... The Earl of Mansfield however prevented so pernicious an act of grace.'
100 *The North-British Intelligencer*, 19 March 1777, p.366. Verse appeared entitled 'The Royal Penitent', paraphrasing Psalm 51, *Scots Magazine* 211, April 1777, pp.211–12.
101 *Caledonian Mercury*, 18 June 1777, p.2.
102 *Westmorland Gazette*, 15 April 1865, p.3. Boswell, *The Life of Samuel Johnson*, vol.2, p.119, Boswell's letter, 9 July 1777, expresses concern about the regard that God's Vicegerent 'will ever show to piety and virtue... Such an instance would do more to encourage goodness, than his execution would do to deter from vice.'
103 *Hampshire Chronicle*, 14 July 1777, p.4. Dodd's case and withholding of mercy, concerned Charles Wesley, see T. Jackson, *The Life of the Reverend Charles Wesley* (2 vols: London: Mason, 1841), vol.2, pp.309–13: praying, at p.310 for the royal bosom to find mercy. Wesleyan attitudes to mercy are a subject in itself; Methodism was supposed to promote 'justice, mercy and truth, the glory of God, and peace

and goodwill among men': R.H. Stone, *John Wesley's Life and Ethics* (Nashville: Abingdon, 2001).

104 W. Dodd, *Thoughts in Prison: In Five Parts. Viz. The Imprisonment. The Retrospect. Public Punishment. The Trial. Futurity. By the Rev. William Dodd, LLD. To Which Are Added, His Last Prayer… and Other Miscellaneous Pieces* (Dublin: Price, etc, 1778), p.241. Efforts to save Dodd through petition to the king and insight into discussion on the Recorder's report appear later e.g. *The Annals of Crime and New Newgate Calendar*, 24 August 1833, p.7.

105 Bryan's *A Biographical and Critical Dictionary of Painters and Engravers, from the Revival of the Art Under Cimabue… To the Present Time: With the Ciphers, Monograms, and Marks, Used by Each Engraver* (1816; London: H.G. Bohn, 1849), p.677, 'it was a time too when royalty exercised all its prerogatives but that of mercy'.

106 'Contributions to the History of Forgery', *Monthly Chronicle* 3, January–June 1839. See *Scots Magazine*, 1 January 1776, p.50; *Shrewsbury Chronicle*, 20 January 1776, p.2.

107 *Hereford Journal*, 7 August 1783; *Newcastle Courant*, 30 August 1781, p.4.

108 *Reading Mercury*, 4 August 1783, p.1.

109 *Northampton Mercury*, 11 August 1783, p.3.

110 *Caledonian Mercury*, 30 July 1783, p.3.

111 *Newcastle Courant*, 6 September 1783, p.3.

112 *Northampton Mercury*, 8 September 1783, p.4.

113 *London Magazine*, August 1783, p.172; W. Creech, *An Account of the Trial of William Brodie and George Smith, Before the High Court of Justiciary, on the 27th and 28th Days of August, 1788* (Edinburgh: Creech, 1788), p.278.

114 *Westmorland Gazette*, 12 February 1820, p.6; 'Royal Notion of Justice', *Examiner*, 14 December 1828, p.2. Probably David Wilcock, who paid a forged guinea note but was pardoned.

115 *Annual Register* 102: 2 (1832) supplement, pp.622–3; T.B. Murray, *Pitcairn, the Island, the People, and the Pastor* (London: SPCK, 1860).

116 *Annual Register* 50 (1808), pp.80–3; *Universal Magazine*, August 1808, p.187; A. Aspinall, ed., *The Correspondence of George, Prince of Wales 1770–1812* vol. 6, *1806–1809* (London: Cassell, 1971), p.2505; *Particulars Respecting the Trial, Condemnation and Execution of Major Henry Alexander Campbell* (Boston: J. Cushing, 1808).

117 R.A. Roberts, ed., *Calendar of Home Office Papers of the Reign of George III. 1773–1775 Preserved in the Public Record Office* (London: HMSO, 1899), pp.10–12, letter of Sir John Fielding to Earl of Suffolk, 1 February 1773.

118 *Oracle and Public Advertiser*, 13 January 1797; 'Principal Occurrences in the Year 1797', *New Annual Register* (London: Robinson, 1798), p.12. A more detailed account is the Old Bailey Proceedings Online (www.oldbaileyonline.org, version 8.0) (accessed 7 September 2019), January 1797, trial of Launcelot Knowles (t17970111-4).

119 'Free Settler or Felon? Convict Ship Lady Shore 1797', http://www.jenwilletts.com/convict_ship_lady_shore_1797.htm (accessed 7 September 2019), cites a Belfast newspaper reporting Knowles had been the Duke of Portland's porter and claimed to be born in Ireland. He was apprehended in 1804 on a Spanish ship off Cadiz. See *Ennis Chronicle and Clare Advertiser*, 7 January 1805, p.2. The *Morning Post* proprietor lost a case for slander when a servant of Portland was implicated in Knowles's fraud, T. Peake, *Additional Cases: Being a Continuation of Cases at Nisi Prius, Before Lord Kenyon, and Other Eminent Judges, Taken at Different Times Between the Years 1795 and 1812* (London: Clarke, 1829), p.141.

120 [P. Colquhoun] *A Treatise on the Police of the Metropolis: Containing a Detail of the Various Crimes and Misdemeanors by Which Public and Private Property and Security Are, at Present, Injured and Endangered: and Suggesting Remedies for Their Prevention* (4th edition; London: Fry, 1797), p.24 (same pagination in third edition). Cited in Radzinowicz, *A History of English Criminal Law and Its Administration*, vol.1, p.185. Colquhoun's 1800 edition was dedicated to the king.
121 *A Treatise on the Police of the Metropolis, Explaining the Various crimes, and Misdemeanours Which at Present Are Felt as a Pressure upon the Community and Suggesting Remedies for Their Prevention by a Magistrate* (London: Fry, 1796), pp.32–3.
122 C. Hamilton, *Transactions During the Reign of Queen Ann; from the Union to the Death of That Princess* (Edinburgh: Creech, 1790), pp.viii–ix.
123 H. Fielding, *An Enquiry into the Causes of the Late Increase of Robbers* (2nd edition: London: Millar, 1751), section 10, 'Of the encouragement given to robbers by frequent pardons'.
124 An ode at St Patrick's Hall, Dublin, *Walker's Hibernian Magazine*, February 1796, p.191. Presumably the attack on the state coach, the day of the state opening of Parliament in October 1795.
125 Note also in 'Universal Prayer', Alexander Pope's lines: 'Teach me to feel another's woe, | To hide the fault I see: | That mercy I to others shew, | That mercy shew to me'. For rendering of the Nicholson episode, see mezzotint by Robert Dighton sold by Carington Bowles, 9 November 1786. Nicholson sent verse appealing to 'Justice with Mercy', D.H. Reiman, N. Fraistat, eds, *The Complete Poetry of Percy Bysshe Shelley* (3 vols; London: Johns Hopkins University Press, 1999), vol.1, p.239.
126 'On the King's Recovery', *London Review and Literary Journal*, March 1789, p.245.
127 *Leeds Intelligencer*, 9 June 1789 [p.2].
128 L. Colley, 'The Apotheosis of George III: Loyalty, Royalty, and the British Nation', *Past and Present* 102 (February 1984), pp.94–129; *Britons: Forging the Nation. 1707–1837* (1992; London: Pimlico, 1996).
129 J. Barrell, *Imagining the King's Death. Figurative Treason, Fantasies of Regicide 1793–1796* (Oxford: Oxford University Press, 2000), p.110, in context of publisher Daniel Eaton's trial for seditious libel in 1794; and the mercy invoked by the radical James Kennedy, p.117. In establishing the secret committee in 1794, Barrell's footnote 28 on p.193 shows the language (threat?) of 'due *Justice* and *Mercy*'.
130 A. Craciun, *British Women Writers and the French Revolution* (Houndmills: Palgrave Macmillan, 2005), pp.70–1, referring to her 'Ode on the 18th of January,' and accompanying prose commentary in *Oracle*, 2 January 1794; A. Goodwin, *The Friends of Liberty: The English Democratic Movement in the Age of the French Revolution* (London: Hutchinson, 1979), p.325.
131 *The Parliamentary Register: Or an Impartial Report of the Debates That Occur in the Two Houses of Parliament*, vol.4, Commons, 17 May 1794 (London: Chapman, 1794), p.39–40, Sheridan. For spurning of 'mercy' by Muir, see Dundas in Commons, 17 May 1794, *Debates on the Report of the Committee of Secrecy in the House of Commons on the 16th and 17th … of May, and in the House of Lords on the 17th and 19th and 22d of the Same Month, 1794* (Edinburgh: Robertson), p.36.
132 Excerpt, *The Historical Magazine*, May 1790, p.186.
133 Hewlett, *The Jubilee*, p.12.
134 Review of 'Beccaria Anglicus', *Letters on Capital Punishments, Addressed to the English Judges. By Beccaria Anglicus* (London: Johnson, 1807) in *Critical Review*, 3rd series 12: 1, September 1807, p.99.

135 J. Taylor, *Relics of Royalty or, Remarks, Anecdotes, and Conversations, of His Late Majesty George the Third* (London: Dean and Munday, 1820), introduction.
136 J. Beresford, *A Discourse in Memory of His Late Majesty, George III* (Leicester: Combe, 1820), p.11.
137 R. Heath, *A King's Example and a People's Duty; a Sermon Preached on Feb. 16, 1820, on Which Evening the Remains of King George the Third Were Interred at Windsor* (London: Rivington, 1820), p.9.
138 *Morning Post*, 3 February 1820, p.3; *Norfolk Chronicle*, 5 February 1820, p.2.
139 R. Huish, *The History of The Private and Political Life of The Late Henry Hunt, Esq., M.P. for Preston* (2 vols; London: Saunders, 1836), vol.1, p.457.
140 *Investigation at Ilchester Gaol in the County of Somerset into the Conduct of William Bridle, the Gaoler* (London: Dolby, 1821). Hunt's situation and implications for the prerogative of mercy from a Commons request to remit the remainder of his sentence figured in Parliament, *Parliamentary Debates*, 24 April 1822, col.41–42.
141 *Exeter and Plymouth Gazette*, 12 April 1845, p.4.
142 The play was criticized as 'Dr Dodd for the Drama', *Court Journal*, see playwright's account, *The Law of the Land, or, London in the Last Century: A Drama in Three Acts (Founded on Fact)* (London: Kenneth, 1837), p.vi. On Lucy Dodsworth's petition, pp.41–2, p.44. For an appreciative but critical review, see *The Athenaeum*, 26 August 1837, pp.629–30.
143 C. White, 'My House in Cecil Street. The Reprieve. Part II', *Ainsworth's Magazine*, 6 (1844), pp.136–40 [p.139].
144 [W. Harvey], *London Scenes and London People: Anecdotes, Reminiscences, and Sketches of Places, Personages, Events, Customs, and Curiosities of London City, Past and Present* (London: Collingridge, 1863), pp.229–30.
145 D. Jerrold, *The History of St Giles and St James*, ch.16, serialized in *Douglas Jerrold's Shilling Magazine* 2: 9 (1845), p.199; reprinted in provincial newspapers.
146 Bleackley, *Some Distinguished Victims of the Scaffold*, p.67. Smith, *George IV*, p.211, emphasizes combined ameliorative efforts by Peel and George IV and refers to the king's abolition of torture (25 March 1822) in Hanover.
147 *Ipswich Journal*, 26 September 1789, p.1.
148 *Chester Courant*, 4 December 1810 [p.2].
149 *The Examiner*, 20 January 1811, p.2. See *Cobbett's Parliamentary Debates*, 28 January 1811, Earl Grey, col.1060, 'may not this line of argument apply to deprive the Regent of that brightest jewel of the royal station – mercy?'
150 *Gentleman's Magazine*, January 1811, p.70; *Knapp and Baldwin's Newgate Calendar and Criminal Recorder* (London: Robins, 1828) vol.4, p.30: 'a feeling that it would be unjust to deprive a human being of life, however enormous his crime, while the fountain of mercy was closed.'
151 *Cheltenham Chronicle*, 24 January 1811, p.1.
152 TNA HO47/46/10, 26 February 1811.
153 TNA HO47/46/9, 16 February 1811. See *Historical Records of Australia* (Sydney: The Library Committee of the Commonwealth Parliament 1916), series 1, vol. 7, p.353, 14 March 1811, for Under Secretary Peel asking for every comfort on board the *Friend*, when transported to New South Wales, due to 'earnest representations' on her behalf.
154 TNA HO47/67/24, 21 April 1811.
155 *Derby Mercury*, 12 September 1811, p.4.
156 J. Watkins, *The Important Results of an Elaborate Investigation into the Mysterious Case of Elizabeth Fenning* (London: Hone, 1815).

157 *Parliamentary Debates from the Year 1803 to the Present Time. Vol. 32. Comprising the Period from the First Day of February to the Sixth Day of March, 1816* (London: Hansard, 1816), 16 February 1816, House of Commons, 'Privately Stealing Bill', col.631.
158 *Caledonian Mercury*, 23 March 1816, p.2, a question raised by Bennet about the many in Newgate under death sentence, 'upon whose cases the Royal opinion had not as yet been taken'. Milton asked if indisposition 'shut up the course and current of the Royal mercy'.
159 *Criminal Recorder: Or, Biographical Sketches of Notorious Public Characters* (2 vols; Nottingham, Dowson, 1815), vol.2, p.627.
160 *Public Ledger*, 27 October 1817, p.4.
161 *Account of the Extraordinary and Shocking Case of George Mathews: Who Was Capitally Convicted at the Old Bailey in February, 1818 on a False Charge of Robbing His Master, Colonel Whaley* (London: Ridgway, 1818), p.viii.
162 *Hull Packet*, 28 April 1818, p.4; *Chester Courant*, 28 April 1818, p.4. [Theodore Hook] 'Precepts and Practice. No. III – Captain Gray', *The New Monthly Magazine* (1835), p.321, claimed 'her active, energetic mind was indefatigably working in every available channel, in order to excite the pity and secure the mercy of the Sovereign'.
163 [C. Bowdler], *On the Punishment of Death, in the Case of Forgery; Its Injustices and Impolicy Maintained* (London: Hamilton, 1818), p.25.
164 W. Anderson, entry on 'Forgery', *The London Commercial Dictionary, and Sea-port Gazetteer* (London: Wilson, 1819), p.288.
165 British Museum, Coventry Bank 1981, 1122.103; Burton and Uttoxeter Bank, 1981,1122.80; Brighton Union Bank, 1981,1122.62.
166 *New Monthly Magazine* 10 (1 October 1818), p.208.
167 The case of John Driscoll, William Weller and George Cashman, executed at Newgate; *Black Dwarf*, 16 December 1818, cols.783–784; see also *Black Dwarf*, 24 March 1819, col.181.
168 *Morning Post*, 10 December 1819, p.4. Fourteen thousand people signed a petition in his case. See *A Full and Circumstantial Report of the Interesting Trial of Henry Stent, Before Mr. Justice Best, at the Sessions House, in the Old Bailey, on Saturday, September 18, 1819, for Maliciously Stabbing His Wife, Maria Stent, on the 5th Day of August Last* (London: Ferriday, 1819).
169 *Journals of the House of Lords*, vol. 52 (1819), 12 May 1819, p.569. In reports of the debate on the Speech, *Morning Post*, 22 January 1819, p.3, and elsewhere, there is a 'politics of the royal prerogative' with MacDonald complaining that ministers curtailed the Regent of the 'noblest, best, and the most divine prerogative', in 'strangely asserting' that petitions for mercy could not be submitted to him.
170 'The Regent's Song; Or, The Song of the Regent', *Gentleman's Magazine*, March 1819, p.256.
171 [J. Crook], *The Voice of the People, in a Memorial to the Prince Regent of Great Britain and Ireland. By an Elector of Westminster* (Westminster: Hay, 1819), p.24; *The Patriot*, 23 October 1819, p.128.
172 *Royal Cornwall Gazette*, 9 June 1837, p.4. Quotation from 'The Insurrection of the Papers. A Dream', *The Works of Thomas Moore, Comprehending All His Melodies, Ballads* (7 vols; Paris: Galignani, 1823), vol.5, pp.221–2.
173 E. Barron, *The Wrongs of Royalty: Being a Continuation of The Royal Wanderer, or, Memoirs of Her Present Majesty Queen Caroline* (London: Rowe, 1820), p.692: printing Denman's speech.

174 Houston, 'Reading and writing Victoria', p.170. The reference is to [C. Bury], *The Murdered Queen! Or, Caroline of Brunswick: A Diary of the Court of George IV* (London: Emans, 1838), p.647.
175 'The Queen's interference for the woman under sentence of death for forgery', *Birmingham Chronicle*, 21 December 1820; J.H. Adolphus, *The Royal Exile; or Memoirs of the Public and Private Life of Her Majesty, Caroline* (18th edition, 2 vols; London: Jones, 1821), vol.2, pp.491–2.
176 *Morning Post*, 15 December 1820 [p.1].
177 M. Airlie, *Lady Palmerston and Her Times* (2 vols; London: Hodder and Stoughton, 1922), vol.1, p.78.
178 *Salisbury and Winchester Journal*, 5 March 1821, p.4; *Hampshire Chronicle*, 5 March 1821, p.4.
179 See HO44/6/107 for the petition of William Baker, 1820, to the King.
180 Defence lawyer Broderick, in W.B. Gurney, *The Trials of Arthur Thistlewood, James Ings, John Thomas Brunt, Richard Tidd, William Davidson, and Others, for High Treason: At the Sessions House in Old Bailey… April, 1820, with the Antecedent Proceedings* (2 vols; London: Butterworth, 1820), vol.2, p.623.
181 *Morning Chronicle*, 13 December 1820, p.3; *Old Bailey Proceedings Online* (www.oldbaileyonline.org, version 8.0, 7 September 2019), September 1820, trial of Thomas Fuller Harnett (t18200918-83). See *Execution of Captain Thomas Fuller Harnett and Ann Price: The Captain for Forging a Bill, and the Woman for Uttering Forged Notes, who Were Executed, Along with Four Others, on Tuesday Last, the 5th December, 1820* (Trongate: Carse, 1820).
182 *Westmorland Gazette*, 22 September 1821, p.2; *Taunton Courier*, 26 September 1821, p.6.
183 *Leeds Intelligencer*, 26 November 1821, p.4; *Bury and Norwich Post*, 28 November 1821, p.4.
184 D. Knighton, *Memoirs of Sir William Knighton, Bart., G.C.H.* (2 vols; London: Bentley, 1838), vol.1, p.170; *Aberdeen Journal*, 12 September 1821, p.3. British texts reported capital punishment as rare e.g. 'Hanover', *Edinburgh Gazetteer* (6 vols; Edinburgh: Constable, 1822), vol. 3, p.211.
185 *Leeds Mercury*, 24 November 1821, p.3.
186 The Ordinary Cotton, reprinted as 'Condemned Sermon for the Eight Men who were Executed on Wednesday', *Westmorland Gazette*, 24 November 1821, p.1.
187 *The State of the Nation at the Commencement of the Year 1822 Considered under the Four Departments of The Finance – Foreign Relations – Home Department – Colonies and Board of Trade* (2nd edition; London: Hatchard, 1822), p. 165; the reply, *An Answer to the State of the Nation at the Commencement of the Year 1822, and the Declarations and Conduct of His Majesty's Ministers Fairly Considered* (London: Ridgway, 1822), p.74.
188 *Royal Cornwall Gazette*, 8 March 1823, p.4.
189 The image, dedicated to John Gardner of Mansfield Place, Kentish Town, 13 June 1823, was sold by Rosebery's of London, 2009.
190 *Morning Post*, 27 November 1824, p.4. See also *The Examiner*, 17 October 1824, p.12. Petitions were addressed to the king-in-council from friends and his wife, *Morning Post*, 8 November 1824, p.4; *Westmorland Gazette*, 13 November 1824, p.2. For correspondence on the justice of withholding royal mercy in this case, see 'W' in *The Kaleidoscope*, 30 November 1824, p.183. For the black seal, see *Bell's Life in London and Sporting Chronicle*, 28 November 1824 [p.1].

191 *The Times*, 13 October 1824, p.3; *Hereford Journal*, 20 October 1824, p.4.
192 *Ipswich Journal*, 9 October 1824 [p.4], referring to the *Newgate Calendar* and Home Secretary's account.
193 *Hampshire Chronicle*, 22 December 1828 [p.3].
194 *The Examiner*, 14 December 1828, p.801, and in amended form in A. Fonblanque, *England Under Seven Administrations* (3 vols; London: Bentley, 1837), vol.1. See *Morning Chronicle*, 11 December 1828, p.2, for subsequent discussion of the royal prerogative.
195 *Sussex Advertiser*, 15 December 1828, p.4. For details of response to these appeals by Home Secretary Peel and members of the Privy Council and communication with the king, see *Oxford Journal*, 13 December 1828, p.4. Petitions were sent to Dublin Castle: Chief Secretary's Office Registered Papers, CSO/RP/1830/2240 (description published http://www.csorp.nationalarchives.ie (accessed 26 July 2018)).
196 *Sussex Advertiser*, 15 December 1828, p.4. The case is preserved in broadsides e.g. *The Life, Trial, and Awful Execution, of Joseph Hunton, Who Was Executed This Morning, December 8th, 1828, in Front of the Debtor's Door at Newgate, for Forgery*.
197 All quotations in the following paragraph are from *The Examiner*, 14 December 1828, p.801.
198 *The Examiner*, 11 September 1831, p.1.
199 *London Standard*, 6 April 1830, p.2, quoting *Limerick Chronicle*.
200 Reports from *Limerick Chronicle*, in *Westmorland Gazette*, 8 May 1830, p.2. Execution was due on 19 April 1830, *Freeman's Journal*, 15 April 1830, p.4. *Clare Sentinel* emphasized the role that the viceroy could play in mercy; see *London Standard*, 12 April 1830, p.3.
201 *London Standard*, 12 April 1830, p.3.
202 *London Standard*, 4 May 1830, p.3.
203 Quoted in *London Standard*, 20 April 1830, p.3.
204 Gatrell, *The Hanging Tree*, ch.20, 'The King in Council', sees George IV's response as one of 'self-distancing' squeamishness and sentiment (pp.269, 551). W.S. Hall, *The Empire of Philanthropy: With a Portraiture of British Excellence as a National Example: a Dramatic Poem with Notes* (London: Hatchard, 1822), notes on the king's mercy in capital punishment and charity, pp.152–3, quoting *Percy Anecdotes*; *The Lady's Magazine*, 30 June 1830, p.386; *Annual Biography and Obituary for the Year*, 1831, p.169, 'Prerogative made no harsh or unbecoming pretensions under the deceased Monarch… Justice was administered in mercy, never was the gracious prerogative of pardon exercised with more readiness.'
205 C.S. Parker, ed., *Sir Robert Peel in Early Life, 1788–1812, as Secretary, 1812–1818, and as Secretary of State, 1822–1827: From His Private Correspondence* (London: Murray, 1891), pp.306–17. The editor speaks of 'several letters creditable to the heart of the King, or of those about him' and reproduces letters, 13 April 1822, on the thirteen-year-old convict Henry Newbury; and on Ward and Desmond on 21 May 1822 – being overruled in efforts to save Ward (p.317). See B. Hilton, 'The Gallows and Mr Peel', ch.5 in T.C.W. Blanning and D. Cannadine, eds, *History and Biography: Essays in Honour of Derek Beales* (Cambridge: Cambridge University Press, 1996).
206 A study of thousands of petitions by B.G. Mortimer, 'Rethinking penal reform and the Royal prerogative of mercy during Robert Peel's stewardship of the Home Office 1822–7, 1828–30', PhD, University of Leicester 2017, follows the line of a humane king operating on a whim, e.g. pp.101–2.

207 *Gentleman's Magazine* 100: 2 (1830), p.161.
208 J. Banvard, *The Life of George IV* (New York: Hurst, 1875), p.572: 'the King always leaned to the side of mercy. It not unfrequently happens that the culprit escapes owing to the scruples of the King.'
209 *Hertford Mercury and Reformer*, 8 December 1835, p.4. See also W. Clark, *The Georgian Era* (4 vols, London: Vizetelly, Branston, 1832), vol.1, p.126.
210 *Bury and Norwich Post*, 7 July 1830, p.1; *Morning Post*, 26 January 1831, p.3; H.E. Lloyd, *George IV. Memoirs of His Life and Reign* (London: Treuttel and Würtz, 1830), pp.465–6.
211 [W.H. Pyne] 'The Greater and Lesser Stars of Old Pall Mall', *Fraser's Magazine*, 1841, pp.677–91 [p.691].
212 J. Alley, *A Sermon Preached at the Parish Church of Saint Mary, Islington, Nov. 16, 1817, Occasioned by the Death of the Princess Charlotte* (London: Rivington, 1818), p.17.
213 The Reverend J.T. Holloway of Whitby, *Select Extracts and Beauties… from… Sermons… on the… Demise… of… the Princess Charlotte, by Divines of the Church Establishment [&c.] by the Editor of the Biographical Memoir of Her Royal Highness* (London: Booth, 1818), p.114.
214 *Royal Correspondence, or, Letters Between Her Late Royal Highness the Princess Charlotte and Her Royal Mother, Queen Caroline of England, During the Exile of the Latter* (London: Jones, 1822), p.29.
215 R. Huish, *Memoirs of Her Late Royal Highness Charlotte Augusta, Princess of Wales* (London: Kelly, 1818), p.277.
216 *Gentleman's Magazine* 122 (December 1817), pp.542–3.
217 E.g. *Sussex Advertiser*, 14 December 1812, p.2, publishing the convict's petition and letter from 'V.H.' See *Old Bailey Proceedings Online* (www.oldbaileyonline.org, version 8.0, 7 September 2019), October 1812, trial of Frances Sage (t18121028-18).
218 'Beneficence', *Percy Anecdotes*, p.6. See J. Coote, *A Biographical Memoir of the Public and Private Life of the Much Lamented Princess Charlotte Augusta of Wales and Saxe-Coburg* (London: Booth, 1817), p.162.
219 *Public Ledger*, 29 June 1826, suggested this was Joseph Michael Hamilton of Dublin, who published *Duelling, The School for Patriots, and Benevolists*, and was a philanthropist, see *Court Magazine*, July 1837, pp.99–101; *The Irish Builder*, 1 August 1870, p.174.
220 Huish, *Memoirs of Her Late Royal Highness Charlotte Augusta, Princess of Wales*, p.487.
221 *Newcastle Courant*, 18 June 1831, p.2. See also *The Life and Memoir of Her Royal Highness Princess Charlotte* (London: Kinnersley, 1818), p. 431.
222 Reviewed in J. Hochstetler, *A History of Criminal Justice in England and Wales* (Winchester: Waterside Press, 2006), ch.12.
223 *A History of England: Combining the Various Histories by Rapin, Henry, Hume, Smollett and Belsham: Corrected by Reference to Furner, Lingard, Mackintosh, Hallam, Brodie, Godwin, and Other Sources; in Three Volumes; from the Invasion by the Romans, B.C. 55 to the Birth of the Prince of Wales, A.D. 1841* (London: Kendrick, 1856), vol. 3, p.1008.
224 *Gentleman's Magazine* 100: 2 (August 1830), p.160.
225 See *Sherborne Mercury*, 6 October 1834, p.2, for comment by the Livery in Common Hall, on the shrievalties of London and Middlesex.
226 *Hertford Mercury and Reformer*, 8 December 1835, p.4.

227 S. Poole, *The Politics of Regicide in England, 1760–1850: Troublesome Subjects* (Manchester: Manchester University Press, 2000), p.166.
228 *Hertford Mercury and Reformer*, 8 December 1835, p.4.
229 J. Peggs, *Capital Punishment: The Importance of Its Abolition: A Prize Essay* (London: Ward, 1839). *Fraser's Magazine*, January 1838, p.69. Abolitionists stressed William IV's clemency and constraint by 'Ministerial Advisers', *The Punishment of Death: A Selection of Articles from the Morning Herald with Notes* (2 vols; London: Hatchard-Elder, 1837), vol.2, p.204.
230 See *The Punishment of Death: A Selection of Articles from the Morning Herald*, vol. 2, p.ii, pp.303, 356, for allusion to William IV's clemency, by 1837. For another report, see *Morning Herald*, 24 November 1835, reported in *Sheffield Independent*, 26 December 1835 [p.3].
231 C. Hindley, *Curiosities of Street Literature: Comprising 'Cocks' or 'Catchpennies', Street-drolleries* (London: Reeves and Turner, 1871), p.53.
232 See petitioning of Adelaide in F. Clune and P.R. Stephensen, *The Pirates of the Brig Cyprus* (London: Hart-Davis, 1962), pp.189–91.
233 G.N. Wright, *The Life and Reign of William the Fourth* (London: Fisher, 1837), p.833.
234 *Selections from the Writings of the Late J. Sydney Taylor, with a Brief Sketch of His Life* (London: Gilpin, 1843), p.283.
235 *London Standard*, 10 July 1837, p.4; *Christian's Penny Magazine*, 22 July 1837, p.232. See also W. Harding, *An Impartial Life of His Late Majesty William the Fourth* (London: Harding, 1837), p.33. J. Sydney Taylor, quoted in *Christian's Penny Magazine*, 22 July 1837, p.236, detected a consistency in William's clemency from the time he presented a petition on behalf of a brother midshipman condemned to death at Jamaica in 1782 for insubordination.
236 *Baptist Magazine* 29 (1837), p.355.
237 R. Huish, *The History of the Life and Reign of William the Fourth, the Reform Monarch of England* (London: Emans, 1837), p.716.
238 'The Death of King William IV', in *Ward's Miscellany* (London: Ward, 1837), p.476.
239 *Coventry Herald*, 7 July 1837, p.3.
240 *New Monthly Magazine*, 1 October 1831, p.434.
241 *The Punishment of Death: A Selection of Articles from the Morning Herald*, vol. 1, p.163.
242 E. Neale, *Life of Edward Duke of Kent* (London: R. Bentley, 1850), p.83.
243 *Eclectic Review*, May 1848, p.529. Fry met Victoria, being requested to visit with William Allen in 1840 (she quoted 'with the merciful Thou wilt shew Thyself merciful', *Memoir of the Life of Elizabeth Fry*, vol.2, p.353). She dined with the Prince and Peel at Mansion House and discussed prisons, punishments becoming too severe, 'my wish that the Queen should be informed of some particulars respecting separate confinement, &c. &c.' 'With Sir Robert Peel, I dwelt much more on the prison subject', *Memoir of the Life of Elizabeth Fry*, vol.2, p.423.
244 See W.J. Anderson, *The Life of F. M., H. R. H. Edward, Duke of Kent: Illustrated by His Correspondence with the De Salaberry Family, Never Before Published, Extending from 1791 to 1814* (Ottawa and Toronto: Hunter, Rose, 1870), pp.15–16. For his sadistic treatment of petty infringements, see D. Thompson, *Queen Victoria*, p.16.
245 W. Kennedy, 'To the Princess Victoria', *The Atlas*, 17 January 1829, p.137; T.D. Barleé, *Miscellaneous Poetry* (Bath: Collings, 1837), pp.8–12; *Court Magazine*, 10, January to June 1837, p.284.

246 The accountant Donald Bain's *Aera Astraea, or, the Age of Justice: An Ode to Her Most Gracious Majesty Victoria* (Edinburgh: Menzies, 1845). See M. Pittock, 'The Culture of Jacobitism', in J. Black, ed., *Culture and Society in Britain, 1660–1800* (Manchester: Manchester University Press, 1997), p.134, on the figure of Astraea, virgin goddess of justice.

Chapter 3

1 [H. Brandreth], *Minstrel Melodies: A Collection of Songs, by the Author of 'Field Flowers'* (London: Longman, Orme, 1839), poem 5 July 1837; reprinted *Aldine Magazine*, 1 May 1839, p.262. For a variant, *Worcestershire Chronicle*, 5 July 1838, p.6.
2 R.E. Hendriks, *Political Fame* (London: W. Pickering, 1847), p.96.
3 *Morning Chronicle*, 17 December 1859, p.4: in the context of sailors who mutinied on the *Princess Royal* and were sent to Winchester gaol.
4 H. Rappaport, ed., *Queen Victoria: A Biographical Companion* (Santa Barbara, California: ABC-CLIO, 2003), p.381.
5 For the queen as generous hearted, see Thompson, *Queen Victoria*, p.29.
6 *Cassell's Illustrated History of England* (London: Cassell, Petter and Galpin, 1863), (8 vols; London etc etc), vol.7, p.386.
7 *The Public Ledger*, St John's (Newfoundland), 13 November 1838.
8 *Eclectic Review* 3, January 1838, p.97.
9 *Stamford Mercury*, 6 July 1838, p.3. For Tory perspective, see *Leinster Express*, 21 October 1837, p.6, on the King of Hanover refusing to imitate the Whig Irish viceroy Mulgrave in public acts of mercy.
10 *Blackwood's Lady's Magazine*, October 1837, p.150.
11 See H.J. Hanham, ed., *The Nineteenth-Century Constitution 1815–1914: Documents and Commentary* (Cambridge: Cambridge University Press, 1969), pp.52–3, for the constitutional position as stated to Edward VII in 1903.
12 Quoted in *Huntingdon, Bedford and Peterborough Gazette*, 11 August 1838, p.2. John Cassell's *Illustrated History of England* (London: Cassell, Petter and Galpin, 1863), vol.7, p.387, describes the speech thus: 'A tone of kindness, mercy, and conciliation, befitting her youth and sex, marked her first speech from the throne.'
13 'Notes of the Month', *Monthly Magazine*, December 1837, p.665.
14 *Parliamentary Debates*, 3rd series, vol.38, 17 July 1837, col.1922. *Anecdotes, Personal Traits, and Characteristic Sketches of Victoria the First, Brought Down to the Period of Her Majesty's Marriage. By a Lady* (London: Bennett, 1840), p.552: 'the whole production of this day derived its chief value from the belief... that the gracious sentiments it expressed emanated from her heart'. *Newcastle Journal*, 25 November 1837, p.3, suggested the Secretary of State, probably responsible for the wording, was unlikely to reduce the capital code: 'he suffers the last sentence of the law to take effect upon a man, whom not only all his townsmen, but the magistracy... recommended as a fit subject for the royal clemency'.
15 *Mirror of Parliament* (1838), second series, vol.1, p.14.
16 *Life of William Allen* (2 vols; Philadelphia: Longstreth, 1847), vol.2, 9 September 1837, p.389. *Chester Chronicle* reproduces a Society of Friends's address to the queen, at St James's Palace, 4 August 1837, referring to William IV's mercy. See RCIN 1073319 and RCIN 1073320, for the volumes. Basil Montagu presented *The Opinions*

of Different Authors upon The Punishment of Death (1809), and *The Debates upon the Bills for Abolishing the Punishment of Death for Stealing the Amount of Forty Shillings in a Dwelling-House... and for Stealing on Navigable Rivers* (1811) to the Prince of Wales, the future George IV.

17   *The Examiner*, 27 September 1856, p.1.
18   *Morning Herald*, reprinted in *London Standard*, 3 May 1838, p.3.
19   *The Parliamentary or Constitutional History of England* (2nd edition, 24 vols; London: Tonson, 1763), vol.21, p.154, and Speaker Lenthall, p.155: 'Justice without Mercy is Wormwood and Bitterness; and Mercy without Justice is too soft a temper for Government: For a Magistrate must have two hands, *plectentem et amplectentem*'. For Cromwell's unmercifulness, see *Don, a Poem. With Historical Notes* (supposedly first printed 1655; Edinburgh: Moir, 1814), pp.61–2 on the wife of a man condemned to death, dragged around the room as she clasped his knees. For Cromwell on mercy, see T. Carlyle, ed., *Oliver Cromwell's Letters and Speeches: With Elucidations by Thomas Cromwell* (2nd edition, enlarged; London: Chapman and Hall, 1846), vol. 3, pp.254–9 (23 January 1655); and D. O'Connell, *A Memoir on Ireland Native and Saxon. Vol.1: 1172–1660* (New York: Casserly, 1843), p.246.
20   See the anti-abolitionist J.W. Watkin, *A Brief Reply to Mr Commissioner Phillips* (London: W. Skeffington, 1858).
21   J. Montgomery, *Journal of Voyages and Travels by the Rev. Daniel Tyerman and George Bennet, Deputed from the London Missionary Society, to Visit Their Various Stations in the South Sea Islands, China, India Etc. Between the Years 1821 and 1829* (2 vols; London: Westley and Davis, 1831), vol.2, p.93; S.L. Kamehiro, *The Arts of Kingship: Hawaiian Art and National Culture of the Kalakaua Era* (Honolulu: University of Hawaii Press, 2009), p.47.
22   A.J. Stephens, *The Book of Common Prayer: With Notes, Legal and Historical* (3 vols; London: Harrison, 1850), vol.2, p.895; R. Pashley, *Pauperism and Poor Laws* (London: Longman, Brown, Green and Longmans, 1852), p.158.
23   *Exeter and Plymouth Gazette*, 7 October 1837, p.2, a banner by Conservative Ladies of the North Division of the county depicting crown, sword of justice and sceptre of mercy, 'emblematical of the State'. See also J.T. Smith on 'Curtana', *Illustrations of the Political and Diplomatic Relations of the Independent Kingdom of Hungary: And of the Interest That Europe Has in the 'Austrian Alliance'* (London: Jeffs, 1861), pp.24–5.
24   W. Huntington, *Spoils Taken from the Tower of London, Without Siege, Violence, Bloodshed, Conquest, or Loss to the Owners. In a Letter to a Friend* (London: n.p., 1788), pp.10–12.
25   A.M. Toplady, *Sermons and Essays* (London: Row, 1793), p.175 (discussing the atonement of Christ); and in 'Other Observations', in *The Posthumous Works of the Late Reverend Mr. A.M. Toplady* (London: Matthews, 1780), p.210: 'To the humble, self empty'd, self renouncing Sinner, even the Sword of Divine Justice is a Curtana, a Sword of Mercy, a Sword without a Point'.
26   'C.', 'On Coronations', *New Monthly Magazine*, 1821, pp.96–104 [p.101].
27   *John Bull*, 18 June 1821, p.214.
28   R. Huish, *An Authentic History of the Coronation of His Majesty, King George the Fourth* (London: Robins, 1821), p.123.
29   *Saturday Magazine* 13: 386, 7 July 1838, pp.4–6 [p.5].
30   *Penny Magazine*, May 31 to June 30 1838), pp.249–56. It is alluded to regarding the Home Secretary, in *Law Magazine* 10 (1838) p.18: 'we are tempted to hope he will

in future wield the sword Curtana of which his office gives him the keeping with somewhat more discretion'.
31 Reported in *Caledonian Mercury*, 7 July 1838, p.4.
32 *Cambridge Independent Press*, 3 August 1844, p.4.
33 M. Richardson, *The Buds of Hope, a Collection of Miscellaneous Poems* (London: Mitchell, 1838), p.7.
34 C.G. Sharpley, *The Coronation, a Poem, in Six Cantos* (London, for the author, 1838), p.46.
35 'Coronation ode for Queen Victoria I', *Blackwood's Edinburgh Magazine*, July 1838, p.140.
36 M. Blessington, ed., *Heath's Book of Beauty* (London: Longman, Orme, Brown, Longmans, 1839), p.247.
37 *Leicestershire Mercury*, 14 July 1838, p.4.
38 'S.S', of Chelsea, *Worcester Journal*, 5 July 1838, p.4, 'While pity shining still the brightest gem… And like a glitt'ring star adorn thy diadem.' R.A. Noah, *Henry and Rosa: A Pathetic Poetical Tale; with a Few Miscellaneous Poems* (London: Stuart, 1846), 'Peace, justice, mercy, loveliest ray | Shine brightly in thy crown… Around the Throne may they entwine, | To grace our lovely Queen', p.51.
39 *Morning Post*, 24 May 1838, p.5.
40 'Lines on the Coronation of Her Most Gracious Majesty Queen Victoria', in E. Brown, *Original Poetry* (Stony Stratford: Sleath, 1839), pp.13–14 [p.13]; and 'Anthem of Joy', pp.21–2 [p.21].
41 'The Night of the Coronation Written in 1838 on Reading the Account of the Coronation of Victoria by Miss Charlotte Barnes of New York', *Southern Literary Messenger* 1840, p.22.
42 *Morning Post*, 10 November 1837, p.3.
43 *Mirror of Literature* 30, supplementary number (November 1837), p.327.
44 *London Daily News*, 2 November 1886, p.3, for justice and mercy in illuminations as mottoes, with blind justice also depicted.
45 *Huntingdon, Bedford & Peterborough Gazette*, 16 March 1839 [p.2].
46 'Chit-Chat', *The Satirist*, 26 November 1837, p.797.
47 A file of petitions and letters for mercy in his case are in HO 17/24/110. *Selections from the Writings of the Late J. Sydney Taylor*, p.311, from *Morning Herald*, 28 October 1837.
48 B. Newman, *Lord Melbourne* (London: Macmillan, 1930), p.229; reproduced also in D.B.W. Lewis, *Four Favourites* (London: Evans, 1948), p.74.
49 *Newcastle Journal*, 29 July 1837, p.3.
50 *John Bull*, 27 August 1838, p.401.
51 *London Standard*, 13 July 1838 [p.4]. Old Bailey Proceedings Online (www.oldbaileyonline.org, version 8, 7 September 2019), July 1838, trial of John Rickey (t18380709-1692); see *London Dispatch*, 29 July 1838, p.4, on Rickey learning of the royal mercy. For detail, see *Freeman's Journal*, 27 June 1838, p.4.
52 The Recorder was involved because the change in the law on murder removed his role in passing sentence of death at the end of the session, giving this to the presiding judge, 'but by a singular omission in the act, he is not empowered to fix a day for the execution'. The Recorder refused this responsibility and the Home Office became involved; see *Oxford University and City Herald*, 21 July 1838, p.4.

53 *Lincolnshire Chronicle*, 17 August 1838, p.2. See also *Lincolnshire Chronicle*, 13 April 1838, p.3. He was, according to *Stamford Mercury*, sent to the 'worst of all penal settlements', 17 August 1838, p.3
54 *John Bull*, 26 August 1838, p.401. The cases were discussed together; the abolitionist *Nottingham Review*, 3 August 1838, p.4, credited the intercession of the Recorder in Rickey's case.
55 *The Torch*, 25 August 1838, p.272. See *The Torch*, 28 October 1837, p.73: 'The Senate saw her blend – with heart elate, | The woman's gentle nature with the Queen!'
56 *Essex Standard*, 3 July 1840, p.4.
57 The radical *Spectator*, on Edward VI's signing of the death warrant for a Kentish heretic, see *Morning Post*'s long excerpt, 12 November 1838 [p.3].
58 *Globe* reprinted in *Caledonian Mercury*, 3 September 1838, p.2.
59 'Royal Mercy', *The Times*, 25 September 1838, p.6, 'Lord John Russell's Mercy', *The Times*, 26 September 1838, p.7.
60 In *Bury and Norwich Post*, 23 August 1837, p.1, followed by comment, 'so that her Majesty will be relieved from the painful duty of ordering executions and will only be called upon to interfere on the side of mercy'
61 *Caledonian Mercury*, 25 May 1837, p.1.
62 *Morning Advertiser*, 19 May 1837 [p.3].
63 The formal wording, 'Her Majesty has approved the finding and sentence of the Court, and has been pleased to extend her most gracious clemency to the prisoner', reprinted *Morning Post*, 10 July 1837, p.2.
64 E.g. *United Service Gazette*, reported in *Morning Post*, 10 July 1837, p.2; *Coventry Herald*, 21 July 1837, p.3; *Norfolk Chronicle*, 29 July 1837, p.4.
65 See S.P. Casteras, 'The wise child and her "offspring": some changing faces of Queen Victoria', in Homans and Munich, eds, *Remaking Queen Victoria*, the image by J. Prentice, reproduced, p.191. The print re-appeared in *The Graphic*, *Illustrated London News*, and elsewhere, attributed to Thomas McLean; also lithograph after J.F. Taylor, 'Queen Victoria on Horseback' (1837).
66 Peggs, *Capital Punishment*, pp.11–12, p.14.
67 *London Standard*, 21 December 1839, p.3. *Australian Temperance Magazine* 3:13 Supplement (2 June 1840), p.200.
68 *The Court Magazine & Monthly Critic and Lady's Magazine* 5 (1840), p.70.
69 *Poverty Bay Herald*, New Zealand, 16 March 1901, p.5.
70 'Did ministers fear the repetition of such as scene as took place when the youthful Queen, on learning that her signature to the sentence of the court-martial above alluded to would cost one of her subjects her life, threw away the pen and exclaimed, "Then I will never sign it?" They are mistaken who suppose that the constitution of England makes the Monarch a Cipher', quoted in *Devizes and Wiltshire Gazette*, 12 April 1838 [p.1].
71 *Sussex Advertiser*, 9 April 1838, p.2. The paper had already, 16 October 1837, p.2, expressed abolitionism, in relation to a female ordered for execution in Paisley.
72 *Sheffield Independent*, 15 September 1838, p.4; see also *Exeter and Plymouth Gazette*, 6 October 1838, p.4. *Sheffield Independent*, 6 October 1838, p.6, published excerpts from Beccaria as a result of the item. Various newspapers credited *Sheffield Iris* as the source.
73 *Sheffield Independent*, 24 November 1838, p.6.
74 *Freeman's Journal*, 24 August 1838 [p.1]; corrections to correspondents, e.g. to 'RPD', *Lloyd's Weekly Newspaper*, 27 November 1853, p.6; and to James Greenwood, *Manchester Courier*, 22 November 1867, p.4.

75 *Blackburn Standard*, 22 August 1838 [p.3].
76 This story was promoted by *Morning Herald*, noted already in *Worcester Journal*, 20 July 1837, p.3 and *Birmingham Gazette*, 24 July 1837, p.4; *Kendal Mercury* reproduced poetry 'as a sort of supplementary evidence of the date of the first publication of the anecdote' (dated June 1838), 'The White Rose blooms on England's throne'. See E. Sidney, *The Life of Lord Hill, G.C.B., Late Commander of the Forces* (London: Murray, 1845), p.360.
77 *London Standard*, 7 May 1838, p.3. The *Dublin Morning Register*, 9 May 1838 [p.2], said the men's release was a fabrication of *Leinster Express* and that the Lord Lieutenant ordered the law to take its course.
78 *Vermont Telegraph*, 3 January 1838, p.60, paragraphed the queen's clemency without identifying this as a military case.
79 S.A. Curzon, *Laura Secord. The Heroine of 1812* (Toronto: Robinson, 1887), p.195; J.G. Hodgins, *Her Majesty the Queen, the Late Prince Consort, and Other Members of the Royal Family: Sketches and Anecdotes, Selected & Arranged Chiefly for Young People* (Montreal: Lovell, 1868), pp.37–8 (the second was a Fenian, soldier Thomas Darragh – *Leeds Mercury*, 17 April 1866, p.6).
80 *Latter Day Saints Millennial Star*, 1879, p.422: 'On a bright, beautiful morning …'; *Wairarapa Daily Times*, 9 June 1879, p.2.
81 P.P. Carpenter, *Words in the War: Being Lectures on 'Life and Death in the Hands of God and Man'* (London: Cash, 1855), p.9.
82 *Excellencies of Woman* (London: G. Stevenson, 1860), pp.39–40.
83 E. Foster, *New Cyclopedia of Illustrations, Adapted to Christian Teaching* (New York: Palmer, 1870), p.450; T. De Witt Talmage, *Every-Day Religion: Being a 4th Series of 50 Sermons* (London: Dickinson, 1876), p.282.
84 *Berwickshire News*, 28 March 1871, p.4.
85 The earliest references c.1850, e.g. *The Christian Miscellany* 5 (1850), p.318. C. Bullock, *The Queen's Resolve* (London: Home Words, 1887), in which she was said to 'frequently [beg] that the lives of the offenders might be spared' (p.154); *Private Life of Queen Victoria by One of Her Majesty's Servants* (New York: Appleton, 1901), p.160; G.A. Henty's *Queen Victoria: Scenes from Her Life and Reign* (London: Blackie, 1901), p.34. See also 'A beautiful incident', *The Christian Miscellany* 5 (1850), p.318. It figures in posthumous newspaper references e.g. *London Journal*, 9 February 1901, p.116.
86 *Exeter and Plymouth Gazette*, 5 May 1891, p.2. See also later coverage of the 'Queen and the Deserter', e.g. *Hampshire Advertiser*, 30 May 1891, p.7.
87 *Liverpool Mercury*, 7 December 1887, p.7.
88 'History and Biography', *Westminster Review* 146.1 (July 1896), pp.702–5 [p.702], reviewing *Two Royal Lives: Queen Victoria. William I, German Emperor*.
89 *London and Paris Observer* 14, 20 May 1838, p.317. Another illustration is J.H. Friston's 'Lord Melbourne instructing a young Queen Victoria', *John Cassell's Illustrated History of England*, vol.7, p.391, dated 1837.
90 'The Death Warrant' in W. Golder, *The New Zealand Survey; A Poem in Five Cantoes. With Notes Illustrative of New Zealand Progress and Future Prospects. Also the Crystal Palace of 1851; A Poem in Two Cantoes. With other Poems and Lyrics* (Wellington, Stoddart, 1867), p.111.
91 The *Sunday School Teachers Magazine*, 1865, p.134; 'Pearl Fisher', 'Britain's Queen', *Our Darlings*, pp.270–4 [p.274]: 'Owing to her tenderness of heart in such matters, an Act of Parliament was passed authorizing the signature to be performed by commission.'
92 *Young Folks Paper*, 29 June 1889, p. 412.

93 O. Winslow, *Life in Jesus: A Memoir of Mrs. Mary Winslow, Arranged from Her Correspondence, Diary, and Thoughts* (New York: Carter, 1860), p.150.
94 *Dundee Courier*, 10 January 1888 [p.2], describes it as a tradition.
95 Reprinted in *The Star* (New Zealand), 10 February 1897, p.2. *Argosy*, vol. 63, January 1897, pp.1–20.
96 RA VIC/ADD/A36/1271, Balmoral, 20 November 1877.
97 *Touchstone*, reprinted in *Illustrated Police News*, 1 December 1877, p.2.
98 E.g. *Sydney Once a Week Magazine*, 1878, 'The Penge Mystery', p.23, reprinting from *Touchstone*.
99 E.g. 'The Queen and Mrs Staunton', in *Sunday School Chronicle* 6, 30 November 1877.
100 Quoted in *Dundee Evening Telegraph*, 19 November 1877 [p.2].
101 *Manchester Evening News*, 22 November 1877, p.2 (and many others), quoting the *Echo*.
102 *Staffordshire Sentinel*, 23 November 1877, p.2.
103 Quoted in *Dundee Evening Telegraph*, 28 November 1877, p.2.
104 *Gwyliedydd* (Rhyl), 1 November 1877, p.7.
105 RA VIC/MAIN/QVJ (W), Princess Beatrice's copy, 14 October 1877.
106 *Brighton Patriot*, 2 May 1837, p.3. See M. Price, *The Perilous Crown: France Between Revolutions, 1814–1848* (London: Macmillan, 2007), p.268; c.f. *Western Times*, 13 November 1834, p.4: 'How differently does the King of the French appear in thus thirsting for the blood of his subjects, from those attributes with which the good spirit of our own King, no less than the principles of the constitution, adorn the throne, making it the fountain of mercy. In France it should seem to be the source of vengeance.' See Knighton, *Memoirs of Sir William Knighton*, vol.2, p.196, for another report on the French king's mercifulness.
107 *Western Times*, 17 April 1852, p.3.
108 *Chelmsford Chronicle*, 23 July 1847, p.2.
109 J. Gregory, *Victorians Against the Gallows. Capital Punishment and the Abolitionist Movement in Nineteenth-Century Britain* (London: I.B. Tauris, 2012), pp.92–4.
110 S. Roberts, *Queen's Coronation: An Address to the Females of Sheffield on the Wickedness, the Barbarity, and the Impolicy of the Punishment of Death in All Classes* (Sheffield: A. Whitaker, 1838). It appears in Roberts's *Yorkshire Tales and Poems* (2nd edition, enlarged, London: Whittaker, 1839), dated 6 February 1839.
111 Roberts, *Yorkshire Tales and Poems*, p.vii.
112 'Scroll of a letter to the Queen, on the Punishment of Death', *Tait's Edinburgh Magazine* 5: 59 (November 1838), pp.725–6. For authorship, John Roberts, *The Irish Unitarian Magazine*, June 1846, p.239 (also reprinting the article), and *Fife Herald*, 29 July 1841, p.92; 19 August 1841, p.104.
113 'Loyal Suggestions Humbly Submitted to the Queen's Most Excellent Majesty by an Æsthetic Student in Morals', *The Monthly Magazine*, n.s., vol.1, May 1839, pp.569–75.
114 *Carlisle Journal*, 24 November 1848, p.3.
115 *Western Times*, 24 November 1849, p.7.
116 *Sheffield and Rotherham Independent*, 25 January 1851, p.2.
117 *Selections from the Writings of the Late John Sydney Taylor*, pp.286–7; A. Midlane, *A Colloquy Between the Gallows and the Hangman. A Poem on the Evils of Capital Punishment with Notes* (London: C. Gilpin, 1851), p.31.
118 *Kendal Mercury*, 12 May 1855, p.6.
119 'Revolting scene in England, in the year of Grace 1866, and under the reign of a female sovereign', *The British Friend*, 1 May 1866, p.118; from 'Analysis and Description of the Report of the Royal Commission on Capital Punishment – 1866', *Social Science Review*.

120 *The Times*, 30 April 1846, p.4.
121 J. Davis, *The Agony of Murder: Written by a Prisoner Describing His Feelings When Under Sentence of Death, and in Most Imminent Danger of Execution* (London: I.R. Taylor, 1859), p.63.
122 J. St Hugh Mills, 'The Incendiary', *New York Mirror*, 22 September 1838, pp.97–8.
123 'Hawthorne', 'My College Friends. No. II. John Brown', *Blackwood's Edinburgh Magazine*, December 1844, pp.763–74 [p.774].
124 G.W.M. Reynolds, *The Mysteries of the Court of London*, vol.8 (vol.2, 4th series: London: Dicks, 1856), p.315.
125 *Monthly Review* 2: 2 (1840), p.265.
126 *The Last Days of a Condemned, from the French, with Observations on Capital Punishment by Sir P.H. Fleetwood* (London: Smith, Elder, 1840), p.vi.
127 *How I Rose in the World* (2 vols; London: C.J. Skeet, 1868), vol.2, p.155.
128 Poole, *The Politics of Regicide*, p.177.
129 See *The Only Correct Account of the Confession and Execution of Fredrick George Manning and Maria Manning for the Murder of Patrick O'Connor* (London: W.M. Clark, 1849), p.8; *An Account of the Last Days, Confessions, and Execution of the Mannings for the Murder of Patrick O'Connor, at Bermondsey* (Leith: Drummond, 1849), p.10.
130 *Sheffield Independent*, 28 April 1849, p.6.
131 *Chester Chronicle*, 21 September 1838 [p.3]. See *Spectator* for late reprieve for Jones, 1 September 1838, p.816. On the assize trial, *London Standard*, 11 August 1838, p.4; *Oxford Journal*, 18 August 1838, p.2.
132 *Chester Chronicle*, 31 August 1838, p.2.
133 *Morning Chronicle*, 27 August 1838, p.3. See *Chester Chronicle*, 7 September 1838, p.3, for defence of Home Secretary against abolitionist *Morning Herald*; and reproduction of *Morning Chronicle* attacking *Herald*'s errors about death warrants.
134 *Huntingdon, Bedford & Peterborough Gazette*, 1 September 1838, p.3.
135 *The Times*, 30 August 1838, p.6.
136 *Journal of the House of Commons* 99 (1844), 17 May, p.310.
137 *The Satirist*, 26 May 1844, p.162.
138 Reprinted in *Hampshire Advertiser*, 3 January 1846, p.6.
139 *Howitt's Journal* 2: 45, 6 November 1847, pp.290–1 [p.291]. Other journalists also appealed to the Queen and matrons of England; see 'Mary Ann Hunt and the "Humanity" of Professing Christians', *The Satirist*, 17 October 1847, p.68; also 'A Cry from a Condemned Cell', *Punch*, 23 October 1847, p.158. On Howitt's abolitionism, A.M. Lee, *Laurels and Rosemary. The Life of William and Mary Howitt* (London: Oxford University Press, 1955), p.168.
140 *Manchester Times*, 16 October 1847, p.2.
141 *Bristol Mercury*, 6 November 1847, p.2. For other appeals to the Queen's mercy, see *Lady's Newspaper*, 2 October 1847, p.313.
142 *The Satirist*, 7 November 1847, p.91.
143 *North Devon Journal*, 26 April 1849, p.2.
144 *London Daily News*, 19 October 1849, p.3. A petition was organized by Gilpin, 59 Dame Street, Dublin: see 'An Appeal for Mercy', directed towards 'women, gentle and merciful in your nature', see *The Advocate: Or, Irish Industrial Journal*, 31 October 1849, p.233.
145 'A Woman's Plea for Mercy', *Punch*, 27 October 1849, p.170.
146 'Charlotte Harris', *The Reasoner*, 14 November 1849, p.317.

147 *Perthshire Advertiser*, reprinted in *Bradford Observer*, 1 November 1849, p.7.
148 'Mercy for Annette Myers', *Punch* 14, 1848, p.107.
149 *The Era*, 2 January 1859, p.9.
150 *Bury and Norwich Post*, 19 January 1864, p.3.
151 *Northampton Mercury*, 16 January 1864, p.3.
152 *Bury Times*, 16 January 1864, p.2.
153 *Reynolds's Newspaper*, 17 January 1864, p.1. *Reynolds's Newspaper*, concerning Ireland, spoke of the 'common hangman' maintaining the authority of our 'beloved and merciful Queen', 15 December 1867, p.1.
154 *Reynolds's Newspaper*, 17 January 1864, p.1.
155 TNA, HO12/146/59140, file on Samuel Wright, letter (unnumbered) by anonymous writer on the queen's mausoleum; letter no.45 linking execution to birth of prince; unnumbered verse, sent 10 January 1864, 'The British Prayer'; and no.35, petitions to Prince of Wales.
156 *Bath Chronicle*, 14 January 1864, p.8.
157 Reverend Newman Hall, *Lloyd's Weekly Newspaper*, 24 January 1864, p.6; *South London Chronicle*, 16 January 1864 [p.2].
158 *Portsmouth Evening News*, 18 December 1891, p.3.
159 'The Quality of Mercy', *The Australian Star*, 4 June 1892, p.4.
160 W.T. Stead, 'What Kind of Sovereign Is Queen Victoria?' *Cosmopolitan Magazine* 29 (June 1900), pp.207–16.
161 *London Pioneer*, 3:1, 14 May 1846, p.33. J. Timbs' *Things Not Generally Known Familiarly Explained: A Book for Old and Young* (London: Bogue, 1856), p.171 sought to correct the misconception. The subject fascinated correspondents: *Notes and Queries* 2nd series 8, 24 December 1859, p.523; 12th series 1, 5 February 1916, pp.111–12; p.211, discussed signing death warrants in Britain and Isle of Man. For corrections of death-warrant error, see *The Cottager* 4 (1824), p.566, from *St James's Chronicle*; a review of Wraxall in *The London and Paris Observer* (Paris: Galignani, 1837), p.55; C.H. Collette, *A Reply to Cobbett's 'History of the Protestant Reformation in England and Ireland'* (London: Partridge, 1869), p.145.
162 'A Queen's Day', *Harper's New Monthly Magazine*, April 1863, pp.657–9 [p.658], reprinted, e.g. *Westmorland Gazette*, 9 May 1863, p.3; *Herts. Guardian*, 20 June 1863, p.7; and magazines such as *The Boy's Miscellany* (London, 1863), p.169.
163 F. Bunsen, *A Memoir of Baron Bunsen* (2 vols; London: Longmans, Green, 1868), vol.2, p.201.
164 *Trewman's Exeter Flying Post*, 13 May 1863, p.8.
165 Reported in *Tavistock Gazette*, 1 March 1867 [p.7].
166 Other jubilee appeals include *Preston Herald*'s lengthy appeal for men condemned for fifteen years' penal servitude for riots in 1878; see *Blackburn Standard*, 11 June 1887, p.6. It was 'known that the queen herself has very strong and pronounced views' against executing women, *Oakes Weekly Republican* (North Dakota), 19 December 1890 [p.7].
167 A.C. Benson and R.B. Brett, eds, *The Letters of Queen Victoria. First Series. A Selection from Her Majesty's Correspondence Between the Years 1837 and 1861. In Three Volumes. Vol.2, 1844–1853* (London: Murray, 1908), p.38, Sir James Graham to the Queen, 13 May 1845.
168 *Salisbury and Winchester Journal*, 2 December 1843, p.2.
169 *Reynolds's Newspaper*, 17 August 1856, p.7.
170 *Reynolds's Newspaper*, 11 July 1858, p.9.

171 *Reynolds's Newspaper*, 20 September 1863, p.3.
172 *Reynolds's Newspaper*, 29 March 1874, p.4.
173 'Anglo-Saxona', 'Alice Wilson, the Murderess', *The Englishman*, 18 January 1879, p.254; see *Newcastle Daily Chronicle*, reprinted in *North London News*, 4 January 1879, p.2 – the release was reported in late December 1878 with headlines like 'A Murderess and Her Majesty's pleasure'.
174 *Reynolds's Newspaper*, 21 August 1887, p.4.

Chapter 4

1   TNA, HO12/107/23139, unnumbered letter by John Passmore Edwards after execution of the octogenarian John Murdoch, to Sir George Grey, 11 August 1856; and TNA, HO12/146/59140, unnumbered letter, 14 January 1864, from Edwards to Sir George Grey, regarding Samuel Wright. Dahomey, a West African kingdom, was associated in the Victorian imagination, with ferocity and barbarity.
2   Material directly addressed to the sovereign in the period, in capital cases, is rarely preserved in the Home Office papers but includes HO45/4054, letters asking for mercy, 'Appeals. Letters to Queen Victoria', dated 1852.
3   R.B. Brett, *After the War* (London: Murray, 1918), p.3.
4   Brett, *After the War*, p.17.
5   She was reluctant to be publicly associated with any popular decision to execute Fenians in 1867, J.H. Murphy, *Abject Loyalty: Nationalism and Monarchy in Ireland During the Reign of Queen Victoria* (Crosses Green, Cork: Cork University Press, 2001), p.156.
6   S. Lee, *Queen Victoria: A Biography* (1904), pp.567–8.
7   RA VIC/MAIN/QVJ (W), Lord Esher's typescript, 12 March–13 March 1838; *Globe*, 14 March 1838, [p.4].
8   RA VIC/MAIN/QVJ (W), Princess Beatrice's copy, 6 May, 8 May 1840.
9   Hobhouse, *Recollections*, vol.5, p.267.
10 RA VIC/MAIN/QVJ (W), Princess Beatrice's copy, 26 February 1879 (on Peace).
11 RA VIC/MAIN/QVJ (W), Princess Beatrice's copy, 29 November 1881.
12 See T.M. Torrens, *The Life and Times of the Right Honourable Sir James R. G. Graham* (2 vols; London: Saunders, Otley, 1863), vol.2, p.577 for Graham's 'leniency' when Lord of the Admiralty, according to Torrens.
13 *Reynolds's Newspaper*, 6 August 1865, p.1. Cited as epigraph to ch.5 in A. Kilday, *A History of Infanticide in Britain, c. 1600 to the Present* (Basingstoke: Palgrave Macmillan, 2013), p.111.
14 *South Eastern Gazette*, 15 August 1854, p.2. For ballads, see 'The Esher Tragedy', published by Harkness of Preston and 'I am Mrs Brough of Esher' by Marks of Whitechapel. *Eclectic Magazine*, May 1855, p.123, reports the 'general dismay' at the verdict.
15 RA VIC/MAIN/QVJ (W), Princess Beatrice's copy, 13 June 1854; *Sporting Review*, July 1854, p.10. J. Ridley, *Bertie: A Life of Edward VII* (London: Chatto and Windus, 2012), p.15, refers to a letter the queen wrote to King Leopold, 13 June 1854, RA VIC/Y99/23.
16 J. Greenwood, *In Strange Company: Being the Experiences of a Roving Correspondent* (London: H.S. King, 1873), p.325.

17   RA VIC/MAIN/B/32/6F, Queen Victoria, Balmoral, 22 November 1880; see also communication by Ponsonby with Harcourt for the queen, RA VIC/MAIN/B/32/9A, 28 November 1880.
18   [F.W. Robinson], *Female Life in Prison by a Prison Matron* (London: Hurst and Blackett, 1863), in Osborne House, RCIN 1040613.
19   RA VIC/MAIN/QVJ (W), Princess Beatrice's copy, 15 January 1864 (visit to Parkhurst – the queen was shown a girl who had killed at least one child by the age of thirteen). The queen visited again in 1845 when it was a boys' prison. See RA VIC/MAIN/QVJ (W), Princess Beatrice's copy, 21 January 1866, on female infanticides in discussion with Lord Chancellor; RA VIC/MAIN/QVJ (W), Princess Beatrice's copy, 30 January 1867, discussing abolition of death penalty for 'destruction of newly born infants', with Walpole of Home Office.
20   J. Marsden, *Victoria & Albert: Art & Love* (London: Royal Collection, 2010), pp.142–3; L.C. Berry, 'Confession and Profession: *Adam Bede*, Infanticide and the New Coroner', in J. Thorn, ed., *Writing British Infanticide: Child-murder, Gender, and Print, 1722–1859* (Newark: University of Delaware Press, 2003), pp.196–217 [p.212].
21   For critique of Grey in this case, see 'Commutation of Capital Punishment', *Saturday Review*, 16 April 1864, pp.470–1; 'The Finale of the Townley Case', *The Economist*, 6 February 1864, pp.165–6; 'The Derbyshire Magistrates and the Home Office', *The Examiner*, 23 January 1864, p.51, 'Was Sir George Grey Justified in Preventing the Infliction of the Sentence of Death upon Townley?' *British Controversialist* (1864), pp.229–31.
22   Since it refers to cousins involved as bankers in a crime, it is likely to be Sir John Dean Paul, who with his cousin, William Strahan, and another, were sentenced to be transported for fourteen years for fraud in 1855: he was released with Strahan from Woking prison in October 1859: see R. Davenport-Hines, 'Paul, Sir John Dean, Second Baronet (1802–1868)', *Oxford Dictionary of National Biography*, Oxford University Press, 2004. *Morning Chronicle* printed a plea for royal mercy, 17 September 1858, p.3. The papers covered the discussion in Parliament of a pardon for Paul and Strahan.
23   RA VIC/MAIN/F/38/37, the Queen to Lady Dunmore, Windsor Castle, 8 November 1855.
24   RA VIC/MAIN/QVJ (W), Princess Beatrice's copy, 12–13 November 1864. 'Ernest C' was Prince Albert's elder brother, Ernest Duke of Saxe-Coburg and Gotha.
25   RA VIC/MAIN/QVJ (W), Princess Beatrice's copy, 19 November 1864.
26   See Ponsonby, *Henry Ponsonby*, p.270. For Harcourt as Home Secretary, see A.G. Gardiner, *Sir William Harcourt* (2 vols; London: Constable, 1923), vol.1, p.391, for his generosity and humanity before law; and P. Jackson, ed., *Loulou: Selected Extracts from the Journals of Lewis Harcourt (1880–1895)* (Madison, NJ: Fairleigh Dickinson University Press, 2006), p.30, entry for 3 November 1881 on infanticide Margaret Messenger.
27   As quoted in Gardiner, *Harcourt*, vol.1, p.398.
28   Diary entry by Hardy, 1 January 1887, defending Home Office over remission for wife murder, in conversation with the queen, A.E. Gathorne-Hardy, *Gathorne Hardy, First Earl of Cranbrook, a Memoir with Extracts from His Diary and Correspondence* (London: Longmans, Green, 1910), p.271.
29   Ponsonby, *Henry Ponsonby*, p.271.

30 Gardiner, *Harcourt*, vol.1, pp.395–6 on remission of punishment for youthful offenders, and on capital punishment as deterrent, pp.396–7.
31 RA VIC/MAIN/B/31/160, Queen Victoria to Sir Henry Ponsonby, Balmoral, 16 November 1880.
32 RA VIC/MAIN/B/32/3A, Queen Victoria, Balmoral. As Ponsonby explained, RA VIC/MAIN/B/32/4, 17 November 1880, 'The Queen is afraid from the number of remissions sent here that you are treating offenders with too great leniency'.
33 RA VIC/MAIN/B/32/6, Harcourt to Sir Henry Ponsonby, 19 November 1880.
34 RA VIC/MAIN/B/32/122, Harcourt to the Queen, 16 August 1881.
35 RA VIC/MAIN/B/32/122A, 17 August 1881. Ponsonby, p.271. On the case, see *Sunderland Daily Echo*, 19 July 1881, p.3.
36 RA VIC/ADDA12/853, Harcourt to Ponsonby, 19 August 1889.
37 RA VIC/ADDA12/854, Queen Victoria, 16 August 1883.
38 RA VIC/MAIN/B/34/4, Harcourt to the Queen, Whitehall, 11 January 1882.
39 RA VIC/MAIN/B/33/19, Harcourt to the Queen, 1884; RA VIC/MAIN/B/33/21, the Queen to Harcourt, 26 June 1884; *Taunton Courier*, 14 May 1884.
40 RA VIC/MAIN/B/33/19, Sir William Vernon Harcourt to the Queen, 23 June 1884; A.G. Gardiner, *Harcourt*, vol.1, pp.399–401 (reprinting Harcourt's letter and the queen's reply, 26 June 1884); P. Jackson, *Harcourt and Son: A Political Biography of Sir William Harcourt, 1827–1904* (Madison, NJ: Fairleigh Dickinson University Press, 2004), pp.89–90.
41 RA VIC/MAIN/B/33/21, the Queen to Harcourt, 26 June 1884; reprinted in Gardiner, *The Life of Sir William Harcourt*, vol.1, pp.440–01.
42 RA VIC/MAIN/B/33/21, the Queen to Harcourt, 26 June 1884.
43 RA VIC/MAIN/A/61/1, 25 February 1885, the Queen to Harcourt; G.E. Buckle, ed., *The Letters of Queen Victoria. Second Series. Vol. 3. 1879–1885*, 23 February 1885, p.612.
44 RA VIC/MAIN/L/16/13, 'For Your Majesty's Signature', Henry Matthews to the Queen, 5 January 1888.
45 RA VIC/MAIN/A/66/116, Lord Salisbury to the Queen, 4 June 1888.
46 Reprinted in press, e.g. *Gloucester Citizen*, 15 August 1887, p.3.
47 See RA VIC/MAIN/QVJ (W), Princess Beatrice's copy, 14 August and 21 August 1887; see also letter of Ritchie of Local Government Board, RA VIC/MAIN/B39/31, 14 August 1887, communicating his impression of the view of the Home Secretary and Justice Stephen to the Queen.
48 RA VIC/MAIN/QVJ (W) 4 October 1888, Princess Beatrice's copy; RA VIC/MAIN/L/16/17-19 (on the East End memorial); RA VIC/MAIN/L16/24, the queen asking Ponsonby if she 'might take the opportunity of writing rather strongly to Mr Matthews'; RA VIC/MAIN/A6718-20, including deciphered telegram from Salisbury responding to suggestion of greater lighting, 11 November 1888; RA VIC/MAIN/B/40/82, 13 November 1888; G.E. Buckle, ed., *The Letters of Queen Victoria. Third Series. A Selection from Her Majesty's Correspondence and Journal Between the Years 1886 and 1901. In Three Volumes. Vol.1. 1886–1890* (London: Murray, 1930), p.449.
49 J.C. Whorton, *The Arsenic Century: How Victorian Britain Was Poisoned at Home, Work, and Play* (Oxford: Oxford University Press, 2010), p.283. See letter from Matthews, 22 August 1889, Buckle, ed., *The Letters of Queen Victoria: Third Series. Vol.1*, and entry on the Queen in C. Jones, *The Maybrick A to Z* (Birkenhead:

Countyvise, 2008), reproducing the queen's letter to Matthews and noting her anger when the American ladies' petition was sent directly to her.
50 A.W. MacDougall, *The Maybrick Case: A Treatise on the Facts of the Case, and of the Proceedings in Connection with the Charge, Trial, Conviction, and Present Imprisonment of Florence Elizabeth Maybrick* (London: Baillière, Tindall and Cox, 1891), pp.557–8, 569.
51 'Tom Merry', 'Whitechapel at Whitehall. Attempted murder of Florence Maybrick. – "Save her," Mr. Matthews', *St Stephen's Review*, 17 August 1889.
52 RA VIC/MAIN/B/41/93-94, Matthews to the Queen, 22 August 1889.
53 RA VIC/MAIN/B/41/94, the Queen to Sir Henry Ponsonby.
54 RA VIC/MAIN/B/44/60, 29 September 1891.
55 'Northumbrian', *Reynolds's Newspaper*, 20 April 1890, p.2.
56 'Memorials to the Queen', *Burnley Express*, 17 August 1889, p.8.
57 'An abortive petition', *Cardiff Times*, 17 September 1892, p.3, reproduced a reply to one petition sent to the queen.
58 *Evening Post*, 12 February 1901, p.2.
59 *Gentleman Farmer* 2 (1897), p.250.
60 'An Open Letter to the Queen', *North American Review* 155: 430, September 1892, pp.257–67 [pp.261–2].
61 'The Maybrick Case Again', *New York Times*, 9 January 1898.
62 'Florence Maybrick Club to the Queen', *New York Times*, 25 May 1899, p.7.
63 *American Lawyer*, vol.7, 1899, p.345.
64 'The Maybrick Case', *American Lawyer*, vol.7, 1899, pp.460–1 [p.461].
65 RA VIC/MAIN/A/76/2, Salisbury to the Queen, 26 January 1900.
66 F. Maybrick, *Mrs Maybrick's Own Story. My Fifteen Lost Years* (New York: Funk and Wagnalls, 1905), p.198. The book advocates a court of criminal appeal.
67 *Preston Chronicle*, 29 March 1890, p.4.
68 *Newcastle Courant*, 12 April 1890, p.1.
69 *Saturday Review*, 12 April 1890, pp.429–30.
70 *Bristol Mercury*, 8 April 1890, p.5.
71 RA VIC/MAIN/A/68/116, the queen, 10 March 1892.
72 RA VIC/MAIN/A/68/125, April 1892. On this case, see C.A. Conley, *Melancholy Accidents: The Meaning of Violence in Post-famine Ireland* (Lanham, MA: Lexington Books, 1999), p.73. See *Western Times*, for Edward Jesty of Exeter's verse, 16 April 1892, p.2 on the case, 'Ode to Mercy'. The Osborne and Montague cases are noted in Dodge's 'Open Letter to the Queen'.
73 RA VIC/MAIN/L/16/62. See A. Davies, '"These Viragoes Are No Less Cruel than the Lads": Young Women, Gangs and Violence in Late Victorian Manchester and Salford', *British Journal of Criminology* 39: 1 (1999), pp.72–89.
74 RA VIC/MAIN/L16/83, Asquith to Sir Henry Ponsonby, 8 April 1893.
75 *Reynolds's Newspaper*, 30 July 1893, p.1.
76 *Tamworth Herald*, 8 December 1894, p.7. See 'The Convict Read. A Telegram to the Queen' *London Daily News*, 4 December 1894, p.6; *Essex Newsman*, 8 December 1894, p.3. On this case, see MEPO3/153; HO144/261/A56481.
77 *Hull Daily Mail*, 8 December 1896, p.4.
78 *Bucks Herald*, 29 February 1896, p.3.
79 V. Mallet, ed., *Life with Queen Victoria: Marie Mallet's Letters from Court, 1887–1901* (London: J. Murray, 1968), p.173. See *The Spectator*, 22 July 1899, p.3 and p.9.
80 *Manchester Guardian*, 19 July 1899, p.7, *Lloyd's Weekly Newspaper*, 23 July 1899, p.15.

81 VIC/MAIN/B/51/15, copy of minute by Matthew Ridley, 15 July 1899.
82 *Parliamentary Debates*, 4th series, vol.74, House of Commons, 13 July, cols.699–700; and 17 July 1899, cols.1001–2. 'Anglophobia – A French Warning to England', *National Review*, September 1899, pp.26–46 [p.34]. See coverage in *le Matin*, 18 July 1899, p.3. The *Fronde* (reported *Pall Mall Gazette*, 28 December 1899, p.2) appealed to the queen concerning the infanticide by Louise Masset, her execution in January 1900 was luridly depicted in the French press.
83 *Le Petit Parisien*, 30 July 1899.
84 C. Strange, 'Capital Case Procedure Manual', *Criminal Law Quarterly*, 1998, p.187.
85 M. MacDonagh, 'The King His Prerogatives and Disabilities', *Good Words* 43 (December 1902), pp.155–9 [p.157].
86 G.E. Buckle, ed., *The Letters of Queen Victoria. Second Series. Vol.2, 1870–1878*, p.223. See 'Death Warrants in the Isle of Man', *Evening Post*, New Zealand, 4 November 1893, p.1; P.W. Edge, 'Law and Practice of Capital Punishment in Isle of Man', *Manx Law Bulletin* 25 (1995) pp.49–61.
87 *Hereford Journal*, 28 December 1842 [p.3].
88 Mrs Hester Banks to Sir George Grey, reprinted in *1864 (37) George Victor Townley. Copy of Correspondence with the Secretary of State for the Home Department, and of Orders or Warrants Issued by Him, Relating to the Case of George Victor Townley*. Banks's letter survives in the Home Office files.
89 RA VIC/MAIN/B/33/22, Harcourt to the Queen, 28 June 1884.
90 'The Gallows and the Jubilee!' *Northern Echo*, 18 November 1886, p.2.
91 *Liverpool Mercury*, 15 March 1887, p.8.
92 RA VIC/MAIN/B/33/19, Harcourt to the Queen, 23 June 1884.

Chapter 5

1 W.C. Townsend, *Modern State Trials* (2 vols; London: Longman, Brown, Green, and Longmans, 1850), vol.1, p.xiii. See T. Smollett, *A Complete History of England Deduced from the Descent of Julius Caesar to the Treaty of Aix la Chapelle, 1748* (London: Rivington and Fletcher, 1758), vol.4, p.426, for a discussion on 'a mild and merciful prince, during whose reign no subject's blood was shed for treason'.
2 J.D. Collet, 'Felonious Speaking', *The Reasoner*, 17 May 1848, p.337.
3 *The Life and Times of Queen Victoria* (London: Cassell, 1901), vol.1, p.31.
4 'A Proclamation', 9 October 1838, *Annual Register* (London: Rivington, 1839), p.315.
5 Letter to queen reprinted in S.J. Reid, *Life and Letters of the First Earl of Durham, 1792–1840* (London: Longmans, Green, 1906), p.205. The phrase 'mercy towards the misguided' is reiterated in Durham's reply to the address of British Wesleyan Ministers in Lower Canada, *A History of the Late Province of Lower Canada: Parliamentary and Political, from the Commencement to the Close of Its Existence as a Separate Province* (5 vols; Quebec: Lovell, 1854), vol.5, p.154.
6 *Annual Register* 80 (London: Rivington, 1839), pp.304–7. The ordinance was annulled as illegal, but Canadians defended the merciful tenor rather than viewing the exile to Bermuda as cruelty; see *A History of the Late Province of Lower Canada*, for extract from *Quebec Gazette*, p.178; and address from Kingston, p.206.
7 *Report and Despatches of the Earl of Durham, Her Majesty's High Commissioner and Governor-General of British North America* (London: Ridgway, 1839), p.299. A

sympathetic treatment of Durham's policy and Sir John Colburne's acts of exemplary justice is in W. Kingsford, *The History of Canada* (Toronto: Rowsell and Hutchison, 1898), vol.10.

8   See *A History of the Late Province of Lower Canada*, p.226, Wofred Nelson, R.S.M. Buchette, Bonaventure Viger, S. Marchessault, H.A. Gauvin, T. Goddu, R. Des Rivieres, and L. Masson, letter of 18 June 1838 from Montreal New Jail.

9   A. Greer, *The Patriots and the People: The Rebellion of 1837 in Rural Lower Canada* (Toronto: University of Toronto Press, 1993), pp.190-1.

10 For an example of a petition, see the District of Niagara reprinted in J.P. Merritt, *Biography of the Hon. W.H. Merritt, M.P.: Of Lincoln, District of Niagara, Including an Account of the Origin, Progress and Completion of Some of the Most Important Public Works in Canada* (St Catherines: Leavenworth, 1875), p.180. Concern about absence of moderation in the response of Arthur and the Executive Council appears in C. Lindsay, *The Life and Times of William Lyon Mackenzie: With an Account of the Canadian Rebellion of 1837, and the Subsequent Frontier Disturbances* (Toronto: Randall, 1862), vol.1, pp.189-90; see also Kingsford, *The History of Canada*, vol.10, p.481.

11 *Upper Canada Gazette*, 11 April 1838, quoted in *Western Herald*, 24 April 1838, p.3.

12 Colonel John Prince, M.P.P., of Sandwich, U.C., in *Western Herald*, 19 July 1838, p.2. Prince's controversial decision to have seven Hunter Patriots shot after the battle of Windsor was later in 1838.

13 *Western Herald*, 8 May 1838, p.90.

14 F.B. Head, *A Narrative* (London: Murray, 1839), p.394, p.399.

15 *Extra Globe*, 19 June 1839. The need to secure the American public's view that justice was administered 'with a great regard to mercy' appears in a despatch on the Durham Report by Arthur to Normanby, 13 May 1839, *Copies of Extracts of Correspondence Relative to the Affairs of Canada* 103, 10 June 1839, No.7, p.34.

16 *London Gazette*, cited in C. Read and R.J. Stagg, *Rebellion of 1837 in Upper Canada* (Ottawa: Champlain Society with Carleton University Press 1985), p.430. See *Western Herald*, 19 June 1838, p.150, on Executive '*mercy*' and an 'equitable exercise of her punitory functions'. *New Vindicator*'s espousal of mercy and forgiveness is critiqued in a letter from a loyalist volunteer soldier, *Montreal Herald*, 20 February 1838 [p.3].

17 *Western Herald*, 4 September 1838, p.229. See *Western Herald*, 18 September 1838, p.2: 'mercy, which according to Shakespeare, endorsed by Sir George Arthur in one of his public documents, "is not strained," has been "strained" in their behalf'.

18 *Examiner*, 5 August 1838, p.481.

19 Speech in Commons on 14 August 1838, reprinted in *Annual Register* (London: Rivington, 1839), p.289.

20 Attorney General Charles Ogden, *Quebec Mercury*, 9 September 1841 [p.1], House of Assembly, 30 August 1841.

21 *Quebec Mercury*, 6 February 1844, [p.2].

22 *Journals of the Legislative Council of the Province of Canada* 8: 1, 18 January 1849.

23 P. Bartley, *Queen Victoria* (Oxford: Routledge, 2016), p.60.

24 G. Merryweather, *Kings, the Devils Viceroys* (New York: the author, 1838), p.271.

25 *Caroline Almanack, and American Freeman's Chronicle, for 1840* (Rochester, New York: Mackenzie's Gazette Office, 1840), p.13, p.20. See *Mackenzie's Gazette* (New York) e.g. 'Left-handed mercy', and 'The Widow of the Martyr', 19 May 1838, on Lower Canada and treatment of Lount's widow, p.15; 7 July 1838, attacks Durham's amnesty, pp.68-9; and a disloyal poem, 'What Is a Queen?' 4 August 1838, p.102. For

scholarly discussion, see B. Wright, '"Harshness and Forbearance": The Politics of Pardons and the Upper Canada Rebellion' in Strange, ed., *Qualities of Mercy*, pp.83–103. Wright notes 'exercise of mercy figured prominently in 1838' (p.83) and looks at the 'calculus of politics' (p.94) in terms of mercy by Arthur and others. See also F.M. Greenwood and B. Wright, eds, *Canadian State Trials: Vol.2: Rebellion and Invasion in the Canadas, 1837–1839* (Toronto: Osgoode Society/University of Toronto Press, 2002).

26 *Caroline Almanack*, p.20.
27 F.B. Head, *A Narrative*, p.334.
28 Ibid., p.131.
29 See in *The Life and Times of William Lyon Mackenzie*, vol.1, p.114, Sir John Colburne's treatment of the libel trial of the newspaper editor Francis Collins. An act of 'mercy' is recorded there, in Lieutenant Governor Sir Francis Bond Head's treatment of Marshall Spring Bidwell, p.65. Colburne's mercy and conciliation in dealing with rebellion in 1837 is highlighted in *The History of Canada*, p.104. On the 'kingly virtue', see petition of Duquette's mother, to Colburne, reprinted in D. M'Leod, *A Brief Review of the Settlement of Upper Canada by the U.E. Loyalists and Scotch Highlanders, in 1783: And of the Grievances Which Compelled the Canadas to Have Recourse to Arms in Defence of Their Rights and Liberties, in 1837 and 1838: Together with a Brief Sketch of the Campaigns of 1812, '13, '14* (Cleveland: Penniman, 1841), pp.282–3.
30 Wright, 'Harshness and Forbearance', p.96. Calls for mercy were uttered in Australia; see 'Clementius', 'The Canadian rebels, now stationed at Longbottom', *The Colonist* (Sydney), 28 March 1840, p.2.
31 *Epitome of Parliamentary Documents in Connection with the North-West Rebellion, 1885* (Ottawa: Maclean, Roger 1886), p.276, petition of setters of Red River, Manitoba, gesturing towards Victoria's 'proverbial' clemency; other petitions use the formula of the queen's 'high prerogative'.
32 *Caroline Almanack*, p.51.
33 *Mackenzie's Gazette*, 29 December 1838, p.2; on British radical response, see G. Martin, *Britain and the Origins of Canadian Confederation, 1837–67* (Vancouver: University of British Columbia, 1995), p.131; and citing Ebenezer Elliott, P.A. Pickering, '"The Hearts of the Millions": Chartism and Popular Monarchism in the 1840s', *History* 88: 290 (April 2003), pp.227–48 [p.245].
34 H. Drapier, 'Chartists' Appeal to the Queen', *Northern Star*, 14 September 1839, p.7.
35 'Victoria. The Star of England. Air of Roast Beef', published by H. Paul of Spitalfields in 1840, reproduced in L. James, *Print and the People, 1819–1851* (London: Allen Lane, 1976), p.346.
36 Plunkett, *Queen Victoria*, p.35. On the monarch in relationship to Chartist appeals to mercy, see M. Sanders, *The Poetry of Chartism: Aesthetics, Politics, History* (Cambridge: Cambridge University Press, 2009), pp.101–2; Thompson, *Queen Victoria*, p.35. On lack of cynicism, see Pickering, '"The Hearts of the Millions"', p.244. See Pickering, '"And your Petitioners &c": Chartist Petitioning in Popular Politics 1838–48', *English Historical Review* 116: 466 (April 2001), pp.368–88, on the parliamentary focus of Chartist petitions.
37 J. and T. Gurney, *The Trial of John Frost for High Treason: Under a Special Commission Held at Monmouth in December 1839 and January 1840* (London: Saunders and Benning, 1840), p.619; reports in press e.g. *Cambridge Independent Press*, 11 January 1840, p.3.

38 *Northern Star*, 1 February 1840, p.1.
39 *The Charter*, 26 January 1840, p.4.
40 *Northern Star*, 1 February 1840; *Northern Liberator*, 8 February 1840, p.3.
41 *The Era*, 2 February 1840, p.227.
42 The handbill reproduced in *Coventry Herald*, 7 February 1840, p.4.
43 *Hull Packet*, 21 February 1840, p.4.
44 *Northern Liberator*, 19 December 1840, p.5.
45 *Northern Star*, 8 February 1840, p.4.
46 *Northern Star*, 12 October 1844, p.7.
47 *Northern Star*, 17 January 1846, p.1.
48 *Northern Star*, 28 March 1846, p.7.
49 'Junius Rusticus', *Northern Star*, 16 January 1841, p.6.
50 *Chartist Circular*, 3 April 1841, p.338.
51 *Northern Star*, 2 January 1841, p.3; see also G. Vargo, 'Chartist Drama: The Performance of Revolt', *Victorian Studies* 61: 1 (Autumn 2018), pp. 9–34 [pp.12–6].
52 *Fraser's Magazine* 22, October 1840, p.394.
53 'Liberty Teaching By Example', *The Examiner*, 27 September 1856, p.1.
54 *Somerset County Gazette*, 17 August 1839, p.3.
55 *The Era*, 18 August 1839, p.6.
56 *Lloyd's Weekly Newspaper*, 8 March 1846, p.7.
57 'Mercy or Blood', *Colonial Times* (Hobart), 17 January 1855, p.2.
58 C. Herbert, *War of No Pity: The Indian Mutiny and Victorian Trauma* (Princeton and Oxford: Princeton University Press, 2008), p.53.
59 *Punch*, 12 September 1857, p.109.
60 '"O God of Battles! Steel My Soldiers' Hearts"', *Punch*, 10 October 1857, p.151. See L. Murdoch, '"Suppressed Grief": Mourning the Death of British Children and the Memory of the 1857 Indian Rebellion', *Journal of British Studies* 51: 2 (April 2012), pp.364–92. The quotation is from *Henry V*, Act 4. See 'Pity for the Poor Sepoys', *Punch*, 10 October 1857, p.154. See W.C. Monkhouse, *The Life and Work of Sir John Tenniel, R.I.* (London: Art Journal office, 1901), p.25.
61 'Letters from a Competition Wallah. Letter IX. British temper towards India, Before, During and Since the Mutiny', *Macmillan's Magazine*, February 1864, pp.288–303.
62 'Mercy and Not Vengeance', *Lady's Newspaper*, 17 October 1857, p.243.
63 Reprinted in C. Hibbert, *Queen Victoria in Her Letters and Journals* (1984; Stroud: Sutton, 2000), p.137.
64 W.L. Arnstein, *Queen Victoria* (Basingstoke: Palgrave Macmillan, 2003), p.103; the Queen to Lady Canning, 8 September and 22 October 1857, in Hibbert, *Queen Victoria in Her Letters and Journals*, pp.137–8. Lady Canning's reflections on clemency are reprinted in J.C. Hare, *The Story of Two Noble Lives, Being Memorials of Charlotte, Countess Canning, and Louisa, Marchioness of Waterford* (2 vols; London: Allen, 1893), vol.2, p.371.
65 Victoria to Lady Canning, 1 July 1858, quoted in Hibbert, *Queen Victoria in Her Letters and Journals*, p.138. RA VIC/MAIN/QVJ (W), Princess Beatrice's copy, 1 November 1857 (conversation with Lord Palmerston). Benson and Brett, eds, *The Letters of Queen Victoria. First Series. Vol.3*, pp.249–367, Canning to the Queen, 25 September 1857; for further correspondence on justice tempered with clemency, see resignation letter by Canning's successor as Governor-General, Ellenborough, 10 May 1858, reprinted p.282. Vernon Smith, president of the Board of Control, July 1857, picking up on a comment by Disraeli: 'As to connecting the name of the Queen

with all that is done in India he thought that whether the Queen or the Company puts down the mutiny no one could imagine that the quality of mercy would not be exercised', *The Indian Administration of Lord Canning, Reprinted from the Bengal Hurkaru* (Calcutta: Hurkaru Press, 1862), p.18.
66 'The Royal Proclamation to India', *Blackwood's Magazine*, January 1859, p.113; 'Proclamation by the Queen in Council, to the Princes, Chiefs and People of India'. For Victoria and Albert drafting the proclamation, T. Martin, *The Life of His Royal Highness the Prince Consort* (London: Smith, Elder, 1879), vol.4, pp.284–7. For reflection on its Christian and merciful message, see *Church Missionary Intelligencer*, January 1859, pp.1–10.
67 'Indicus', *Christian Observer*, August 1858, p.759.
68 J.M. Ludlow, *Policy of the Crown Towards India* (London: Ridgway, 1859), p.7.
69 Ludlow, *Policy of the Crown Towards India*, p.207, citing Fredrick Cooper's acts as a 'sham of leniency'. On the prerogative, I quote H.S. Cunningham, *Earl Canning and the Transfer of India from the Company to the Crown* (Oxford: Clarendon Press, 1911), p.175.
70 *Allen's Indian Mail*, 11 February 1859, p.135, from magistrate of Shahabad, Alonzo Money. See also Ram Gopaul Ghose, 3 November 1858, in J.K. Majumdar, ed., *Indian Speeches and Documents on British Rule 1821–1918* (Calcutta: Longman, Green, 1937), p.77.
71 *London Evening Standard*, 15 April 1859, p.5, vote of thanks to civil and military officers, House of Lords, 14 April 1859, the Earl of Derby, praising Montgomery, resident in Oude, 'with her Majesty's proclamation in his hand, and making the best use of the promises of mercy which that proclamation set forth'.
72 M. Moaddel, *Islamic Modernism, Nationalism, and Fundamentalism: Episode and Discourse* (Chicago: University of Chicago Press, 2005), p.63; Taylor, *Empress: Queen Victoria and India*, p.197.
73 *The Indian National Congress, Containing an Account of Its Origin and Growth, Full Text of All the Presidential Addresses, Reprint of All the Congress Resolutions, Extracts from All the Welcome Addresses, Notable Utterances on the Movement, Portraits of All the Congress Presidents* (Madras: Natesan, 1909), p.323.
74 Ibid., p.373. For a critical view, see R. Chatterjee, *The Consolidation of the Christian Power in India* (Calcutta: Prabasi Press, 1927), p.91; for pro-Victoria view, see R.C. Dutt, *The Economic History of India in the Victorian Age: From the Accession of Queen Victoria in 1837* (London: Kegan Paul, Trübner, 1908), p.231.
75 J.B. Crozier, 'The Government of India Problem: A Study in Applied Sociology', *Fortnightly Review* 91: 541 (January 1912), pp.91–105 [pp.98–100].
76 D. Naoroji, *Poverty and Un-British Rule in India* (London: Sonnenschein, 1901), p.583.
77 See R. Dutt, *Indian Poetry. Selections Rendered into English Verse* (London: Dent, 1904), p.70. For acts of royal mercy, see B.N. Ramusack, *The New Cambridge History of India. III.6. The Indian Princes and Their States* (Cambridge: Cambridge University Press, 2004), p.133.
78 M. Mukerjee, *India in the Shadows of Empire: A Legal and Political History (1774–1950)* (Oxford University Press, 2009).
79 *Report on the Administration of Bengal, 1877–78* (Calcutta: Bengal Secretariat Press, 1878), p.66.
80 *Gloucestershire Echo*, 19 February 1887, p.3; *Carlisle Journal*, 25 February 1887, p.4.

81 Cited in *Voice of India*, February 1887, p.86; see also Bengali daily *Dainik* (Calcutta), in *Report on Native Papers for the Week Ending 12th February 1887*, p.170, for summary translations of Indian-language/Indian-owned newspaper items, produced for the colonial state and digitized in South Asia Open Archives via jstor.org.
82 B.W. Savile, *How India Was Won by England Under Clive and Hastings* (London: Hodder and Stoughton, 1881), p.238.
83 Giuseppe Norfini's jubilee bust of the 'Kaisar-i-Hind' for the Oriental University Institute includes swords of justice and mercy.
84 D.M. Morrison, *India and Imperial Federation* (London: Sampson Low, Marston, 1902), p.100.
85 R. Chakrabarty, review of A. Roy, *Nationalism as Poetic Discourse in Nineteenth-Century Bengal* (2003), in *Bengal: Past and Present* 123 (2004), p.84.
86 S.M. Tagore, *Victoria-gítika, or Sanskrit Verses, Celebrating the Deeds and the Virtues of Her Most Gracious Majesty the Queen Victoria and Her Renowned Predecessors* (Calcutta: I.C. Bose, 1875).
87 Lord Clarendon reported in *The Greville Memoirs: A Journal of the Reigns of King George IV, King William IV, and Queen Victoria* (8 vols; London: Longmans, Green, 1898), vol.8, p.130. J.B. Norton, *Topics for Indian Statesmen* (London: Richardson, 1858), pp.6–61, refers to *Lahore Chronicle* and *Friend of India*, contrasted with humane *Morning Star* (England) and *Athenaeum* in India.
88 6 January 1893, p.18 in *Report on Native Papers Published in the Bombay Presidency. For the Week Ending 14th January 1893*.
89 *Report on Native Papers for the Week Ending the 22nd December 1877*, pp.5–6. Extended discussion on mercy in capital sentences appeared in *Jámi-ul-Ulúm* (Moradabad) after sentence of death on a co-wife; see *Selections from the Vernacular Newspapers Published in the North-Western Provinces & Oudh, Received Up to the 18th September 1900*, pp.469–70. Later references include *Report on Native Papers Published in the Bombay Presidency. For the Week Ending 13th November 1909*, p.20, non-exercised prerogative of mercy towards Sarvottam Rao, editor of *Swardi*, in *Jain* and *Indu Prakash*; *Selections from Indian-Owned Newspapers Published in the United Provinces*, no.48 (1915), p.1220, *Abhyudaha* (Allahabad), 20 November 1915 and *Pratap* (Cawnpore), 22 November 1915, praising viceregal tempering of justice in punishing a Lahore conspiracy.
90 He was executed on 13 August 1891, Buckle, ed., *The Letters of Queen Victoria: Third Series. Vol. 3. 1879–1885*. For native commentary, see e.g. *Gujarati*, 16 August 1891 in *Report on Native Papers Published in the Bombay Presidency. For the Week Ending 22nd August 1891*, pp.21–2.
91 *Derby Daily Telegraph*, 10 January 1893, p.2; *The Star* (Guernsey), 12 January 1893, p.1. Referring to *The Code of Criminal Procedure*, see *The Pocket Criminal Procedure Code: Containing Also the Indian Penal Code* (Calcutta: Secular Press, 1889), with proviso, 'Nothing herein contained shall be deemed to interfere with the right of Her Majesty to grant pardons, reprieves, respites, or remissions of punishment' (p.155). This section was an amendment of 1874 to the Code.
92 'Anglo-Indian', 'Lord Curzon's Services to India', *North American Review* (January 1903), pp.68–79 [p.71]. After 1916, the prerogative was delegated to the viceroy by Royal Warrant, A.K. Ghose, *Public Administration in India* (Calcutta: University of Calcutta Press, 1930), p.24.
93 G.F. Pardon, *Illustrious Women Who Have Distinguished Themselves for Virtue, Piety, and Benevolence* (London: Blackwood, 1852), pp.29–30.

94 The colonial governor Sir George Grey, interviewed by Lady Isabel Somerset's *Woman's Signal*, 3 May 1894, p.290.
95 RA VIC/MAIN/QVJ (W), Princess Beatrice's copy, 24–25 January 1843.
96 RA VIC/MAIN/A/13/61, Sir Robert Peel to the Queen, 24 January 1843.
97 Benson and Brett, eds, *The Letters of Queen Victoria. First Series. Vol.1. 1837–1843*, 25 January 1843.
98 RA VIC/MAIN/QVJ (W), Princess Beatrice's copy, 26 January 1843. The queen referred to Oxford in RA VIC/MAIN/QVJ (W), Princess Beatrice's copy, 17 June 1840.
99 RA VIC/MAIN/QVJ (W), Princess Beatrice's copy, 5 February 1843.
100 Benson and Brett, eds, *The Letters of Queen Victoria. First Series. Vol.1*, 4 March 1843.
101 RA VIC/MAIN/Y/91/5, Queen Victoria to King Leopold, 14 March 1843.
102 RA VIC/MAIN/QVJ (W), Princess Beatrice's copy, 5 March 1843.
103 RA VIC/MAIN/A/14/1, Sir Robert Peel to the Queen, Whitehall, 'Sunday Morning'.
104 RA VIC/MAIN/C/3/43; VIC/MAIN/QVJ (W), Princess Beatrice's copy, 10 July 1840.
105 RA VIC/MAIN/QVJ (W), Princess Beatrice's copy, 10 July 1840. See Poole, *The Politics of Regicide*, pp.186–7.
106 RA VIC/MAIN/QVJ (W), Princess Beatrice's copy, 17 June 1842; RA VIC/MAIN/C/6/34, Victoria, Buckingham Palace, 18 June 1842.
107 J. McCarthy, *A History of Our Own Times from the Accession of Queen Victoria to the Berlin Congress* (4 vols; London: Chatto and Windus, 1879), vol.1, p.160
108 RA VIC/MAIN/M/67; the letter by the queen to Albert is RA VIC/MAIN/M/67/40, dated 29 June 1842. An account of royal mercy in these cases receiving, presumably, Victoria's imprimatur was Theodore Martin's official *Life of His Royal Highness the Prince Consort* (2nd edition; London: Smith, Elder, 1875), vol.1, p.141, and a letter from Albert to his father explaining the risks from the 'vindictiveness' of the common people.
109 RA VIC/MAIN/M/67/42, Sir James Graham, 30 June 1842.
110 RA VIC/MAIN/M/67/43.
111 RA VIC/MAIN/M/67/44.
112 RA VIC/MAIN/M/67/77.
113 *John Bull*, 25 June 1842, p.302; reprinted elsewhere, e.g. *The Age*, 26 June 1842, p.3.
114 [S. Warren], 'Modern State Trials. Part II', *Blackwood's Edinburgh Magazine* 68, November 1850, pp.545–72 [p.552].
115 RA VIC/MAIN/C/6/35.
116 Martin, *Life of His Royal Highness the Prince Consort*, vol.1, p.141.
117 *The Court, Magazine, Monthly Critic and Museum*, July 1842, p.24.
118 See RA VIC/MAIN/C/6/36, 17 July 1842, for the queen's gratification that the bill passed quickly through both Houses.
119 *The Spectator*, 9 July 1842, p.662.
120 Ibid.
121 *Pictorial Times*, 25 April 1846, p.257, discussing responses to attempts on Victoria and Louis Philippe's lives.
122 The phrase in S. Warren, *Miscellanies Critical, Imaginative and Juridical* (2 vols; London: Blackwood, 1855), vol.2, p.126.
123 RA VIC/MAIN/L/14/104.
124 RA VIC/MAIN/L/14/106, Queen Victoria, Windsor Castle, 2 March 1882.
125 RA VIC/MAIN/L/14/111, Queen Victoria.
126 RA VIC/MAIN/L/14/107, Gladstone to Sir Henry Ponsonby, 10 Downing Street, 3 March 1882; RA VIC/MAIN/L/14/116, Gladstone to the Queen, 10 Downing Street;

RA VIC/MAIN/L/14/117, Gladstone to Sir Henry Ponsonby, 10 Downing Street, 9 March 1882.
127 RA VIC/MAIN/L/14/118, the Queen.
128 Ibid.
129 RA VIC/MAIN/L/14/133, the Queen, Windsor Castle, 19 April 1882.
130 RA VIC/MAIN/L/14/134, the Queen, Windsor Castle, 19 April 1882.
131 RA VIC/MAIN/L/14/139, Sir Henry Ponsonby to the Queen, 20 April 1882.
132 RA VIC/ADDA12/725, the Queen, Balmoral castle, 27 May 1882.
133 RA VIC/MAIN/L/14/111, the Queen.
134 'An Episode in English History – Assassination of Mr Perceval, in 1812', *Dublin University Magazine* 62, August 1863, pp.177–89 [p.178].
135 RA VIC/MAIN/L/14/140.
136 RA VIC/MAIN/L/14/141, Sir Henry Ponsonby to Gladstone, Windsor Castle, 23 April 1882.
137 Ibid. See RA VIC/MAIN/D/32/53, Gladstone to the Queen, 3 May 1882, on changes in the form of the verdict passed upon MacLean; RA VIC/MAIN/L/15/13, Gladstone's letter to the Queen, 20 August 1883, on the Trial of Lunatics Bill, in which the guilt of someone insane would be recorded, the insanity would now be specially found and cause the accused to be detained at Her Majesty's pleasure, in the belief that the verdict of guilt had a 'deterrent effect upon persons not entirely responsible for their actions'. This was enacted.
138 *Morning Post*, 9 April 1900, p.3.
139 *Pall Mall Gazette*, 20 June 1902, p.7; *The Sketch*, 8 August 1900, p.92.

Chapter 6

1 J.S. Buckingham, *America, Historical, Statistic, and Descriptive* (2 vols; New York: Harper and Brothers, 1841), vol.1, p.iv.
2 B. Gregory, 'Staging British India', ch.4 in J.S. Bratton, R.A. Cave, B. Gregory, M. Pickering, H.J. Holder, *Acts of Supremacy: The British Empire and the Stage, 1790–1930* (Manchester: Manchester University Press, 1991), p.170.
3 E. Copley, *A History of Slavery and Its Abolition* (2nd edition, London: Houlston, 1839), p.642.
4 C. Midgley, *Women Against Slavery: The British Campaigns, 1780–1870* (London: Routledge, 1992), p.65. See L. Dimock, 'Queen Victoria, Africa and Slavery: Some Personal Associations', paper presented to AFSAAP Conference 2009, accessed at afsaap.org.au (2 February 2019). For context, see C.H. Wesley, 'The Abolition of Negro Apprenticeship in the British Empire', *Journal of Negro History* 23: 2 (April 1938), pp.155–99.
5 Yet, *Christian Observer*, May 1843, p.313, 'he unhappily concurred with his father and brothers and was found with the Duke of Clarence in the divisions against the abolition'.
6 *Leicester Chronicle*, 22 July 1837, p.2.
7 Ibid.
8 *Birmingham Journal*, 15 July 1837, p.7.
9 *Monthly Magazine*, November 1837, p.452.

10 *Newcastle Courant*, 2 February 1838, p.3. See also G. Thompson, *Anti-Slavery Crisis: Policy of Ministers. Reprinted from the Eclectic Review, for April, 1838. With a Postscript on the Debate and Division in the House of Commons, on the 29th and 30th of March* (London: W. Ball, 1838), p.25.
11 *Parliamentary Debates*, 3rd series, vol.150, 'Negro Emancipation', House of Lords, 20 February 1838, cols.1313–14.
12 H. Brougham, *The British Constitution: Its History, Structure and Working* (London: Griffin, Bohn, 1861), pp.330–1.
13 G. Lerner, *The Feminist Thought of Sarah Grimké* (New York: Oxford University Press, 1998), p.52. The letter, 26 October 1837, in Boston Public Library, is digitized, https://ark.digitalcommonwealth.org/ark:/50959/2z10z220t
14 W. Bevan, *The Operation of the Apprenticeship System in the British Colonies. A Statement, the Substance of Which Was Presented and Adopted at the Meeting of the Liverpool Anti-Slavery Society, Dec. 19th, 1837, Etc* (Liverpool: Marples, 1838).
15 *The Friends' Intelligencer* 1, 16 August 1838, p.144. For other figures, see Wesley, 'The Abolition of Negro Apprenticeship in the British Empire', pp.178–9. On Dublin female abolitionist appeals to the queen, see C. Kinealy, *Daniel O'Connell and the Anti-Slavery Movement* (2011; Abingdon: Routledge, 2016), p.56.
16 E. Breitenbach, L. Fleming, S.K. Kehoe, and L. Orr, eds, *Scottish Women: A Documentary History, 1780–1914* (Edinburgh: Edinburgh University Press, 2013), p.251.
17 *Leeds Mercury*, 10 February 1838, p.6.
18 *Birmingham Journal*, 30 December 1837, p.4.
19 *Carlisle Journal*, 12 May 1838, p.3.
20 See *Essex Standard*, 27 April 1838, p.4 for all the quotations from Sturge's speech.
21 *Bradford Observer*, 4 January 1838, p.2.
22 *Northern Star*, 28 April 1838, p.6.
23 *Bristol Mercury*, 28 April 1838, p.4.
24 *Exeter and Plymouth Gazette*, 5 May 1838, p.3.
25 *York Herald*, 28 April 1838, p.3.
26 *West Kent Guardian*, 2 June 1838, p.2.
27 *Chelmsford Chronicle*, 13 July 1838, p.2.
28 E.g. *Baptist Magazine*, March 1840, p.129.
29 *Leicestershire Mercury*, 7 July 1838, p.4.
30 *Sheffield Independent*, 23 June 1838, p.6.
31 *Leicester Journal*, 29 June 1838, p.4. See also 'Theta', *Fife Herald*, 28 June 1838, p.70.
32 *Poems* (Cambridge: Metcalf, 1846), p.111. For other verse extolling the queen in relation to abolition, see H. Holmes, *English Kings, or Sketches of British History: From the Invasion of Caesar* (Romsey: Lordan, 1843), p.55.
33 P.W. Scher, 'Uneasy Heritage: Ambivalence and Ambiguity in Caribbean Heritage Practices', in R. Bendix, A. Eggert, A. Peselmann, eds, *Heritage Regimes and the State* (Göttingen: Universitätsverlag Göttingen, 2012), p.89.
34 *Periodical Accounts Relating to the Missions of the Church of the United Brethren Among the Heathens* (London: Brethren Society, 1838), p.453.
35 D.L. Eudell, *The Political Languages of Emancipation in the British Caribbean and the US South* (Chapel Hill: University of North Carolina Press, 2002), p.43. See also G. Horne, *Negro Comrades of the Crown: African Americans and the British Empire Fight the U.S. Before Emancipation* (New York: New York University Press, 2012). See

Papers Relative to the West Indies: Ordered, by the House of Commons, to Be Printed 15 March 1839, Part 4, for letters.
36 J. Coffey, '"Yours for the Jubilee": The Abolitionists' Scriptural Imagination', in *Exodus and Liberation: Deliverance Politics from John Calvin to Martin Luther King Jr* (Oxford: Oxford University Press, 2014), p.114.
37 *Liverpool Mercury*, 3 August 1838, p.7. The legislation, passed on 11 April 1838, was 'An Act to amend the Act for the Abolition of Slavery in the British Colonies' [1 & 2 Vict. c. 19].
38 James Curry, speech reproduced in J.W. Blassingame, ed., *Slave Testimony: Two Centuries of Letters, Speeches, Interviews Autobiographies* (Baton Rouge, LA: Louisiana State University Press, 1977), p.144, 'under the free government of Queen Victoria'.
39 *Proceedings of the General Anti-slavery Convention*, p.28.
40 Ibid., p.120; p.114.
41 J. Pierpont, *Antislavery Poems of John Pierpont* (Boston: Johnson, 1843), p.33.
42 R.W. Winks, *The Blacks in Canada: A History* (New Haven, CT: Yale University Press, 1971), p.329. See R.J. Branham and S.J. Hartnett, *Sweet Freedom's Song: 'My Country "Tis of Thee' and Democracy in America"* (New York: Oxford University Press, 2002), note 34 on Victoria's popularity for abolitionists e.g. Joshua McCarter's *The Emancipation Car, Being an Original Composition of Anti-Slavery Ballads, Composed Exclusively for the Underground Railroad* (1854).
43 W. Goodell, *Slavery and Anti-slavery. History of the Great Struggle in Both Hemispheres* (New York: Harned, 1852), p.373.
44 *The Friend*, 6 April 1839, p.213; *Friends Intelligencer*, 1 March 1839, p.235.
45 S. Rubek [John Burke], *Stanzas to Queen Victoria, and Other Poems* (New York: Brady, 1866), p.135
46 RA VIC/MAIN/QVJ (W), Princess Beatrice's copy, 16 May 1838.
47 RA VIC/MAIN/QVJ (W), Lord Esher's typescript, 25 June 1838.
48 RA VIC/MAIN/QVJ (W), Lord Esher's typescript, 5 October 1838. Melbourne's reception of a delegation of the Central Negro Emancipation Committee was unfavourable; see Wesley, 'The Abolition of Negro Apprenticeship in the British Empire', p.181.
49 *Proceedings at the First Public Meeting of the Society for the Extinction of the Slave Trade and for the Civilization of Africa Held in Exeter Hall on Monday 1st June 1840 His Royal Highness Prince Albert President of the Society in the Chair* (London: Clowes, 1840). See M. Taylor, 'Prince Albert and the British Empire', in F. Bosbach and J.R. Davis, ed., *Prinz Albert – Ein Wettiner in Grossbritannien/Prince Albert – A Wettin in Britain* (Munich: Saur, 2004); S. Drescher, *The Mighty Experiment: Free Labor Versus Slavery in British Emancipation* (New York: Oxford University Press, 2002), p.166.
50 Henry le Jeune, 'The Liberation of Slaves' (1847), oil on canvas, RCIN 406241. The Royal Collection includes a copy of *Uncle Tom's Cabin* given by Victoria to Prince Albert in 1853.
51 *York Herald*, 4 December 1874, p.3.
52 *British Friend*, February 1856, p.33, from *The Nonconformist*, 23 January 1856, citing *The Inquirer*, 19 January 1856 (a Unitarian newspaper); and correction in *The Athenaeum*, 26 January 1856, p.107, which suggested the political consequence of making public comments on a question that threatened the Union led to her dismissal and there was no intention to dedicate the book to the queen. See

A.M. Murray, *Letters from the United States, Cuba and Canada* (2 vols; London: Parker, 1856).
53 F.M. Bladen, *Historical Records of New South Wales: Papers Relating to King, 1803–1805*. (Sydney: Potter, 1897), vol.5, pp.153–4 (Governor King pardoning conditional emancipists). See discussion of mercy in G.D. Woods, *A History of Criminal Law in New South Wales: The Colonial Period, 1788–1900* (Sydney: Federation Press, 2002), pp.5–6.
54 *Launceston Examiner*, 2 March 1844, p.7. Reprinted 20 December 1845, p.432.
55 'The Prerogative of Mercy', *The Argus*, 17 January 1855, p.4.
56 W.H. Cooper, *The Crisis: A Treatise upon Certain So-Called Constitutional Principles Recently Asserted, with Respect to the Right of Petition, the Privileges of Parliament, and the Prerogative of Pardon* (Sydney: Kelly, 1875), p.19, p.22; it criticized petitions *against* royal mercy as 'not merely unconstitutional, but… absolutely without precedent' (p.16). On the impact of the case, see Woods, *A History of Criminal Law in New South Wales*, p.6.
57 'The Prayer of the Coloured Men', *Evening News* (Sydney), 9 June 1879, p.3, Sir George Innes did not think the queen would interfere: 'She could not, without enormous expense in telegraphing being incurred, be put in possession of all the facts of the case. And it would be a very strong measure for the Queen to take to interfere thus with the Executive, it is presided over here by a Lieutenant-Governor of almost unequalled experience in the administration of the criminal law.'
58 'The Blackfellow Executed', *Evening News*, 10 June 1879, p.3.
59 Howard Association, Report, 1887, p.11.
60 *Queensland Figaro and Punch*, 11 June 1887, p.922; 18 June 1887, p.3. See J.W. Knight linking Queensland women and a female monarchy with mercy, *The Brisbane Courier*, 6 June 1887, p.5. Thompson would be the only woman hanged in Queensland. Jubilee mercy was discussed in 'Jubilee Libertini', *The Week* (Brisbane), 25 June 1887, p.22, reprinted in *The Telegraph* (Brisbane), 27 June 1887, p.2, on Christopher Pickford.
61 From the letter from Parkes to Governor Carrington, quoted extensively in W. Kukulies-Smith and S. Priest, 'The Mount Rennie Rape Case of 1886: Politics, Mercy and Justice in Late Nineteenth Century Australia', ch.9 in P. Easteal, ed., *Justice Connections* (Newcastle upon Tyne: Cambridge Scholars, 2013), pp.220–39 [p.231]. See L. Trainor, *British Imperialism and Australian Nationalism: Manipulation, Conflict and Compromise in the Late Nineteenth Century* (New York: Cambridge University Press, 1994), pp.74–5. Detailed material on prerogative, petitions from the accused, police reports, newspaper clippings are in Carrington's personal papers; see description of the album in 'miscellaneous papers', Reel M926, in *Lord Carrington, Papers, 1860–1928 Reels M917-37*, National Library of Australia State Library of New South Wales, 1972. For royal prerogative in relation to the crime, see *Daily Telegraph* (Sydney), 6 January 1887, p.5.
62 'Mount Rennie Outrage', reprinting letter from 'Civis', *Launceston Examiner*, 20 December 1886, p.3. Sir Henry Parkes set out the queen's prerogative in capital cases, 16 January 1880 in the Legislative Assembly: see 'Capital Punishment', *Hay Standard* (New South Wales), 4 February 1880, p.2, indicating limits to prerogative were opposed to the advice of her responsible ministers.
63 *Maryborough Chronicle*, 29 June 1887, p.2.
64 *Australian Star*, 23 April 1897, p.8; *Sydney Morning Herald*, 23 April 1897, p.3. Newspaper commentaries reveal local campaigns; e.g. Townsville Municipal Council

call for clemency for Coombemartin and Ayrshire Downs prisoners linked to the socialist E. Lowry, a Townsville alderman, *Queenslander* (Brisbane), 8 May 1897, p.1016. For critical discussion about prisoner release, a decade later, see *Sydney Morning Herald*, 23 April 1897, p.4, editorial arguing that with legal reforms, there was no reason for the prerogative.

65 See *The Advocate* of Melbourne, 26 June 1897, p.2; and 'Jubilee Clemency', *Southern Cross*, 20 August 1897, p.5.
66 From Melbourne correspondent of *The Times*, 22 June 1897, p.5.
67 *The Argus* (Melbourne), 4 October 1853, p.4. I draw on S. Petrow, 'Fear, panic and Persecution: *The Argus* and Victorian Anti-convict Legislation in the 1850s', abstract of paper, November 2016, http://www.anzsoc2016.com/1736 (accessed 2 February 2019). The prerogative was exercised by colonial government after the 1890s; see 'The Prerogative of Mercy', *The Ballarat Star* (Victoria), 19 August 1892, p.4; *Daily Telegraph* (Sydney), 18 August 1892, p.5.
68 'The Quality of Mercy', *Australian Star* (Sydney), 4 June 1892, p.4. One of the foundational constitutional documents of the commonwealth of Australia has mercy among border ornaments, Queen Victoria's Letters Patent constituting the Office of the Governor-General, 29 October 1900.
69 Printing John Norton's 'A Plea for Prisoners', An Open letter to Sir Wm Jno. Lyne, K.C.M.G., MP', *Truth* (Brisbane), 16 December 1900, p.4.
70 M.G. Fawcett, *Life of Her Majesty Queen Victoria* (Boston: Roberts, 1895), p.192.
71 A.B. Keith, *Responsible Government in the Dominions* (3 vols; Oxford: Clarendon Press, 1912), vol.3, ch.4.
72 'Rejoice oh! Greatly', Supplement to *Weekly Freeman*, 4 June 1887, p.4 published associated verse.
73 See 'The New Era', the title given to the publication of George V's proclamation after the royal assent to the Government of India Act of 1919, *The Times*, 24 December 1919, p.10, which includes the king-emperor's direction to exercise this clemency to political prisoners if compatible with public safety.
74 R.B. Seeley, *The Life and Reign of Edward I* (London: Seeley, Jackson, Halliday, 1872), p.351.
75 W.T. Denison, *Varieties of Vice-regal Life* (2 vols; London: Longmans, Green, 1870), vol.2, p.190.
76 A. Chernock, 'Queen Victoria and the "Bloody Mary of Madagascar"', *Victorian Studies* 55: 3 (Spring 2013), pp.425–49.
77 *Christian World Magazine*, July 1866, p.58.
78 D.C. Boulger, *The History of China* (revised edition; 2 vols; London: Thacker), vol.2, p.491. On Cixi as Guanyin, D. Ling, *Two Years in the Forbidden City* (New York: Moffat, Yard, 1911), p.225.
79 R. Wilson, *The Life and Times of Queen Victoria* (4 vols; London: Cassell, 1897), vol.3, p.228.
80 RA VIC/MAIN/QVJ (W), Princess Beatrice's copy, 14 November 1864 (*Globe*); 24 November 1864 (German press).
81 Original telegram in French, RA VIC/MAIN/J/66/111, 2 June 1898.
82 RA VIC/MAIN/J/66/117, 2 July 1898.
83 W.C. Harris, *The Highlands of Æthiopia* (2nd edition, 3 vols; London: Longman, Brown, Green, and Longmans, 1844), vol.3, p.390.
84 *Narrative of a Journey from Calcutta to Europe by the Way of Egypt in the Years 1827 and 1828*, quoted in *The Lady's Magazine*, June 1829, p.301.

85 'The Rival Brothers' in *The Romance of History. India* (3 vols; London: Churton, 1836), vol.1, p.137.

Chapter 7

1 'A Boy's History of England', *Boys' Journal* (London: Vickers, 1867), p.590.
2 S.A. Weltman, 'Victoria and Ruskin's Domestic Ideology' in Homans and Munich, eds, *Remaking Queen Victoria*, pp.115–22 [p.119].
3 *New Palace of Westminster* (London: Warrington, 1862), p.13; reiterated for francophone visitors, in *Le Nouveau Palais de Westminster* (London: Warrington, 1859), p.13.
4 See 'Resolutions… Proposed by Mr Gally Knight', Appendix, no.9, *Third Report from Commissioners on the Fine Arts* (London: Clowes, 1844), p.25, for early reports of the scheme, *Globe*, 9 December 1852, p.1.
5 A.N. Wilson, *Prince Albert: The Man Who Saved the Monarchy* (London: Atlantic Books, 2019), p.108; E. Martin, 'Queen Victoria, Prince Albert and the Patronage of Contemporary Sculpture in Victorian Britain 1837–1901', PhD, University of Warwick, Department of History of Art, December 2013, 2 vols; vol.1, p.115 for the echo of crown, peers, and Commons.
6 On the royal visit, *Lady's Newspaper*, 21 February 1857, p.114. For images of the figures, see *Engravings from Original Compositions Executed in Marble at Rome by John Gibson* (London: Colnaghi, Scott, 1861); J. Harrington, *The Abbey and Palace of Westminster* (London: Sampson Low, Marston, 1869); T. Archer, *Our Sovereign Lady, Queen Victoria: Her Life and Jubilee* (London: Blackie, 1888), vol.4, before p.129.
7 RA VIC/MAIN/QVJ (W), Princess Beatrice's copy, 16 February 1857.
8 T. Mathews, *The Biography of John Gibson, R.A., Sculptor, Rome* (London: Heinemann, 1911), p.178.
9 *The Land We Live In, A Pictorial and Literary Sketch-Book of the British Empire* (London: Orr, 1855), vol.2, p.210.
10 'The Gibson Bequest', *The Architect* 16, 5 August 1876, p.77.
11 *London Guide: A Handbook for Strangers Showing Where to Go, How to Get There, and What to Look At* (London: G.F. Cruchley, 1862), p.80.
12 *The Eleventh Report of the Commissioners on the Fine Arts. With Appendix* (London: Eyre and Spottiswoode, 1858), p.8.
13 See *The New Palace of Westminster* (London: Warrington, 1862), p.20 on stylistic mismatch; on scale, *Art-Journal* 9 (1870), p.79; on expression of clemency, *The Critic*, 16 April 1855, p.189; *Art-Journal* 9 (1870), p.79.
14 *The Athenaeum*, 14 December 1861, p.801; 3 February 1866, p.172.
15 A.J.C. Hare, *Walks in London* (2 vols; London: Daldy, Isbister, 1878), vol.2, p.389; *Kelly's Post Office Guide to London in 1862* (London: Kelly, 1862), p.328.
16 Prudence, Temperance, Fortitude, Faith, Hope, and Charity, as noted by *The Child's Companion* (London: Religious Tract Society, 1844), p.14, which hoped it would be the abode, among other qualities, of clemency. On Marochetti's work, see albumen print by Camille Silvy, 1861, National Portrait Gallery collection, NPG Ax55523; and C. Blanc, *Gazette des Beaux Arts* (Paris, 1864), pp.566–7 [p.566]. The Victoria Memorial outside Buckingham Palace and Albert Memorial have representations of Justice.

17 For Mary's signing of Jane Grey's death warrant, see engraving by George Cruikshank from W.H. Ainsworth, *The Tower of London: An Historical Romance* (1840; London: Routledge, 1854), opposite p.352. Victoria, romantic worshipper of Mary Stuart, discussed her guilt for Darnley's murder in her journals; see Vallone, *Becoming Victoria*, p.120, for her critique of Elizabeth's lack of pity for her cousin. Charles Piloty depicted Mary's reception of the death warrant: see frontispiece and text, *Art Journal* (New York: Appleton, 1878), p.377. Portraits of monarchs signing death warrants included Elizabeth signing Essex's, by Alexander von Liezen-Mayer (1873); J.S. Copley's painting of Charles I signing Strafford's; and Mary signing Jane Grey's by Daniel Huntingdon (1847). On John Pettie's portrait of King Edward VI, see *Freeman's Journal*, 22 March 1879, p.6; *The Times*, 5 May 1879, p.11; J. Hayward, *The Life and Raigne of King Edward the Sixth* (London: Parridge, 1630), p.7. For Laslett Pott's 'Signing His First Death Warrant', see *Liverpool Mercury*, 21 March 1893, p.6. Paintings of similar royal acts, and efforts to supplicate for mercy, in continental Europe include Eilif Peterssen's 'Christian II Signing the Death Warrant of Torben Oxe' (1875–1876) and Eugénie Servières, 'Ines de Castro with Her Children at the Feet of Alfonso IV, King or Portugal' (1822), where royal clemency is appealed to.

18 Faed, 'From the picture in the collection of John Pinder Esq. Manchester', *Art-Journal*, 1 March 1868, p.48. See British Museum, 1872,1012.6271. Also 'Alfred liberating the family of Hastings', by Henry Singleton, published by William Bromley in 1798, see Keynes, 'The Cult of King Alfred the Great', p.316 and British Museum copy, 1858,1009.157.

19 *Illustrated London News*, 1 May 1847, pp.281–2.

20 *Illustrated London News*, 28 February 1846, p.16, the poem opening: 'Oh Woman! In our adverse hour… Thou art the type of mercy here | And angels hallow thy control.'

21 M. Stone, 'Intercession of Queen Philippa for the Citizens of Calais', in C. Dickens, ed., *A Child's History of England* (1862). For a lithograph by the American John Sartain, see *The Eclectic Magazine*, May 1861.

22 Strohm, 'Queens as Intercessors' in P. Strohm, *Hochon's Arrow: The Social Imagination of Fourteenth-Century Texts* (Princeton, NJ: Princeton University Press, 1992), pp.95–119. A. Strickland, *Lives of the Queens of England, from the Norman Conquest* (2 vols; London: Colburn, 1840), vol.2, p.364, negotiated the problem of this queen on battlefields: 'Her courage was wholly moral courage and her feminine feelings of mercy and tenderness led her.' For F.M.L. Yates, *Letters Written During a Journey to Switzerland in the Autumn of 1841* (2 vols; London: Duncan and Malcolm, 1843), vol.1, p.5, 'She arose like a pleading angel who had obtained mercy for the condemned.'

23 G.M. Murphy, *Reynolds's Newspaper*, 17 January 1864, p.5.

24 A.H. Wall, *Fifty Years of a Good Queen's Reign. A Book for the Royal Jubilee of 1886–1887* (London: Ward and Downey, 1886), p.252. On Elizabeth I, see C. Kingsley, *Westward Ho* (2 vols; Leipzig: Tauchnitz, 1855), vol.1, p.283: 'It is the fashion now to call her a despot but unless every monarch is to be branded with that epithet whose power is not as circumscribed as Queen Victoria's is now, we ought rather to call her the most popular sovereign.' See 'A.S.', 'The Old Queen; or, The Death-Warrant of Essex', *The London Reader: of Literature, Science, Art and General Information* 1.16 (29 August 1863), pp.506–8. On the relationship to the previous century, see F. O'Gorman and K. Turner, eds, *The Victorians and the Eighteenth Century: Reassessing the Tradition* (2004; London: Routledge, 2017).

25 *Northern Star*, 4 January 1845, p.7.

26 D. Jerrold, 'Elizabeth and Victoria', *Illuminated Magazine*, vol.1, May 1843, p.6.

27 G.W.M. Reynolds, *Canonbury House, or, the Queen's Prophecy* (1858; London: Dicks, 1870), p.23, p.217.
28 *Cork Examiner*, 21 August 1863, p.2.
29 Marcus Bickford, reported in *Proceedings and Debates of the Constitutional Convention of the State of New York* (5 vols; Albany: Weed, Parsons, 1868), vol.1, p.437.
30 Quoted in review of C. Wordsworth, *Sequel to Letters to M. Gondon on the Destructive Character of the Church of Rome, Both in Religion and Polity*, in *Dublin Review*, June 1848, pp.269–95 [p.278].
31 S.J. Hale, *Woman's Record: Or Sketches of All Distinguished Women* (New York: Harper and Brothers, 1853), p.808; by contrast E. Holt, *The Public and Domestic Life of His Late Most Gracious Majesty, George the Third: Comprising the Most Eventful and Important Period in the Annals of British History* (2 vols; London: Sherwood, Neely and Jones, 1820), vol.1, p.214.
32 *Hamilton Advertiser*, 29 November 1862, p.1.
33 'The Quality of Mercy Is Not Strained', *Judy*, 5 June 1867, p.70; the cartoon is overleaf.
34 S. Beedle, *An Essay on the Advisability of Total Abolition of Capital Punishment* (London: Nichols, 1867), p.7; A.L. Merrill and H.D. Northrop, *Life and Times of Queen Victoria* (Washington, DC: [Office of the Librarian of Congress] 1901), p.240, 'again the Queen was moved to tears in public'.
35 G.W.E. Russell, *Collections and Recollections (Series II)* (London: Nelson, 1909), p.35.
36 The use of the adjective is frequent: A. Manning, *Queen Philippa's Golden Booke* (London: Hall, 1851), p.i; 'T.W.L.' 'The Children's Jubilee', *Newcastle Chronicle*, 9 July 1887, p.8; 'From Queen To King', *Shipley Times and Express*, 2 February 1901 [p.4].
37 E. Eastlake, ed., *Life of John Gibson, R.A., Sculptor* (London: Longmans, Green, 1870), pp.205–6.
38 'England's Mission to the East', in 'Eta Mawr', *The Story of Count Ulaski: Aurelia: Or, the Gifted: And Other Poems* (London: Provost, 1870), p.163.
39 On the playwright's dilemma, *Female Revenge: Or, the British Amazon: Exemplified in the Life of Boadicia* (London: Cooper, 1753), p.16. On Bonduca, see 'The Tragedy of Bonduca', reprinted in *Fifty Comedies and Tragedies Written by Francis Beaumont and John Fletcher* (London: Macock, 1679), p.40. On Boudicea, see M. Vandrei, *Queen Boudica and Historical Culture in Britain: An Image of Truth* (Oxford: Oxford University Press, 2018); R. Hingley and C. Unwin, *Boudica: Iron Age Warrior Queen* (London: Hambledon Continuum, 2005); A. Fraser, *Warrior Queens: Boudicea's Chariot* (London: Weidenfeld and Nicolson, 1988).
40 E.g. R.W. Morgan, *The British Kymry, or, Britons of Cambria: Outlines of Their History and Institutions* (Ruthin: Clark, 1857), p.102; Boadicea is the pattern for patriotic rallying round Victoria, if threatened, in Lloyd's 'Ode on the Princess Victoria', *A Collection of English Poems and Odes* (London: Longman, Rees, Orme, Brown, Green and Longman, 1834), p.3.
41 'A Lady', *Anecdotes, Personal Traits, and Characteristic Sketches of Victoria the First, Brought Down to the Period of Her Majesty's Marriage* (London: Bennett, 1840), p.337; 'The Modern Queen Boadicea leading her Captive in Chains', a lithograph from *The Tickler*, no.7 (9 December 1837), Royal Collection, RCIN 605957.
42 G. Jones, *The History of Ancient America: Anterior to the Time of Columbus; Proving the Identity of the Aborigines with the Tyrians and Israelites; and the Introduction of Christianity into the Western Hemisphere by the Apostle St. Thomas* (3rd edition; London: Longman, Brown, Green and Longmans, 1843), p.269.

43 S. Maunder, *Select British Biography: From the Rude and Warlike Days of Boadicea to the Victorian Era* (London: Longman, Orme, Brown, 1839).
44 'The Queens Before the Conquests', *Gentleman's Magazine*, December 1854, pp.539–48 [p.541].
45 J. Giles, *Story Book of English for the Use of Little Children* (London: Law, 1851), p.10.
46 *Public Opinion*, 12 June 1869, p.754; on status as royal sculptor, see *English Illustrated Magazine*, 1898, which calls the Celt 'this early Victoria'.
47 Vandrei, *Queen Boudica*, pp.150–1.
48 M. Trevelyan, *Britain's Greatness Foretold: The Story of Boadicea, the British Warrior-Queen* (London: Hogg, 1900), pp.xii–xiii.
49 *The Woman's Signal*, 7 January 1897, p.6; *Fun*, 8 February 1898, p.42.
50 W.L. Arnstein, *Queen Victoria*, p.101, citing diarist Charles Greville; Arnstein, 'The Warrior Queen: Reflections on Victoria and Her World', *Albion* 30: 1 (Spring 1998), pp.1–28; and U. Keller, *The Ultimate Spectacle: A Visual History of the Crimean War* (2001; Abingdon: Routledge, 2013), ch.5.
51 Mrs T.K. Hervey, 'Victoria', *Illustrated London News*, 13 May 1854, p.446.
52 Description and engraving, *Illustrated London News*, 2 February 1856, p.109.
53 *The Times*, 5 January 1855, p.6; see R. Bates, '"All Touched My Hand": Queenly Sentiment and Royal Prerogative', *19: Interdisciplinary Studies in the Long Nineteenth Century* 20 (2015), pp.1–25. The assessment is from *Illustrated London News*, 2 February 1856, p.109.
54 *The Examiner*, 19 January 1856, p.35; *London Evening Standard*, 28 April 1883, p.5.
55 The queen's letter to Nightingale and an account of Nightingale wearing the brooch appear in C. Gere, *Victorian Jewellery Design* (London: Kimber, 1972), p.244.
56 D. Urquhart, *The Edinburgh Review and the Affghan War: Letters Reprinted from the Morning Herald* (London: Maynard, 1843), p.53; *Hereford Times*, 14 February 1857, p.10.
57 O'Neill's words under the auspices of Northampton Liberal Association, *Northampton Mercury*, 22 November 1879, p.5, cited in Taylor, *Empress: Queen Victoria and India*, p.38.
58 Ponsonby, *Henry Ponsonby*, p.47: a sergeant who had embezzled.
59 G.K. Chesterton, 'The Poet Laureateship', *Illustrated London News*, 5 July 1913, p.4.

Conclusion

1 E. Harrison, 'Pageantry and Politics', *The Nineteenth Century and After* 68 August 1910, pp.220–6 [p.220].
2 G.K. Chesterton, 'The Queen and the Suffragettes', *What's Wrong with the World* (London: Cassell, 1910), pp.173–4 [p.173].
3 Asserted for example in C. Petrie's chapter on 'Monarchy' in *The English Genius* (London: Eyre and Spottiswoode, 1938), p.135.
4 'Vigil', *Northern Whig*, 31 July 1899, p.2.
5 Reverend J.S. White, St Andrew's Presbyterian Church, *Maitland Daily Mercury*, 5 February 1901, p.5: 'Her late Majesty loved mercy… Her reign set forth the divine quality of mercy in a higher degree and to a greater extent than that of any of her predecessors'.
6 *Ealing Gazette*, 2 February 1901, p.8.

7   *Essex Newsman*, 9 February 1901, p.3, grand jury of Essex.
8   *London Daily News*, 28 February 1907, p.7.
9   S. Lee, *Edward VII: A Biography* (2 vols; London: Macmillan, 1927), vol.2, p.39.
10 S. Nowell-Smith, *Edwardian England 1901–1914* (London: Oxford University Press, 1964), p.25; M. MacDonagh, *Parliament: Its Romance, Its Comedy, Its Pathos* (Westminster: King, 1902), p.16.
11 E. Alexander, *Chief Whip. The Political Life and Times of Aretas Akers-Douglas First Viscount Chilston* (London: Routledge and Kegan Paul, 1961), p.309; and p.311 for Alexandra's humane sympathies and anxiety about two women to be hanged in February 1903. See S. Lee, *King Edward VII. A Biography. Vol.2 The Reign* (London: Macmillan, 1927), p.42, for his views on capital punishment for murder.
12 Hanham, ed., *The Nineteenth-Century Constitution 1815–1914*, pp.52–3.
13 Michael Bentley asserts royal power's persistence: 'Power and Authority in the Late Victorian and Edwardian Court', ch.9 in A.J. Olechnowicz, ed., *The Monarchy and the British Nation 1780 to the Present* (Cambridge: Cambridge University Press, 2007), pp.163–87.
14 See *Coventry Evening Telegraph*, 18 February 1901, concerning labourer Samson Silas Salmon. It is corrected elsewhere, e.g. *Worcestershire Chronicle*, 23 February 1901, p.4. For mercy in the post-Victorian monarchy, see 'The Prerogative of Mercy', *The Justice of the Peace*, 30 April 1910, p.206.
15 'Hope for Reprieve. How Apted May Obtain the Royal Mercy', *Leominster News*, 14 March 1902, p.6.
16 *Portsmouth Evening News*, 10 September 1904, p.5; *Southern Daily Echo*, 12 September 1904, p.2. See 'The Beck Inquiry. Interest of the King', *Evening Star*, 10 September 1904, p.4.
17 H. Cohen, *The Spirit of our Laws* (London: Sweet and Maxwell, 1906), p.285.
18 'The Royal Clemency. Release of prisoners', *Homeward Mail from India, China and the East*, 21 November 1908, p.24. For discussion of such a gesture during the coronation, see 'Show Mercy', *Western Times*, 18 June 1902, p.4; 'London Letter', *Bradford Observer*, 6 February 1901, p.8.
19 'The King's Clemency', *Sunderland Daily Echo*, 23 January 1902, p.3, case of Wilhelm Jahr. On Lynch, see 'An Amusing Instance of Royal Mercy', *Wicklow People*, 20 July 1907, p.12; for nuances of Edward VII's scruples about clemency towards Lynch, see letter to Herbert Gladstone, 21 July 1906, reprinted in Lee, *King Edward VII*, vol.2, p.41.
20 C. Hibbert, *Edward VII: The Last Victorian King* (1976; Basingstoke: Palgrave Macmillan, 2007), p.212.
21 On Connemara clemency; 'Royal Clemency, Country Woman's Petition Granted', *Belfast News-letter*, 31 July 1903, p.5; *Dublin Daily Express*, 31 July 1903, p.5. On the Irish tour in 1903, see J. Loughlin, 'Crown, Spectacle and Identity: The British Monarchy and Ireland under the Union 1800–1922', ch.4 in Olechnowicz, *The Monarchy and the British Nation*, pp.125–6.
22 On Alexandra's mercy, E. Legge, *More About King Edward* (Boston: Small, Maynard, 1913), pp.371–2. See W.R.H. Trowbridge, *Queen Alexandra. A Study Of Royalty* (London: Unwin, 1921), pp.215–16.
23 Trowbridge, *Queen Alexandra*, p.216; note the astringent comment on royalty and charity, compared with the personal virtue of compassion, p.221.
24 Letters reprinted in Lee, *King Edward VII*, vol.2, pp.42–3 (the quotation about the halfpenny press, 17 April, Frederick Ponsonby to Herbert Gladstone, on the king's behalf).

25 *Truth* (Brisbane), 18 January 1903, p.5.
26 *Parliamentary Debates*, 4th series, vol.192, House of Commons, 15 July 1908, cols. 847–9.
27 *Royal Cornwall Gazette*, 26 May 1910, p.6.
28 'The Character of King Edward VII', *Quarterly Review*, reprinted in R.B. Brett, *The Influence of King Edward, and Essays on Other Subjects* (London: J. Murray, 1915), p.31; 'The King and the Beggar Maid', *The Graphic*, 2 March 1929, p.299.
29 *Aberdeen Press and Journal*, 16 May 1910, p.6.
30 *Westminster Gazette*, quoted in *Dublin Daily Express*, 24 May 1910, p.2.
31 *Walsall Advertiser*, 31 January 1914, p.7.
32 'King's Pardon for Driver Caudle', *Nottingham Evening Post*, 1 November 1913, p.5.
33 'Lord Morley's Opportunity', *London Daily News*, 9 May 1910, p.5; 'An Opportunity in India', *London Daily News*, 10 May 1910, p.5. For discussion of mercy, see S.L. Karandikar, *Lokamanya Bal Gangadhar Tilak: The Hercules and Prometheus of Modern India* (Poona: the author, 1957), p.344; the campaign for mercy for Tilak began 1897: see *Report on Native Papers Published in the Bombay Presidency. For the Week Ending 4th December 1897*, p.22.
34 'An Opportunity in India', *London Daily News*, 10 May 1910, p.5. See also 'The Quality of Mercy', *Globe*, 11 May 1910, p.1.
35 For example, prisoners sentenced after strikes in coal mines, New South Wales, *Sydney Morning Herald*, 17 May 1910, p.9; 'The First Official Act. The Clemency of the Crown', *Daily Telegraph* (Sydney), 25 October 1910, p.7. For his speech in Jaipur, November 1905, praising the maharajah's charity, see *His Majesty King Georges Speeches In India* (Madras: Naetsan, n.d.), p.19.
36 *India*, 12 January 1912, p.22.
37 On the king and queen's interest in clemency for the Mayor of Cork, see D. Hannigan, *Terence MacSwiney: The Hunger Strike That Rocked an Empire* (Dublin: O'Brien, 2012); queen's private secretary's letter, *Londonderry Sentinel*, 2 September 1920, p.2; 'Royal Clemency. Mr Balfour and Constitutional Practice', *The Scotsman*, 31 August 1920, p.5. For the king's attitude towards his prerogative in a military context, see I.F.W. Beckett, 'King George V and His Generals', in M. Seligman and M. Hughes, ed., *Leadership in Conflict* (Barnsley: Leo Cooper, 2000).
38 *The Spectator*, quoted in *Newcastle Journal*, 6 December 1915, p.4.
39 See J. Rowbotham and M. Glencross, eds, *Monarchies and the Great War* (London: Palgrave Macmillan, 2018).
40 P. Williamson, 'The Monarchy and Public Values, 1900–1953', ch.8 in Olechnowicz, *The Monarchy and the British Nation 1780 to the Present*, pp.246–52.
41 Trowbridge, *Queen Alexandra*, p.215.
42 'The Character of Kingship', *Nash's Pall Mall Magazine* 93: 493 (June 1934), pp.10–93. The words are Malcolm's, *Macbeth*, act 4, scene 3.

Select Bibliography

For reasons of space, primary source newspapers and articles in periodicals are excluded: full details are in the Endnotes. The primary and secondary print sources and image references are also select: full details are cited in the Endnotes.

Primary

Archives

The Royal Archives, Windsor

    RA VIC/ADD/A/36/1271
    RA VIC/ADD/A/12/725, 853-854
    RA VIC/MAIN/A/13/61
    RA VIC/MAIN/A/14/1
    RA VIC/MAIN/A/61/1
    RA VIC/MAIN/A/66/116
    RA VIC/MAIN/A/67/18-20
    RA VIC/MAIN/A/68/116, 125
    RA VIC/MAIN/A/76/2
    RA VIC/MAIN/B/31/160
    RA VIC/MAIN/B/32/3A, 4, 6, 6F, 9A, 122-122A
    RA VIC/MAIN/B/33/19, 21-22
    RA VIC/MAIN/B/34/4
    RA VIC/MAIN/B39/31
    RA VIC/MAIN/B/40/82
    RA VIC/MAIN/B/41/93-94
    RA VIC/MAIN/B/44/60
    RA VIC/MAIN/B/51/15
    RA VIC/MAIN/C/3/43
    RA VIC/MAIN/C/6/35-36
    RA VIC/MAIN/D32/53
    RA VIC/MAIN/F/38/37
    RA VIC/MAIN/L/13/138-139
    RA VIC/MAIN/L/14/104, 106-107, 111, 116-118, 133-134, 139-141
    RA VIC/MAIN/L/15/13
    RA VIC/MAIN/L/16/13, 17-19, 24, 62, 83
    RA VIC/MAIN/M/67/40, 42-43
    RA VIC/MAIN/M/67/77
    RA VIC/MAIN/Y/91/5
    RA VIC/MAIN/QVJ (W) Queen Victoria's Journals (digitized versions)

Select Bibliography

The National Archives, Kew

    Home Office papers
    HO12/107/23139
    HO12/146/59140
    HO17/126/2 accessed via findmypast.co.uk digitization
    HO17/126/3 accessed via findmypast.co.uk digitization

Note: other materials cited in Endnotes from Home Office, Metropolitan Police and State Paper files (HO, MEPO and SP) are references to TNA catalogue information.

Old Bailey Proceedings Online

www.oldbaileyonline.org, version 8.0 (accessed 7 July 2019)

National Library of Scotland

Blaikie. SNPG.1.16; Blaikie.SNPG.18.6; Blaikie.SNPG.19.5; Blaikie.SNPG.19.10 'Jacobite prints and broadsides' digital collection, digital.nls.uk

National Archives, Republic of Ireland

Chief Secretary of Ireland's Office Registered Papers
    CSO/RP/1830/2240
    Description published http://www.csorp.nationalarchives.ie (accessed 26 July 2018)

British Library

Churchill Archive, digitized database published by Bloomsbury Publishing
    CHAR 12/10/36-37, 20 June 1911

Oxford, Bodleian Library, John Johnson Collection of Printed Ephemera, Crime 1 (78).

Recorder's report fate of Greenacre decided. 1837 in *The John Johnson Collection: An Archive of Printed Ephemera*
    http://johnjohnson.chadwyck.com.plymouth.idm.oclc.org (accessed 7 July 2019)

Printed Sources

Official Publications and Parliamentary Debates

Epitome of Parliamentary Documents in Connection with the North-West Rebellion, 1885
    (Ottawa: Maclean, Roger 1886)
House of Commons Papers. 1864 (37) George Victor Townley. Copy of Correspondence with the Secretary of State for the Home Department, and of Orders or Warrants Issued by Him, Relating to the Case of George Victor Townley
Journal of the House of Commons, vol.99 (1844)

Journals of the House of Lords, vol.52 (1819)
Journals of the Legislative Council of the Province of Canada to May 30, 1849, in the Twelfth Year of the Reign of Queen Victoria, Being the Second Session of the Third Provincial Parliament of Canada. vol.8, Session 1849
Mirror of Parliament. Second Series, Commencing with the Reign of Queen Victoria. vol.1 (London: Longman, Orme, Brown, Green and Longmans, 1838)
Parliamentary Debates from the Year 1803 to the Present Time. vol.18. *Comprising the Period from the 1st of November 1810, and the 28th of February 1811* (London: Hansard, 1811)
Parliamentary Debates from the Year 1803 to the Present Time. Vol.32. *Comprising the Period from the First Day of February, to the Sixth Day of March, 1816* (London: Hansard, 1816)
Parliamentary Debates, 3rd series, vols.36, 38, 49, 150, 156, 331 (1837–1870); 4th series, vols. 74 (1899), 192 (1908)
Parliamentary Debates, New Series; Commencing with the Accession of George IV. vol.6 *comprising the period from the Fifth Day of February to the Twenty-Second Day of April, 1822* (London: Hansard, 1822)
Parliamentary Debates, New Series; Commencing with the Accession of George IV. vol.7 *Comprising the Period from the Twenty-Fourth Day of April to the Sixth Day of August, 1822* (London: Hansard, 1823)
Report and Despatches of the Earl of Durham, Her Majesty's High Commissioner and Governor-General of British North America (London: Ridgways, 1839)
Report on the Administration of Bengal, 1877–78 (Calcutta: Bengal Secretariat Press, 1878)
Sessional Papers Printed by Order of the House of Lords. Session 1839. Copies or Extracts of Correspondence Relative to the Affairs of Canada 103, 10 June 1839
Third Report of the Commissioners on the Fine Arts, with Appendix. Command Papers (1844). XXI.169

Books and chapters in books before 1930

A Diary of Royal Movements and of Personal Events and Incidents in the Life and Reign of Her Most Gracious Majesty Queen Victoria (London: Elliot Stock, 1883), vol.1
A Full and Circumstantial Report of the Interesting Trial of Henry Stent, before Mr. Justice Best, at the Sessions House, in the Old Bailey, on Saturday, September 18, 1819, for Maliciously Stabbing His Wife, Maria Stent, on the 5th Day of August Last (London: Ferriday, 1819)
A History of the Clemency of Our English Monarchs: From the Reformation, Down to the Present Time. With Some Comparisons (London: N. Mist, 1717)
A History of the Late Province of Lower Canada: Parliamentary and Political, from the Commencement to the Close of Its Existence as a Separate Province (5 vols; Quebec: Lovell, 1854), vol.5
A Letter from the Countess of Nithsdale with Remarks by Sheffield Grace (London: n.p., 1827)
A Report of Some Proceedings on the Commission for the Trial of the Rebels in the Year 1746, in the County of Surry: And of Other Crown Cases: To Which Are Added Discourses upon a Few Branches of the Crown Law (London: Brooke, 1792)
A Sermon Occasioned by the Death of His Late Majesty: Preached on Saturday the 29th of November, 1760, in the Synagogue of the Portuguese Jews in London. By Isaac Mendes Belisario … Translated from the Spanish (London: Brotherton, 1760)

A Sermon Preach'd at St. James's Church, Westminster, on June the 7th, 1716: Being the Day of Publick Thanksgiving to Almighty God for the Suppression of the Late Unnatural Rebellion (London: J. Tonson, 1716)

A Sermon upon the Death of Queen Anne: Of Blessed Memory, Who Departed This Life Aug. 1. 1714. Preached at Chelmsford in Essex, August 15. 1714. By George Noon (London: Keble, 1714)

Acherley, R. *The Britannic Constitution: Or, The Fundamental Form of Government in Britain* (London: A. Bettesworth, 1727)

Adolphus, J.H. *The Royal Exile; or Memoirs of the Public and Private Life of Her Majesty, Caroline* (18th edition, 2 vols; London: Jones, 1821), vol.2

Ainsworth, W.H. *The Tower of London: An Historical Romance* (1840; London: Routledge, 1854)

Airlie, M. *Lady Palmerston and Her Times* (2 vols; London: Hodder and Stoughton, 1922), vol.1

Alley, J. *A Sermon Preached at the Parish Church of Saint Mary, Islington, Nov. 16, 1817, Occasioned by the Death of the Princess Charlotte* (London: F.C. and J. Rivington, 1818)

Almon, J. *A Review of the Reign of George II* (2nd edition, London: Wilkie, 1762)

Anecdotes, Personal Traits, and Characteristic Sketches of Victoria the First, Brought Down to the Period of Her Majesty's Marriage. By a Lady (London: Bennett: 1840)

Apotheosis Basilike; or, a Pindarick Ode, upon the Pious and Blessed Transit of that Most Excellent Prince James the II. King of Great Britain (n.p., 1708)

Arnot, H. *The History of Edinburgh, from the Earliest Accounts to the Present Time* (Edinburgh: Creech, 1779)

Atterbury, F. *An Argument to Prove the Affections of the People of England to Be the Best Security of the Government, Humbly Offered to the Consideration of the Patrons of Severity, and Applied to the Present Juncture of Affairs* (London: W. Jones, 1716; reprinted, London, 1746)

Badger, C. *Friendly Admonitions to Parents, and the Female Sex in General; with Reflections on Moral and Religious Subjects; Intended for the Benefit of the Rising Generation* (London: Cadell and Davies, 1803)

Bain, D. *Aera Astraea, or, The Age of Justice: An Ode to Her Most Gracious Majesty Victoria* (Edinburgh: Menzies, 1845)

Beccaria, C. *An Essay on Crimes and Punishments: By the Marquis Beccaria of Milan. With a Commentary by M. de Voltaire* (Edinburgh: Donaldson, 1788)

Benson, A.C. and R.B. Brett, eds, *The Letters of Queen Victoria. First Series. A Selection from Her Majesty's Correspondence between the Years 1837 and 1861. In three volumes. Vol.1 1837–1843* (London: J. Murray, 1908); *Vol.2 1844–1853* (London: Murray, 1908); *Vol.3 1854–1867* (London: Murray, 1908)

Bentham, J. *The Works of Jeremy Bentham. Published under the Superintendence of His Executor, John Bowring* (Edinburgh: Tait, 1843), vol.9

Blackstone, W. *Commentaries on the Laws of England. Book the fourth. By William Blackstone, Esq. Solicitor General to Her Majesty* (Oxford: Clarendon Press, 1769)

Bleackley, H. *Some Distinguished Victims of the Scaffold* (London: Kegan Paul, Trench, Trübner, 1905)

[Bowdler, C.] *On the Punishment of Death, in the Case of Forgery; Its Injustices and Impolicy Maintained* (London: Hamilton, 1818)

Brathwaite, *Astraea's Teares: An Elegie upon the Death of That Reverend, Learned and Honest Judge, Sir Richard Hutton, Knight* (London: Nevil, 1641)

Brett, R.B. *After the War* (London: Murray, 1918)

Brett, R.B. *The Influence of King Edward, and Essays on Other Subjects* (London: J. Murray, 1915)
Brett, R.B. *The Training of a Sovereign. An Abridged Selection from 'The Girlhood of Queen Victoria', Being Her Majesty's Diaries between the Years 1832 and 1840* (New York: Longmans, Green, 1914)
Brougham, H. *Historical Sketches of Statesmen Who Flourished in the Time of George III: To Which Is Added Remarks on Party and an Appendix* (Paris: Baudry, 1839)
Butler, S. *The Mercy of God; Especially Considered with Reference to Our Present Situation. A Sermon Preached at St. Julian's, Shrewsbury. Sept. 14, 1800* (Shrewsbury: Eddowes, 1800)
C.L, *The Advantages of the Success of the House of Stewart to the Crown of Great Britain Demonstrated* (London: Noble, 1747)
Campbell, J. *The Lives of the Lord Chancellors and Keepers of the Great Seal of England: From the Earliest Times Till the Reign of King George IV* (8 vols, London: Murray, 1869), vol.8.
Campbell, J. *V.R.I. Queen Victoria: Her Life and Empire* (London: Eyre and Spottiswoode, 1901)
Caroline Almanack, and American Freeman's Chronicle, for 1840 (Rochester, New York: Mackenzie's Gazette Office, 1840)
Chambers, R. *History of the Rebellion in Scotland in 1745, 1746*, vol.2 (Edinburgh: Constable, 1827)
Chesterton, G.K. *The Napoleon of Notting Hill* (London: Bodley Head, 1904)
Chesterton, G.K. 'The Queen and the Suffragettes', reprinted in *What's Wrong with the World* (London: Cassell, 1910), pp.173–5
Clarke, H.G. *A Critical Examination of the Cartoons, Frescos, and Sculpture, Exhibited in Westminster Hall. To Which Is Added the History and Practice of Fresco Painting. By Henry G. Clarke, Assisted by Eminent Artists* (London: Clarke, 1844)
Cobden, E. *The Blessedness of the Merciful: A Sermon Preached before the Sons of the Clergy at Their Anniversary Meeting in the Cathedral-Church of St Paul, April 14, 1743* (London: Cooper, 1743)
Cohen, H. *The Spirit of Our Laws* (London: Sweet and Maxwell, 1906)
Colquhoun, P. *A Treatise on the Police of the Metropolis, Explaining the Various Crimes, and Misdemeanours Which at Present Are Felt as a Pressure upon the Community and Suggesting Remedies for Their Prevention by a Magistrate* (London: Fry, 1796)
Cooper, W.H. *The Crisis: A Treatise upon Certain So-called Constitutional Principles Recently Asserted, with Respect to the Right of Petition, the Privileges of Parliament, and the Prerogative of Pardon* (Sydney: Kelly, 1875)
Creech, W. *An Account of the Trial of William Brodie and George Smith, before the High Court of Justiciary, on the 27th and 28th Days of August, 1788* (Edinburgh: Creech, 1788)
Criminal Recorder: Or, Biographical Sketches of Notorious Public Characters (2 vols; Nottingham, Dowson, 1815), vol.2
Dacre, B. *Winifred, Countess of Nithsdale: A Tale of the Jacobite Wars* (New York: Sadlier, 1869)
Davis, J. *The Agony of Murder: Written by a Prisoner Describing His Feelings When under Sentence of Death, and in Most Imminent Danger of Execution* (London: I.R. Taylor, 1859)
De Lolme, J.L. *The Constitution of England, or an Account of the English Government; in Which It Is Compared with the Republican Form of Government, and Occasionally with the Other Monarchies in Europe* (1771; London: Spilsbury, 1775)
De Witt Talmage, T. *Every-Day Religion: Being a 4th Series of 50 Sermons* (London: Dickinson, 1876)

Denison, W.T. *Varieties of Vice-Regal Life* (2 vols; London: Longmans, Green, 1870), vol.2
Dodd, W. *Thoughts in Prison: In Five Parts. Viz. The Imprisonment. The Retrospect. Public Punishment. The Trial. Futurity. By the Rev. William Dodd, LLD. To Which Are Added, His Last Prayer… and Other Miscellaneous Pieces* (Dublin: Price, etc., 1778)
Edinburgh Gazetteer (6 vols; Edinburgh: Constable, 1822), vol. 3
Encyclopaedia Perthensis; or Universal Dictionary of the Arts, Sciences and Literature (2nd edition; Edinburgh: Brown, 1816) vol.14
Eusden, L. *Three Poems; the First, Sacred to the Immortal Memory of the Late King; the Second, on the Happy Succession, and Coronation of His Present Majesty* (London: Roberts, 1727)
Execution of Captain Thomas Fuller Harnett and Ann Price: The Captain for Forging a Bill, and the Woman for Uttering Forged Notes, Who Were Executed, Along with Four Others, on Tuesday Last, the 5th December, 1820. To Which Is Added, the Captain's Dying Letter, and the Woman's Wonderful Behaviour (Trongate: Carse, 1820)
Farrar, F.W. *Mercy and Judgment: A Few Last Words on Christian Eschatology, with Reference to Dr. Pusey's 'What Is of Faith?'* (London: Macmillan, 1881)
Fawcett, M.G. *Life of Her Majesty Queen Victoria* (Boston: Roberts, 1895)
The Federalist. On the New Constitution, (2 vols; New York: Hopkins, 1802), vol.2
Female Revenge: Or, the British Amazon: Exemplified in the Life of Boadicia (London: Cooper, 1753)
Fonblanque, A. *England under Seven Administrations* (3 vols; London: Bentley, 1837), vol.1
Foot, J. *An Appeal to the Public, Touching the Death of Mr. George Clarke, Who Received a Blow at Brentford on Thursday the Eighth of December Last, of Which He Languished and Died on Wednesday the Fourteenth of the Same Month* (London: Davis, 1769)
The Form and Order of the Service That Is to Be Performed: And of the Ceremonies That Are to Be Observed, in the Coronation of Her Majesty Queen Victoria, *in the Abbey church of St. Peter, Westminster, on Thursday the 28th of June, 1838* (London: Eyre and Spottiswoode, 1838)
Free, J. *Common Safety The Cause and Foundation of Human Society* (3rd edition; London: for the author, 1769)
Fry, K., and F. Cresswell, eds, *Memoir of the Life of Elizabeth Fry, with Extracts from Her Journal and Letters. Edited by Two of Her Daughters* (2 vols; London: J. Hatchard/Gilpin, 1847), vol.2
Gardiner, A.G. *Sir William Harcourt* (2 vols; London: Constable, 1923), vol.1
Gladwin, F. *The Persian Moonshee* (London: Wilson, 1801)
Golder, W. *The New Zealand Survey* (Wellington: Stoddart, 1867)
Greenwood, G. *Queen Victoria, Her Girlhood and Womanhood* (Montreal: Dawson, 1883)
Gurney, J. and T. Gurney, *The Trial of John Frost for High Treason: Under a Special Commission Held at Monmouth in December 1839 and January 1840* (London: Saunders and Benning, 1840)
Harding, W. *An Impartial Life of His Late Majesty William the Fourth* (London: Harding, 1837)
Head, F.B. *A Narrative* (London: Murray, 1839)
Heath, R. *A King's Example and a People's Duty; a Sermon Preached on Feb. 16, 1820, on Which Evening the Remains of King George the Third Were Interred at Windsor* (London: Rivington, 1820)
Heathcote, R. *The Irenarch; or, the Justice of the Peace's Manual. II. Miscellaneous Reflections upon Laws, Policy, Manners, Etc. III. An Assize-Sermon [on Micah VI. 8] Preached at Leicester. 12 Aug. 1756* (London: n.p., 1781)

Henty, G.A. *Queen Victoria: Scenes from Her Life and Reign* (London: Blackie, 1901)
Hewlett, J. *The Jubilee; or, Motives for Thanksgiving Derived from a Consideration of the Character and Conduct of King George the Third, a Sermon* (London: Rivington and Johnson, 1809)
His Majesty King Georges Speeches In India (Madras: Naetsan, n.d.)
Howell, T.B. *A Complete Collection of State Trials and Proceedings for High Treason and Other Crimes and Misdemeanors from the Earliest Period to the Year 1783, with Notes and Other Illustrations* (21 vols; London: Longman, Hurst, Rees, Orme and Brown, 1816), vol. 17
The House That Jack Built; the Real or Constitutional House That Jack Built (London: Asperne, 1819)
Howell, T.B. and T.J. Howell, *A Complete Collection of State Trials* (London: Longman, Hurst, Rees, Orme and Brown, 1820), vol.27
Huish, R. *An Authentic History of the Coronation of His Majesty, King George the Fourth* (London: Robins, 1821)
Huish, R. *The History of the Life and Reign of William the Fourth, the Reform Monarch of England* (London: Emans, 1837)
Huish, R. *The History of the Private and Political Life of the Late Henry Hunt, esq., M.P. for Preston: His Times and Cotemporaries* (2 vols; London: Saunders, 1836), vol.1
Huish, R. *Memoirs of Her Late Royal Highness Charlotte Augusta, Princess of Wales* (London: Kelly, 1818)
The Indian National Congress, Containing an Account of Its Origin and Growth, Full Text of All the Presidential Addresses, Reprint of All the Congress Resolutions, Extracts from All the Welcome Addresses, Notable Utterances on the Movement, Portraits of All the Congress Presidents (Madras: Natesan, 1909)
'Integritas', *Truth, but No Treason: Or, Oppression Often the Cause of Rebellion. Being a Necessary Caution to the People of Great Britain, That They Do Not, Whilst They Are Laudably Endeavouring to Keep Out the One, Widen the Door for the Other,... Humbly Dedicated to the King, by an Englishman* (London: Wood, 1748)
Jackson, T. *The Life of the Reverend Charles Wesley* (2 vols; London: Mason, 1841), vol.2
Jeaffreson, J.C. *A Book about Lawyers* (2 vols; London: Hurst and Blackett, 1867), vol. 2
Jerrold, C. *The Early Court of Queen Victoria* (New York: Putnam, 1912)
Johnston, N. *The Excellency of Monarchical Government, Especially of the English Monarchy: Wherein Is Largely Treated of the Several Benefits of Kingly Government, and the Inconvenience of Commonwealths* (London: Clavel, 1686)
Keith, A.B. *Responsible Government in the Dominions* (3 vols; Oxford: Clarendon Press, 1912), vol.3
Knighton, D. *Memoirs of Sir William Knighton, Bart., G.C.H.: Keeper of the Privy Purse during the Reign of His Majesty King George the Fourth. Including His Correspondence with Many Distinguished Personages* (2 vols; London: Bentley, 1838)
Larwood, J. *Forensic Anecdotes: Or, Humour and Curiosities of the Law and of the Men of Law* (London: Chatto and Windus, 1882)
Lawford, F.G.V. *Our Queen, and Other Poems* (London: Digby, Long, 1895)
Lee, S. *Queen Victoria: A Biography* (London: Smith, Elder, 1904)
Legge, E. *More about King Edward* (Boston: Small, Maynard, 1913)
Lovell, E. *Justice and Mercy Equal Supporters of the Throne; or, The Duty of the Magistrate to Employ His Sword against the Stubborn and Rebellious* (London: Corbett, 1716)
Lowndes, M.B. *His Most Gracious Majesty King Edward VII* (London: Grant Richards, 1901)

The Loyalist's House That Jack Built (9th edition; London: S. Knights, n.d)
MacDougall, A.W. *The Maybrick Case: A Treatise on the Facts of the Case, and of the Proceedings in Connection with the Charge, Trial, Conviction, and Present Imprisonment of Florence Elizabeth Maybrick* (London: Baillière, Tindall and Cox, 1891)
Mackintsosh, J. *The Miscellaneous Works of the Right Honourable Sir James Mackintosh: Complete in One Volume* (London: Longman, Brown, Green and Longmans, 1851)
[Madan, M.] *Thoughts on Executive Justice with Respect to Our Criminal Laws Particularly on the Circuits* (London: Dodsley, 1785)
Martin, T. *Life of His Royal Highness the Prince Consort* (2nd edition; London: Smith, Elder, 1875), vol.1
Martin, T. *The Life of His Royal Highness the Prince Consort* (London: Smith, Elder, 1879), vol.4
Mathews, T. *The Biography of John Gibson, R.A., Sculptor, Rome* (London: Heinemann, 1911)
Maybrick, F. *Mrs Maybrick's Own Story. My Fifteen Lost Years* (New York: Funk and Wagnalls, 1905)
Merryweather, G. *Kings, the Devils Viceroys* (New York: the author, 1838)
More, H. *Hints towards Forming the Character of a Young Princess* (London: Cadell and Davies, 1805)
More, H. *Slavery, A Poem* (London: Cadell, 1787)
Murray, A.M. *Letters from the United States, Cuba and Canada* (2 vols; London: Parker, 1856)
Narrative of the Celebration of the Jubilee of Her Most Gracious Majesty Queen Victoria, Empress of India in the Presidency of Madras (2nd edition; London: Macmillan, 1887)
[Neale, E.] *Dark Deeds. By the Author of 'The Gaol Chaplain'* (London: Vickers, 1857)
New Palace of Westminster (London: Warrington, 1862)
Parker, C.S. ed. *Sir Robert Peel in Early Life, 1788–1812, As Secretary, 1812–1818, and as Secretary of State, 1822–1827: From His Private Correspondence* (London: Murray, 1891)
[Peck, F.] *Sighs upon the Never Enough Lamented Death of Queen Anne* (London: Clements, 1719)
Peggs, J. *Capital Punishment: The Importance of its abolition: a Prize Essay* (London: Ward, 1839)
'Percy, S. and R. Percy', *Percy Anecdotes. Anecdotes of Crime and Punishment* (1822; London: Cumberland, 1826)
'Percy, S. and R. Percy', *Percy Anecdotes. Vol.8. Anecdotes of Justice* (London: Cumberland, 1826)
Philip, R. ed. *The Works of John Bunyan: With an Introduction to Each Treatise, Notes, and a Sketch of His Life, Times, and Contemporaries* (3 vols; Glasgow: Blackie, 1850), vol.1
Philipps, C. *Vacation Thoughts on Capital Punishment* (London: Cash, 1857)
Private Life of Queen Victoria by One of Her Majesty's Servants (New York: Appleton, 1901)
Proceedings at the First Public Meeting of the Society for the Extinction of the Slave Trade and for the Civilization of Africa Held in Exeter Hall on Monday 1st June 1840 His Royal Highness Prince Albert President of the Society in the Chair (London: Clowes, 1840)
The Punishment of Death: A Selection of Articles from the Morning Herald, with Notes (2 vols; London: Hatchard, 1836–7), vols 1–2
Pyle, T. *The Wisdom of a Government in Distributing Punishment or Mercy to State-criminals. A Sermon Preached at the Lent-assizes Holden at Thetford in Norfolk, on March 23 1715* (London: J. Wyat, 1716)

Rae, P. *The History of the Rebellion Rais'd Against His Majesty King George I. By the Friends of the Popish Pretender... To Which Is Now Added, A Collection of Original Letters, and Authentic Papers, Relating to That Rebellion* (London: Millar, 1746)

Reddington, J. ed. *Calendar of Home Office Papers of the Reign of George III: 1760-1775; Preserved in Her Majesty's Public Record Office* (London: Longman, and Trübner, 1878)

Reddington, J. ed. *Calendar of Home Office Papers of the Reign of George III. 1766-1769, Preserved in her Majesty's Record Office* (London: Longman, and Trübner, 1879)

Reeve, H. ed. *The Greville Memoirs: A Journal of the Reigns of King George IV and King William IV* (3 vols; London: Longmans, Green, 1874), vol.2

Reeve, H. ed. *The Greville Memoirs: A Journal of the Reigns of King George IV, King William IV, and Queen Victoria* (8 vols; London: Longmans, Green, 1898), vol.8

Reid, S.J. *Life and Letters of the First Earl of Durham, 1792-1840* (London: Longmans, Green, 1906)

Rennell, T. *The Ruinous Effects of Faction, Discord and Mutiny* (London: Rivington, 1797)

Report of the Trial of Thomas Hunter, Peter Hacket, Richard M'Neil, James Gibb, and William M'Lean: Operative Cotton-spinners in Glasgow, Before the High Court of Justiciary, at Edinburgh, on Wednesday, January 3, 1838, and Seven Following Days, for the Crimes of Illegal Conspiracy and Murder (Edinburgh: Clark, 1838)

Reynolds, G.W.M. *Canonbury House, or, The Queen's Prophecy* (London: Dicks, 1870)

Reynolds, G.W.M. *The Mysteries of the Court of London*, vol.8 (vol.2, 4th series: London: Dicks, 1856)

Roberts, R.A. ed. *Calendar of Home Office Papers of the Reign of George III. 1773-1775 Preserved in the Public Record Office* (London: HMSO, 1899)

Roberts, S. *Queen's Coronation: An Address to the Females of Sheffield on the Wickedness, the Barbarity, and the Impolicy of the Punishment of Death in All Classes* [sic] (Sheffield: A. Whitaker, 1838)

Roberts, S. *Yorkshire Tales and Poems* (2nd edition, enlarged, London: Whittaker, 1839)

[Robinson, F.W.] *Female Life in Prison by a Prison Matron* (London: Hurst and Blackett, 1863)

Royal Correspondence, or, Letters between Her Late Royal Highness the Princess Charlotte and Her Royal Mother, Queen Caroline of England, during the Exile of the Latter (London: Jones, 1822)

Schomberg, J.J. *Elements of the British Constitution: Containing a Comprehensive View of the Monarchy and Government of England* (2nd edition, London: Painter, 1824)

Selections from the Writings of the Late J. Sydney Taylor, With a Brief Sketch of His Life (London: Gilpin, 1843)

Sharpley, C.G. *The Coronation, a Poem, in Six Cantos* (London: for the author, 1838)

Sidney, E. *The Life of Lord Hill, G.C.B., late Commander of the Forces* (London: Murray, 1845)

Smedley, E., H.J. Rose, and H.J. Rose, eds, *Encyclopaedia Metropolitana, or, Universal Dictionary of Knowledge* (London: Fellowes, 1845), vol.22

Smith, F.E. *Fourteen English Judges* (London: Cassell, 1925)

Smith, G.B. *Life of Her Majesty the Queen Compiled from All Available Sources* ('People's Edition', London: Routledge, 1887)

Smollett, T. *A Complete History of England: From the Descent of Julius Caesar, to the Treaty of Aix la Chapelle, 1748* (3rd edition; London: Rivington and Fletcher, 1758-99), vol.4, vol.10

Somervile, W. *The Chace, a Poem* (3rd edition: London: Hawkins, 1735)

Southey, R. *Authentic Memoirs of Our Late Venerable and Beloved Monarch, George the Third* (London: Jones, 1820)

The State of the Nation at the Commencement of the Year 1822 Considered under the Four Departments of The Finance – Foreign Relations – Home Department – Colonies and Board of Trade (2nd edition; London: Hatchard, 1822)

Stephens, A. *Memoirs of John Horne Tooke, Interspersed with Original Documents* (2 vols; London: Johnson, 1813), vol.1

Stephens, T. *The Book of the Constitution of Great Britain* (Glasgow: Blackie, 1835)

Stevenson, G. *A Dissertation on the Atonement. In Three Parts* (Philadelphia: Towar, 1832)

Strickland, A. *Lives of the Queens of England, from the Norman Conquest* (2 vols; London: Colburn, 1840), vol.2

Strickland, A. *Lives of the Queens of England* (revised edition, 8 vols; London: Colburn, 1852), vol.8

[Swift, J.], *Travels into Several Remote Nations of the World. In Four Parts* (London: Motte, 1726), vol.1

Tagore, S.M. *Victoria-gítika, or Sanskrit Verses, Celebrating the Deeds and the Virtues of Her Most Gracious Majesty the Queen Victoria and Her Renowned Predecessors* (Calcutta: I.C. Bose, 1875)

Tallack, W. *Penological and Preventive Principles, with Special Reference to Europe and America* (London: Wertheimer, Lea, 1889)

Torrens, T.M. *The Life and Times of the Right Honourable Sir James R. G. Graham* (London: Saunders, Otley, 1863), vol.2

Townsend, W.C. *The Lives of Twelve Eminent Judges of the Last and of the Present Century* (2 vols; London: Longmans, 1846), vol.1

Townsend, W.C. *Modern State Trials* (2 vols; London: Longman, Brown, Green and Longmans, 1850), vol.1

The Trial of Joseph Gerrald, before the High Court of Justiciary, at Edinburgh, on the 13th and 14h of March, 1794, for Sedition: With an Original Memoir, and Notes (Glasgow: Muir, Gowan, 1835)

Trowbridge, W.R.H. *Queen Alexandra. A Study Of Royalty* (London: Unwin, 1921)

Urquhart, D. *The Edinburgh Review and the Affghan War: Letters Reprinted from the Morning Herald* (London: Maynard, 1843)

Victoria, Queen, *More Leaves from the Journal of a Life in the Highlands, from 1862 to 1882* (5th edition; London: Smith, Elder, 1884)

Wakefield, E.G. *Facts Relating to the Punishment of Death in the Metropolis* (London: Ridgway, 1831)

Wall, A.H. *Fifty Years of a Good Queen's Reign. A book for the Royal Jubilee of 1886–1887* (London: Ward and Downey, 1886)

Walpole, H. *Memoirs of the Reign of George the Second*, ed., Lord Holland (2nd edition; London: Colburn, 1846), vols 1–2

Watkin, J.W. *A Brief Reply to Mr Commissioner Phillips* (London: W. Skeffington, 1858)

Watkins, J. *The Important Results of an Elaborate Investigation Into the Mysterious Case of Elizabeth Fenning* (London: Hone, 1815)

Wills, W. *The Law of the Land, Or, London in the Last Century: A Drama in Three Acts (Founded on Fact)* (London: Kenneth, 1837)

Wilson, R. *The Life and Times of Queen Victoria* (2 vols; London: Cassell, 1891, 1893)

Wright, G.N. *The Life and Reign of William the Fourth* (London: Fisher, 1837)

Secondary

Books and chapters in books mostly published after 1930

Abruzzo, M. *Polemical Pain: Slavery, Cruelty, and the Rise of Humanitarianism* (Baltimore: Johns Hopkins University Press, 2011)
Andrew, D.T. and R. McGowen, *The Perreaus and Mrs. Rudd Forgery and Betrayal in Eighteenth-Century London* (Berkeley: University of California Press, 2001)
Arnstein, W.L. 'Queen Victoria and Religion', in G. Malmgreen, ed., *Religion in the Lives of English Women, 1760-1930* (London: Croom Helm, 1986)
Aspinall, A. ed. *The Correspondence of George, Prince of Wales 1770-1812. vol. 6. 1806-1809* (London: Cassell, 1971)
Baines, P. *The House of Forgery in Eighteenth-Century Britain* (Aldershot: Ashgate, 1999)
Barrell, J. *Imagining the King's Death. Figurative Treason, Fantasies of Regicide 1793-1796* (Oxford: Oxford University Press, 2000)
Bartley, P. *Queen Victoria* (Oxford: Routledge, 2016)
Beattie, J.M. *Crime and the Courts in England, 1660-1800* (Oxford: Oxford University Press, 1986)
Bennett, T., L. Grossberg and M. Morris, eds, *New Keywords: A Revised Vocabulary of Culture and Society* (Oxford: Blackwell, 2005)
Bentley, M. 'Power and Authority in the Late Victorian and Edwardian Court', ch.9 in A.J. Olechnowicz, ed., *The Monarchy and the British Nation 1780 to the Present* (Cambridge: Cambridge University Press, 2007)
Berry, L.C. 'Confession and Profession: *Adam Bede*, Infanticide and the New Coroner', in J. Thorn, ed., *Writing British Infanticide: Child-Murder, Gender, and Print, 1722-1859* (Newark: University of Delaware Press, 2003), pp.196–217
Bresler, F.S. *Reprieve: A Study of a System* (London: Harrap, 1965)
Buckle, G.E. ed. *The Letters of Queen Victoria. Second Series. A Selection from Her Majesty's Correspondence and Journal between the Years 1862 and 1878. In Three Volumes. Vol.1. 1862-1869* (London: Murray, 1926); *Vol.2 1870-1878* (London: Murray, 1926); *Vol.3 1879-1885* (London: Murray, 1928)
Buckle, G.E. ed. *The Letters of Queen Victoria. Third Series. A Selection from Her Majesty's Correspondence and Journal Between the Years 1886 and 1901. In Three Volumes. Vol.1 1886-1890* (London: Murray, 1930); *Vol. 2 1891-1895* (London: Murray, 1931); *Vol.3 1896-1901* (London: Murray, 1931)
Bull, M. *On Mercy* (Princeton: Princeton University Press, 2019)
Carter, S. and M. Nugent ed. *Mistress of Everything: Queen Victoria in Indigenous Worlds* (Manchester: Manchester University Press, 2016)
Casteras, S.P. 'The Wise Child and Her "Offspring": Some Changing Faces of Queen Victoria', in Homans and Munich, eds, *Remaking Queen Victoria* (Cambridge: Cambridge University Press, 1997), pp.182–99
Chadwick, R. *Bureaucratic Mercy: The Home Office and the Treatment of Capital Cases in Victorian Britain* (New York: Garland, 1992)
Colley, L. *Britons: Forging the Nation. 1707-1837* (1992; London: Pimlico, 1996)
Dabhoiwala, F. 'Writing Petitions in Early Modern England', ch.6 in M.J. Braddick and J. Innes, *Suffering and Happiness in England 1550-1850: Narratives and Representations; A Collection to Honour Paul Slack* (Oxford: Oxford University Press, 2017), pp.127–48

de Waele, M. 'Conflict Resolution Under the First Bourbons', in A. Forrestal and E. Nelson, eds, *Politics and Religion in Early Bourbon France* (Basingstoke: Palgrave Macmillan, 2009), pp.132–53.

Dixon, T. *The Invention of Altruism: Making Moral Meanings in Victorian Britain* (Oxford: Oxford University Press for the British Academy, 2008)

Dowling, M.B. *Clemency and Cruelty in the Roman World* (Ann Arbor, MI: University of Michigan Press, 2006)

Duncan, S. *Mary I: Gender, Power and Ceremony* (New York: Palgrave Macmillan, 2012)

Duncan, S. '"Most Godly Heart Fraught with al Mercie": Queens' Mercy During the Reigns of Mary I and Elizabeth I', ch.3 in C. Levin and R. Bucholz, eds, *Queens and Power in Medieval and Early Modern England* (Lincoln: University of Nebraska Press, 2009), pp.31–50

Durston, G.J. *Fields, Fens and Felonies: Crime and Justice in Eighteenth-Century East Anglia* (Hook: Waterside Press, 2016)

Eder, M. *Crime and Punishment in the Royal Navy of the Seven Years' War, 1755–1763* (Aldershot: Ashgate, 2004)

Finnegan, R. *Why Do We Quote? The Culture and History of Quotation* (Cambridge: Open Book Publishers, 2011)

Fortier, M. *The Culture of Equity in Early Modern England* (Aldershot: Ashgate, 2005)

Fortier, M. *The Culture of Equity in Restoration and Eighteenth-Century Britain and America* (Aldershot: Ashgate, 2015)

Gardiner, A.G. *The Life of Sir William Harcourt* (2 vols; London: Constable, 1923)

Gatrell, V.A.C. *The Hanging Tree: Execution and the English People 1770–1868* (Oxford: Oxford University Press, 1994)

Gere, C. *Victorian Jewellery Design* (London: Kimber, 1972)

Giloi, E. *Monarchy, Myth, and Material Culture in Germany, 1750–1950* (Cambridge: Cambridge University Press, 2011)

Green, T.A. *Verdict According to Conscience: Perspectives on the English Criminal Trial Jury, 1200–1800* (Chicago: University of Chicago Press, 1985)

Greenwood, F.M. and B. Wright, eds, *Canadian State Trials: Vol.2: Rebellion and Invasion in the Canadas, 1837–1839* (Toronto: Osgoode Society/University of Toronto Press, 2002)

Greer, A. *The Patriots and the People: The Rebellion of 1837 in Rural Lower Canada* (Toronto: University of Toronto Press, 1993)

Gregory, B. 'Staging British India', ch.4 in J.S. Bratton, R.A. Cave, B. Gregory, M. Pickering, H.J. Holder, *Acts of Supremacy: The British Empire and the Stage, 1790–1930* (Manchester: Manchester University Press, 1991), pp.150–78.

Hanham, H.J. ed. *The Nineteenth-Century Constitution 1815–1914: Documents and Commentary* (Cambridge: Cambridge University Press, 1969)

Hardie, F. *The Political Influence of Queen Victoria, 1861–1901* (London: Oxford University Press, 1935)

Harootunian, H.D. 'The Benjamin Effect: Modernism, Repetition, and the Path to Different Cultural Imaginaries', ch.4 in M.P. Steinberg ed., *Walter Benjamin and the Demands of History* (Ithaca: Cornell University Press, 1996)

Hay, D. 'Property, Authority and the Criminal Law', in D. Hay, P. Linebaugh, J.G. Rule, E.P. Thompson, and C. Winslow, *Albion's Fatal Tree: Crime and Society in Eighteenth-Century England* (London: Allen Lane, 1975), pp.17–63

Hibbert, C. *Edward VII: The Last Victorian King* (1976; Basingstoke: Palgrave Macmillan, 2007)

Hilton, B. 'The Gallows and Mr Peel', ch.5 in T.C.W. Blanning and D. Cannadine, eds, *History and Biography: Essays in Honour of Derek Beales* (Cambridge: Cambridge University Press, 1996), pp.88–112

Hingley, R. and C. Unwin, *Boudica: Iron Age Warrior Queen* (London: Hambledon Continuum, 2005)

Hochstetler, J.A. *A History of Criminal Justice in England and Wales* (Winchester: Waterside Press, 2006)

Houston, G.T. 'Reading and Writing Victoria: The Conduct Book and the Legal Constitution of Female Sovereignty', ch.9 in M. Homans and A. Munich, *Remaking Queen Victoria* (Cambridge: Cambridge University Press, 1997), pp.159–81.

Houston, G.T. *Royalties: The Queen and Victorian Writers* (Charlottesville, VA: University Press of Virginia, 1999)

Jay, M. *Fin-de-siècle Socialism and Other Essays* (New York: Routledge, 1988)

Jones, C. *The Maybrick A to Z* (Birkenhead: Countyvise, 2008)

Keith, A.B. *The Constitution of England from Queen Victoria to George VI* (2 vols., London: Macmillan, 1940), vol.1.

Keller, U. *The Ultimate Spectacle: A Visual History of the Crimean War* (2001; Abingdon: Routledge, 2013)

Kesselring, K.J. *Mercy and Authority in the Tudor State* (Cambridge: Cambridge University Press, 2003)

Kilday, A. *A History of Infanticide in Britain, c.1600 to the Present* (Basingstoke: Palgrave Macmillan, 2013)

King, P. *Crime, Justice and Discretion in England, 1740–1820* (Oxford: Oxford University Press, 2000)

Kukulies-Smith, W. and S. Priest, 'The Mount Rennie Rape Case of 1886: Politics, Mercy and Justice in Late Nineteenth Century Australia', ch.9 in P. Easteal, ed., *Justice Connections* (Newcastle upon Tyne: Cambridge Scholars, 2013), pp.220–39

Lacey, H. *The Royal Pardon: Access to Mercy in Fourteenth-century England* (York: York Medieval Press, 2009)

Lee, S. *King Edward VII. A Biography. Vol.2 The Reign* (London: Macmillan, 1927)

Lemmings, D. *Law and Government in England During the Long Eighteenth Century: From Consent to Command* (Basingstoke: Palgrave Macmillan, 2011)

Loughlin, J. 'Crown, Spectacle and Identity: The British Monarchy and Ireland Under the Union 1800–1922', in A.J. Olechnowicz, ed., *The Monarchy and the British Nation, 1780 to the Present* (Cambridge: Cambridge University Press, 2007), pp.108–36

Majumdar, J.K. ed., *Indian Speeches and Documents on British Rule 1821–1918* (Calcutta: Longman, Green, 1937)

Marsden, J. *Victoria & Albert: Art & Love* (London: Royal Collection, 2010)

May, A.N. *The Bar and Old Bailey, 1750–1850* (Chapel Hill: University of North Carolina Press, 2003)

McGeary, T. *The Politics of Opera in Handel's Britain* (Cambridge: Cambridge University Press, 2013)

McGowen, R. '"Making Examples" and the Crisis of Punishment in Mid-Eighteenth-Century England', in D. Lemmings, ed., *The British and Their Laws in the Eighteenth Century* (Woodbridge: Boydell, 2005), pp.182–205

McLynn, F. *Crime and Punishment in Eighteenth Century England* (1989; London: Routledge, 2013)

Meyler, B. *Theaters of Pardoning: Sovereignty and Judgment from Shakespeare to Kant* (Ithaca: Cornell University Press, 2019)

Monod, P.K. *Jacobitism and the English People, 1688–1788* (Cambridge: Cambridge University Press, 1989)
Morris, M. *The British Monarchy and the French Revolution* (New York: Yale University Press, 1998)
Munich, A. *Queen Victoria's Secrets* (New York: Columbia University Press, 1996)
Munslow, A. *The Future of History* (Basingstoke: Palgrave Macmillan, 2010)
Murphy, J.H. *Abject Loyalty: Nationalism and Monarchy in Ireland During the Reign of Queen Victoria* (Crosses Green, Cork: Cork University Press, 2001)
Murphy, P.T. *Shooting Victoria: Madness, Mayhem, and the Rebirth of the British Monarchy* (New York: Pegasus Books, 2012)
Nussbaum, M. *Anger and Forgiveness: Resentment, Generosity, Justice* (New York: Oxford University Press, 2016)
Pittock, M. 'The Culture of Jacobitism', in J. Black, ed., *Culture and Society in Britain, 1660–1800* (Manchester: Manchester University Press, 1997), pp.124–45
Plank, G.G. *Rebellion and Savagery: The Jacobite Rising of 1745 and the British Empire* (Philadelphia: University of Pennsylvania Press, 2006)
Plunkett, J. *Queen Victoria: First Media Monarch* (Oxford: Oxford University Press, 2003)
Pocock, J.G.A. 'Concepts and Discourses: A Difference in Culture? Comment on a Paper by Melvin Richter', in H. Lehmann and M. Richter, eds, *The Meaning of Historical Terms and Concepts. New Studies on Begriffsggeschichte* (Washington DC: German Historical Institute, Occasional Paper No.15, 1996), pp.47–58
Ponsonby, A. *Henry Ponsonby. Queen Victoria's Private Secretary* (London: Macmillan, 1943)
Poser, N.S. *Lord Mansfield: Justice in the Age of Reason* (Montreal: McGill-Queen's University Press, 2013)
Prest, W.R. *William Blackstone: Law and Letters in the Eighteenth Century* (Oxford: Oxford University Press, 2012)
Prochaska, F. *Royal Bounty: The Making of a Welfare Monarchy* (New Haven: Yale University Press, 1995)
Radzinowicz, L. *A History of English Criminal Law and Its Administration from 1750: The Movement for Reform, 1750–1833*, vol.1 (London: Stevens, 1948)
Ramusack, B.N. *The New Cambridge History of India. III.6. The Indian Princes and Their States* (Cambridge: Cambridge University Press, 2004)
Rappaport, H. ed., *Queen Victoria: A Biographical Companion* (Santa Barbara, California: ABC-CLIO, 2003)
Read, C. and R.J. Stagg, *Rebellion of 1837 in Upper Canada* (Ottawa: Champlain Society with Carleton University Press, 1985)
Sanchez, G. *Pity in Fin-de-Siècle French Culture: 'Liberté, Égalité, Pitié'* (Westport, CN: Praeger, 2004)
Sankey, M.D. *Jacobite Prisoners of the 1715 Rebellion: Preventing and Punishing Insurrection in Early Hanoverian Britain* (Aldershot: Ashgate, 2005)
Sapire, H. '"We Have Seen the Son of Heaven? We Have Seen the Son of Our Queen": African Encounters with Prince Alfred on His Royal Tour, 1860', ch.1 in S. Carter and M. Nugent, ed., *Mistress of Everything: Queen Victoria in Indigenous Worlds* (Manchester: Manchester University Press, 2016), pp.25–53
Shagan, E.H. *The Rule of Moderation: Violence, Religion and the Politics of Restraint in Early Modern England* (Cambridge: Cambridge University Press, 2011)
Sharpe, K. *Rebranding Rule: The Restoration and Revolution Monarchy, 1660–1714* (New Haven, CT: Yale University Press, 2013)

Skinner, Q. *Visions of Politics*, vol. 1 *Regarding Method* (Cambridge: Cambridge University Press, 2002)
Smith, E.A. *George IV* (London: Yale University Press, 1999)
Smith, H. *Georgian Monarchy: Politics and Culture, 1714–1760* (Cambridge: Cambridge University Press, 2006)
Strange, C. ed., *Qualities of Mercy: Justice, Punishment, and Discretion* (Vancouver: University of British Columbia Press, 2011)
Taylor, A. *'Down with the Crown': British Anti-Monarchism and Debates About Royalty Since 1790* (London: Reaktion, 1999)
Taylor, M. 'The British Royal Family and the Colonial Empire', in R. Aldrich and C. McCreery, eds, *Crowns and Colonies: European Monarchies and Overseas Empires* (Manchester: Manchester University Press, 2016), pp.27–50
Taylor, M. *Empress: Queen Victoria and India* (New Haven: Yale University Press, 2018)
Thompson, D. *Queen Victoria. A Woman on the Throne* (1990; London: Virago, 2001)
Trainor, L. *British Imperialism and Australian Nationalism: Manipulation, Conflict and Compromise in the Late Nineteenth Century* (New York: Cambridge University Press, 1994)
Tuckness, A. and J.M. Parrish, *The Decline of Mercy in Public Life* (New York: Cambridge University Press, 2014)
Vandrei, M. *Queen Boudica and Historical Culture in Britain: An Image of Truth* (Oxford: Oxford University Press, 2018)
Vernon, J. *Politics and the People: A Study in English Political Culture, c.1815–1867* (Cambridge: Cambridge University Press, 1993)
Villeponteaux, M. *The Queen's Mercy: Gender and Judgment in Representations of Elizabeth I* (New York: Palgrave Macmillan, 2014)
Walvin, J. *Victorian Values* (London: Deutsch, 1987)
Williams, R. *The Contentious Crown: Public Discussion of the British Monarchy in the Reign of Queen Victoria* (Aldershot: Ashgate, 1997)
Williamson, P. 'The Monarchy and Public Values, 1900–1953', in A.J. Olechnowicz, ed., *The Monarchy and the British Nation 1780 to the Present* (Cambridge: Cambridge University Press, 2007), pp.246–52
Wilson, A.N. *Prince Albert: The Man Who Saved the Monarchy* (London: Atlantic Books, 2019)
Winn, J.A. *Queen Anne: Patroness of Arts* (Oxford: Oxford University Press, 2014)
Woods, G.D. *A History of Criminal Law in New South Wales: The Colonial Period, 1788–1900* (Sydney: Federation Press, 2002)
Wright, B. '"Harshness and Forbearance": The Politics of Pardons and the Upper Canada Rebellion', in C. Strange, ed., *Qualities of Mercy: Justice, Punishment, and Discretion* (Vancouver: University of British Columbia Press, 2011), pp.83–103.
Yates, F.A. *Astraea. The Imperial Theme in the Sixteenth Century* (London: Routledge and Kegan Paul, 1975)

Articles

Arnstein, W.L. 'The Warrior Queen: Reflections on Victoria and Her World', *Albion* 30:1 (Spring 1998), pp.1–28
Bates, R. '"All Touched My Hand": Queenly Sentiment and Royal Prerogative', *19: Interdisciplinary Studies in the Long Nineteenth Century* 20 (2015), pp.1–25

Beattie, J.M. 'The Royal Pardon and Criminal Procedure in Early Modern England', *Historical papers/Communications historiques* 22: 1 (1987), pp.9–22

Chernock, A. 'Queen Victoria and the "Bloody Mary of Madagascar"', *Victorian Studies* 55: 3 (Spring 2013), pp.425–49

Colley, L. 'The Apotheosis of George III: Loyalty, Royalty, and the British Nation', *Past and Present* 102 (February 1984), pp.94–129

Davies, A. '"These Viragoes Are No Less Cruel than the Lads": Young Women, Gangs and Violence in late Victorian Manchester and Salford', *British Journal of Criminology* 39: 1 (1999), pp.72–89

Devereaux, S. 'Imposing the Royal Pardon: Execution, Transportation, and Convict Resistance in London, 1789', *Law and History Review* 25: 1 (Spring 2007), pp.101–38

Dixon, T., 'The Tears of Mr Justice Willes', *Journal of Victorian Culture* 17: 1 (2012), pp.1–23

Edge, P.W. 'Law and Practice of Capital Punishment in Isle of Man', *Manx Law Bulletin* 25 (1995), pp.49–61

Hankey, J. 'Victorian Portias: Shakespeare's Borderline Heroine', *Shakespeare Quarterly* 45: 4 (Winter, 1994), pp. 426–48

Herrup, C. 'The King's Two Genders', *Journal of British Studies* 45: 3 (July 2006), pp.493–510

Keynes, S. 'The Cult of King Alfred the Great', *Anglo-Saxon England* 28 (1999), pp. 225–356

King, P. and R. Ward, 'Rethinking the Bloody Code in Eighteenth-Century Britain: Capital Punishment at the Centre and on the Periphery', *Past & Present* 228: 1 (1 August 2015), pp.159–205

Leja, M. 'Keyword', *American Art* 23: 1 (Spring 2009), pp.34–5

MacKay, L. 'Refusing the Royal Pardon: London Capital Convicts and the Reactions of the Courts and Press, 1789', *The London Journal* 28: 2 (2003), pp.21–40.

Murdoch, L. '"Suppressed Grief": Mourning the Death of British Children and the Memory of the 1857 Indian Rebellion', *Journal of British Studies* 51: 2 (April 2012), pp.364–92

Pickering, P.A. '"The Hearts of the Millions": Chartism and Popular Monarchism in the 1840s', *History* 88: 290 (April 2003), pp.227–48

Pickering, P.A. '"And Your Petitioners &c": Chartist Petitioning in Popular Politics 1838-48', *English Historical Review* 116: 466 (April 2001), pp.368–88

Ree, J. 'Civilizing Efforts', *History Workshop Journal* 87 (2019), pp.294–300

Rodgers, D.T. 'Keywords: A Reply', *Journal of the History of Ideas* 49: 4 (October–December 1988), pp.669–76

Rosenberg, S. '"The Justice of Queen Victoria": Boer Oppression, and the Emergence of a National Identity in Lesotho', *National Identities* 3: 2 (2001), pp.133–53

Strange, C. 'Capital Case Procedure Manual', *Criminal Law Quarterly* 41: 2 (1998), pp.184–97

Thomas, K. 'Diary', *London Review of Books*, 32: 11 (10 June 2010), pp.36–7

Thomas, P.D.G. 'Thoughts on the British Constitution by George in 1760', *Bulletin of the Institute of Historical Research* 60: 143 (October 1987), pp.361–3

Wesley, C.H. 'The Abolition of Negro Apprenticeship in the British Empire', *Journal of Negro History* 23: 2 (April 1938), pp.155–99

Wiener, M.J. 'The Sad Story of George Hall: Adultery, Murder, and the Politics of Mercy in Mid-Victorian England', *Social History* 24: 2 (1998), pp.174–95

Unpublished

Dimock, L. 'Queen Victoria, Africa and Slavery: Some Personal Associations', paper presented to AFSAAP Conference 2009, at afsaap.org.au (accessed 2 February 2019)

Martin, A. 'Queen Victoria, Prince Albert and the Patronage of Contemporary Sculpture in Victorian Britain 1837–1901', unpublished PhD (2 vols), University of Warwick, Department of History of Art, December 2013, vol.1

Mortimer, B.G. 'Rethinking Penal Reform and the Royal Prerogative of Mercy During Robert Peel's Stewardship of the Home Office 1822–7, 1828–30', unpublished PhD, University of Leicester, 2017

Index

abolition of slavery (1834) and apprenticeships 1, 5–6, 12, 19, 126, 128–30
Acherley, Roger 22–3
Addison, Joseph 44
Adelaide, Queen (wife of William IV) 66
Afghanistan, Victorian British army in 148
Alfred (Australian aborigine, 1879) 131
Alfred, King 15
Almon, John 51
American Revolution 155
animal welfare 7
animals, and mercy 7, 10–11
Anne, Queen (1665–1714), and mercy 41–2, 107, 142
Ansell, Mary Ann (murderer, 1899) 104
Anti-Jacobin Review 36
Apotheosis Basilike 41
archives, and mercy 16–17, 124
Archives, Royal, and Victoria on mercy 16, 91, 93–106
Arnot, Hugh 23
Arthur, Sir George 108
assassination, attempts on monarchs 54, 112, 119–24
Astraea 41, 67
atonement 1–2, 7, 84
Australasia, and royal mercy 114, 130–3

Bagehot, Walter 25
Bean, William 122
Beattie, J.M. 14
Beccaria, Cesare 25, 51
Beck, Adolf 152
benevolence 8, 10–11, 14–15, 19, 21, 32, 36, 42, 47–8, 53–6, 58–9, 66, 83, 118, 127, 135
Bentham, Jeremy 7, 22
Berry, Elizabeth (murderer, 1887) 105
Best, William Mawdsly 22
Biddulph, Sir Thomas (keeper of Privy Purse) 83

birthdays, royal 31, 67, 103
Blackstone, Sir William 23, 47
Boer War 145, 152
Brough, Mary Ann (infanticide 1854, royal wet nurse) 95
Brougham, Henry 35, 59, 65, 109 127
Browning, Elizabeth Barrett 144
Browning, Robert 5
Bunyan, John 2
Buxton, Thomas Fowell 130
Byng, John (admiral, executed 1757) 48

Cadman, Josiah (forger, 1821) 60
Cameron, Archibald (Jacobite executed 1753) 47
Campbell, Major Henry Alexander (duellist, executed 1808) 53
Canada 108–11, 129
Canning, Charles John (Governor-General of India, nicknamed 'Clemency') 116
capital punishment, and anti-capital punishment 17, 22, 34, 49, 51, 56–7, 59, 62, 65, 67, 72, 75–7, 83–91, 94–5, 97, 99, 104–5, 112–13, 120, 122, 125, 130–2, 134, 141, 143–4, 153
Carlos I, King of Portugal (1863 – 1908) 134
Caroline, Queen (wife of George IV, 1768 – 1821) 59
Caroline, Queen of Ansbach (wife of George II, 1683–1737) 44, 47
Cato Street conspiracy (1820) 59
Cawnpore, Angel of 114
Charlotte, Princess of Wales (1796–1817) 21, 63–5
Charlotte, Queen (wife of George III, 1744–1818) 21, 53–4, 56
Chartism and chartists 88, 111–14, 119–20, 122, 142, 148
Chesterton, G.K. 11, 149

chivalry 5
Christianity, and mercy 1–3, 7, 10, 13, 22, 37, 78–9, 84, 90, 116–17, 131, 135, 137, 155
Churchill, Winston (home secretary) 16, 32
Cixi, empress dowager of China (1835–1908) 134
clemency 22, 24, 29, 31–2, 35, 41–4, 46, 48–9, 53–4, 59–61, 66, 72, 74–5, 77–8, 86, 90, 101, 104, 107–9, 111–14, 116–19, 130, 132, 135, 138–40, 144, 151, 153, 155
Collet, John Dobson 107
compassion 1–2, 8, 15, 36, 39, 44, 48, 56, 72, 76–7, 89, 97
Comyn, Peter (arsonist, executed 1830) 24, 62
Constitution, and imagery 21, 138
Constitution, and mercy 21–39, 58, 66, 70, 76, 105, 127, 133, 138, 152
Convicts Prevention Act (State of Victoria, 1853) 132
Cooper, Charles Purton 26, 28
Copley, Esther 126
coronation ritual; coronation oath 3, 23–24, 29, 38, 66, 72, 109, 117, 170 n.25
Courvoisier, François (murderer, 1840) 94
Cowper, William 129
'Crewe tragedy' (murder in 1890) 103
Crimean War 32, 140, 145–6
criminal law, Scotland 23
Criminal Law Reform, Commission (1833) 65
Cromwell, Oliver 2, 72
Cross, Richard Assheton (home secretary) 82, 97
crown, aureate; of mercy 21
Cruikshank, George 26, 61, 151
Culloden, Battle of (1746) 46–7
Cumberland, Duke of (William Augustus, youngest son of George II, 1721–1765) 46–7
Cumberland, Duke of (Ernest Augustus, fifth son of George III, 1771–1837) 69–70
Curtana, and sword of mercy 72–3, 74, 87, 114, 149, 154

Curzon, George (1st Marquess Curzon) 119

Dahomey 91, 93
Daniel, Thomas (murderer, 1760) 49
De Clementia (Seneca) 13
De Lolme, Jacques 33
death warrants 25, 27, 47–8, 75, 77, 79–81, 84–5, 88, 105, 107, 112–13, 130, 151–2
Derwentwater, third earl (James Radclyffe, executed 1716) 44
Dickens, Charles 11–12
dictionaries 58, 145
Dodd, Dr William (forger, 1777) 51
Doddridge, Philip 22
Durham, Lord John George Lambton, (1st Earl, governor general of British North America) 108–9
Dyce, William 5
Dykes, Oswald 42
Dymond, Alfred 85

Earbery, Mathias 44
Edward VI, King of England 44, 81, 220 n.17
Edward VII, King of Great Britain 151–3
Elizabeth I, Queen of England 13, 140, 142, 144, 220 n.17
Emmet, Robert (executed 1803) 35
encyclopaedias 24
England, Church of 14, 37, 72
enlightenment and mercy 13, 16
equity 2, 13, 19, 23, 33, 58, 72, 117–18
Esher, Viscount (Reginald Brett, 2nd Viscount) 93
Ethiopia 135
Ewart, William 57, 85
Eyre, Sir James (Recorder of London) 26

feminine embodiment of mercy 5–6, 82, 144
Fenianism 144
Fenning, Eliza (executed, 1815) 58
Fielding, Henry 47, 54
Fonblanque, Albany 61
forbearance 2, 7, 10, 37, 77, 111
forgery 14, 17, 51, 53, 56, 58

forgiveness 7, 13, 53, 66, 153
Fortier, Mark 19
Foster, Sir Michael (Recorder of Bristol) 23
Francis, John (would-be regicide, 1842) 28, 120–1
Frost, John 32, 112–13
Fry, Elizabeth 36, 67
Furley, Mary (infanticide, 1844) 35, 87, 94

Gardiner, Francis (bushranger) 131
Gatrell, V.A.C. 62
Gay, John 46
George III, King (1738–1818) 14, 16–17, 21, 24, 26, 48–57, 143
George IV, King (1716–1830) 24, 32, 41, 57–63, 73
George V, King (1865–1936) 32, 151, 153–5
Gerrald, Joseph (trial, 1794) 33
Gibson, John (and statue of Mercy) 138–40
Gilpin, Charles 85, 88
Gladstone, William Ewart 123–4
Glorious Revolution 14
Goldsmith, Oliver 44
gothic revival 5
Government of India Act (1858) 12
Graham Sir James (home secretary) 29–30, 87, 94, 121
Greenacre, James (murderer, 1837) 26
Grey, Sir George (home secretary) 29, 94–6
Grimké sisters (Sarah and Angelina) 127
Gurney, John (judge) 35, 87

Hale, Matthew 36
Hamilton, Gail (*nom de plume* of Mary Dodge) 102
Hannah, Robert 46
Hanover, kingdom of 47, 60, 191 n.182
Harcourt, William Vernon (home secretary) 94–5, 97–9, 105–6
Harris, Charlotte (murderer, 1849) 88
Hawaii, kingship 72
Hawkins, Henry (judge) 35
Hay, Douglas 1–2, 13–14
Herrup, Cynthia 13
Hetty Sorrel (character in *Adam Bede*) 95

Heyrick, Elizabeth 126
Heywood, Peter, and mutiny on *Bounty* 53
Hill, Rowland (commander in chief of the British army) 78
History of Clemency of Our English Monarchs 44
history paintings 46, 140, 145
Hogarth, William 46–7
Hohenzellerns 155
Home Secretary 16, 24–5, 27–9, 32–3, 35–6, 49, 57–8, 61, 63, 75, 82, 87, 90, 93–105, 113, 120–1, 152
Howitt, Mary 88
Humanitarian League 10–11
humanitarianism 6, 8, 10–11
Hunt, Henry 56, 66
Hunt, Mary Ann (murderer, 1847) 88
Hunton, Joseph (utterer of forged bill, 1828) 61

India 6–7, 10, 12, 15, 31, 114–19, 133, 152–3, 155
infanticide 77, 90–1, 94–5, 105
Ireland 32, 35, 73, 78, 94, 133, 144, 152–3, 155
Isle of Man, and capital punishment 105

Jacobins 18
Jacobite propaganda 41, 43–4
Jacobites 46–7
Jamaican Revolt (1865) 6
Jeffreys, Judge 35
Jerrold, Clare 17
Jerrold, Douglas 142
Johnson, Samuel 47
jubilee 8, 10, 21, 31, 55, 90–1, 103, 105, 118, 129, 131–3
judicial portraiture, and mercy 37
judges, and mercy 33–7
judges, and monarchy 38
judges, unmerciful 35–6
Judy 143–4, 149
Junius (anonymous writer, 1769–1772) 49
jurors, and mercy 17, 33–4, 36, 57, 61, 76, 99, 103, 105, 112
justice 1–3, 5–6, 8, 11, 13–15, 17, 19, 21–4, 33–7, 41–4, 46–9, 51–2, 54–8, 61–7, 72, 74, 77, 81, 83, 88, 91, 96, 101, 108–9,

111–12, 114–19, 125–8, 130–1, 133, 137–40, 143–5, 151, 153, 155
justices of the peace 32, 36–7

Keith, Arthur 133
Kennedy, Matthew (and Patrick and Polly Kennedy) 49, 51
Kent, Duke of (Prince Edward, fourth son of George III, 1767–1820) 67
Kentish, Nathaniel Lipscomb 130–1
Kesselring, Krista 13
keywords 18–19
King in Council 17, 26–7, 39, 57, 61, 151
Koh-i-noor 6
Knowles, Launcelot (access to mercy 1797) 53–4

Lacey, Helen 12
Law, Charles Ewan (Recorder of London) 27
Lee, Sidney 28, 151
Leslie, Charles 22
Lewis, Sir George Cornewall (home secretary) 33
Lipski, Israel (murderer, 1887) 101
Lives of the Lord Chancellors (Campbell) 34–5
Lount, Samuel (executed 1838) 108
Lowes, John (attempted murder, 1837) 77

Macaulay, Catherine 23
Macaulay, Thomas Babington 10
Mackenzie, William Lyons 109
Mackintosh, Sir James (judge) 57
MacLean, Roderick (would-be regicide, 1882) 122–3
Maclise, Daniel 5
McNaghten, Daniel (homicide, 1843) 119–20
Madagascar 134
Madan, Martin 26
Manning, Maria (murderer, 1849) 87
Margarot, Maurice (transported for sedition 1794) 54
Marochetti, Carlo 140
Mary I, Queen (1516–1558) 142
Mary II, Queen (1662–1694) 41
Matthews, Henry (home secretary) 100–3

Matthews, Peter 108
Maybrick, Florence (murderer, 1889) 101–3
Measure for Measure (Shakespeare) 5, 44, 59
medieval mercy 12, 32
Mehmet Ali, ruler of Egypt (1769–1849) 135
Melbourne, Lord (William Lamb, 2nd Viscount) 27, 69, 75–6, 81, 94, 120, 129, 130
Merchant of Venice, The (Shakespeare) 3–4
Mercy, as child's name 11
Mercy, goddess of, Guanyin 134
mercy and imperialism 6–7, 15, 19, 110, 118, 124–5, 130, 133–4
mercy, 'reign' of in poetic language 1, 64
mercy, throne of 2, 59
Midgley, Clare 127
Montague, Anne Margaret (homicide, 1892) 103
Montgomery, James 74
Morphew, John 46
Morris, William 31
Muir, Thomas (transported for sedition 1794) 54
Mukherjee, Mithi 117
Mulgrave, Constantine Henry Phipps, Lord (Marquess of Normanby) 32, 73
Müller, Franz (murderer, 1864) 87, 134
Murphy, Paul 15
'Mutiny', in India and mercy 116–17

Napoleon 155
newport rising (1839) 112
newspapers, and mercy 14, 17, 29, 37, 41, 48, 53, 61, 64–5, 78, 82–3, 90, 101, 103, 105–6, 114, 117–18, 124, 153
Nicholson, Margaret (would-be regicide, 1786) 54
Nightingale, Florence 146–7
Nithsdale, Earl (William Maxwell, 5th Earl), and Countess Winifred 46
Non-British monarchs, and mercy 134–5, 155
Norbury, Lord (John Toler, 1st Earl of Norbury, judge) 35
Northern Star 88, 111–13, 125, 142
Nussbaum, Martha 7

Old Bailey 25, 34, 53, 58, 60, 66
Old Bailey Online 19, 34
Oliver Twist, and Queen Victoria 12
opera, and depiction of mercy 16
Osborne, Ethel (convicted of larceny and perjury, 1892) 103
Oxford, Edward (attempted regicide) 120

Page, William (attempted murder, 1839) 77
Palmer, Thomas 54
Palmerston, Lord (Henry John Temple, 3rd Viscount, home secretary) 5
Papineau, Louis-Joseph 108
Paton, John (of Grandham, Jacobite) 44
Patriotism and mercy 24, 155
Peel, Sir Robert 119, 121
Peggs, James 66
Penge murder (1877) 82, 131
Perrie, William (murderer, 1837) 75
Perreau brothers (Robert, Daniel, executed for forgery 1776) 51–2
Peterloo massacre 36, 59
petitions, to the crown (and royalty) 29, 46–7, 49, 53, 58, 65, 83, 85–9, 102, 112, 127, 130–1
philanthropy 2, 6–8, 10, 15, 31, 126
Philippa, Queen (wife of Edward III, 1313–1369) 140–1
Phipps, Charles 95, 97
pity 13, 19, 31, 44, 74, 81, 88–9, 95, 114–15, 144, 153
Plunkett, John 15
poetry and mercy 7, 15–18, 48, 54, 63, 73–4, 81, 83, 89
Ponsonby, Sir Henry 97–8, 102, 124
Poole, Steve 86
Porteous riots (Edinburgh, 1736) 47
Portia (character in *The Merchant of Venice*) 5, 8
Portia, actors' portrayal of, in eighteenth and nineteenth century 4
power, and mercy 1–2, 5–7, 10, 12–13, 15, 16, 21–2, 25, 31, 49, 54, 57, 60–1, 74, 76, 90, 102–3, 105, 113, 118, 129, 138
Prerogative, Royal 5, 7, 9, 11–13, 21, 24–5, 27–9, 49, 51, 54, 56–9, 61–2, 67, 78, 87, 89, 90, 97, 101, 104, 107–8, 111, 117–19, 122, 127, 130, 131–4, 142, 152
Presidential (US) prerogative of mercy 24
Prince Albert, and assassination 120; capital punishment 102; Indian rebellion 116; mercy in art 138, 144–6; slavery 130
Prochaska, Frank 15
progress, and mercy 8, 142
propaganda, and mercy 43, 85, 128, 155
providence 117, 124
Punch cartoons 96, 108, 114–16
Pye, Henry James (poet laureate) 54
Pyne, William Henry 63

Quakerism and Quakers 6, 67, 70, 85, 88, 125–7, 129, 143
'Of Queen's Gardens' (John Ruskin, 1864) 6

race, and mercy 6–7, 31, 118
Rai, Lajput 133, 154
Ranavalona I, queen of Madagascar (1778–1861) 134
Rasoherina, queen of Madagascar (1814–1868) 134
rebellion, and amnesty 108
Rebellion, in Canada 1837–1838 108–11
Recorder of London 25–7, 34, 53, 56, 58, 60–1, 63, 66, 76, 86
Red Cross, Royal (founded 1883) 147
Reformation, Protestant 13, 44
Regency (1811–1820) and mercy 57–9
regalia, and symbolism of mercy (*see also* crown, curtana, orb, sceptre, sword of mercy) 2, 18, 72–3, 87, 114
regicide 19, 28, 54, 86, 145
republicanism 15, 131
republicanism, and mercy 54
Restoration, The 13
Reynolds, George W.M. 86, 142
Reynolds's Newspaper 101, 141
Richmond, John (murderer, 1881) 98
Rickey, John (homicide) 75
Ridley, Sir Matthew White (home secretary) 104
Riel, Louis (executed 1885) 111
Ripper, Jack the 11

Robinson, Mary 54
Roberts, Samuel 84
Romilly, Samuel 57–8
royal births, and mercy 89, 133
royal deaths, and mercy 32
royal marriages, and mercy 32
royal proclamation, India (1858) 117
royal visits, and mercy 32
Rudd, Margaret (forgery case, 1776) 14
rumour 75, 78, 83, 91
Ruskin, John, defining mercy 7
Russell, Lord John (home secretary) 27, 66, 76, 94, 109, 114, 144
Ryland, William Wynne (engraver, forger, 1783) 52–3

Salisbury, Lord (Robert Gascoyne-Cecil, 3rd Marquess) 100–3, 134
sceptre, of mercy 49, 60, 67, 74, 111–12, 135
Schomberg, J.J. 36
Seneca 13
sepoys 118
sermons 11, 42–3, 48, 64, 66, 81, 85
sermons, assize 24, 36
Sesame and Lilies (by John Ruskin) 6, 137
Shelley, Percy Bysshe 22
Sheridan, Richard Brinsley 57
Sharpe, Kevin 13, 41
Shagan, Ethan 13
Shakespeare, William 51, 133
Sidmouth, Lord (Henry Addington, 1st Viscount, home secretary) 58, 60
Silvester, John (Recorder of London) 26
Slavery *and* slave trade, *see* abolition of slavery and apprenticeships
Smith O'Brien, William 78
Smith, Hannah 42, 44
Smith, Sydney 85
Society for the Abolition of Capital Punishment 85, 90
Somervile, William 7
Spurgeon, Charles 81
Statuary and mercy 23, 37, 137–40
Staunton, Mrs (mother of homicides) 82–3, 131
Stead, William Thomas 90
Stockmar, Baron (Christian Friedrich) 90
Strange, Carolyn 14, 33

Stuart, Charles Edward 43
Stuart dynasty and mercy 42–3
Sturge, Joseph 126, 127–8
Sussex, Augustus Frederick, Duke of 66, 70, 84, 126
suffragettes, and discourse of mercy 151, 153
sympathy 1–2, 6, 8, 15, 34, 36, 83, 85, 88, 93, 108, 113, 138, 144, 146–7
Symson, David 42

Tahiti, kingship 72
Taylor, John Sydney 66, 75, 120
Taylor, Miles 15, 117, 148
telegrams, for mercy 101, 104
Tenniel, John 96, 114–15
Terror, The (French revolution) 24
Terry, Ellen 3–4
The Times 61, 85, 114
theatre 56
'Think again, I pray you!' (anecdote of royal mercy) 77–81
Thompson, George 127
Thornycroft, Thomas 145
Tichborne movement 1
Todd, Alpheus 28
Tolpuddle martyrs 66
Tooke, John Horne 26, 49, 51
Tories, and politics of mercy 13, 22, 32, 73, 75–6, 114
Tomahawk (1795) 24
tomahawk, and scalping 110
Townley, George (murderer, 1864) 29, 95, 105
transportation 28, 32, 35, 49, 54, 75–6, 78, 87, 113, 120
truth (coupled with mercy) 37, 42, 48, 54, 64
Tyranny, and George III 49

Uncle Tom's Cabin 130

Valpy, Richard 24
Viceroy of Ireland 32
Victoria Beatrix 117
Victoria Humana 8, 148
Victoria, Queen of Great Britain and Empress of India, attitude to administration of justice (letter of

1865) 97; attitude to animal welfare 7, 10; attitude to capital punishment 27, 69; attitude to abolition of capital punishment, alleged 90, 105; attitude to Florence Maybrick 101; attitude to infanticide 95; attitude to remission of sentences 97–9; attitude to slavery 129–30; attitude to wife-murder 97
Victoria, Queen, in fiction 86
Victoria, Queen, interest in murder cases 94, 97, 101, 104
Victoria, Queen, mercy in her private journals and published works 3
Victoria, Queen, mercy in her religious education 3
Victoria, Queen, relationship with home secretaries, *see* under named home secretaries
Victoria, Queen, role in relationship to Recorder of London's Report 25–8
Victoria, Queen in artwork, as benevolent 8; as Queen Philippa of Hainault 141; between justice and clemency 138–40; compared with Elizabeth I 142; between Justice and Fenian 143
Victoria, as benevolent 8–9; as mother (appealed to) 29, 82, 85–6, 88, 103–4, 112–14, 116–18, 131, 144; as tearful 15, 75, 81, 144; as warrior queen 145

Victoria Vindex 117, 148
Villeponteaux, Mary 13
Virgin Mary 6
virtues 1, 5, 10–12, 15, 41–2, 48–9, 51, 54, 64, 67, 69, 72, 88, 138, 140
vivisection, and anti-vivisection 94
Voltaire, commentary on Cesare Beccaria 25

Wales, Prince Frederick of (1707–1751) 47
Wellington, Duke of (Arthur Wellesley, 1st Duke) 24, 62, 77–8
Whigs, and politics of mercy 23, 28, 32, 42, 57, 76, 113
Whitechapel murders (1889) 101
Wilberforce, William 129
Wilcox, Emily (murderer, 1884) 99
Wilkes, John 49
William III 41
William IV 41, 65–6
Williams, Raymond 18
Williams, Richard 15
women, merciful disposition 5–6, 15, 84, 86, 88, 113, 145
working-class, and mercy 15, 89
Wright, Barry 111
Wright, Samuel (murderer, 1864) 15, 89

www.ingramcontent.com/pod-product-compliance
Lightning Source LLC
Chambersburg PA
CBHW072140290426
44111CB00012B/1929